Wakefield Press

WOTAN'S DAUGHTER

Richard Davis is an internationally acclaimed writer specialising in biographies. He was encouraged to pursue a career in writing by Patrick White, Alan Marshall and Ivan Southall. This biography of Marjorie Lawrence, *Wotan's Daughter*, issued here in a new edition, is one in a series devoted to the lives of notable Australian musicians. Others include biographies of June Bronhill and Stuart Challender (both published by Wakefield Press) and of pianists Geoffrey Parsons and Eileen Joyce. More are planned for the future. These have enjoyed international critical success and earned Richard the Joan Sutherland and Richard Bonynge Award for the Arts. Richard is also the author of some lighter books and teaches Creative Writing. His popular Creative Writing courses attract students from around Australia and overseas.

By the same author

Biographies

Anna Bishop: The Life of an Intrepid Prima Donna

Eileen Joyce: A Portrait

Among Friends: Geoffrey Parsons

Wotan's Daughter: The Life of Marjorie Lawrence (hardcover edition)

Close to the Flame: The Life of Stuart Challender

A Star on Her Door: The Life and Career of June Bronhill

Other books

The Ghost Guide to Australia

Great Australian Ghost Stories

WOTAN'S DAUGHTER
The life of
MARJORIE LAWRENCE

RICHARD DAVIS

Wakefield Press

Wakefield Press
16 Rose Street
Mile End
South Australia 5031
www.wakefieldpress.com.au

First published 2012
This paperback edition published 2021

Copyright © Richard Davis, 2012, 2021

All rights reserved. This book is copyright. Apart from any fair dealing for the purposes of private study, research, criticism or review, as permitted under the Copyright Act, no part may be reproduced without written permission. Enquiries should be addressed to the publisher.

All photographs are from the Marjorie Lawrence Papers, and were generously provided by the Special Collections Research Center, Morris Library, Southern Illinois University, Carbondale, Illinois.

Edited by Penelope Curtin
Cover design by Stacey Zass
Typeset by Wakefield Press

ISBN 978 1 74305 846 6

 A catalogue record for this book is available from the National Library of Australia

 Wakefield Press thanks Coriole Vineyards for continued support

This book is respectfully dedicated to the memory of
Sheila Prior, AM, BEM, DLJ
1914–2004

Sheila Prior devoted her life to working in an honorary capacity for various community organisations and for the arts. During a thirty-two-year tenure as Founding President and Chairperson of the Australian Opera Auditions Committee Inc., Sheila was instrumental in raising more than two million dollars. These funds were used to support talented Australian singers, conductors and instrumentalists.

Nothing is impossible, nothing hopeless if you have courage and faith in God. Don't ever lose your sense of humour. If you can keep laughing you are safe. I have walked hand in hand with God. He has given me strength. It has made every impossible thing, possible.

Marjorie Lawrence

Contents

Foreword to the first edition	*Dame Joan Sutherland* and *Richard Bonynge*	viii
Foreword to this edition	*Wayne Groom*	ix
Preface	*Richard Davis*	xi
Chapter One	'Push the Pram for Baby'	1
Chapter Two	Stitches and Scales	12
Chapter Three	Innocents Abroad	26
Chapter Four	Mademoiselle Lawrence	36
Chapter Five	Triumph in the Sun	49
Chapter Six	Doubts, Delays and Disputes	58
Chapter Seven	L'Étoile de l'Opéra	72
Chapter Eight	Apple Pie and Horseplay	86
Chapter Nine	Storm Clouds Gathering	100
Chapter Ten	Lucky Strikes and Jackboots	112
Chapter Eleven	Homecoming	126
Chapter Twelve	The Glory Years	138
Chapter Thirteen	'Was ich liebe, muss ich verlassen'	152
Chapter Fourteen	'Master of my fate and captain of my soul'	166
Chapter Fifteen	Chin-up Girl	179
Chapter Sixteen	Off to War	192
Chapter Seventeen	Twilight of the Gods	203
Chapter Eighteen	Interrupted Melody	215
Chapter Nineteen	Professor Lawrence	229
Chapter Twenty	'Leb' wohl'	241
Notes		253
Appendix	Discography of Marjorie Lawrence's Recordings	279
Bibliography		299
Index		303

Foreword to the first edition

Joan Sutherland, OM, AC, DBE and Richard Bonynge, AC, CBE

I first heard the glorious voice of Marjorie Lawrence just before my fourteenth birthday in September 1944 in Sydney. I can still hear her incomparable sound in Dido's 'Lament' as if it were yesterday. Five years later Joan and I adored her Sydney concerts – she gave at least six in June and July 1949.

Her sublime final scene from *Götterdämmerung*, her 'O don fatale', her 'Divinités du Styx' remain with me forever. If only I had heard her Valentine in *Les Huguenots* at the Opéra in Paris in 1936!

She came to La Scala in 1966 to see Joan as Donna Anna and we spent a memorable evening after the opera. We later had the indescribable pleasure of being in the same concert together for the United Nations in New York in 1976. Marjorie sang 'Waltzing Matilda' from her wheelchair and the entire audience was in tears. How privileged we were to share even a tiny part in her life.

In our opinion the voice of Marjorie Lawrence was the only Wagnerian comparable to Kirsten Flagstad and certainly one of the three greatest ever to come from Australia.

Bravo to Richard Davis for the long-awaited biography, which restores a great singer to her rightful place in operatic history.

Foreword to this edition

Wayne Groom, Producer, Australian International Pictures

It was Louise Woodcock who gave me Richard Davis's book *Wotan's Daughter* to read. The cover was handsome, a stunning photo of Marjorie Lawrence in full Brünnhilde dress, wearing a helmet and holding a spear and shield, an image from another era.

Louise is a pianist who travelled the world playing concerts with her talented violinist husband, Ronald Woodcock. She thought I might like the book. I thought not. I had little interest in opera, despite being a filmmaker for 40 years.

I read the book to please Louise, and ended up making a feature-length documentary, *Marjorie Lawrence: The world at her feet*, about the great soprano's spectacular life. Richard Davis's wonderful biography of Marjorie Lawrence is a revelation. His meticulous research over three continents, his vivid storytelling and his affectionate, objective view of Marjorie's achievements and shortcomings, are riveting. I couldn't put the book down.

Perhaps the greatest puzzle of Marjorie's astonishing life is that she is so little remembered by the Australian public. Marjorie became arguably the greatest Wagnerian soprano in the world in the 1930s, singing at the Paris Opera and The Met, wowing audiences and receiving glowing critiques. She became friends with President Roosevelt and Queen Elizabeth (the present Queen's mother). M-G-M made a movie of her life which won an Academy Award, and she was decorated with the Légion d'honneur by the French Government. Yet most Australians don't know her name.

Those who do remember Marjorie love her fiercely. Conductor Brian Castles-Onion carefully curated a beautiful box set of CDs of her performances. Singer John Bolton Wood admires her voice, and Marjorie is regularly celebrated by the Richard Wagner Society in Victoria.

Of course, Marjorie's greatest fans are in Winchelsea and Dean's Marsh, in country Victoria, where as a teenager Marjorie rode her horse in surrounding paddocks singing opera, imitating her hero, Dame Nellie Melba. Even today, 100 years later, dedicated archivists in the Winchelsea Historical Society still curate her artefacts, letters and photos.

Richard Davis, in his dedicated, unassuming scholarly manner, has done Australia a great service by 'rediscovering' Marjorie's life, preserving her achievements for posterity. On a more personal note, his brilliant biography sent my cinematographer, Dr Carolyn Bilsborow, and me on a thrilling journey of discovery.

Meeting Richard Davis was a treat, although from the outset he was suspicious of my credentials. During our interview, when I stumbled over the pronunciation of *Götterdämmerung*, he remarked casually, 'You don't know much about opera do you?'

Interviewing Ita Buttrose in the ABC boardroom in Sydney was surreal. Ita was so enthusiastic about Marjorie Lawrence, sharing an amazing but little known Buttrose family connection with Marjorie. I won't tell you what it is, but it is historically important and had a major influence on Marjorie.

Marjorie had a hugely successful career, transitioning from her father's Winchelsea farm to performing in the great opera houses of the world during the 1930's. How she did it is hard to comprehend, a mixture of extraordinary talent, a prodigious drive to succeed and a great work ethic.

Despite Marjorie's success, life delivered her a cruel blow, a nightmarish, freaky moment of unbelievable sadness that few could have survived. Brian Castles-Onion suggested we should not concentrate on this tragedy, insisting Marjorie be remembered for her magnificent voice. We agreed, but as we delved into Marjorie's life, we discovered precious USA archival footage, during and after the crisis, that revealed an amazing character trait Marjorie possessed – her fortitude. This is critical to understanding who Marjorie was and perhaps, in retrospect, why she has been misunderstood.

Dame Kiri Te Kanawa immediately embraced Marjorie's story when we contacted her to voice the narration for our documentary. She unhesitatingly agreed to lend her prestigious name to our film, not charging a fee. Excited, Carolyn and I dashed over to Auckland, overcoming Covid fears, and drove four hours on a narrow country road to Dame Kiri's home. She was a delight! Her voice and affection for Marjorie shine through her narration. Kiri confessed she identifies with Marjorie's journey, from farm girl to the urban centres of Europe and the United States.

Thank you, Richard Davis, for writing your wonderful biography of Marjorie Lawrence. Carolyn and I salute you. Your *Wotan's Daughter* changed our lives, as good books tend to do. I hope our documentary reaches your high standards and helps to celebrate Marjorie's remarkable existence.

Preface

Richard Davis

On 20 April 1955 the world premiere of one of the few successful opera films to come out of Hollywood was given in Melbourne, Australia. Within days the film was released across Australia, then the United States and Great Britain. It received rave reviews wherever it was shown. Audiences flocked to see it and the film netted millions of dollars for Metro Goldwyn Mayer.

The film was called *Interrupted Melody* and was based on a best-selling book of the same name. It told the story of an Australian country girl named Marjorie Lawrence who rose to become one of the world's great opera singers before being struck down by a crippling disease. Audiences reached for their handkerchiefs as they watched the film's glamorous star, Eleanor Parker, fight pain, disability and depression to get back on her feet – metaphorically and physically – and to return to the opera stage, aided and abetted by Glenn Ford, playing the heroine's devoted husband. The film combined rags to riches, romance, glamour, tragedy, courage and ultimately triumph, along with good acting and the best representation on screen up to that time of opera staging and opera singing.

The question therefore arises: why, with a successful book and a successful film chronicling Marjorie Lawrence's life, is a modern biography needed? A number of sound reasons answer this question, the most obvious being that Marjorie had another thirty years of active life *after* the book was published.

Secondly, the book *Interrupted Melody* was ghost-written for Marjorie as her autobiography, with all the information it contains supplied by her and not independently verified by the ghost writer. By comparison with the autobiographies of most prima donnas, *Interrupted Melody* is delightfully candid, but when the book was written Marjorie was still active as a singer and therefore selective about what she revealed, omitting or underplaying anything that might have been harmful to her career. Marjorie also took a great deal of poetic licence in reporting certain events, especially those of her early years, and in some cases the ghost writer (expert though he was) embroidered them further.

Thirdly, although modesty was not a particularly conspicuous trait in Marjorie's character (it is rare among prima donnas), she is modest about her own accomplishments in *Interrupted Melody*. Nowhere in the book will the reader find the kind of objective analysis of her voice and her singing necessary to fully appreciate her art. Nor will the reader find comparison between Marjorie and other Wagnerian sopranos, also necessary if she is to be accorded her rightful place among them.

The film of *Interrupted Melody* takes enormous liberties with the already dubious content of the book, and admirable though it may be as cinema, if we of the past who is ripe for re-evaluation. Apart from vintage record collectors, Wagner historians, a small claque of her devoted former students and the fading memories of some very elderly opera goers, she is largely forgotten – a fate she does not deserve. There is plenty of convincing evidence in the form of personal recollections, contemporary criticism and sound recordings to prove beyond doubt that she is worthy of much wider recognition and a place among the greatest Wagner singers of all time.

Equally compelling is just how inspiring Marjorie's personal story is. She was not the first and will not be the last celebrity to fall victim to a crippling disease at the height of her career, but few have fallen from so high or climbed back so far. In her lifetime Marjorie's indomitable spirit served as an inspiration to others suffering disease and injury, and there is no reason why it should not serve the same commendable purpose for all time.

It is my sincere hope that this biography will swing the spotlight back onto Marjorie Lawrence, fill the omissions and correct the inaccuracies of the autobiography and the Hollywood movie and restore this courageous Australian to her rightful place in musical history. If it does, it will be due in no small part to the many people who generously shared their knowledge, opinions, reminiscences, records, recordings, enthusiasm, advice and encouragement with me.

I am deeply indebted to Her Majesty Queen Elizabeth II who graciously shared her recollection of Marjorie with me and gave me permission to quote her. Also to Dalton Baldwin, James Bantin, Tom Bath, Mark Beasley, Judith Bent, Mike Blyth, Janet Brien, Matthew Briggs, Katherine Brisbane, AM, Monica Bullen, Ita Buttrose, AO, CBE, L. Carroll, Ann E. Case, Victoria Chance, Karen Clayton, Colleen Cole, Marlene Cook, Keith Curry, Madeleine Curtis, Violet Dandy, Michael Dixon, Annette Drysdale, the late Peter Egan, OAM, Jean-Jacques Eggler, Lauris Elms, AM, OBE, Norman Falconer, Ann Fischer, Hedwig Fojt, Deborah Franco, Christina Garrett, Pat Gladden, Suzetta Glenn, Dr Elaine Harriss, Pamela Hinde, Lorilee Huffman, Eric Jones, Tony Jordan, June Knight, the late Dr Frank Lappin, Neil Lawrence, Richard Le Sueur, Judith Lincoln, Patricia M. Lloyd, Diane Longinotti, John Lucas, James K. McCully, Dave McHaney, Ron Millard, Charles Miller, Angela Moore-Swafford, Prof. Allison Nelson Loebbaka, Gloria Norton, Norma Paley, Mavis Palmer, Elizabeth Phillips, Dr John A. Phillips, Dr Raeschelle Potter-Deimel, Murray Richmond, Liz Robbins, Diane Russell, Helen Ryan, Pamela Sanabria, Ian Schram, Patricia Schroeter, John Preston Smith, Mariella Soprano, Margaret Stewart, Prof. David Tunley, AM, Patti Vance Hays, Florence Waite, Joseph Ward, OBE, Jonathan Mark Winchester, John Woods, Judy Wright, Dr John M. Yarborough, Edward Young and Sue Zellers.

I also gratefully acknowledge the assistance provided to me by the Bibliothèque-musée de l'Opéra and the Archives Nationales de France, Paris; The Bibliothèque & Archives de la Ville de Lausanne; the Libraries of the University of Queensland; National Library of Australia; State Library of Victoria; Canberra School of Music

Preface

Library; Gold Coast City Council Library Services; Caltech, Pasadena; Garland County Historical Society, Arkansas; Kosciusko County Historical Society, Indiana; Winchelsea & District Historical Society; Geelong Historical Society; Lorne Historical Society; the Geelong Heritage Centre, and the Musicological Society of Australia; Geelong Advertiser; Camperdown Chronicle; Colac Herald; Torquay Surf Coast Times; Geelong Independent and Gramophone Magazine, London. I am also grateful to Southern Illinois University Press for permission to quote from their edition of *Interrupted Melody*.

A special debt of gratitude is owed to Richard Bonynge, AC, CBE, for encouraging me to write this book and contributing the splendid foreword, and to the late Dame Joan Sutherland, OM, AC, DBE, who graciously added her imprimatur to Richard's words.

I also wish to thank David Carlson, Dean of Library Affairs at Southern Illinois University and Pamela Hackbart-Dean and her expert team at the Special Collections Center, Morris Library, who provided access to 'The Marjorie Lawrence Papers' and offered willing assistance during my research. Also to Dr Dona Bachman and her team at the university museum who granted me access to their collection of Marjorie's stage costumes and memorabilia, and to Janine Wagner and her team at the School of Music. To all these friends and colleagues at Southern Illinois University, I offer sincere thanks for their hospitality during my visit to Carbondale in 2010.

I am also indebted to Dr H.D. (Erik) Dervos, who generously provided me with access to his extensive collection of recordings of Marjorie Lawrence, helped me with my research and offered much good advice, and to Dr Jeffrey Gawler, FRCP, who generously undertook an expert reassessment of Marjorie's medical condition for me.

I also acknowledge with profound gratitude the financial assistance provided to me for this project by the Australian Opera Auditions Committee Inc. through the 2011 Joan Sutherland and Richard Bonynge Award. This group of dedicated supporters of the arts has provided assistance to singers and other practitioners in the arts over many years. I am also grateful to Michael Bollen and his team at Wakefield Press and to my editor Penelope Curtin, all of whom brought their expert skills to the production of this book.

Finally, may I offer my thanks to you, the reader of this book, and express a sincere hope that you enjoy reading Marjorie's story as much as I enjoyed writing it.

Richard Davis

Chapter One
'Push the Pram for Baby'

Australia as a nation was just six years old when Marjorie Lawrence was born. Until the Earl of Hopetoun, representing the octogenarian Queen Victoria, proclaimed the Commonwealth of Australia on 1 January 1901, the six Australian states had been individually answerable to their imperial masters in Whitehall. Marjorie's formative years coincided with the formative years of her nation and she would be a young woman before Australia had a purpose-built national capital. In the meantime, Melbourne, the capital of Marjorie's home state of Victoria, would serve as the seat of the new nation's parliament.

Melbourne was the richest and grandest city in the new Commonwealth, built on the proceeds of nineteenth-century gold rushes, but in 1907 subsistence living on unpromising land and hardship reminiscent of the pioneering era could be encountered not far from 'Marvellous Melbourne'. A drive south-west of Melbourne for about six hours in a horse-drawn buggy (or a bit less in one of those new-fangled motor cars) would lead to the village of Deans Marsh, centre of a small farming and sawmilling community in the northern foothills of the Otway Ranges. Deans Marsh comprised a smattering of humble, well-kept commercial buildings, a community hall, a church and about a dozen modest houses, one of which was the home of the Lawrence family.

Marjorie's father, William Lawrence, was a first-generation Australian, the son of an Englishman who had come to Victoria as a free settler in the 1850s.[1] 'Bill', as he was universally known, was a resourceful, no-nonsense man described by a contemporary as 'tough as goat's knees, but kind of heart'. He was also good looking with broad shoulders, sound limbs and a pleasing face adorned with the masculine trademark of the time – a large, drooping moustache.

Bill Lawrence turned the heads and the hearts of many local girls in his youth, but took his time to choose a bride. In his late thirties he fell in love with twenty-seven-year-old Elizabeth Smith, the daughter of a local farmer. 'Lizzie', as her family called her, had a forthright personality to match Bill's and was by all accounts a beauty, having inherited her Irish mother's dark good looks.[2]

The courtship of Bill Lawrence and Elizabeth Smith, as may seem appropriate for the future parents of an opera star, was musical. Elizabeth played the wheezy reed organ for services in St Paul's, the village church; Bill had a fine baritone voice and joined the church choir to be near his sweetheart. Both were talented amateur musicians, Elizabeth playing the piano as well as she played the organ and Bill invariably seconded to provide the music at local dances with his concertina or his home-made one-string fiddle. When not singing in the choir, Bill, accompanied by his sweetheart, was also a dab hand at comic music hall songs and the sentimental ballads of the day.[3]

Bill and Elizabeth Lawrence were married in 1898 and set up house in a modest timber cottage in Deans Marsh.[4] In neatly kept paddocks behind the house they established a mixed farm, growing oats, potatoes and other small crops, and kept a couple of cows, horses, some sheep, pigs and poultry.

Children soon began to arrive: first a son, Lindsay, born in 1899, then another son, Edwin (known as 'Ted' or 'Snowy') in 1901 and a daughter, Eileen, the following year. In 1904 and 1905 two more baby boys were born: Percy and Alfred. In later years Percy figured prominently in Marjorie's career, sharing many of her triumphs, but little Alfred, like so many infants in times past, sickened and died before his first birthday.

As well as being a competent man of the land, Bill Lawrence was also an enterprising man of business. If he had lived in our time he might have become a property developer or an angel investor. He devised several schemes to supplement his meagre income from the farm and to support his growing family. At different times he established, operated and sold off for a profit a butcher's shop, a bakery, a smith and a saddlery. Such enterprise earned him the respect of the community and the devotion and gratitude of his family, who prospered from his foresight and hard work.

On 17 February 1907, Bill and Elizabeth's sixth child and second daughter was born, like all of her siblings in the big bed in the front bedroom of the Lawrence house. The names Marjorie and Florence were chosen for her, presumably because they were popular and fashionable at the time, as there had been no Marjories or Florences in recent generations of either parent's family. In a land where sobriquets are valued more than proper names, Marjorie was speedily shortened to 'Marge', and the nickname 'Babe' applied to her by her father.[5]

Marjorie described herself as 'a thin, unlovely individual with wispy, straw-coloured hair', and no one gazing on the little girl as her mother proudly showed her off to family, friends and neighbours in the small community could have predicted that she would one day conquer the glamorous international world of grand opera. Nor could anyone have predicted the tragedy that was about to strike the Lawrence family.

A few weeks after Marjorie's first birthday, Elizabeth Lawrence found she was pregnant again. Having enjoyed straightforward pregnancies in the past, she was alarmed to find that this time she was in considerable pain. A doctor in the region's principal town, Winchelsea, examined Elizabeth and confirmed that she was pregnant. He also found a lump in her stomach, which he suspected was a malignant tumour.

A distraught Bill and a frightened Elizabeth drove back to Deans Marsh with the doctor's prognosis ringing in their ears: 'If you were not pregnant Mrs Lawrence, I would recommend the immediate removal of the tumour, but to do so now would almost certainly kill your baby. On the other hand, if you are not operated on and my suspicions are correct, then the tumour may kill you.'

Bill and Elizabeth faced an impossible choice. As Christians and devoted to the family ethos, they were horrified at the thought of being responsible for killing their unborn child, but the alternative seemed too great a sacrifice for Elizabeth, her loving husband and their five young children to make. A wait-and-see policy was adopted and it was hoped (and prayed for) that Elizabeth would give birth to a healthy child then be able to receive life-saving treatment for the tumour.

In the months that followed Elizabeth's cancer spread from her stomach to her liver, and by the time she was due to go into labour it was apparent she might not survive the ordeal. It was also apparent that a house filled with young children was not the place for her confinement, so after Christmas, Elizabeth went to stay with one of Bill's sisters, Louisa Prime, in the neighbouring town of Birregurra.

On 8 January, Elizabeth gave birth to a son. The child survived. He was named Thomas after Elizabeth's brother-in-law Thomas Prime, but in later life was always known by his second name, Allan. Elizabeth never left the bed the Primes had provided for her. Eight days after giving birth, she died and the following week was laid to rest in Bambra Cemetery near Deans Marsh.

Of the shocked and tearful children who gathered around their mother's grave on that hot summer afternoon in 1909, Lindsay, Ted, Eileen and Percy would retain vague but precious memories of their mother. Age denied little 'Marge' and her newborn brother that comfort, but as she would observe later, infancy also spared Marjorie the emotional trauma her father and her older siblings suffered. Innocence also prevented her from realising how her existence complicated the plans a bewildered Bill Lawrence then had to make to keep his household functioning.

It was decided that a motherless home was no place for a newborn baby boy or a two-year-old girl. Both Allan and Marjorie would eventually return home, but for the time being Allan was made a ward of Thomas and Louisa Prime and raised by them at Birregurra, while Marjorie was sent to live with her grandmother, Julia Lawrence, in the home where Bill Lawrence had spent his youth, at Pennyroyal, a few miles from Deans Marsh.

Julia Lawrence, widowed matriarch of the family and in her mid-seventies when her little granddaughter came to live with her, was an important early influence on Marjorie. Years later Marjorie would speculate that the streak of toughness in her own character which served her career so well was a legacy from her beloved 'Grandma'. Julia Lawrence was typical of the strong-bodied and strong-willed pioneering women who imposed civilisation on remote pockets of the Australian wilderness, and if age had made her body frail her spirit remained unassailable.

Julia had come to Australia in 1854, married Henry Lawrence at Geelong, established a wayside inn on the road to Winchelsea and produced eight children in quick succession, including Marjorie's father.[6] Julia's trials began when Henry Lawrence became an invalid and the inn became insufficient to house and support her large family. She acquired a tract of virgin bushland at Pennyroyal and there carved out a farm, using timber cleared from the property to build a homestead. Forty years later Marjorie would recall the time she spent at Pennyroyal with affectionate nostalgia:

> *Grandmother still lived in the original old homestead which had grown soft and beautiful with the years and my move there made the lives of several people, including mine, immeasurably happier. At my father's place I had been pretty much a pest, but at Pennyroyal I was the only child in the house and treated like a princess. Grandmother bought me a complete new wardrobe and she and her old housekeeper could not have given me more care and adulation had I been a real princess.*[7]

Marjorie was well on the way to becoming in her own words 'a spoiled brat' when Julia Lawrence died just before Christmas in 1910 and Marjorie returned to her family home. There, as she recalled:

> *I was subjected to a toughening process over the next few years, the common lot of any member of a largish, rough and tumble family not over endowed with worldly riches.*

In her absence Bill Lawrence had acquired a housekeeper, the first of several who were paid to manage his house and supposedly look after his children. These women sometimes brought their own children with them, adding to the squeeze in the Lawrence house and leading to juvenile warfare. Some were overfond of liquor, one stole from the family cashbox, and several became infatuated with the still-handsome Bill Lawrence and set about trying to become the next Mrs Lawrence.

Bill missed his 'Lizzie' terribly. Years later Percy Lawrence would remind Marjorie how their father always became 'pretty useless' for a week or two around the middle of January and deeply depressed on the anniversary of their mother's death. Bill was also lonely and the attraction these housekeepers felt towards him may have in some cases been reciprocated, but his brood always put a stop to any romance before it took hold.

> *We Lawrence children had read our fairy stories and we knew what evil creatures stepmothers could be. We made up our collective mind there would be no*

stepmother in our house. Whenever we sensed the possibility of father's installing one, we would forget our bickering and team up to make the life of the woman so miserable as to dissipate her passion and cause her to flee the place.

Marjorie was personally responsible for the demise of one of these hapless creatures, whom she later admitted might have made a suitable wife for her father. Little 'Marge' climbed into a tree and began to howl loudly enough to be heard for miles. Neighbours and passers-by gathered to listen to her. 'I won't come down until that woman goes away! She doesn't like me! She *beats* me!' Marge bellowed while her brothers and sisters, gathered around the base of the tree, added a chorus of 'Poor Marge' and 'Poor Babe'.

Were Australians a people given to lynching, I think that poor housekeeper might have ended her days there and then dangling at the end of a rope. As it was, she rushed into the house, packed her bags and caught the next train back to Melbourne.

When Marjorie's sister Eileen ('Lena' to her devoted brothers and her little sister) reached the age of fourteen she took over the running of her father's household and the threat of infiltration by evil stepmothers passed. Bill Lawrence never remarried, focusing his energies instead on his children and his multifarious business interests.

From an early age, Marjorie was expected to do her share of tasks around the house and farm – washing dishes, making beds, weeding the vegetable patch and helping to tend the animals and poultry. She also learned to ride – the day her father threw her onto the bare back of their placid mare, Bazil. Marjorie developed a lifelong love of horses and quickly became a first-class horsewoman, eagerly taking every opportunity to ride wherever she encountered horses over the next thirty or so years.

Marjorie's schooling began in 1912 when she was sent to William Burt's School on the Deans Marsh to Lorne road. By her own admission she was an unruly student, chattering in class and getting up to mischief in the schoolyard, neither of which endeared her to her teachers, but she was also a precocious learner with a highly retentive memory. Years later those attributes would serve her well when she began to study and learn operatic roles. As she grew older she would attend other schools in the Deans Marsh area, collecting her share of merit certificates, sporting awards and detentions.

In *Interrupted Melody* Marjorie claims that she could not remember a time when she did not want to sing – 'During most of my waking hours little tunes bubbled out of me almost unbidden' – and at age five little Marge had her first opportunity to display her vocal prowess in public.

The Sunday school teacher at St Paul's had asked for volunteers to sing solos in a local concert and Marjorie eagerly put up her hand. At the concert on the following Saturday, when it came time for Marjorie to perform she sailed confidently out onto the makeshift stage pushing a doll's pram, her blonde hair trimmed with new blue ribbons. When the 'oohing' and 'aahing' subsided, she launched into a rendition of 'Push the Pram for Baby', one of the hit numbers from Lionel Monckton's new musical *Our Miss Gibbs*, although her rendition was more notable for its volume than its vocal finesse.

Marjorie enjoyed holding the audience's attention as she rattled through the song's sentimental lines and mimed the actions ('Push the pram for baby, dear little dimpled baby; turn the corners gently, mind you don't collide'), but at least one of her older brothers was mortified by what he perceived as his baby sister's shameless exhibitionism. From the back of the church, eleven-year-old Ted interjected loudly: 'Go 'ome, Marge, Dad wants ya!', but Marjorie was not fooled by the ploy. She finished her song and basked in the prima donna's reception the audience gave her. From that day onwards, she claimed, her heart was set on becoming a singer.

Soon after this Marjorie began taking piano lessons. A Miss Jenkins drove over in her buggy from Birregurra once a week to give Marjorie and her brother Percy lessons on the old upright piano that took pride of place in the front room of the Lawrence house. Nothing is known of Miss Jenkins, but she must have been a competent teacher. Percy played the piano well throughout his life and dreamed of becoming a concert pianist until he sustained a serious injury to a finger in a farm accident. Marjorie learned enough from Miss Jenkins to be able to accompany herself in private once her career became established.

All the Lawrence children had musical voices, including little Allan who was reunited with his brothers and sisters at Deans Marsh when he reached school age. Marjorie's eldest brother, Lindsay, came closest to matching her vocal amplitude, with a fine baritone voice resembling his father's and which was much in demand for benefit concerts, patriotic ceremonies and weddings. As they came of age, each of the children joined the choir of St Paul's, where their aunt, Emma Smith, had replaced their mother as organist.

In 1917 the old vicar at St Paul's retired and was replaced by the Reverend Alex Pearce from Melbourne, the first serious musician Marjorie had met and the first to recognise the exceptional quality of her voice. Alex Pearce was a romantic figure – tall, distinguished-looking and seeking solace in a small bush parish following the recent death of his young wife. Most of the females in the congregation developed a crush on the handsome young widower, including Marjorie, and when it was discovered that he had been on the stage before joining the ministry, was a fine pianist and had trained choirs which had successfully competed at the prestigious South Street Eisteddfods in Ballarat, his appeal quadrupled.[8]

Pearce immediately set about improving the choir at St Paul's, dispensing with those whose voices had been tolerated too long and recruiting younger singers like the Lawrences who could cope with the more sophisticated and 'serious' choral repertoire he was determined to introduce. In number and quality, the choir of the tiny sun-bleached wooden church in Deans Marsh could not hope to compete with the great choral societies of the capital, but in terms of broadening their and the community's experience of good music Pearce seemed truly to be a godsend – not least to Marjorie.

Pearce quickly recognised that ten-year-old Marjorie's voice was exceptional; powerful for her age, wide ranging and beginning to show the velvety texture and deep resonance of a future mezzo-soprano or contralto. Marjorie was soon promoted to principal soloist with the choir and a whole new world of music was revealed to her, which she joyfully embraced.

> *With the advent of Alex Pearce, singing for the first time became a serious business for me. Until then I had sung when and how the spirit moved me. The new minister put curbs on my carolling and endeavoured to show me that music was like grammar; that there were rules for governing its construction and interpretation. At first I found the restrictions of musical law and order irksome and singing ceased to be fun. But, as we learned excerpts from the cantatas of Bach and the oratorios of Handel, Stainer and Mendelssohn, I found a new and deeper joy in being able to sing.*

As well as being an innovative choir master, Pearce was also a strict one and while she revelled in the opportunities she was being given, the larrikin in Marjorie rebelled at Pearce's insistence on long, frequent and rigorous rehearsals.

> *Many was the time that Alex Pearce's choir practice was delayed while that good man left the other singers and strode down to a large pond that lay between our farm and the church, compelled me to desist from my favourite sport of catching tadpoles, and hustled me off, frequently dripping wet, to sing.*

Marjorie's voice was soon being heard in concerts organised by Pearce all over the Deans Marsh, Winchelsea and Colac area and across the Otways in the coastal resort of Lorne. More often than not it was the Lawrence family who were the staples at these events, Marjorie topping the bill with Lindsay and Ted (who had a pleasant tenor voice) in support and Percy at the piano. Marjorie wondered later in life if the good people of that part of the western district might not have got heartily sick of 'trios by the Lawrence family', 'duets by the Lawrence family' and endless 'solos by the Lawrence family'.

'Welcome Home' concerts for troops returning from the First World War also provided opportunities for these youngsters to show off their talents. Thirty years on Marjorie would write:

> *I sometimes speculate now upon what the feelings of the returning heroes must have been when they realized they had fought to preserve a way of life that produced precocious, stagey little girls who warbled that 'life was only made for laughter'.*

If war-weary soldiers and work-weary farmers had sometimes been ambivalent about their appreciation of Marjorie, the municipal leaders of Deans Marsh were not. To them Marjorie represented an opportunity to put their small town 'on the map'. One of these, Shire President Mountjoy, bestowed on Marjorie the title 'Our Little Melba', making reference to the most famous of Australian women at the time, the internationally acclaimed 'Queen of Song', Dame Nellie Melba.

Marjorie liked the appellation and was probably unaware at the time that almost every promising young female singer in Australia had been accorded the same title since Melba conquered the opera world in the 1890s. Marjorie knew little about Melba beyond what she had read in newspapers, but she did know the great singer's exquisite soprano voice. A friend of the family in Deans Marsh had a wind-up gramophone and a collection of fragile shellac records. Prominent among these and frequently played in Marjorie's presence were some of Melba's lilac-labelled His Master's Voice recordings and some blue-label Columbia's by another great Dame, the stalwart English contralto Clara Butt. Because of the extraordinary range of Marjorie's voice she was able to imitate both these women, which, in itself presented a dangerous dilemma.

> *I could not make up my mind whether I wanted to become a contralto like Butt or a soprano like Melba. I spent hours at a time out in the paddocks in the evening riding like a fury without saddle or bridle in the bright moonlight – and singing at the top of my voice. First I would be Butt, growling away at 'Land of Hope and Glory', then Melba letting off the pyrotechnics of the 'Mad Scene' from 'Lucia' – to the utter bewilderment of stupid-looking sheep who gathered round to listen and to the interest of the neighbours who would greet one another the next morning with: 'Marge was out again last night. The breeze was blowing in our direction'.*

There are those familiar with Marjorie's recordings but not her career who would say she never fully made up her mind which register suited her best. At different times in her career she essayed both soprano and contralto roles, often singing them with a distinctly lighter (but not Melba-like) or darker (but hardly Butt-like) tone.

Singing on horseback in the cool night air also set a precedent Marjorie followed for the rest of her life. While she watched other singers coddle themselves in scarves and stuffy rooms, for Marjorie fresh air was invigorating and exposure to the elements, she believed, toughened her body and her voice. While that might sound like a dangerous philosophy for a singer with a fragile voice and a fragile constitution, it suited Marjorie, who was blessed with a robust frame and resilient vocal cords.

In 1921 when Marjorie was fourteen, Bill Lawrence sold the little farm in Deans Marsh and bought a larger property three miles from Winchelsea, the regional centre on the Barwon River. Here he built a more spacious house and expanded his farming and business interests, climbing as Marjorie put it, 'a rung or two up the local social ladder'. Bill also bought the family's first motor car – a black T-Model Ford – which sons but not daughters were taught to drive.

Many factors were now at work directing Marjorie towards a career as a singer, along with a few, equally forceful, working in the opposite direction. If one single event could be said to have convinced Marjorie that her future lay in singing, it was an unplanned and unexpected encounter she had with a player-piano salesman shortly after the move to the new property.

Being a local musical celebrity did not excuse Marjorie from her share of the work on the new farm and riding into Winchelsea once a week to buy supplies was one of her chores. It was on one of these shopping expeditions that Marjorie heard the sound of a piano being played very proficiently from inside a large van parked in the centre of the town. Intrigued by this, Marjorie rode over to the van, which turned out to be a mobile furniture showroom.

> *As I looked in I saw the owner, a stout, pleasant looking man, playing a player-piano and doing it very well. The instrument was equipped with all kinds of gadgets and he was using them to get beautiful and thoroughly musical effects. The man smiled and beckoned me in. He was playing a ballad I knew and, standing alongside him, I began to sing and despite the fact that his instrument was a Pianola, I never before had sung with so sensitive an accompanist. A crowd gathered but we kept on with our concert, my marketing completely forgotten.*

For each of the next three or four days, Marjorie found an excuse to ride into Winchelsea, but as she discovered it was impossible to give daily recitals in the main street of one's home town without its becoming general knowledge.

> *When father heard the news, he read the riot act to me, warning me of the dangers of talking to strange men – but not before my musician friend, whose name I never did discover, had told me I should go to Paris to study.*

Exactly why this musical salesman should have suggested Paris rather than London, Milan, Berlin or anywhere else to Marjorie, she never knew. It may have been because Melba had gone there to study, but whatever the reason, it would prove prescient advice. To Paris Marjorie would eventually go, and although this became her goal from this time onwards, it would take several years and much hard work before it was realised.

As the years passed, Marjorie's voice strengthened, along with her determination to become a professional singer. By 1923, when she turned sixteen, she realised that if she was to avoid squandering the magnificent gift she had been given, she needed an expert singing teacher to guide her. While there was no one suitable in Winchelsea, there were several in Melbourne. The reaction from Marjorie's father when she asked if she might travel up to Melbourne to consult some professional singing teachers, with a view to taking lessons, shocked and disappointed her.

> *Dad was violently opposed to the idea. Singing in the home, in church, at local gatherings was all very well, but going to Melbourne for lessons might lead anywhere – even to the professional stage! No daughter of his, he raged, was going on the stage. And he was surprised and hurt that I should even contemplate leaving the home he had worked and striven to make comfortable and happy for us all. I didn't argue. That would have been futile. When Dad's mind was made up, it remained made up. I knew that if I were to go to Melbourne to study singing I would have to do what is popularly described as 'running away from home'.*

Marjorie confided the plan she had hatched to her sister Lena and brother, Ted. 'You can't do it, Marge,' they said, 'not until you're eighteen; 'til then Dad could get the coppers onto you and they'd bring you home'. Marjorie doubted that her father (whose love for her was never in doubt) would have done anything quite so drastic, but she could imagine him following her to Melbourne and dragging her home in disgrace. It was not a risk Marjorie was prepared to take, so she bided her time – for two frustrating years.

To occupy herself and to equip herself with a skill that might provide employment when she finally got to Melbourne, Marjorie began taking sewing lessons (along with a group of other young girls) from a petite, hawk-featured Englishwoman in her early forties who had come to live in the district – a Mrs Boddington.

> *Ada Boddington fascinated me. She had an elegance and* savoir-faire *rare among the women of our community. Perhaps it was their realization that she was 'different', which caused some of them to dislike her. Frequently I heard her referred to as a 'red-ragger', because of her suffragist activities. While we sewed, Ada would regale us with tales of the famous and glamorous people she had known or seen in England, which further whetted my desire to see the world outside Winchelsea.*

To this day there are folk in the Winchelsea district who remember Ada Boddington as an embarrassing rebel who upset the community's respectable complacency and they hint at activities she was involved in which appalled their parents. For all that, Ada Boddington was an expert needlewoman and the skills she passed on to Marjorie enabled the future struggling singing student to save a great deal of money by making her own clothes. 'Boddie', as Marjorie came to call her, also proved to be a keen supporter of Marjorie's ambitions.

Also during this waiting period, Marjorie had her first romance – with a young man named Patrick Considine, whom she described as 'a hefty lump of Australian manhood', and for a while it seemed she might abandon her musical ambitions in favour of domestic ones. 'Pat' Considine was the stepson of Tom Ryan, a jovial Irishman who ran the Barwon Hotel in Winchelsea.

> *Falling in love was a horribly serious business for me and Pat, so serious we were utterly miserable for the entire period of our romance. Our parents were even less happy, if that were possible, when we announced that we wished to marry. My father and Pat's parents were on friendly terms, but the idea of his daughter marrying a Catholic horrified him as much as her wanting to be a professional singer. The Ryans were no happier at the prospect of their son taking a Protestant for a wife.*

Pat Considine made it clear to Marjorie that he expected her to convert to Roman Catholicism before they married, an expectation that prompted the end of their relationship. This was the first of many passionate affairs Marjorie would enter into with handsome and not always suitable men, but for the rest of her life Marjorie had a soft spot for her first love 'Pat' and he for her.

As her eighteenth birthday approached, Marjorie began to plan her departure for Melbourne – but keeping her plans hidden from her father. After reading that John Brownlee, the new sensation among Australian singers abroad, had been taught by the Melbourne singing teacher Ivor Boustead, Marjorie decided gaining admission to his classes would be her objective once she reached the capital. Apart from Lena and Ted, Marjorie also shared her plans with Percy and Allan. Percy, a favourite sibling of Marjorie's, promptly announced that he would be accompanying her.

Marjorie turned eighteen on 17 February 1925 and two days later she and her fellow conspirators put their plan into action. The train to Melbourne left Winchelsea railway station at seven in the morning, but Bill Lawrence was normally up and about by six, so it was decided that Marjorie and Percy needed to be away by five.

On that still summer morning, just as the sun was colouring the distant hills with a pink glow and the magpies were beginning their carolling, Percy and Allan stealthily pushed the T-model Ford down the long driveway towards the Winchelsea road. Ted in the meantime kept watch at the house in case their father stirred. Allan cranked the car into life and then drove Marjorie and Percy to the station. There, to the amusement of the station master, brother and sister remained hidden behind some crates until the train arrived. Allan sneaked the car home and back into its shed. Bill Lawrence woke up a few minutes later to learn that two of his brood had flown the nest.[9]

For Marjorie the first stage of the adventure that would eventually lead her to Paris had begun, and, if she felt guilty about deceiving her father, she was comforted by the certain knowledge that she was following her destiny and could take no other possible course.

Chapter Two
Stitches and Scales

Marjorie and Percy knew only one person in Melbourne – a distant cousin named Linda Kahle who had once holidayed with them at Winchelsea. Some weeks before their departure Marjorie had written a letter to this cousin suggesting a reciprocal visit, her choice of words leaving little room for a refusal. The response they sought came back a few days later; an invitation for Marjorie and Percy to stay with the Kahle family in their home in the Melbourne suburb of Coburg – for one week.

Linda Kahle met Marjorie and Percy on their arrival in Melbourne and was alarmed to discover that her country cousins had brought most of their possessions with them, and were hoping to stay indefinitely. She explained that while they were welcome to stay as long as they liked, her parents could not afford to support them. Marjorie retorted confidently: 'Don't worry, Linda, we're both going to get jobs and I'm going to become a famous singer, so we'll pay your Mum and Dad for our rooms and our meals … soon'.

Before leaving home, Marjorie had also written to Ivor Boustead and arranged for an audition with him on the afternoon they arrived. Boustead was one of the most respected and fashionable singing teachers in the city – and his reputation had soared since John Brownlee's success. In later years Marjorie often wondered what the dapper and erudite teacher must have made of her, with her freckles, her unkempt hair and her homemade clothes, as he ushered her into his studio.[1]

> *Boustead's studio was filled with photos of famous singers and grateful pupils all inscribed to him. He sat down at his large, black piano and asked me what I would like to sing. I produced the sheet music for the great soprano aria 'Ocean, Thou Mighty Monster' from Weber's* Oberon *which I had been keeping in reserve for just such an occasion. Boustead played and I sang. My voice sounded tremendous in the little studio and even I was thrilled at the reverberating tones I produced. When I finished with a great flourish Boustead said nothing. Then he thumped a chord, and told me to sing some scales. Higher and higher we went*

and my voice flew up the scale with the confidence of a steeplejack. 'That was a top D you sang then, young woman' he said and I replied as bold as you like 'I imagined it was'. My boldness vanished though, and I was nothing more than a very excited girl when he added 'You have a magnificent natural voice – one of the best I've ever heard'. My impulse was to throw my arms around Boustead's neck and kiss him, then I wanted to laugh and cry at the same time.[2]

Boustead quizzed Marjorie about her experience and her situation and told her to go away and find a job and come back when she was settled, and that he would be delighted to teach her. Marjorie raced back to Coburg to share the good news with Percy and to tell him they must find jobs the next day.

I felt there was not a moment to lose. At eighteen one begins to imagine one is getting old! I feared I was so ancient that if I did not push ahead with my singing I would be an old woman before I achieved anything.[3]

Marjorie had probably heard that in earlier times many young singers by the time they reached eighteen had some training behind them, while a few of the more precocious had even made their professional debuts, so there was an undercurrent of genuine if unnecessary concern behind her urgency.

If impressing Ivor Boustead had been easier than Marjorie had expected, finding work proved much harder. Percy got a job pulling drinks at a soda fountain in Collins Street, promptly flooded the establishment and several customers with aerated ice water and was marched off the premises by the proprietor before the end of his first (and last) shift.

Marjorie answered advertisements for seamstresses but found to her dismay that all the Melbourne factories used large electric sewing machines and her treadle machine skills and delicate hand stitching were not in demand. She did land a job as a 'finisher' in a workshop in Flinders Lane, sitting with a dozen other women at a large work table sewing buttons onto dresses all day.

Monotonous though the work was, Marjorie might have stuck at this job but for a rule of silence imposed by the employer. Sitting from eight in the morning till five in the afternoon without speaking was too much for chatterbox Marjorie and she left after a week. Her next job was also in a clothing workshop – a couple of blocks further along Flinders Lane – and here she did Cornelli work, embossing and other fancy stitching. This was slightly less monotonous work, the pay was better (thirty shilling per week instead of twenty-four) and speaking was permitted.

Percy settled into a job as an insurance salesman and quickly discovered he had a talent for persuading people to part with money in exchange for security. Soon he was earning good wages and commissions and, combined with Marjorie's thirty shillings, brother and sister soon had a modest but sound financial footing.

Marjorie began taking lessons with Ivor Boustead at the end of March, 1925, just one month after she had arrived in Melbourne. Twice each week, Mondays and

Thursdays during her lunch hour, she would run two blocks from Flinders Lane to Little Collins Street and bound up the stairs to Boustead's studio. Marjorie's talent blossomed under Boustead's expert guidance and for the rest of her life she remained grateful to him for endowing her with a reliable, basic vocal technique that would serve her for decades to come. Many years later, when Boustead was an elderly man but still teaching, she would write:

> *For every honest person who teaches singing there are a hundred charlatans and Australia is no more free from this pestilence than any other part of the world. It was a lucky day when I found my way to Ivor Boustead's studio. He is honest and conscientious. I never had to unlearn anything he taught me and when Cécile Gilly accepted me into her studio in Paris three years later she simply took up where Boustead left off.*

Boustead made Marjorie sing scales and vocal exercises for months on end, but he also allowed her to study some songs and, later, operatic arias which he felt were right for her voice – songs in contralto keys and arias written for contraltos. Boustead acknowledged the exceptional range of his pupil's voice but insisted she use the top of her voice very sparingly until she was fully developed, vocally and physically. Pieces like 'Ocean, Thou Mighty Monster' with its 'B's and top 'C' were set aside, while Boustead made her concentrate on perfecting the lower and middle parts of her voice. When her Paris teacher, Cécile Gilly, famously pronounced a few years later that Marjorie was a dramatic soprano Boustead pointed out that he had known that all along, but had chosen a course that would allow the transition from contralto to soprano to occur naturally and safely when Marjorie's vocal equipment was ready for it. It was perhaps the best legacy any teacher could have given Marjorie at the time.

The temptation to allow Marjorie to show off her sumptuous top notes must have been great for both student and teacher, for voices of Marjorie's kind are extremely rare. Singers are seldom endowed with natural dramatic soprano voices and most, including some of the most famous, begin as lyric sopranos or lirico-spintos (lyric sopranos with a bit more vocal heft) singing lighter roles and then train (or occasionally force) their voices to encompass the dramatic soprano repertoire when they reach maturity. Young singers like Marjorie who can effortlessly do justice to an aria like 'Ocean, Thou Mighty Monster' at eighteen are few and far between.

Marjorie relished her lessons and Boustead enjoyed training the 'magnificent natural voice' to respond to the demands of great music and teaching Marjorie to command it wisely. So engrossed did teacher and pupil become that the lessons often ran over time. Back at the clothing workshop in Flinders Lane, Marjorie's colleagues covered for her many times, doing her work as well as their own, but on one occasion their efforts failed.

The proprietor of the workshop also ran a dress shop across town which kept her occupied most of the time, but on this fateful afternoon she decided on a snap inspection of the workshop. When Marjorie rushed back thirty minutes late, the proprietor was waiting for her and sacked her on the spot. Marjorie begged for another chance explaining where she had been and what she had been doing, but the woman was adamant.[4]

Around this time the Kahles at Coburg had been making it clear that Marjorie and Percy had overstayed their welcome and their board was too far in arrears, so Percy found 'digs' in a boarding house and Marjorie took a job as a live-in housekeeper for two spinsters in a gloomy old house in Clifton Hill. Had she not been desperate, this was a job she would never have taken, and accepting it proved a mistake. In exchange for the use of the household piano and a pokey bedroom on an enclosed veranda, Marjorie did all the cooking, washing, sweeping and scrubbing and had to pay her 'employers' six shillings a week for her meals.

Lena came to Marjorie's aid by secretly sending her ten shillings each fortnight from the housekeeping money, but that stopped after a few weeks. Lena wrote, when the fortnightly letter arrived but without the ten-shilling note:

Dad is still very angry about what you and Perc did. He keeps saying he can't understand where he went wrong and that he always tried to make a good home for you. Anyhow, when he found me putting the money in an envelope addressed to you he took it and he says I must not send you any more.[5]

Marjorie's situation now became desperate. She told the spinsters they would have to find another household slave and went searching for other work. This time she advertised for a paid position as housekeeper in a house with a piano she could use for singing practice and received a promising reply from a Mrs Gregory who ran a boarding house at Middle Park.

I went to see her and quickly felt she was sceptical about me, but her house was pleasant and there was a good looking piano in the corner of the room where she interviewed me. I made up my mind I would be living under the Gregory roof before the week was out. The few months I had been in Melbourne had sharpened my wits and made me a shrewder person and this new shrewdness came to my aid in dealing with Mrs Gregory. Unmistakably she was Irish or of Irish descent, so when a pause came in the interview I asked 'Would you like me to sing for you?' and before she had time to reply I sat at the piano and sang 'Killarney', spreading the words of the song inches thick with sentiment.

Tears ran down the old lady's cheeks. She came over to the piano and put an arm around my shoulder. 'Almighty God has been good to you, my dear,' she said, 'will you move in tomorrow or at the end of the week?'

Marjorie worked hard for Mrs Gregory and earned every penny of the five shillings per week she was paid, along with free board and unlimited use of the piano. As the months passed a warm relationship developed between them and Marjorie began to feel more at peace with the world and her (at least temporary) contentment was reflected in her singing, which was showing rapid improvement, to the extent that by the winter of 1926 Boustead decided Marjorie was ready to enter her first singing competition.

In the nineteenth and early twentieth centuries annual eisteddfods and singing competitions flourished in cities and towns across Australia offering young artists the opportunity to compete against each other, gain performance experience and useful feedback from competent adjudicators, along with substantial cash rewards for the victors.

The major Victorian competitions were held in Melbourne, Ballarat, Bendigo and Geelong, but it was decided that Marjorie should try her luck in a smaller one at Colac. Staying at the Lawrence farm while competing at Colac was not an option. Even if Bill Lawrence had agreed, Boustead would have counselled against Marjorie exposing herself to the emotional turmoil of a strained reunion while trying to do her best in the competition. Lena arranged for Marjorie to stay with another prominent family in the district – the Batsons, whose daughter Yvonne was then Marjorie's best friend. If Bill Lawrence had been aware that his errant offspring was in the district and singing in Colac, he kept his distance and made no attempt to contact her.

Excited at the prospect of singing in public for the first time since commencing her training with Boustead, Marjorie dismissed any unsettling thoughts of her family from her mind and concentrated on competing in the Colac events. She had entered seven sections of the Colac Competition and came equal first in the 'Sacred Song' category, singing 'O Rest in the Lord' from Mendelssohn's *Elijah* (a piece she had first sung with Alex Pearce) and second in the 'Secular Song' section with Wilfred Sanderson's 'My Dear Soul'. The adjudicator was the veteran professor Joshua Ives, the first professor of music at Adelaide University. He noted:

> *Marjorie Lawrence's voice displayed fine promise. This competitor has musical instincts seeking expression. Intonation, phrasing and facial expression were excellent.*[6]

Another distinguished musical pedagogue heard Marjorie at Colac. Fritz Hart, director of the Albert Street Conservatorium in Melbourne approached her after the competition and suggested a place might be found for her in his institution if she was interested. Marjorie of course was flattered and delighted by his attention. The Albert Street Conservatorium enjoyed the patronage and support of the now officially retired Dame Nellie Melba, who taught there when she was in Australia, and Professor Hart was a major power in the Australian musical scene. A week later Marjorie received a letter from Hart requesting that she and her father call on him and that Marjorie sing for Mary Campbell, the principal resident voice teacher at the conservatorium.

Marjorie wrote to Bill Lawrence to ask that he join her at the interview with

Hart. To her surprise and delight a reply came by return mail, with Bill saying that he was pleased she had done well at Colac and that he would travel to Melbourne and accompany her to see 'this professor'. The letter was signed 'Your loving Dad'.

Father and daughter (and Percy) were reunited under the clocks at the entrance to Flinders Street Railway Station, twenty months after Marjorie and Percy had absconded. That afternoon Bill Lawrence accompanied Marjorie to the Albert Street Conservatorium, feeling proud and self-conscious in equal measure.

The interview went well and, when Marjorie sang for Hart and Campbell, both expressed their approval. At the end of the interview Hart assured Marjorie that a place would be found for her at the conservatorium and that he was sure Dame Nellie would be delighted with the decision. However, there was one aspect of the encounter that Marjorie would later deeply regret. When Professor Hart asked if she was currently taking lessons with anyone, Marjorie foolishly answered 'No'. To make matters worse, Marjorie had not told Ivor Boustead about Fritz Hart's interest in her and only confessed to him that she had spoken to Hart *after* her interview at the conservatorium. Boustead was not impressed, but as he was fond of Marjorie and not of Hart, he laid the blame entirely on the conservatorium director.[7] Boustead did, however, pose an ultimatum. Marjorie must choose – either him or the conservatorium. Marjorie came to her senses and tearfully asked for Boustead's forgiveness, but that did not end the affair. Without realising it, Marjorie had made an enemy in Hart.

A week later a letter arrived for Marjorie from Hart saying he had received a note from Boustead accusing him of attempting to steal one of his pupils and demanding Marjorie explain to Boustead that she had told him she was not studying with anyone when they met. Hart concluded by saying how dreadfully disappointed he was that Marjorie would not be coming to the conservatorium 'for Dame Nellie's sake as well as your own'.

If Marjorie was upset by the bitter lesson she had learned about loyalty, this at least was part-compensated by the reconciliation with her father. When Boustead closed his studio for the summer break, Marjorie and Percy went home to Winchelsea to spend Christmas. In the new year Percy returned to his job in Melbourne, but Marjorie (with Mrs Gregory's blessing) stayed on for a couple of weeks. It was, she would later claim, one of the happiest times of her life. Lena's cooking tasted like ambrosia, Bazil was there to be ridden over the paddocks and Molly, her favourite cow, to be lovingly milked. A tennis court had been built behind the house a few months earlier and Marjorie spent most of those hot, sultry days bashing tennis balls around with her brothers Ted and Allan or happily sharing the household chores with Lena.

Bill had an even bigger surprise for Marjorie. He took her into town on Boxing Day morning and proudly showed her his latest business venture: the Globe Theatre, a timber, fibro-cement and corrugated iron building with an auditorium seating 200 and sporting dressing rooms, a box office, a projection booth and a large screen above a small stage. Bill Lawrence had brought Hollywood to Winchelsea, and Marjorie promised him that one day when she came home world-famous, the first concert she would give would be in his theatre. Marjorie kept her word, but Bill Lawrence was not there to witness the event.

Marjorie returned to her job and her lessons with Boustead in February and to a new aspect of her training. Most of the arias Marjorie had studied were in Italian and Boustead had taught her the Italian words parrot-fashion, a practice that satisfied neither pupil nor teacher, so with Boustead's blessing and using part of a small weekly allowance Bill Lawrence had agreed to pay her, Marjorie began taking Italian language lessons from an Italian woman who taught from her front room in Fitzroy. Marjorie's excellent memory stood her in good stead and before long she had a basic grasp of 'poetic' Italian – although she discovered when she later visited Italy that vernacular Italian was markedly different from operatic Italian! Having an understanding of what she was singing greatly improved Marjorie's renditions of arias like 'O don fatale' from Verdi's *Don Carlos*. This aria was a favourite of hers at the time because, although Boustead made her sing it in a lower key than originally written by the composer, Princess Eboli's show-stopping solo gave her the opportunity to show off a couple of her resplendent upper notes.

In March 1927 Marjorie entered the Royal South Street Competition in Ballarat, the most prestigious musical contest in Australia at the time and in later years a vehicle for advancing the careers of many notable singers, including Sylvia Fisher, John Lanigan, Keith Neilson, Robert Allman, Lauris Elms and Kiri te Kanawa. Marjorie entered five sections, but not the coveted 'Sun Aria' sponsored by the Melbourne *Sun-Pictorial* newspaper since Boustead did not believe she was ready for this award.

Marjorie believed she sang well at Ballarat, but she failed to gain a place in any section. The adjudicator for all the vocal sections that year was Fritz Hart. Professor Hart is not remembered as a vindictive man, but it is not impossible that he allowed his recent disappointing experience with Marjorie to colour his judgment. Thorold Waters, the outspoken music critic of the *Sun-Pictorial* and later a stalwart supporter of Marjorie, believed that was the case, and so did she.

Ivor Boustead did not entirely share their view. He had noted a tiredness and lack of drive in his favourite pupil since her return from Winchelsea. He astutely used the results from Ballarat as the catalyst for a reassessment of Marjorie's prospects and her personal circumstances. He realised that if Marjorie was to have the professional singing career she aspired to and was capable of, she needed the supportive atmosphere of home and family. Although he would be reluctant to see her leave his care, Boustead also impressed upon Marjorie that it was crucial she begin making plans to further her studies overseas. Marjorie for her part acknowledged the drudgery and exhaustion of heavy housework at Mrs Gregory's boarding house and the difficulty she had in finding time between her duties to practise. She also freely admitted that spending Christmas at home had left her feeling desperately homesick. As to travelling overseas, Marjorie had nurtured the dream of Paris all these years, but had not been able to save any money towards realising her goal.

As a first step, Boustead suggested he write to Marjorie's father, explain the situation and suggest that she give up her job, return home to live and travel to Melbourne for her lessons. Given Bill Lawrence's softened attitude, there seemed a reasonable chance of his agreeing. In Boustead's long and sincere letter he assured Marjorie's father of his absolute faith in his daughter's talent and confidence in her ability to succeed at an international level if she were given the support she needed and, in Boustead's opinion, fully deserved.

Bill Lawrence capitulated. He had been missing 'Babe' as much as she had him since her return to Melbourne and he took little persuading. He did however place one condition on her return home. In his letter Boustead had mentioned that Marjorie's next challenge would be the 1928 Geelong Eisteddfod, at which another Sun Aria prize would be offered and which Marjorie would enter. The ever practical Bill Lawrence made it a condition that if Marjorie failed in Geelong as in Ballarat, she must give up her aspirations for a professional career and 'settle down'. Marjorie agreed, and her father's ultimatum proved to be the inducement she needed to succeed in Geelong.

Marjorie packed her bags and returned home the following week to an enthusiastic welcome – a welcome that included the proud purchase of a new motor car in celebration of the prodigal daughter's return. Marjorie quickly fitted back into the routine of farm life and, as she kept her first diary for part of this year, we know that her mornings were taken up with milking the cows, washing, ironing and sewing, and her afternoons were given over to practice using a new piano Bill Lawrence had bought to replace the old one from Deans Marsh.

Twice a week Marjorie travelled to Melbourne by train for her singing lessons with Ivor Boustead (which now lasted as long as Boustead's schedule would allow) and her Italian lesson with the woman in Fitzroy. Relieved of the burden of having to spend most of her energy earning a living and with the security of family support and encouragement, Marjorie's voice and her singing improved in leaps and bounds.

By the time of the 1928 Geelong Competition she was at her youthful peak – not yet an accomplished or experienced artist and still confined to the contralto range, but confident of the power and beauty of the sounds she could produce. In preparation for this competition, Marjorie enlisted the help of a talented young local pianist named Ray Dickson and together they worked on the pieces Marjorie and Boustead had suggested would demonstrate her talent.

The Geelong Competition (or Cumunn na feinne, to give it its traditional Welsh title) was held over three days in the Palais Royal, a sizeable theatre in the centre of Geelong. Lena was to accompany Marjorie to Geelong and Bill and Marjorie's brothers would stay at home to await news. Marjorie always took great delight in recounting how her brother Lindsay was so preoccupied with thoughts of her on the final day of competition that he forgot to open the seed shoot on the horse-drawn wheat-planting machine, his oversight not discovered until the following spring when no crop appeared.

Marjorie entered all fourteen adult solo singing sections in the Geelong competition, including the Sun Aria, and won every one. The adjudicator for the majority of the sections was an organist from New Zealand, Purcell Webb. When Marjorie sang 'O don fatale', he noted on his comments sheet: 'Nice full voice, sings with expression, good declamation, words distinct'. When Marjorie sang 'Annie Laurie' he wrote: 'Good colouring, very artistic', and with 'O thou that tellest good tidings to Zion' from Handel's *Messiah*, it was one word underlined: 'Excellent'.

The Sun Aria contest was held on the last day of the competition and judged by Thorold Waters, who had not heard Marjorie in the earlier sections of the competition. For this most important test Marjorie sang an aria from a now forgotten opera, *Nadeshda*, by the English composer Arthur Goring Thomas. Marjorie would have preferred to have sung 'O don fatale', but Boustead convinced her that Natalia's aria from *Nadeshda* would be a better choice and he was right. 'O, my heart is weary' spans two octaves (from A-flat below middle C to A above the stave) and contains passages marked *resolutto* (resolutely), *con dolore* (with pain), *maestoso* (majestically) and *animando* (animatedly), giving Marjorie ample opportunity to display the range of her voice and her blossoming dramatic powers.

Thorold Waters was bowled over by Marjorie's performance and found it hard to contain his enthusiasm. As she left the platform, he whispered to Marjorie's accompanist, 'Where in the hell did you find *her*?' Dickson merely smiled. Marjorie was not Dickson's discovery, but Waters would soon be trying to convince the world that she was his.

Marjorie was the twenty-eighth competitor to sing and had listened intently to the twenty-seven who preceded her, many of whom were experienced singers who had come to compete only in the Sun Aria and collectively represented a much higher standard of singing than Marjorie had encountered in the previous days. By the time her turn came she was convinced she had no chance and, after singing, insisted on returning to the friend's home in Geelong where she and Lena had based themselves and had to be coaxed and cajoled into returning to the Palais Royal that evening to hear the results. To add to Marjorie's gloom she discovered on arriving back at the theatre that all the other contestants had changed into evening dress – she was wearing an overcoat on top of the homemade blouse and skirt she had sung in. It was late before Thorold Waters rose to his feet to announce the winner of the radio station 3LO's gold medal and the Sun Aria prize.

'T.W.'s' musical critiques in the *Sun-Pictorial* were notable for their verbosity and the speech he made that night was long. Midnight was approaching before he finally announced that both prizes had been won by 'one of the most exciting young singers it has ever been my privilege to hear, a singer with a voice of gold whom I predict will have an illustrious career in opera … number twenty-eight, Miss Marjorie Lawrence'. No one was more surprised than Marjorie and no one prouder than Bill Lawrence when the triumphant Marjorie came dashing through the front door at Winchelsea at 2.30 in the morning shouting 'Dad! Dad! I won! I won!'[8]

The 3LO medal came with an engagement to give four short recitals from the station's studios in Melbourne for a fee of twenty pounds and the Sun Aria carried a cash prize of the same amount. Combined with the smaller cash prizes awarded in the other sections of the competition, Marjorie estimated she had won more money in three days than she would have earned at Mrs Gregory's boarding house in three years.

More importantly, winning the Sun Aria made Marjorie a statewide celebrity. At this time singing competitions were followed with avid interest by the newspaper-reading population and the Sun Aria drew almost as much hype and excitement as a football final. Newspapers reported on the phenomenal success of 'Miss Marjorie Lawrence of Winchelsea' and quoted Thorold Waters and Purcell Webb at length. When Ivor Boustead was interviewed he told journalists that Marjorie was a wonderful pupil with a remarkable facility for learning and that he hoped that she would soon be able to travel overseas, probably to Paris where he hoped his former pupil, John Brownlee, now based there, would be able to direct and advise her in her studies. An excited and slightly overawed Marjorie thanked everyone and confirmed that she hoped to go overseas, Paris having been her goal for longer than she could remember.

The first published photos of Marjorie began to appear in the press at this time. They show a plumpish figure and a broad face topped with a mop of hair (now described as copper-coloured), plain but pleasant features, widely spaced teeth and a slightly embarrassed expression. The days when audiences and critics would remark on Marjorie's glamour were still a long way off. Her unsophisticated clothes add to the impression these photos give of a strong and healthy country girl endowed with courage and determination – which exactly describes Marjorie in 1928.

Those who had not yet heard Marjorie's voice had their opportunity through her recitals on radio 3LO in June. With Ray Dickson again in support, Marjorie sang items she had sung in Geelong as well as 'Er, der Herrlichste von allen', the second song from Schumann's song cycle *Frauenliebe und -leben*, the Page's aria from Meyerbeer's *Les Huguenots*, 'Le Roi de Thule' from Berlioz's *La Damnation de Faust* and that perennial standby of all contraltos, 'Softly awakes my heart' from *Samson et Dalila* by Saint-Saëns. Although she sang all these pieces in English, the Schumann gave a foretaste of her singing of German lieder, which would develop into a significant component in her career, and the three arias anticipate her mastery of many roles in French opera. The success of these broadcasts led to invitations to sing on other radio stations and offers flooded in for Marjorie to sing in concerts in the capital and in regional centres around Melbourne. She continued her lessons with Boustead and juggled a now encouragingly full schedule, appearing wherever she and Boustead deemed it rewarding to her reputation and helpful to her experience.

Marjorie was delighted with her success, but if there was a chance of her success going to her head, two embarrassing situations and one frustrating event would bring her back to earth with a bump. The first occurred when she sang with an orchestra for the first time – at a rehearsal in a suburban hall in Melbourne with a small orchestra conducted by Percy Code.

> *I strode out and stood at the very front of the stage, so that I was standing back to back and several feet away from the conductor. It never occurred to me but what he [sic] and the orchestra would follow my singing. Our first number was to be Beethoven's 'In questa tomba oscura'. We began with great gusto, but about half way through I was shocked to discover that I was a bar ahead of the orchestra. I might have continued so, but suddenly the orchestra stopped and I received a tap on my shoulder from the conductor's baton. 'Young lady,' he said sternly, 'don't you realise you are supposed to follow me?' I was speechless with embarrassment and blushed to the roots of my hair. 'I'm very sorry,' I muttered, 'I've never sung with an orchestra before'. The conductor smiled kindly and said 'You should have told me, my dear. Now come back here, stand beside me and let's begin again.'* [9]

The second event almost put an end to Marjorie's career before it had begun. After the success of her Italian language lessons, Marjorie decided she also needed English elocution lessons, so without consulting Boustead, she enrolled in the studio of the Melbourne drama teacher Mostyn Wright. Wright was a colourful, flamboyant character who was delighted to have Marjorie join his classes and, in addition to teaching her to project her speaking voice and colour it with exaggerated inflections, he also cast her in one of his stage productions. Just six weeks after winning the Sun Aria, Marjorie made her stage debut in Melbourne's Queen's Hall performing a long speaking role in *The Humble Exalted*, a comedy written by Mostyn himself.

When Marjorie turned up for her next lesson with Boustead she was almost voiceless. After she croaked through a scale, he asked 'What in God's name have you been doing?' Marjorie confessed and Boustead gave her another ultimatum. She could either continue singing or become the leading lady of the Mostyn Players, but she could not do both. If she persisted in speaking as Mostyn had taught her, Boustead assured her she would destroy her singing voice. It was not a hard decision and a thoroughly chastened Marjorie returned to Winchelsea and communicated with her family in whispers for the next few days while the ever-obliging Boustead placated Mostyn Wright.

The Albert Street Conservatorium incident resurfaced yet again, causing

Marjorie intense frustration and, ultimately, disappointment. Just as the municipal leaders of Deans Marsh had done a decade earlier, the more powerful civic leaders of the city of Geelong rallied around Marjorie after she won the Sun Aria, motivated like those in Deans Marsh by a mixture of altruism and self-interest. Foremost among these was Howard Hitchcock, a former lord mayor of the city and now representative for the Western District in the upper house of the Victorian Parliament.

Hitchcock claimed friendship with Dame Nellie Melba, who was currently in Melbourne supervising the last of the three touring opera companies she had imported to Australia in partnership with the theatrical entrepreneurs, J.C. Williamsons. Hitchcock promised Marjorie that he would arrange for her to sing for Melba, in the hope that the famous diva might bestow her approval on Marjorie and perhaps offer practical assistance as she had done for several other young Australian singers. Hitchcock's friendship with Melba was close enough for the request to be considered, but not as close as the diva's friendship with Fritz Hart. The answer came back that Dame Nellie was far too busy to hear Miss Lawrence. Hitchcock asked repeatedly over a period of several weeks, with the same excuse (if it was that) offered on each occasion, until the final request was left unanswered.

Marjorie does not mention Fritz Hart at all in *Interrupted Melody* and attributes Melba's response to the older singer's fear of a rival to her supremacy among Australian singers, but this supposes an impossible degree of foresight on Melba's part. The Albert Street Conservatorium debacle of two years earlier and Hart's animosity towards Marjorie seem much more likely to have been at the heart of the matter. Whether Melba's patronage would have helped Marjorie or not is debatable anyway, as most of Dame Nellie's female protégées turned out to be seven-day wonders. Nevertheless at the time it was a disappointment to Marjorie and her supporters. While always acknowledging Melba's superlative voice and singing technique, Marjorie could not resist taking a thinly disguised swipe at Dame Nellie in *Interrupted Melody* when she referred to 'aged, rather ridiculous women refusing to quit the scene and imposing themselves on the public after their voices are gone'.

Marjorie did make one positive gain from Melba's activities in 1928. The Melba–Williamson Opera Company played in Melbourne for eight weeks and Marjorie was able to see her first operas on stage. She gloried in Verdi's *Aida* sung by a stellar cast – Hina Spani in the title role, Francesco Merli as Radames and John Brownlee as Amonasro – and marvelled at the spectacular Toti dal Monte as Lucia di Lammermoor.

If Melba was unwilling to hear Marjorie, John Brownlee was not. After the Melbourne opera season the young baritone took temporary leave from the company to undertake a concert tour of his home state. Either Hitchcock, James Galbraith (head of the Geelong competitions) or Ivor Boustead – or possibly all three – approached the easygoing Brownlee and asked if he would listen to a promising young girl from the area where he had grown up with a view to assisting her to study in Paris. Brownlee agreed willingly, and he and Elena Daniela, the soprano supporting him on the tour, listened to Marjorie sing half a dozen pieces, accompanied by their pianist William G. James, the future head of music at the Australian Broadcasting Commission.

Following the audition Brownlee was interviewed by the press and was fulsome in his praise of his young compatriot:

> *Marge Lawrence has a wonderful voice of extraordinary range and she shows marked musical ability. There's no doubt she has a great career ahead of her – she certainly has everything going for her. I have assured Mr Boustead that if Marge can come to Paris where I am now based, I will do all in my power to help her – including arranging for her to audition for Madame Cécile Gilly, one of Europe's foremost singing teachers and the wife of my own teacher, Dinh Gilly.*[10]

Brownlee's interest added to the impetus to raise money for Marjorie to travel overseas and to study full-time in Paris. It also helped to convince Bill Lawrence that something remarkable he had previously underestimated was unfolding and that he had to set aside his personal reservations. He agreed to provide the financial support Marjorie would need if she went to Paris, by paying her a monthly allowance of forty pounds – evidence of his material success in Winchelsea, his faith in Marjorie and his generosity. Benefit concerts were also arranged to raise money to cover Marjorie's travelling expenses.

Plans for Marjorie's departure now began in earnest. Howard Hitchcock used his influence to secure a deluxe cabin on the Aberdeen and Commonwealth Shipping Company's liner *Jervis Bay* scheduled to leave Melbourne for Europe at the end of October.[11] There was long and heated discussion in the front room of the Lawrence house about the need for someone to go with Marjorie as companion and chaperone – and who that should be. Lena was the obvious choice but she was still running the house and was now engaged to be married. Percy offered his services, but a woman was considered more appropriate. Finally and somewhat reluctantly on Bill's part, Ada Boddington was approached and readily agreed, persuaded no doubt by the opportunity the adventure would offer her to visit her own family in England.

As all of these discussions were taking place and the preparations for departure being made, Marjorie gave farewell concerts throughout the Western District. At the end of August a note arrived from Brownlee inviting her to sing with him at a concert he was giving to aid the Geelong Hospital in the Palais Royal on 1 September. Marjorie read the note with delight and excitement. Although she had shared platforms with other artists before, she had never sung with anyone as famous as Brownlee.

On the first occasion that Marjorie met Brownlee and while they tucked into a lunch of fish and chips, she had asked him if he thought she should lose some weight. The jovial baritone had laughed and said: 'Good Lord no, a voice like yours needs a substantial body to support it'. However, for this landmark concert, Marjorie decided she had to look as shapely and attractive as possible. Ada Boddington and Mrs Hitchcock were enlisted to help. The Hitchcock family were Geelong's leading haberdashers and Bill Lawrence parted with fifteen pounds for one of their new *'a la mode'* dinner gowns in pink plush and decorated with beads for Marjorie to wear.

> *These dear ladies, who knew much more about dressing than I did also got hold of a long corset into which I was laced and which made me look like a fugitive from a Mack Sennet comedy. Then they insisted on encompassing my breasts in one of those old fashioned bodices, the lacy, bony, uncomfortable precursor of the modern brassiere. When this monstrosity was put on me it gave me the appearance of a very cross pouter pigeon.*

Marjorie kept the pink dress (her first item of evening wear) and eventually took it to Paris with her. She also kept fond memories of that concert. Despite the constricting undergarments, she sang her two solos well and she knew it. As an encore she joined Brownlee in the duet 'Là ci darem la mano' from Mozart's *Don Giovanni.*

The next time Marjorie sang with John Brownlee would be on the stage of the Paris Opéra, when they were stars of equal brilliance.

Chapter Three

Innocents Abroad

A few weeks before Marjorie sailed for Europe she made four recordings for the Australian branch of the Aeolian Company in Melbourne. Marjorie, or her family or supporters, paid for these private recordings and, although they were allocated catalogue numbers and carried Aeolian's standard pink 'Vocalion' label, they were never issued commercially; small numbers were pressed to order (at seven shillings and sixpence each) and largely purchased as gifts. Considering how few of these discs were pressed, it is remarkable that any copies survive, but survive they do, allowing us to hear what the twenty-one-year-old Marjorie sounded like before her fame extended beyond Australia.

For the time these discs were well recorded, in what the company proudly described as its 'state-of-the-art recording studio' in Coppin Street, Richmond. Taking the catalogue numbers as a guide, the first item Marjorie recorded was Beethoven's song 'In questa tomba oscura', followed by 'O don fatale' from *Don Carlos*, the song 'Ring, Bells, Ring' by Maude Craske Day and finally a piece that became a favourite encore of Marjorie's throughout her singing career: Laura Lemon's ballad 'My Ain Folk'.

Played at eighty revolutions per minute (the standard speed for Vocalion discs), these recordings reveal a deep, resonant contralto voice and a style of singing that shows clear indebtedness to Marjorie's model Clara Butt. The tone is rich in the Beethoven song and the effect is suitably tomb-like. The heavily truncated version of 'O don fatale' (cut down to fit onto a three-minute disc) hints at why Ivor Boustead suggested Marjorie sing something else at the Ballarat competition. Marjorie gives a good display of *legato* singing in the central section, but the faster beginning and end of the aria sound choppy and there is little attempt to convey the character's emotional roller-coaster ride so beautifully translated into music by Verdi. The two popular items come off best. Marjorie sounds more relaxed and comfortable (as well she might at this stage in her career) with drawing room ballads. She had probably been singing 'My Ain Folk' for a decade before she made this recording and Marjorie relishes the tune and the words, without over-sentimentalising what is essentially a syrupy piece.

At best these recordings are curiosities, but they are important for our understanding of the singer that Marjorie would later become. Clearly that sound foundation in the lower register Boustead was striving for had been established before she left his studio and we catch glimpses of Marjorie's upper register, but as yet there is little in between. This makes the two registers (upper and lower) sound like two different voices. There are also a few stylistic signposts pointing to the future, such as a tendency to introduce *portamenti* (sliding between notes) at unexpected moments in the music, which would become hallmarks of Marjorie's mature style.[1]

Marjorie farewelled the people of Winchelsea and Geelong at two final concerts. In Winchelsea the 'pictures' at the Globe Theatre were suspended for one night, and the locals, including the entire Lawrence family and a large contingent from Deans Marsh, assembled to hear Marjorie sing. Supported by local artists, the Western District's favourite daughter was decked out in her pink beaded evening gown.

At the conclusion of the Winchelsea concert Marjorie was presented with a travelling rug made from local wool – 'to remind you of the district where you grew up and the people who are so proud of you'. The soft, thick rug would prove useful when Marjorie arrived in Europe at the beginning of winter, but neither she nor any of the good folk who gathered around her after the concert shaking her hand and admiring their gift could ever have imagined that it would end up stolen by German soldiers when Hitler's army marched into Paris twelve years later.

After the Geelong concert, Howard Hitchcock, still smarting from his failure to keep his promise about Melba, made a fervent speech in which he predicted Marjorie would eclipse *all* other Australian-born female singers. He then presented Marjorie with a leather-bound, gold-embossed address book, which fortunately did not share the fate of the rug. Marjorie used that little book for the next twenty years and it survives, worn soft and dog-eared, among Marjorie's papers.

At a farewell party for Marjorie on her last night at home, the Lawrences gathered around the piano and sang together for a final time, at the end of the evening her father, brothers and sister singing the old hymn 'God be with you till we meet again' for her. It was typical of the Lawrences and many families in what Patrick White called this land of callused hearts, to express their feelings in song rather than words, but the sentiments were no less sincere.

The liner *Jervis Bay* was scheduled to sail from Prince's Pier, Port Melbourne at 4.30 on the afternoon of 23 October, bound for Southampton, the port from which Grandma Lawrence had embarked seventy-four years earlier. Passengers had been requested to board the ship by 3.30 pm, but the Lawrences, en masse, had arrived hours before. They had inspected the cabin Marjorie and Boddie would be sharing for the next five weeks and had organised for a couple of rather shaky family photos to be taken in the pale sunlight on deck. This was the last time all the Lawrence 'kids' were photographed together with 'Dad' in their midst. Bill Lawrence, now in his late sixties and with his moustache turned snowy white, looks dejected and preoccupied in the photographs. Marjorie looks tense and excited, decked out in a voluminous rabbit skin coat and hanging on for dear life to a capacious handbag.

In *Interrupted Melody* Marjorie gives a fictional and romanticised account of the departure of the ship, describing a sea of coloured paper streamers, her Dad standing forlornly on the wharf and Marjorie, blinded by tears, singing his favourite song to him from the ship's railing. What actually happened was much more prosaic. Instead of a call for all those going ashore to leave the ship, an announcement was made that the *Jervis Bay*'s sailing would be delayed for several hours because of a massive storm in the Great Australian Bight. As time passed father and brothers began to fidget; there were cows at home that needed milking, a long drive ahead of them with early morning chores the next day, and lightning and thunder fast approaching.

Marjorie sadly farewelled her family, with Bill reassuring her that he would arrange her journey home if things didn't go to plan or if she became homesick. He also said in an aside Marjorie was not supposed to hear, 'Oh well, I'll never see *her* again'. Tears flowed and Marjorie's last glimpse of her family came as they hurried into the watery gloom on Prince's Pier.

The *Jervis Bay* finally sailed at midnight and the first twelve hours of the voyage were an ordeal, with Marjorie and Boddie taking refuge in their bunks and remaining there as the steamer ploughed through mountainous seas, gale-force winds and torrential rain, finally limping into Port Adelaide, their first port of call. By the time the ship steamed out of Fremantle into the broad, blue expanse of the Indian Ocean two days later, the weather and the passengers had brightened and Marjorie and Boddie slipped effortlessly into the gay milieu of shipboard life.

As a companion Ada Boddington was a great success, but as a chaperone she failed miserably. One of the senior officers on the ship took a fancy to her and she was soon off flirting with him, leaving Marjorie to take care of herself. Also on board was a young Englishman named William Baker who chanced his luck with Marjorie. 'Bill' Baker, who was in the diamond business, an agent for a company based at Johannesburg, was on his way home to Birmingham from New Zealand. Athletic, blonde-haired, snappily dressed, full of charm and by Marjorie's standards, alluringly sophisticated, he was just a year older than she – and Marjorie fell for him.

When the ship docked at Colombo, Marjorie and her new beau went ashore with a group of other young people. They engaged a fleet of rickshaws and visited what they thought was a famous tea house. There they lounged on divans smoking cigarettes in preposterously long holders, savouring the scent of the nutmeg flowers that filled the air and feeling delightfully exotic. Suspicion dawned when the nubile young women who served them began making suggestive gestures at the menfolk. The party beat a hasty retreat. The 'tea house' turned out to be the most famous brothel in the city.

Colombo had other exotic attractions on offer. Someone suggested a drive to Moratura Beach, south of the city, which was famous for nude bathing. Having swum naked in creeks and dams with her brothers all through her childhood Marjorie was not particularly troubled by the concept of nudity, but she and her companions were alarmed when a large crocodile suddenly appeared on the beach scattering bathers. Another hasty retreat was made, this time back to the ship.

Between their departure from Colombo and the ship's entry into the Red Sea, Marjorie was involved in an embarrassing incident, but not one of her making. Marjorie and Boddie had barely spoken to the captain of the *Jervis Bay*, a portly, bewhiskered old salt, since coming on board and were surprised when a steward knocked on their cabin door and presented them with a handwritten note from the captain inviting 'Marjorie and companion' to join him for dinner that night. When the two presented themselves at the captain's table at eight as instructed, the captain's first words to Marjorie were: 'Thank you so much for the flowers, my dear. How thoughtful of a young girl like you.' Marjorie responded with: 'What flowers?' It transpired that the captain had received a large floral arrangement accompanied by a card reading: 'With the compliments of Marjorie'. A young violinist named Marjorie Schmitt who was travelling to Belgium hoping to study with the great violin virtuoso Eugène Ysaÿe had joined the ship at Port Adelaide, but the captain had assumed that the flowers were from Marjorie Lawrence. In fact, they were from Marjorie Schmitt. Despite this incident Marjorie and Boddie enjoyed a splendid meal along with the other privileged guests that evening and Boddie showed Marjorie how to eat asparagus, a delicacy she had never tasted before. Marjorie Schmitt had her turn at the captain's table the following night.

Sailing through the Suez Canal fascinated Marjorie. Ships going in opposite directions passed each other with what seemed like only feet separating them, while Arabs leading camels plodded along the shore line in the shadows of the gigantic grey steel ships. It was an extraordinary juxtaposition of modern and ancient cultures, and when the sun set, the howling of jackals could be heard from both banks.

Twenty-one days out of Melbourne, the *Jervis Bay* entered Port Said, where feluccas with dark red sails clustered along the shore and naked boys dived into the sea to retrieve coins thrown by the ship's passengers. Marjorie and Bill Baker went ashore and explored the city. Marjorie was appalled by the filth in the streets and the stinking smells that hung in the still air. As dusk approached and what the couple decided were 'rum-looking coves' began to appear on the streets, they beat yet another hasty retreat to the safety of the *Jervis Bay*.

Long romantic nights in tropical waters and shared adventures brought Marjorie and the young Englishmen closer together and sex seemed the inevitable next stage in their relationship, until Marjorie dropped the news that this was to be a new experience for her. Bill Baker backed off rapidly, leaving Marjorie wondering whether virginity was to be her permanent lot. The two settled back into a friendship, although marriage was spoken of and Baker promised to write to Marjorie when he reached home. The pair also made plans to meet later in London. Nothing came of it and Marjorie heard no more about Bill Baker until a woman approached her after a concert in Birmingham in 1945 and introduced herself as Bill's sister. Her brother, the woman said, was then living in South Africa, but still spoke fondly of Marjorie. Like Pat Considine, Bill Baker never married.

As the *Jervis Bay* steamed through the Mediterranean, Marjorie received a request from the captain to sing at the Armistice Day service he was to conduct on deck. Before the assembled passengers and crew and with noisy gulls squawking overhead, Marjorie sang Elgar's 'Land of Hope and Glory' accompanied by the ship's dance band. It was the first time her voice had been heard publicly outside her homeland.

The *Jervis Bay* docked at Southampton on 17 November. Marjorie and Boddie travelled to London by train and then on to the Midlands for a brief visit to Boddie's parents, and from there to Paris. For this last stage of their journey the pair took the train to Dover, a ferry across the channel to Calais and finally another train to Paris, arriving at Gare Saint-Lazare on a wet afternoon, feeling bedraggled, lost and confused. Marjorie's dream of reaching Paris had finally come true, but at the time she wondered if it would prove to be a nightmare. Rolling green paddocks, bright sunshine, friendly 'Aussie' faces and the familiar drawl seemed to belong to a different universe.

The travel company that had booked the trip from London for the pair had also arranged for Marjorie and Boddie to stay at the Hôtel Louvre Sainte-Anne just off Avenue de l'Opéra. The distance between the station and the hotel is no more than two kilometres, but neither of them knew that. They waved down a taxi and explained in broken English that they wanted to be taken to the 'Saint Anne Hotel'. The driver pegged them as strangers (and gullible ones at that) and drove half way around central Paris before dropping them in Rue Sainte-Anne and demanding twenty-nine francs, three times the amount the journey should have cost.

From the taxi Marjorie had caught glimpses of the Opéra – Paris's grand opera house – known to Parisians as the 'Palais Garnier' in honour of its architect. Marjorie insisted that before they unpack she and Boddie walk up Avenue de l'Opéra to see the building at close range. The women stood on the busy Place de l'Opéra and stared in awe at the intricately carved stone façade of what is still the grandest of all opera houses, crowned with busts of famous composers and adorned with colossal gilded statues. 'I'm going to sing there one day', Marjorie told her companion. 'Of course you are, Marge dear', Boddie replied but neither of them was convinced.

John Brownlee had returned to Paris ahead of Marjorie and she had written to the baritone giving him the date of their arrival and the name of their hotel.

Time and again Marjorie asked at the hotel reception desk if there was a message for her from Monsieur Jean Brownlee, but none came. Finally after three days she mustered the courage to ring Brownlee's apartment in the suburb of Nieully-sur-Seine. The singer's sister, Jess, answered the telephone. When Marjorie explained who she was, Jess Brownlee (who was always fiercely protective of her brother) informed her impatiently that 'John has the flu and is far too sick to see you'. Marjorie was about to retaliate with some words the singer's sister probably hadn't heard since leaving Australia, when Jess Brownlee added: 'However, he has arranged an audition for you with Madame Gilly at four on Thursday afternoon, so make sure you're there'. Marjorie's relief was immense as Jess Brownlee gave her Cécile Gilly's address, spelling out the words carefully while Marjorie scribbled them down on a scrap of paper.

The following Thursday, two hours before the appointed time and clutching the scrap of paper and a street map she had bought to guide her, Marjorie climbed the lower slopes of the hill leading up to Montmartre and located number 58 Rue de la Rochefoucauld, an address that would become like a second home to her over the next couple of years.[2] She hung around in the street filling in time until just before the appointed time and then rang the doorbell. A maid showed Marjorie to the top floor and ushered her into 'Madame's' studio, a spacious room with a grand piano and a small stage with burgundy-coloured proscenium drapes. A beautiful, dignified looking woman with skin like ivory and touches of grey through her hair sat in the centre of the room. Beside her stood John Brownlee, a beaming smile on his face.

Marjorie's French extended no further than *'Bon jour, Madame'* and if Gilly had any English she was not about to waste it on this gauche bumpkin from Australia. Brownlee acted as interpreter, but Gilly wasted no time on small talk. 'Chantez, chantez, Mademoiselle', she ordered.

A young female pianist appeared from nowhere and Marjorie climbed onto the little stage, while Gilly and Brownlee retreated to the other end of the room. Marjorie sang 'O don fatale' in Italian, and 'O, My Heart is Weary' in English. Gilly then came forward, her face expressionless, and waved the pianist off the piano stool. She sat at the piano herself and struck a key indicating with an imperious gesture that Marjorie was to sing the same note. As Boustead had made her do years before, Marjorie followed Gilly, singing scales and isolated notes that took her from the bottom to the top of her voice.

Although Marjorie had sung very little since leaving Australia, she knew she was singing well, speculating that the enforced rest might have been beneficial to her voice. When Gilly finally stopped playing and exclaimed: 'Ah, une soprano dramatique ... une soprano *Wagnerienne*!' and Marjorie saw the look of satisfaction on Brownlee's face, she knew she had done well.

The exchanges that followed had to be translated by Brownlee. Gilly said she would teach Marjorie and asked where she was living. When Marjorie mentioned the hotel, Gilly threw her hands in the air and said a hotel was not the right place for a student to live and that Marjorie should be living with a French family where she could learn the language and steep herself in 'the glorious culture of France'. Gilly added that she knew such a family and would arrange an introduction to them for Marjorie and her companion. Marjorie departed from 58 Rue de la Rochefoucauld with her head spinning, her feet barely touching the ground and her confidence renewed.

Next day a petite and friendly woman named Marguerite Palustre arrived at the Hôtel Louvre Sainte-Anne and introduced herself to Marjorie and Boddie. Mademoiselle Palustre was a teacher of languages who specialised in teaching French to English-speaking singing students, including several from Madame Gilly's studio. Madame Gilly, she explained, had charged her with escorting Marjorie and 'Madame Boddington' to meet the family of Monsieur and Madame Grodet.

Palustre had a small automobile and as she drove Marjorie and Boddie back up the hill towards Montmartre she explained tactfully that the Grodets were very respectable people who had fallen on hard times and supported themselves by taking in foreign students as lodgers. The little car swung into Avenue Trudaine, a kilometre further up the hill from Gilly's house and stopped outside number twenty-seven. The southern side of this broad tree-lined avenue was (and is) typical of residential streets in central Paris, with a continuous line of five-story buildings dating from the Haussmann era, all facing straight onto the street and graced by tall windows, ornate pediments and cast-iron balconies.

Without the thought of singing to distract her, Marjorie felt more uncomfortable meeting the family she might soon be living with than she had confronting Madame Gilly. She recalled with amusement:

> *I was wearing a two-tone dress made out of heavy wool – one of my homemade Winchelsea numbers. The skirt was a dull brown and the top insipid beige with a large floppy bow on the neckline. This was matched with flat-heeled shoes and my big, all purpose handbag. The Grodets looked me up and down and frowned and all I could do was giggle!*[3]

Monsieur Emile Grodet and Madame Marie Grodet de Lacratelle were both elderly, courtly and spoke no English. Also at the meeting was their son, Henri, a tall, slim, dark-haired young man in his mid-twenties. Marjorie thought young Grodet very charming and wondered if she was being introduced to the first of those immoral Frenchmen she had heard about.

The Grodets owned the third level of the building and already had lodgers occupying some of their eight bedrooms. The house was filled with oversized antiques, tinkling chandeliers and old paintings – relics of the Grodets' wealthier days, Palustre explained in an aside to Marjorie. The décor seemed excessively ornate to Marjorie who knew nothing about antiques, and the plumbing in the communal bathroom looked primitive, but as the rent was low and the location ideal, a deal was struck. Marjorie and Boddie moved to Avenue Trudaine the next day.

As Marjorie got to know the Grodets she discovered much about them that was interesting and endearing. Emile Grodet was a *Chevalier de la Légion d'honneur* and had been the mayor and leading industrialist in the town of Noisy-le-Grand in the Marne Valley, until his partner ruined their business. Grodet had to sell off all his assets except the house in Paris to pay the debts the partner had incurred in their joint names. Marjorie described him as 'charming, courteous in old-fashioned ways and a fervent patriot who still fancied himself as a ladies' man'.[4]

Madame Grodet de Lacratelle, who retained her family name, was an aristocrat and an essayist, a deeply religious woman who was beginning to lose her eyesight when Marjorie came to live with them. Later she would proudly explain to Marjorie that she had grown up in a château, could trace her family back for centuries, was related to three members of the Académie française and as a girl had conversed with Lamartine and Victor Hugo.[5]

The first meal Marjorie and Boddie shared with the Grodets, like so many of Marjorie's experiences of recent times, quickly developed into a farce. Seated around the massive dining table were 'Madame' and 'Monsieur', who ate with great formality and scowled if anyone spoke in any language other than French (suspecting the offender might be slandering them), Marjorie and Boddie (whom the Grodets called Madame *Boddin-tune* to her great annoyance) and several other boarders, including Einar Johansen, a young Danish piano student who alone among the other residents spoke some English.[6]

The food was good but not plentiful and Boddie caused annoyance by demanding that she must have a salad. The Grodets' old maid, Lucienne, was despatched grumbling to the pantry to cobble together a dish the Grodets never ate and considered decidedly bourgeois. When the main course was served Marjorie experimented with one of the French phrases she had learned: 'Passez-moi le pot de moutarde, s'il vous plait', but the Grodets were not impressed at this early stage in their acquaintance with the strange women from a land they believed was populated largely by *les kangaroos* and *les chiens sauvage*. When coffee was served Marjorie discovered a new taste sensation: camembert cheese, another food that became a lifelong passion for her.[7]

Trips to the bathroom were also comical. Still suspicious of all French men, Marjorie would only venture to the communal bathroom in company with Boddie. The other residents thought these antipodeans very odd as they scuttled along the hall arm in arm and swathed in unbecoming bathrobes and leather slippers. A rumour soon spread through the house that they were '*les lesbiennes*' even though they had separate bedrooms.

Marjorie's room had a French window opening onto a tiny balcony overlooking the street and opposite the house was the Lycée Rollin, a famous boys' school where the alumni included the painters Manet, Moreau and Utrillo.[8] Marjorie spent many hours at the window watching the boys in their distinctive uniforms going back and forth to school in the wan winter sunlight or icy driving rain, thinking all the while about her brothers back home. To John Brownlee she confessed that she wasn't sure how well she would be able to cope with big city living, apartment dwelling, dusty antiques and bleak weather, and how she longed for the sunshine and greenery of Australia. 'You'll have to get used to it like I did', her compatriot told her. 'It's no use complaining. You can't get out in the paddocks here, Marge. This is *Paris*.'[9]

Marjorie did get used to it and came to understand and love Paris, claiming it as her second home, but this took time. Typical of the knowledge that did not filter through to her for some time was that on the opposite side of the Lycée Rollin and a mere one hundred metres from her window was Boulevard de Rochechouart, location of several of Paris's most famous *maison closes* and the haunt of legions of streetwalkers and dirty postcard sellers. Henry Miller wrote that 'semen ran thick in the gutters of Boulevard de Rochechouart'. For a while at least Marjorie remained blissfully ignorant of such realities and fortunately for her, the only 'Miller' read in the Lawrence household back home was the local grocer's advertising.

Einar Johansen helped Marjorie acclimatise, as did Henri Grodet. Johansen became a friend and Henri became Marjorie's latest boyfriend and, quite possibly, her first lover. Henri showed Marjorie over Paris, including to the top of the Eiffel Tower and on picnics to the Bois de Boulogne. He also introduced her to the delights of French cuisine and Paris café society and took her for the first time to the Opéra to hear Brownlee sing Telramund in Wagner's *Lohengrin*.

Another member of the Grodet family was helpful to Marjorie's acclimatisation. A few weeks after Marjorie arrived one of the Grodet daughters returned home after a disastrous marriage to a brutal Armenian silk merchant. Emilie – known to everyone as 'Mimi' – was as tall as her brother and had the same pale skin and doleful eyes, features which made Henri attractive, while she simply looked wan. But Mimi was kind of heart and immediately became fond of Marjorie. Soon Mimi was accorded the title 'best friend', supplanting Yvonne Batson in far-off Australia.

For all her lack of beauty, Mimi was a French woman through and through and she took it upon herself to inject some chic into Marjorie's fashion sense and improve her appearance, beginning by helping Marjorie to choose a couple of hats. 'Only servants go into the street without *le chapeau, cheri*', Mimi admonished her sternly.

The need for Mimi's sartorial advice was reinforced when Marjorie and Boddie were invited by Jess Brownlee to a tea party, attended by several elegant French woman and another Australian, Louise Hanson-Dyer, millionairess, patron of the arts and unofficial *chargé d'affaires* of the Australian community in Paris. Marjorie thought she acquitted herself well enough that afternoon, but as she was leaving her hostess took her aside and told her bluntly that her frock was a disaster, her hair needed thinning out and slicking down and her flat shoes were beyond the pale.

Under Mimi's guidance Marjorie began to wear fewer layers of clothing, replaced her woolly Australian underwear with some more feminine items, got her hair *coiffured* and began to take interest and care in the details of dressing. The transformation from 'young bumpkin' to 'glamorous woman' began, and just occasionally progressed a little too far. After Jess Brownlee's rebuke, Marjorie went out and bought herself a skin-tight dress and the highest-heeled pair of shoes she could find. She turned up for her next singing lesson wearing this outfit and with her hair severely slicked down. Madame Gilly screamed 'Mon Dieu! You look like *une putain*. Go home immediately and change and don't come back till you are *Marjoree* again!' The slinky dress and the towering shoes were relegated to the back of Marjorie's wardrobe and never worn again.

Early in the new year, Boddie announced that she was returning to Australia. There had never been a firm agreement between the two women about how long Boddie would keep her company, but Marjorie had envisaged it running to months rather than weeks and she was surprised and nervous at the prospect of being left 'alone', although Mimi, Henri and the senior Grodets assured her they would take care of her.

The Grodets kept their word and Mimi proved a reliable friend and later a staunch ally when Marjorie began to build her career. Henri provided much more than that and it was the great regret of his and Mimi's lives that Marjorie did not marry Henri and that the two women did not become sisters in the legal sense. 'Henri was handsome, charming and lovable,' Marjorie would recall wistfully years later, 'but I was focused on making a career as a singer and I was not about to make the mistake I nearly made with Pat Considine'.[10] Monsieur and Madame Grodet soon warmed to Marjorie, recognising her Aussie ebullience, enthusiasm and ready laugh as virtues, not signs of frivolousness. They became like doting grandparents to her and in years to come they would follow her triumphs with pride, while she agonised over the misfortunes that befell them.

Chapter Four

Mademoiselle Lawrence

Despite the Great Depression (which took a little longer to reach France than it did other major industrialised countries), Paris could justifiably claim to be the artistic hub of the world in the late 1920s and early 1930s – a magnet for painters, writers and, to a lesser extent, musicians from around the globe.

If Marjorie had wandered down Rue de la Boétie, a couple of kilometres from Avenue Trudaine, there was a good chance she might have spotted Pablo Picasso coming or going from his studio, or Salvador Dali exhibiting himself in any of the hundreds of fashionable cafés around the city. If she had been so inclined, she might have shaken hands with Henry Miller, T.S. Elliot, Colette, F. Scott Fitzgerald or James Joyce (whom she did eventually meet) at Sylvia Beach's 'Shakespeare and Company' bookshop on the Left Bank.

In the frenetic years following the end of the First World War, style had replaced substance and hedonism had replaced heroism in 'The City of Light'. *Haute couture* was being reinvented by Coco Chanel and Elsa Schiaparelli and the houses of Guerlain and Coty were doing the same for *parfum*. At the Folies-Bergère Josephine Baker could be seen shaking her derriere, while the Penobscot Indian, Molly Spotted Elk, performed her controversial tribal dance at Bricktop's cabaret 'up the hill' on Montmartre.

Musical activity was only slightly less spectacular. If they were in town, Louis Armstrong or Django Reinhart might have been encountered doing a 'turn' at one of the city's famous nightspots. Stravinsky was quietly producing a string of masterpieces in his apartment in Rue du Faubourg-St-Honoré; Ravel, though he lived in the country, popped up to town frequently, while the group of composers calling themselves *Les Six* were active, and would-be composers were flocking to the composition classes of Nadia Boulanger, described by Ned Rorem as the most influential teacher since Socrates.

The greatest singers of the time visited Paris and sang as guests at the Opéra and in the city's historic concert halls, but if foreign singers found ready acceptance in Paris, French singers of this period found less of a welcome when they ventured abroad. It was not that the great French singers of the day (Ninon Vallin, Germaine Lubin, Georges Thill etc.) were not first-class artists with fine voices; it was rather a matter of taste, their 'Gallic' style of singing finding less acceptance outside France than the more torrid and lachrymose outpourings of their counterparts from south of the Alps.[1]

It might be said that Marjorie qualified for inclusion in the Paris musical fraternity from the moment she began lessons with Cécile Gilly, albeit at the lowest level. Being a pupil of Madame Gilly carried status, for among connoisseurs of singing in Paris, Cécile Gilly was legendary. Marjorie had her first lesson with Madame two days after she moved in with the Grodets and thereafter four times a week. Gilly proved to be an exacting and demanding teacher, which Marjorie could cope with, but she was also cold and unfriendly towards her new pupil. Easygoing and affable Marjorie found this difficult to cope with and she left Rue de la Rochefoucauld in tears many times during the first months. Marjorie had little choice but to persevere and it was well she did, because Cécile Gilly proved to be the ideal teacher for the present state of Marjorie's voice, her current level of accomplishment and her aspirations to be a dramatic soprano.

As *maîtresse* and *pupille* came to know one another better, their relationship improved. Like the elder Grodets, Gilly probably mistook Marjorie's ebullience for a lack of commitment or dedication, but after Marjorie proved that she internalised and applied what she was taught and had demonstrated that she was willing to work very hard, Gilly softened. Another factor must have been the teacher's awareness of the quality of the pupil's voice. At that time Gilly had about twenty other students, including the Australian coloratura soprano Rita Miller, but none of these had the spectacular voice Marjorie was blessed with. It would not have been too long before she realised that she had a potential star on her hands, one of those rare gilt-edged assets no singing teacher, no matter how famous they are, can afford to let slip through their fingers.[2]

Marjorie also came to understand why her teacher was 'a tough cookie', as she later described her in an American journal. Madame Gilly had had a hard life. As Cécile Roma she had enjoyed a successful career as a mezzo-soprano in France and had then married the charismatic French-Algerian baritone Dinh Gilly (Brownlee's future teacher). In 1909 both were engaged by the Metropolitan Opera in New York and made their debuts with the Met's subsidiary company at the New Theatre, Dinh as Albert in Massenet's *Werther* and Cécile in the small role of Amarante in Lecocq's *La Fille de Madame Angot*. Dinh made a good impression and moved straight into the principal company. Cécile did not. When the Met gave a season in Paris in 1910, she was included in that company to sing minor roles and never returned to America.[3] After that her husband kept her perpetually pregnant and off the stage, while his career blossomed *and* while he pursued a long love affair with another soprano, the famous Emmy Destinn.

After the birth of their third child, Dinh Gilly abandoned his wife to live openly with his mistress in her castle in Bohemia. With a young family to care for and support single-handedly, Cécile Gilly turned to teaching and, although she had built an enviable reputation by the time Marjorie came along, it had been a struggle, made harder by the continuing interference of her husband. As Marjorie described, the still infatuated Cécile welcomed him into her home and her bed whenever he deigned to visit her and she bore Gilly two more children. The struggle had been long and the toll it had exacted on Madame had left its mark.

From the outset, Gilly trained Marjorie as a soprano. The dark-toned contralto voice that had ponderously negotiated 'In questa tomba oscura' and 'O Rest in the Lord' a few months earlier was set aside and the bright-toned dramatic soprano that had been kept in check for so long was allowed to emerge and develop in its place. But the transition was not accomplished lightly.

> *Madame Gilly boasted, quite justifiably, that she was 'the flag-bearer of technique' and day after day for many weeks she permitted me to sing nothing but scales and exercises and when at last she allowed me to sing some arias they were excerpts from the operas of Handel, Mozart and Rossini or the cantatas of J.S. Bach, calculated to lighten up my voice and strengthen my technique.*[4]

Gilly also developed and strengthened the 'middle' section of Marjorie's voice – the notes linking the upper and lower registers that are so conspicuously missing in the recordings Marjorie had made before leaving Australia. This had the effect of integrating the registers into a seamless progression of notes and eliminating any audible 'gear changing'.

By mid-1929 Gilly was beginning to coach Marjorie in complete opera roles. The title role in Gluck's *Alceste*, which Gilly herself had sung on stage in France and Marjorie would later sing at the Met in New York, was the first. For this she renewed her acquaintance with the young pianist who had accompanied her at her audition with Gilly, who had turned out to be Madame's eldest daughter, Renée, just a year older than Marjorie and assisting her mother while she prepared for a career of her own as a mezzo-soprano.[5]

Cécile Gilly insisted that her pupils learn every note of any role they studied before she began to instruct them on interpretation, and helping Marjorie do this was Renée Gilly's task. Marjorie's diaries for the years she studied in Paris show that she spent as much time working with Renée as she did with Cécile, although Marjorie never acknowledged Renée's contribution when she came to discuss or write about her training.

Once again Marjorie's excellent memory came to her aid as she learned Alceste and then a sequence of other parts with Renée coaching and prompting her from the piano – note by note and phrase by phrase for hour upon hour. Within a few months she had mastered another five roles: the title role in *Aida*, Valentine in Meyerbeer's *Les Huguenots*, Donna Anna in *Don Giovanni*, Salomé in Massenet's *Hérodiade* and the title role in Ponchielli's *La Gioconda* – all but the last, roles she would sing on stage when her career commenced. Aida, Donna Anna and Gioconda were learned in Italian first and then in French to accommodate the practice in France's opera houses of singing almost everything in French. In each case Marjorie then moved on to study the vocal and histrionic intricacies of performing these roles with Madame Gilly.

Six principal roles in six months may seem like an inflated claim, but time and again throughout her career, Marjorie proved that she could learn shorter parts in a couple of weeks and longer ones in a month – or two, at the most – and the proof of how efficient she was at this lies in the almost complete absence of criticism against her for lapses in either words or music.[6]

Marjorie also began French lessons with Marguerite Palustre and soon had an idiomatic command of the language, which allowed her to communicate easily and to sing roles in French with verisimilitude.

> *Mademoiselle Palustre set me taxing exercises. For a word like 'Dieu' which crops up frequently in opera, I had to repeat over and over again 'Dieu grand', 'Dieu bon', 'Dieu de toute clémence' etc. This was very important as it was not possible to get into the Opéra as a regular if one sang French with a foreign accent.*[7]

It seems that, from the beginning of her studies in Paris, it was the unanimous objective of all Marjorie's teachers to get her onto the roster of the Paris Opéra. Setting aside the question of national pride in the company itself – every Parisian believes the Opéra is, always has been and always will be the best in the world – there were good musical reasons for Marjorie to set her sights on a stage career. At this point in the development of her voice she had the capability to sing what the French call 'Falcon' roles. These are a range of taxing soprano roles in French operas requiring power, endurance, a solid middle register and a strong upper register, rising to a top 'D'. Good examples are Valentine in *Les Huguenots*, which Marjorie had learned, and Rachel in Halévy's *La Juive*, which she would soon set about learning.

The operas in which these roles occur are performed most often in France and the Falcon parts are difficult to cast. Lighter-voiced sopranos find them heavy-going and most Wagnerian sopranos lack the agility to sing them. Marjorie could and did sing these roles and in later years when she joined the ranks of the Wagnerians, she was one of the few who retained enough vocal agility to be able to continue to sing them.

Cornélie Falcon, the French soprano after whom these roles were named, also had a 'wild' quality about her singing – a calculated abandon which excited audiences. Marjorie also possessed that quality, which was confirmed by an unexpected commentator. One morning when Marjorie was having a lesson with Cécile Gilly, the maid interrupted and announced anxiously: 'Monsieur est ici', and into the studio strode Dinh Gilly.

The famous baritone was now in his fifties and had retired from the stage, but he was still charismatic. We can probably be confident of Marjorie's reaction to his shock of black hair just starting to turn grey, his misshapen nose (it had been broken more than once) and his dark-ringed eyes. It was now apparent to Marjorie why so many women had fallen for this man and she found herself feeling a little flushed in his presence. Monsieur Gilly insisted the lesson continue and he sat down to listen to Marjorie. Later he exclaimed: '*Magnifique!* She is like a young horse this one!' Then he remonstrated with his wife: 'For God's sake, Cécile, don't try to tame her. There are too many tame creatures in the world today!' [8]

Cécile Gilly was not about to tame 'the young horse', but she did feel the need to curb some of the extracurricular activities Marjorie was pursuing which she felt might be harmful to her pupil's voice and studies. Marjorie had found indoor tennis courts and indoor swimming baths not far from Avenue Trudaine and indulged in long bouts of ball bashing and swimming. Madame took her aside one day and remonstrated with her about wasting energy on *les sports* when she could have been studying or practising her singing – or preparing for *le concert*. Marjorie dutifully agreed but did not give up these typically Aussie pursuits; she simply never mentioned them again within Gilly's hearing.

The concert Gilly referred to was a twice-yearly event she organised in her studio to highlight the talents of her students to invited guests from the city's musical fraternity. At the next, on 12 June 1929, Marjorie sang 'Divinités du Styx' from *Alceste* and the taxing aria 'Bel raggio lusinghier' from Rossini's *Semiramide*. The noble *Alceste* aria remained in Marjorie's repertoire throughout her career and we have a fine 'off air' recording of it by which we can judge Marjorie's accomplishment in it, but of 'Bel raggio' we have nothing. It would be fascinating to know how Marjorie coped with the rapid scales and stratospheric top notes of this aria, but we can only guess. There are no reports of this concert, which rates as Marjorie's semi-public and pre-professional debut in Paris.

Gilly must have been pleased with Marjorie's performance for she invited her, along with other students, to vacation with her in the historic old town of Euse in the Midi-Pyrénées, during August. Madame had a summer villa there called 'Mont Fleurie' which could house about two-thirds of the students and the rest were billeted in the town. As this trip took place before the time Gilly softened towards Marjorie, she was not one of the privileged ones chosen to stay at the villa. Instead she, Rita Miller and a girl from New Zealand named Gladys Petrie were installed in a cottage in the village – an annex to the local auberge – with Marguerite Palustre to guard them. Three high-spirited antipodeans living across the road from a pub was a sure recipe for trouble, and fun and games began almost immediately, with 'Marge' as the ringleader.

Madame had presented each of the girls with two pairs of thick white stockings and instructed them to wear them at all times in order to satisfy the strict moral standards of rural France. The trio found these far too hot and the young women could be found on the first few afternoons sunbathing on the verge in front of the cottage, hatless, stockingless and sipping aperitifs smuggled from across the road.

The food the auberge supplied was good but insufficient to satisfy the large appetites the girls had, so they made frequent sorties on the auberge's orchard after dark, stealing peaches and pears. To protect their legs from mosquitoes, the trio donned their white stockings for these raids, and that proved their undoing. The owner of the auberge spotted six white legs in the moonlight one night and apprehended them loaded with baskets of his fruit.

Next morning Madame came storming down from the villa like an avenging fury, waving a furled umbrella and complaining about the disgrace Marjorie, Rita and Gladys had brought upon her. The girls and their ineffectual chaperone were removed to a quaint old farm house, where it was hoped they could do less damage.

Some American girls were already installed at the farmhouse and Marjorie had a room across the hall from one of them – a rather fey creature named 'Janie' who spent her time writing fairy stories. Years later when Marjorie sang at the Civic Opera House in Chicago for the first time, 'Janie' turned up and introduced herself as Jane Crusinberry, author of radio serials and a household name in America.

There were also bats in the bedrooms, ducks in the kitchen and a flighty horse in the yard called 'Colibri' whom nobody had ever been able to ride. Marjorie bet the other girls that she could ride 'Colibri' and leapt onto the horse's back. The horse bolted and Marjorie clung to its mane. It was not long before Marjorie had settled the animal and was doing what she had done in Winchelsea – tearing along with the wind blowing in her face and singing at the top of her voice. This time it was Donna Anna's 'Vengeance' aria from *Don Giovanni*. Colibri headed towards Gilly's villa and without reins Marjorie could do little to divert him. As rider and horse shot by, an outraged Madame threw up a window and shouted: '*Marjoree! Marjoree!* You'll break your neck ... and you're singing *sharp*!'

Back in Paris, another Australian, Norma Gadsden, came to live at the Grodets and to study with Cécile Gilly. Gadsden was also a dramatic soprano who later turned to Wagner, subsequently becoming a respected singing teacher under her married name of Madame Dominique Modesti. Gadsden hoped that Marjorie would smooth paths for her as Brownlee had done for Marjorie, but according to Lauris Elms who studied with the Modestis and heard the story directly from Gadsden, Marjorie saw the newcomer as a rival for the affections of Henri Grodet and the attention of Cécile Gilly. No doubt she was uncooperative and the two Victorians never became what Australians call 'mates', but Marjorie's diary does show they socialised frequently and sang together on stage on a couple of occasions.

As the autumn of 1929 turned into winter and the anniversary of Marjorie's arrival in Paris approached, she continued her studies with Cécile Gilly and her coaching with Renée Gilly, adding five more roles to her repertoire: Rachel in *La Juive*, Marguerite in Berlioz's *La Damnation de Faust*, Sélika in Meyerbeer's

L'Africaine, Santuzza in Mascagni's *Cavalleria Rusticana* and the title role in Puccini's *Madama Butterfly*. Of these she would sing Rachel several times on stage, Sélika just twice and the others not at all, and yet their learning added to her knowledge and her versatility and, she hoped, hastened the day when the doors of the Opéra would open to her.

On 26 November Marjorie made what could be described as her 'official' debut in Paris in a concert at the prestigious Salle Gaveau. Unlike the earlier studio concert, this one was open to the public, but as Marjorie had to pay for the privilege of singing rather than *be* paid for it, it hardly qualifies as her professional debut. Philippe Gaubert, principal conductor at the Opéra, a minor composer and a major friend of Cécile Gilly's approached Gilly for performers for a small concert of his own music. Gaubert came to the studio and listened to a handful of pupils chosen by Gilly, including Marjorie. The next day the successful students received a note from Madame impressing on them the generosity of the opportunity they were being offered and informing them that if they paid her an agent's fee of 100 francs each, they could avail themselves of it. Such pragmatism might have seemed out of place in an artistic milieu, except in Paris.

Marjorie duly paid her 100 francs and sang Gaubert's orchestral song cycle *Au Jardin de l'infante* (settings of poems by Albert Samain) with members of the Paris Conservatoire Orchestra, conducted by the composer. Because the concert took place on a Sunday, none of the critics from the newspapers attended, so although there are no reviews there is plenty of other evidence that Marjorie's singing was successful. She alone among the singers was asked for an encore and with Gaubert beaming down from the podium, she repeated the final song in the cycle. Gilly was so pleased with her performance that any lingering reservations she may have had about 'Marjoree' vanished and she was promoted to the position of 'star' pupil. However, when Maestro Gaubert suggested that the star pupil should immediately audition for the Opéra, Gilly prudently replied 'Not yet, she is not ready'.

According to a report in *Australian Musical News* based on a letter from Marjorie to James Galbraith (of the Geelong Eisteddfod), Cécile Gilly was so impressed by Marjorie's performance at Gaubert's concert that she paid to have another set of private recordings made of Marjorie singing – 'some of which were to be sent home to Australia for Christmas'.[9] There is no evidence to corroborate this claim, but it is tantalising to think that Marjorie's voice might have been recorded in 1929. There is the possibility that such recordings might have preserved Marjorie's singing of the *Semiramide* aria, Donna Anna's 'Vengeance' aria or excerpts from any of the operas she was currently studying, but if these recordings were made, none is known to survive.

The Australian press had taken sporadic interest in Marjorie's progress since her departure from Australia. Small articles appeared in *Australian Musical News*, usually as a result of letters from Marjorie to Boustead or Galbraith or reports from Thorold Waters, who had visited Marjorie in Paris. The general press took less interest, only occasionally inserting a paragraph, but as the result of a bizarre series of events, one Australian newspaper made a contribution to Marjorie's success at the Gaubert concert by providing the gown she wore that evening.

While Marjorie was staying at Euse in August she had received an unexpected visit from the Paris representative of a newspaper, identified by Marjorie as the Melbourne *Sun*. They chatted about Australia and the newspaper man made casual and vague reference to an error his newspaper had printed about Marjorie and how he would like to buy her a gift by way of recompense. Marjorie answered that she would love a nice concert gown for when her career got underway. The wily newspaper representative then produced a typed document which Marjorie signed, relinquishing any right to further compensation for the error. 'Now, when you get back to Paris you can go to any shop you choose and buy yourself a dress up to the value of 2000 francs and tell them to bill me for it', he said as he hastily stowed the document in an inner pocket of his jacket.[10]

Marjorie got her dress – a magnificent creation in emerald green, trimmed with white swan's down, which cost 3500 francs, but the newspaper paid up without a murmur. Later she found out the nature of the 'error' and realised that her naivety had robbed her of the opportunity for even more substantial compensation. The New York correspondent of the newspaper had cabled a story to Australia about the murder–suicide of the American actors Louis Bennison and Margaret Lawrence – Bennison had shot Lawrence then himself. A careless sub-editor in Australia had changed 'Margaret Lawrence' to 'Marjorie Lawrence' and so for a brief period some Australians believed it was their Sun Aria winner who had met that grim fate.

While Marjorie was enjoying her first public triumph in Paris other events were taking place at home in Winchelsea of which she was unaware. On 14 August Bill Lawrence made a new will, revoking an earlier one. Then, just as the family were sitting down to lunch on Christmas Day, he dropped dead. On Christmas afternoon a telegram arrived at the Grodets for Marjorie informing her that 'Dad' was dead. Marjorie was devastated and the memory of her father's overheard words the year before must have come back to her with numbing force. A week later a letter from Lena explained that Bill Lawrence had been buried at Bambra Cemetery beside their mother and near their grandparents and that, as soon as the will was read, she would let Marjorie know how the estate was to be divided.

The Grodets comforted Marjorie and Madame Grodet whisked her off to the nearby church of Notre Dame de Lorette to pray for the soul of *'le pauvre Papa'*. In her grief Marjorie found comfort in this charming old classical-style church at the bottom of 'The Street of Martyrs' and briefly thought about embracing Roman Catholicism, but was deterred by the notion of how *'Papa'* would have reacted if he had known what she was considering.[11]

Cécile Gilly kept her busy by assigning her a new role to study, one Marjorie had been longing to tackle – Puccini's Tosca. Marjorie threw herself into learning the role and remembered later that whenever anyone visited Gilly's studio around this time, her teacher would make her sing the passage in Act Three where Tosca describes killing the villainous Baron Scarpia, rising to a resplendent top C, and then dropping two octaves on the next note. Marjorie might well have empathised with Puccini's hard-pressed heroine at this time for she was facing a catalogue of woes of her own.

Marjorie claimed that following her father's death the allowance he had been sending her had ceased to arrive. In *Interrupted Melody* she wrote:

> *Ever since my arrival in Paris a monthly draft had arrived from my father which enabled me to pay for lessons, living expenses and other essentials and father had assured me that if anything happened to him he had instructed the family that the money should continue to come to me. My allowance had been adequate, but no more. I had not been able to save anything out of it. It was Percy who broke the news to me that my eldest brother, Lindsay, who had become head of the family, had decided no more money should be sent me. I had been away two years and already cost father too much money, Lindsay had told a family council: if I could not learn to sing in two years I never would.*[12]

When *Interrupted Melody* came out in Australia in 1949, Lindsay Lawrence went into print himself with a letter to Geelong's principal newspaper refuting Marjorie's accusations that her allowance had been stopped and maintaining that the money she had received was in the nature of a loan which she had agreed to repay.[13]

Marjorie was touring Australia when Lindsay's letter was published and on being shown it, she sent a reply to the same newspaper explaining that the letter had been a painful shock to her and that she had no wish to engage in public controversy over their unhappy differences.[14] In private she strongly contradicted the claim that the allowance her father had offered her was ever a loan, but admitted that when she had asked Lindsay for money after their father's death she had made a commitment to repay him when she could afford to, both parties recognising that repayment might be years away.

Marjorie's bank statements for 1930 support Lindsay's claim that he had cabled money to her, albeit with less regularity than their father – fifty pounds in January, and further identical sums in April, May, July and September, not an inconsiderable total, given the hardship of depression and drought then being experienced by Victorian farmers, and probably a substantial drain on his own pocket.[15]

There was a further shock in store for Marjorie when she received advice of the dispositions in Bill Lawrence's new will. In it he bequeathed the largest portion of his estate (valued for probate at 17,707 pounds) to Lindsay in the form of an immediate payment of one thousand pounds free of probate or estate duty, plus all of his father's farm machinery, livestock, crops and motor car. Lena was to receive a payment of six hundred pounds and Allan, four hundred pounds. The balance of the estate was to be sold, debts repaid and the remainder divided into five equal shares, one each for Lindsay, Ted, Eileen, Percy and Marjorie – but not Allan, who was now twenty.[16] Ted, Percy and Allan immediately contested the will jointly and lodged a caveat with the probate office to suspend its processing.[17]

Marjorie believed Lindsay had coerced their father into making the new will to benefit himself and, according to living family members, Ted never spoke to his elder brother again. Whether either is true is strongly disputed by different branches of the family, but Marjorie's enmity towards Lindsay is understandable, with her discovery that he (as chief executor of the will) would not release her share until she repaid him a substantial part of the sum she owed him. Marjorie refused and even had she been willing to repay her brother, she did not have the money.[18]

Relations between members of the Lawrence family were never the same after this wrangling, and Bill Lawrence's estate was not finalised for seventeen years. There were desperate times during those years (including the present one in Paris) when Marjorie could have used her legacy. By the time she received it in 1947 it had been eroded to a pittance.

When the disruption to Marjorie's allowance occurred, her friends in Paris rallied around. Cécile Gilly and Marguerite Palustre told her she could suspend payment for lessons and repay them when her career got underway. Gilly also bought her a badly needed new pair of shoes. Monsieur and Madame Grodet made a similar offer to suspend her board, but knowing how desperate their own situation was, Marjorie insisted on paying them a reduced rate. As an expression of his devotion to her, Henri Grodet offered to get a second job and support her. Another Australian student of Gilly's, Emily Skyring, whose family were well off, pressed two 1000-franc notes onto her saying 'Listen Marge, I hear you're broke and things are pretty tough with you. You have a better voice than me and I reckon you'll do something with it. I want you to spend this on whatever you need.'[19] Marjorie managed with the concessions from her teachers, Skyring's gift and rather a lot of small amounts she reluctantly accepted from Henri Grodet. Later she would pay back all these staunch supporters in full, although none expected it at the time.

Another good 'mate' from the Australian community in Paris was Archie Longden, whom she met at the Brownlees and who also came from Geelong. Longden was a young, music-loving accountant who lived in a garret near the École Militaire and dreamed of becoming a concert promoter. Among all her friends in Paris, only Longden left a written account of their friendship:

> I remember when I first met Marge. She rushed into the room talking voluble French and carrying a bundle of music. After that we went many times to the opera and heard the famous Wagner singers of the day – Lotte Lehmann and Frida Leider singing the roles in which Marge would later have such success. We were both poor so sat in the gallery or 'hen roost' as it is called in Paris and by risking our necks could sometimes see half the stage! However the seats only

cost eight francs and as I used to take along the words and Marge the score, we thoroughly enjoyed ourselves.[20]

Marjorie and Archie also discovered a mutual love of circus and often went together to the Cirque d'Hiver' in the Marais and Cirque Medrano on the notorious Boulevard de Rochechouart, both establishments made famous in the paintings of Toulouse Lautrec and Picasso. At Cirque d'Hiver they laughed until they cried at the musical antics of the clown 'Grock', and at the Medrano they gasped as the glamorous tightrope walker 'Barbette' revealed herself at the end of the act as Mr Vander Clyde, a cowboy from Texas.

What Henri Grodet thought of Marjorie's friendship with Longden is not on record, but there is no evidence that their relationship ever got beyond mateship, while her romance with Grodet continued to blow hot and cold for another six years. The Grodets did not approve of *le cirque* so Henri escorted Marjorie to the cinema instead. Marjorie found French-language films helped her to develop her French accent and Henri translated any parts of the dialogue she didn't understand, often to the annoyance of other ticket holders. The reverse applied when they indulged in an English-language movie and then there were fewer objections from the audience who listened attentively to Marjorie's running commentary in French.

Marjorie's lessons with Marguerite Palustre came to an end during 1930 and she began to take German lessons instead. This coincided with Cécile Gilly's decision that it was time Marjorie began to study the operas of Richard Wagner. Marjorie would learn the great Wagner soprano roles in French, but knowledge of German was preparation for the day when she would have to relearn them in their original language to sing them beyond the borders of France. Learning German proved more difficult than learning French as Marjorie had no one apart from her teacher to converse with and her progress was slow.

Marjorie continued to study regularly with Cécile Gilly and work with Renée Gilly through 1930 and 1931, adding another nine roles to the twelve she had already learned: Charlotte in Massenet's *Werther*, the title roles in Richard Strauss's *Salome* and Reyer's *Salammbô*, Brunhilde in Reyer's *Sigurd* and five Wagner parts: Elisabeth in *Tannhäuser*, Brangäne in *Tristan und Isolde*, Kundry in *Parsifal* and two of the Brünnhildes: in *Die Walküre* and *Siegfried*.[21]

Marjorie would never sing Charlotte (a mezzo-soprano role occasionally appropriated by sopranos) or Salammbô on stage and Reyer's Brunhilde was a concession to the popularity of his opera *Sigurd* in France – a treatment by a French composer of the same Nordic legends that inspired Wagner's Ring Cycle. Marjorie would sing in *Sigurd* on stage several times and make excellent recordings of Brunhilde's solos.

Richard Strauss's Salome, based on a play by Oscar Wilde, would become a signature role for Marjorie, sung to acclaim on four continents and while she was learning this role at Gilly's studio it provided an encounter that was to have long-reaching impact on her career:

> Mary Garden was with Madame Gilly at the time to do some kind of a 'refresher' course, and I arrived at the studio one day to discover that the famous soprano was on hand to initiate me into the wonders of Strauss' Salome.[22]

Scottish by birth, American by upbringing and French by inclination, Mary Garden was one of the most exciting and original artists of her day. She had created the role of Mélisande in Debussy's *Pelleas et Mélisande* in 1902 and sung Strauss's Salome all over the world with a heady mix of success and scandal. At this time Garden was still singing but her career was winding down. It was a stroke of good fortune that she then had the time and the patience to help Marjorie come to grips with the very difficult music of *Salome* and help her to develop a credible portrayal of Strauss's psychotic and erotic teenager, who has to both sing and dance on stage.

The first extract from a Wagner opera Gilly taught Marjorie was in some ways the most challenging of all, Brünnhilde's Immolation Scene from the final act of *Götterdämmerung*, the concluding opera in the Ring Cycle. While that might seem a strange choice as an introduction to the composer and the multifarious role of Brünnhilde, it did give Marjorie a view of her ultimate destination – dramatically and musically – before she embarked on the long journey through three operas and about eight hours of music.

The first complete Wagner role Marjorie learned was Elisabeth from *Tannhäuser*, followed by Brangäne from *Tristan und Isolde*, another 'mezzo' role occasionally appropriated by young dramatic sopranos in the past. Both these roles would figure in Marjorie's career when it finally got underway. Kundry in *Parsifal* was studied next, a role to which Marjorie was ideally suited and which she would eventually sing on stage. With these roles under her belt Marjorie set out on that journey through the 'Ring', learning the relatively short but extremely arduous part of Brünnhilde in *Siegfried*, then the same character in *Die Walküre*. She would tackle the rest of Brünnhilde in *Götterdämmerung* in 1932.

Marjorie enjoyed learning these challenging parts and they gave her the opportunity to explore and gauge her true vocal stamina and to immerse herself in the trials and tribulations of Wagner's warrior maid, a character she found both sympathetic and infinitely rewarding. Just occasionally, enthusiasm overcame prudence. While Marjorie was practising Brünnhilde's battle cry from *Die Walküre* with Renée Gilly at the piano one day, Cécile shouted up from a lower floor 'You sound like a *train whistle!*'

Another great soprano turned up at Gilly's studio while Marjorie was learning these roles: the Russian Félia Litvinne. Litvinne was then living in retirement in Paris, but in her day she had been a leading Wagnerian soprano and an acclaimed exponent of several other roles now in Marjorie's repertoire. Litvinne had been

Paris's first Isolde and first Brünnhilde in *Götterdämmerung*. Like Garden, Litvinne was able to offer sound advice based on practical experience gained on the world's great opera stages, in her case for over forty years. It is also not difficult to find echoes of Litvinne's singing style in Marjorie's. Comparison of their recordings reveals the same vigorous cut and thrust when singing the heroic music of the warrior maid and the same verbal acuity in the treatment of Wagner's text, qualities that may well have been part of a legacy from the older singer to the younger. Another legacy was a small collection of Litvinne's own stage costumes, which she presented to Marjorie. After some alteration (carried out by Marjorie herself, who was half the older singer's girth), these were gratefully added to the wardrobe Marjorie was assembling in preparation for the time she would be required to provide all her own costumes.[23]

This was an intense period of learning for Marjorie and she quite rightly indulged herself with a couple of short summer holidays in the company of Mimi Grodet. In 1930 they visited the resort town of Vichy in the Auvergne and in 1931 went further afield to Rome, staying in a cheap hotel near the Trevi fountain. Marjorie dragged Mimi around the locations where the fictitious story of *Tosca* is set. They strolled through the cool gloom of the church of Sant'Andrea della Valle, stared at the Palazzo Farnese and climbed to the roof of the Castel Sant'Angelo, from which Tosca spectacularly leaps to her death at the end of Puccini's opera. But not everything in Italy was so appealing or as gratifying – it was while on this trip that Marjorie discovered how inadequate her Italian was. Furthermore, the tourists encountered an air of menace and a tension in the city they could not ignore. Squads of Mussolini's 'black shirts' paraded about, graffiti on walls proclaimed 'Il Duce ha sempre ragione' ('The Duce is always right') and Fascist flags flapped from rooftops and balconies.

This was Marjorie's first brush with Fascism on an organised scale. At the time and in the excitement of a first holiday in the eternal city, it is doubtful whether Marjorie appreciated the full import of what she witnessed. But the fact that she noted her impressions indicates that the seeds of concern were sown. In a short time Fascism and Nazism would wreak havoc on the lives of many of her friends and thwart some of Marjorie's own plans.

Chapter Five

Triumph in the Sun

As the months passed Marjorie became evermore impatient to commence her stage career. By the end of 1931 she had a repertoire of twenty-one principal roles, several of which were greatly in demand in opera houses and hard to cast because of their vocal demands and extreme difficulty. Marjorie also knew that she now had full command of her voice and was capable of making such splendid sounds that she longed to share them with the world at large.

To add to her frustration, several of Cécile Gilly's other students, including one or two who had arrived *after* Marjorie, had made their stage debuts and were enjoying the material rewards of success. Rita Miller, for example, was now principal coloratura soprano of the opera company at Toulon in the south of France and receiving laudatory reviews for her singing of Lucia di Lammermoor, Delibes's *Lakmé* and Gilda in Verdi's *Rigoletto*. 'Patience, *ma petite*,' Gilly kept telling Marjorie, 'you are destined for bigger things'. Madame was right, but at twenty-four and with boundless energy and a unique talent, patience did not come easily to Marjorie.

After the Gaubert concert there had been other small concerts and a couple of false starts at a stage career. Most of the concerts had been in the suburbs of Paris – low-key, Sunday afternoon affairs featuring young hopefuls, talented amateurs and professional has-beens. For singing 'Divinités du Styx' in a suburban town hall Marjorie received the princely fee of twenty-five francs but paid exactly that amount to get to and from the venue in taxis.

The most rewarding concert engagements came through another old friend of Cécile Gilly's: Gustave Bret. Maestro Bret turned up at Gilly's studio one day seeking a contralto soloist to sing with the Paris Bach Society, of which he was founder and conductor. Gilly decided that singing Bach (and Handel) in the lower register would do Marjorie's voice no harm and Bret was delighted to have a soloist who could sing both contralto and soprano parts. Thereafter Marjorie performed regularly with Bret's group in L'Église Réformée de l'Étoile near the Arc de Triomphe. Perhaps the highlights of her association with this group were two performances of Bach's *St Matthew Passion*, in which Marjorie sang the alto solos.

Breaking into opera was not so easy. Both Gilly and Marjorie knew that very few singers made their professional debuts on the stage of the Paris Opéra. Even those whose subsequent careers were based at the Opéra had to prove themselves elsewhere before graduating to the country's *premiere* house. To meet that requirement, Marjorie needed to gain some stage experience and a few good notices before attempting her assault on the Opéra.

With Gilly's blessing, Marjorie auditioned for the role of Tosca in a scratch production of Puccini's opera being mounted at Nanterre. The impresario listened in awe as Marjorie sang Tosca's aria 'Vissi d'arte' and the passage from the last act that had been her showpiece at Gilly's studio. He then threw up his hands. 'Mille pardons, Mademoiselle,' he said, 'but if I put you on the stage, the audience would give my other singers "the bird".[1] You are too good for my little company. You should be at the Opéra.' Marjorie must have felt like screaming.[2]

On another occasion when she auditioned for an out-of-town company, the director asked if she knew a certain role; it was not in her repertoire and Marjorie answered honestly, and as there was nothing else for her to sing, she was not engaged. When she reported what had happened to Gilly, Madame flew into a rage. 'Never, *never* say you do not know a role! If it is in your range, you can always *learn* it.' Practical though that advice may have been, it almost landed Marjorie in serious trouble a few months later.

Marjorie also auditioned with the director of the Nouveau Théâtre de Vaugirard near the Luxembourg Palace on the Left Bank. He was mounting two concerts and told Marjorie that if she sang at both without a fee, he would engage her as prima donna for a season of opera he was planning for 1932. Marjorie agreed and, looking every inch the prima donna in her emerald-green dress, she sang the Semiramide aria, 'Les Regrets' from Benjamin Godard's 'dramatic symphony' *Le Tasse* and Martini's delectable *Plaisir d'amour*. The concerts were a sell-out, but when Marjorie called at the theatre the day after the second one, she was told the opera season had been cancelled. Mimi and Marjorie consoled themselves with a slap-up lunch neither could afford at the fashionable Café Coupole nearby.

Marjorie's breakthrough came the following November. It seemed Cécile Gilly knew everybody who was anybody in the city, for it was yet another of her contacts, Eugène Charabot, member of the French Senate, who passed word to her that the Monte Carlo Opéra needed an extra soprano for its forthcoming winter season. Charabot, who knew the director of the company, volunteered to write to him.

The Monte Carlo Opéra was not the Paris Opéra, Madame explained, but it was just about the next best thing. The theatre was elegant, the audiences fashionable, the orchestra and chorus well disciplined, the conductors distinguished and the soloists were stars of international repute who vied to sing there. Garden and Litvinne had both sung at the Monte Carlo Opéra and so had Melba, Caruso, Chaliapin and countless other great singers in the company's fifty-year history. The

Monte Carlo Opéra also had a reputation for presenting new works (most notably Puccini's *La Rondine*, which had had its premiere there in 1917) and as a launching pad for young sopranos who went on to have great careers.

An appointment was made for Marjorie to audition for the director of the company, Raoul Gunsbourg, at his Paris home near the Nouveau Théâtre de Vaugirard, three days before Christmas. Mimi accompanied Marjorie to provide moral support and also out of curiosity to see Gunsbourg, who was the current owner of the château where her mother had grown up. When the two women arrived at Gunsbourg's they found a distinguished-looking, elderly man also waiting to enter. Marjorie immediately recognised him as Marcel Journet, the revered French bass who was nearing the end of a long and illustrious career which had taken him to most of the world's great opera houses. Journet bowed to Marjorie and Mimi and stood back to allow them to enter.[3]

When Marjorie was shown into the presence of Raoul Gunsbourg she received a shock. His opera house in Monte Carlo might have been elegant, but there was nothing elegant about '*Monsieur le directeur*'. Gunsbourg was squat, repellently ugly and had a lecherous twinkle in his eye which belied his seventy-two years. When he grasped Marjorie's hand and slobbered over it, she began to understand why so many young sopranos were given a chance to make their debuts with his company.[4]

Seated at Gunsbourg's piano was a wizened little man Marjorie later found out was named Louis Narici and who most people believed was the composer of the six operas that had been performed and published under Gunsbourg's name. Narici played and Marjorie sang 'Un bel dì' from *Madama Butterfly*, followed by 'Divinités du Styx'. For all his eccentricities, Gunsbourg was a good judge of voices and according to Marjorie he stopped her halfway through the Gluck aria and conducted her into the next room. He sat down at a large desk and indicated a chair for Marjorie. Gunsbourg reached for a blank contract form and commenced writing. The conversation that followed went something like this: 'Do you sing Elisabeth in *Tannhäuser*, Mademoiselle?' 'Oui, Monsieur.' '*Tosca?*' 'Oui, Monsieur.' '*La Damnation de Faust?*' 'Oui, Monsieur.' 'Elsa in *Lohengrin?*' 'Oui, Monsieur.' 'Valentine in *Les Huguenots?*' 'Oui, Monsieur.' 'Isolde?' 'Oui, Monsieur.' 'Do you sing Isolde in French *and* German, Mademoiselle?' 'Naturellement, Monsieur.'[5]

As Marjorie answered Gunsbourg scribbled on the contract. When he reached the end of the page he signed it with a great flourish and then reached for another blank form. He scribbled away at that for a few minutes then asked: 'Do you know all of "Butterfly", Mademoiselle?' 'Oui, Monsieur.' 'And *La Tetralogie?*' 'Oui, Monsieur,' came the predictable reply.[6]

'Tres bien, Mademoiselle', said the beaming impresario after he signed the second form. 'Here is a contract to sing for me in the season starting in the new year, and another for the following season. You will make your debut as Elisabeth in *Tannhäuser* on January twenty-first, the opening night. Also, you will see there is an opera called *L'Escarpolette*, which is my own latest creation. I will send you the score and you will look at the role of Marinette. Now, what do you say, Mademoiselle?'

Gunsbourg escorted Marjorie back to the first room where Marcel Journet was talking to Narici. Gunsbourg asked Marjorie to sing again and she chose 'Vissi d'arte'. Impresario and famous singer listened and at the end of the aria Journet reached over Narici and turned the score back to the scene between Tosca and Scarpia in the first act. 'Venez, venez, mon enfant', Journet said. Narici played and Marjorie and Journet sang through the entire scene.

> *Never had I enjoyed singing so much. Journet's luscious voice rolled out, challenging me to match his tones. Narici did incredible things with the piano and old Gunsbourg who, whatever else he might have been, was a genuine music lover, smiled his happiness. As for Mimi, she sat on the edge of her chair incredulous that it was I, her friend, singing with the fabulous Journet.*[7]

Journet praised Marjorie and Gunsbourg slobbered over her hand again. The impresario also asked after the health of Madame Grodet and whispered to Mimi that she was 'a very beautiful girl'. After that the women made a hasty exit.

Marjorie and Mimi went straight to Cécile Gilly's studio, Marjorie waving the two contracts triumphantly. Gilly was as delighted as they, but insisted on scrutinising the documents. 'Mon Dieu,' she said, 'you have agreed to Elsa, Isolde in French and German and the *whole* Ring! And what is this *L'Escarpolette*?' Marjorie explained what *L'Escarpolette* was and reminded Gilly of the advice she had given her earlier about never refusing a role. Madame nodded sagely and replied, 'Well, *ma chérie*, you are going to be *very* busy before you go to Monte Carlo'.

Gilly pointed out that such contracts were drawn up listing all the roles the impresario *might* want the singer to undertake and that if Marjorie was lucky she would not be called on to sing the roles she did not know.[8] She also pointed out that the shrewd Gunsbourg had secured Marjorie's services ridiculously cheaply – at a flat fee of 7500 francs for the first season, regardless of how often she sang, and 15,000 for the second season (which was only a slightly more reasonable figure) and with no expenses or advances. Such considerations could not dampen Marjorie's jubilation however. She was going to make her stage debut on the opening night of a season at a famous opera house – and in a mere four weeks.[9]

With Cécile and Renée Gilly's help Marjorie made a quick study of the role of Elsa in Wagner's *Lohengrin* and Marinette in *L'Escarpolette*, but it was mutually agreed that if she was called on to sing either the *Götterdämmerung* Brünnhilde or Isolde during the forthcoming season, she would make some excuse. As it transpired Marjorie was not required to sing either role by Gunsbourg – or most of the others listed on her contract.

As the four weeks passed, information filtered through about the forthcoming season in Monte Carlo. The roster of artists was to include, as well as Marjorie, three other sopranos – the beautiful Eidé Norena from the Paris Opéra, the vibrant Hungarian dramatic soprano Maria Nemeth, both of whom were established international stars – and the Japanese Tamaki Miura, who specialised in the role of Madame Butterfly. Others stars included Spanish mezzo-soprano Conchita Supervia, Italian tenor Giacomo Lauri-Volpi and France's leading tenor, Georges Thill. Marjorie grew evermore excited and more nervous as the time to depart for Monte Carlo approached.

The ever faithful Mimi accompanied Marjorie to Monte Carlo. They travelled overnight on *le train de grand luxe* to Nice and then transferred to a smaller rattly service to Beausoleil, a hilly picturesque town overlooking the Principality of Monaco. After investigating hotel prices in Monte Carlo (the opera season took place during the resort's busiest months), Marjorie and Mimi decided a cheap hotel on the French side of the border was their best option. Hôtel Mondial at Beausoleil turned out to be 'cheaper' than they had expected. Their shared room was so tiny they had to keep climbing over their trunks, and the mattresses on the beds were filled with smelly straw. Mimi set up the tiny paraffin stove in one corner and using the frying pan she had brought with them cooked their first meal. Later they would discover an Italian family restaurant nearby and indulge in the occasional plate of pasta, but economy dictated endless egg dishes and sausages fried on the diminutive stove.

Next morning Marjorie and Mimi ventured down the hill for their first glimpse of the opera house, located next door to the famous Casino de Monte-Carlo. Marjorie excitedly pointed out the posters pasted on the front of the building advertising the opening night *Tannhäuser* with her name listed in large letters along with Georges Thill, who was to sing the title role, and the rest of the cast. 'My eyes swam when I saw my name posted on that billboard', Marjorie recalls in *Interrupted Melody*.

The first rehearsal for *Tannhäuser* took place on 17 January, four days before the opening night. Marjorie sang well and after Elisabeth's entrance aria, 'Dich, teure halle' (or in this case, 'Salut a toi, noble demeure', because in Monte Carlo everything was also sung in French), the orchestra put down their instruments and applauded her. Georges Thill was very considerate about Marjorie's lack of stage experience and she found that singing with this splendid artist, one of the great tenor voices of the century, inspired her to excel herself. After the rehearsal Thill took her aside and said: '*Mademoiselle*, you have a magnificent voice, but your acting … you are so stiff. You must let me help you. Come to my hotel tomorrow afternoon for tea and I will show you all the moves.'

Marjorie was flattered by the famous tenor's solicitousness and readily accepted his offer, but when she arrived at Thill's luxurious hotel suite the next day she discovered the moves he had in mind had nothing to do with opera.

Scarcely had we finished our tea which Georges had ordered directly I arrived when he began making love to me. He asked what I was thinking about and I foolishly said 'Someone dear'. Egoist that he was, Georges thought I meant him and kept murmuring 'C'est moi, c'est moi, ma cherie!' as he enfolded me in his arms. It was a surprise attack and I had to think fast. Not only was Georges agile but he was the sexiest man I had ever met.[10]

Common sense prevailed and when Thill went to answer his telephone, Marjorie made her escape. She had too much to think about to get emotionally entangled with one of her fellow artists forty-eight hours before making her all-important stage debut.

For the general rehearsal the following day (to which the public were admitted) Marjorie brought along the costume she had bought for this role, but the old wardrobe mistress, who had taken a liking to her, found her a more spectacular one in *bleu de France* with a delicate gold coronet that glinted on her copper-coloured hair.

Make-up proved more of a problem. Marjorie had told Gunsbourg that she was familiar with stage make-up, assuming it was no different from street make-up. With Mimi's help she coated her face with white grease paint to which she added only lipstick. In the break between the second and third acts, Gunsbourg came rushing into Marjorie's dressing room shouting: 'What have you done? Such a beautiful girl and you look like a *cloon*!' Gunsbourg then grabbed a rabbit's foot brush and vigorously applied rouge to Marjorie's cheeks, forehead and chin. When she returned to the stage she looked even more like a clown.

On 21 January 1932, Marjorie made her stage debut singing a role she would sing only twice more in her entire career. The small opera house was packed with a fashionable audience that included the ruler of the principality, Prince Louis II. As a good luck token, Marjorie wore a small silver brooch in the shape of a key. The person who had lent it to her claimed it had been given to Flora Macdonald by Bonnie Prince Charlie, and although Marjorie acquitted herself splendidly, some luck was required to overcome a couple of mishaps.[11]

Elisabeth does not appear until the second act of *Tannhäuser*, which gave Marjorie and Mimi ample time to work themselves up into a state of nervous panic. The wardrobe mistress made Marjorie drink a concoction of raw eggs and cognac, which made her desperately thirsty, and Mimi had to fetch her several glasses of water. When the time finally arrived for Marjorie to make her entrance, she stumbled over a piece of wood a careless stage hand had left in the wings and lurched onto the stage.

After 'Dich, teure halle' the audience applauded her and at the end of the second act they gave her an ovation. Flushed with pride and relief, Marjorie acknowledged the audience with a deep bow which dislodged her coronet. Showing the deftness of an Aussie kid who had played 'catch' throughout her childhood, Marjorie caught the coronet as it slid over her forehead and jammed it back on her head. The audience stopped the performance again in the final act to applaud her singing of Elisabeth's Prayer, and at the end of the opera Marjorie had to take two solo curtain calls, an honour accorded only to Thill among the other cast members.[12]

Back in Marjorie's dressing room she and Mimi hastily changed into evening clothes in the not unrealistic expectation that someone – Gunsbourg or Thill most likely – would take them out to celebrate. Thill did call in to offer his congratulations, as did other singers and the conductor, while the tenor presented Marjorie with a photograph of himself inscribed: 'To my dear comrade, Marjorie. A souvenir of your debut at Monte Carlo from Georges Thill – someone who will never forget you.'

Gunsbourg bustled in, made a short speech praising his judgment in engaging Marjorie and then bustled out again, leaving Marjorie and Mimi alone. Then, just as both women were gathering up their belongings to return to an empty hotel room, a stage hand arrived bearing a note. Marjorie opened it and read it aloud: 'My dear, you will be one of the greatest. I cannot come to see you but I wish you every success.' It was signed 'Clara Butt'. All thoughts of neglect vanished.[13]

Gustave Bret had travelled down to Monte Carlo in his capacity as music critic of the journal *L'Intransigent*. In the next issue he wrote: 'Mademoiselle Lawrence's voice, technique and dramatic expression created a sensation'. The critic of the Nice *L'Eclaireur* was most fulsome in his praise, reporting that Marjorie sang notes of a quality unheard before, that her singing was 'infinitely perfect' and that her debut had been the most successful at the house since Chaliapin in 1906. The correspondent of a local English-language newspaper in his review accused Gunsbourg of lying about Marjorie's professional status, saying she was far too good to be the debutante Gunsbourg had claimed her to be.[14]

There do not appear to have been any in-depth, analytical reviews written about this performance. Perhaps that is not surprising given the hedonistic atmosphere in the town at this time. The names of the aristocrats and socialites in attendance at the opening night of the opera and their magnificent evening gowns filled the columns of the local press. Moreover, *Tannhäuser* was hardly a novelty and this cast in their respective roles (apart from Marjorie) were already familiar. All posterity has been left are the platitudes reprinted above, and our knowledge of Marjorie's progress as a singer is sketchier for the lack of anything more substantial.

Another who had travelled to Monte Carlo to attend Marjorie's debut was her friend John Brownlee. Some months later, when he was interviewed for *Australian Musical News* and asked about young singers needing to prepare thoroughly for their debuts, he said:

> *Look at young Marjorie Lawrence! Now, there's a girl of grit. People in Australia cannot possibly realise what it meant when Marjorie made her big success at the Monte Carlo Opera. I was there that night and I heard her sing.*

> She was wonderful. She came through with flying colours. It was a furore. She could never have created such an impression without the greatest assurance and grit and strong knowledge of her job.[15]

After her sensational debut, Gunsbourg must have regretted committing most of the other dramatic soprano parts during the season to his established dramatic soprano star, Maria Nemeth, although for a while it seemed Marjorie might yet sing Tosca. Gunsbourg asked Marjorie to understudy Nemeth as Tosca and also as Salomé in Massenet's *Hérodiade*.

Tosca was planned to open early in the season with Lauri-Volpi singing Cavaradossi, but when rehearsals began Nemeth had not arrived in Monte Carlo. Marjorie sang the title role during all of the rehearsals, relishing the opportunity to sing with another famous tenor, but the public never had the opportunity to hear her. Lauri-Volpi had insisted on the public being excluded from the general rehearsal and Nemeth showed up the day before the first performance.

Marjorie's only other assignment that season in Monte Carlo was Gunsbourg's new 'creation', *L'Escarpolette*, and it was a work Marjorie quickly learned and even more quickly forgot.[16] *L'Escarpolette* (*The Swing*) was a one-act pastiche cobbled together by Gunsbourg using the melodies of the popular song writer Paul Delmet. As it seems likely that Narici did the musical arrangements, the only part of the work that could truly be credited to Gunsbourg was the libretto. Set in the eighteenth century and involving the love of a peasant girl for a viscount, the work was dramatically feeble and musically trite.

Marjorie was assigned the role of the peasant girl, Marinette, and the only singer of international repute in the cast was the baritone Arthur Endrèze, an American by birth and an established star at the Paris Opéra, who played a nameless 'Old Professor'. Gunsbourg lavished resources on this cherished work, including nine rehearsals, spectacular costumes, powdered wigs and 'chocolate box' sets, but to little effect. *L'Escarpolette* survived three performances and then sank into oblivion.[17]

Marjorie's contract required that she stay in Monte Carlo during the full six weeks of the opera season but the small amount of work Gunsbourg was able to give her meant she had time on her hands. On the afternoon of 5 March she gave a concert in St Paul's Anglican Church in Monte Carlo, assisted by Jean Stokking, a minor tenor from the opera company. Gunsbourg himself attempted to assist with the problem of Marjorie's spare time by offering the same kind of dalliance Thill had sought, but his advances were even less welcome than the tenor's. Gunsbourg invited Marjorie and Mimi to lunch at the luxurious Hôtel de Paris where he lived when in Monte Carlo and before the meal presented each of them with a string of pearls. These he claimed were *ancien* family heirlooms. When Marjorie failed to respond to innuendos and pats on the thigh, Gunsbourg focused his attention on Mimi but got no further with her. This tiresome meal had a hilarious codicil.

When Marjorie and Mimi attended a performance of *Madama Butterfly* at the opera house the following night, they giggled silently when Tamaki Miura came on stage wearing an identical string of pearls. Marjorie speculated that the lecherous impresario probably had these 'heirlooms' mass-produced.

On a couple of occasions Marjorie and Mimi took coffee at the famous Café de Paris, opposite the Hôtel de Paris. Here Marjorie caught the eye of the darkly handsome pianist who entertained the patrons. He came to their table, introduced himself as Jean Matross and asked if he might escort Marjorie and Mimi home. After Gunsbourg, Matross was a breath of fresh air and Marjorie described him as 'a dinger of a bloke'.[18] The women were flattered and readily accepted. All the way up the hill to Beausoleil the pianist whistled bits of *Tristan und Isolde*, which endeared him to Marjorie, but not to Mimi, who sensed something sinister about their new companion. Marjorie met up with Matross several times after that and he played for her while she practised. Matross also suggested Marjorie should run away with him, marry him and buy a little love nest for them to live in.

This affair came to abrupt end when Mimi remembered where she had heard the pianist's name and seen his face before. It was in the Paris newspapers. He had been tried for the murder of an English woman at the channel resort of Le Touquet and the theft of her jewellery, but was acquitted through lack of evidence. When Marjorie angrily confronted Matross with this, he denied the crimes, but Marjorie sent him packing anyway.

Marjorie attracted other admirers before leaving Monte Carlo, including an Italian student named Guido, whom she also rejected when she discovered he was ten years her junior. Guido brought a final offering to his 'amore' at the train station on the morning Marjorie and Mimi returned to Paris – a large basket of oranges which burst and sent fruit rolling all over the platform.

The six weeks in Monte Carlo had passed quickly, with Marjorie succeeding in the first major test of her career with, as John Brownlee put it, 'flying colours'. Gunsbourg had promised her she would open the 1933 season as Madame Butterfly and sing all the performances of *Tosca*. As the train rolled out of the station and climbed along the coast towards Nice, Marjorie could look back with satisfaction at her achievement and forward with pleasure to a new phase in her career.[19]

Chapter Six

Doubts, Delays and Disputes

Marjorie returned in triumph to Paris in April 1932 and to Cécile Gilly's studio. Madame kept repeating 'I knew you could do it', while some of Marjorie's fellow students took her out to celebrate with a magnum of champagne at a bar near Place Pigalle. Marjorie got soundly drunk for the first and last time in her life and had to be smuggled into her room at the Grodets.

With what was left of the money she had earned at Monte Carlo, Marjorie offered to pay some of her outstanding fees to Cécile Gilly, but Gilly would not accept the money, saying 'Your success is enough for the time being'. Marjorie paid Henri Grodet what she owed him and pressed some money onto his parents, who had repapered her room in her absence.

Marjorie now set about learning the complete role of Brünnhilde in *Götterdämmerung*, while Gilly began pulling strings to secure her an audition with Jacques Rouché, *directeur-général* of the Paris Opéra. Philippe Gaubert's support was enlisted and he promised to put in a good word for her and to get Marjorie's name onto the list for the next general audition of singers. Gaubert, or another of Madame's contacts at the Opéra, passed on the very useful tip that Rouché was dissatisfied with the singers he had available for the role of Ortrud in *Lohengrin*. Gilly seized on this opportunity and *Götterdämmerung* was temporarily set aside while she and Marjorie revisited *Lohengrin* and the role of the pagan schemer, the foil to Elsa, the latter being the part Marjorie had earlier studied from same opera.[1]

A formal request for the audition, detailing Marjorie's success in Monte Carlo, was written by Gilly and posted to Rouché. In early June a reply came confirming that Rouché would hear Marjorie at four on the afternoon of 16 June. In typical fashion, Marjorie dashed to the market at the bottom of the Sacré Cœur steps and bought a remnant of mauve georgette to make herself a new dress for the occasion. In *Interrupted Melody* Marjorie reports that she was still struggling to get the hem on the skirt straight on the morning of the audition and that the music was far less problematic.

Gustave Bret agreed to accompany Marjorie at the audition and they met at the opera house stage door. The auditions were to be conducted on the stage, so when they entered, Marjorie and Bret were ushered into the palatial artists' salon behind the stage. There they found several other nervous singers with their accompanists about to face the same trial.

When Marjorie and Bret finally walked out onto the vast stage, she recognised several people sitting in the darkened stalls, including Rouché, Gaubert and two of the company's leading singers, tenor José de Trevi and bass-baritone André Pernet. Marjorie had heard both these singers on that stage and would join them there eventually, but first she had to convince the elderly, stern-looking, heavily bearded *directeur-général* that she was worthy of that opportunity.

Marjorie rightly claimed that confidence in her voice and good preparation, along with the success she had achieved in Monte Carlo, had given her a new degree of self-assurance, but that assurance deserted her that afternoon. 'I was terrified,' Marjorie later admitted, 'but as had happened to me before and would happen many times again, I was able to dig a bit deeper and summon up something extra to carry me through occasions like that'.[2]

Marjorie sang 'Divinités du Styx', and the end of the aria was greeted with stony silence. Rouché then asked if she knew anything else. 'I would like to sing Ortrud's Invocation from the second act of *Lohengrin*', Marjorie replied. 'We would certainly like to hear you sing that, Mademoiselle', Rouché said and Marjorie fancied the *directeur-général* sat up a little straighter in his seat.

Marjorie began: 'O dieux de haine' ('You gods forsaken') and pitched the exposed A-sharp on the first syllable of 'haine' perfectly and with an audacity that made everyone else in the theatre sit up. At the end of the short piece Marjorie hurled the final notes out into the vast auditorium with all the power and brilliance she could muster. Gaubert, de Trevi and Pernet rewarded her with warm applause, but Rouché remained stern-faced. He waited until the applause petered out and then dismissed Marjorie and Bret with a cursory 'Merci, Mademoiselle ... Monsieur'. Marjorie went home not sure whether she had succeeded brilliantly or failed miserably. Confirmation that she had at least made some impression came two days later with a note from Rouché's secretary asking her to call on the *directeur-général* two mornings hence.

Mimi went with Marjorie to the opera house on this occasion and waited in an anteroom while Rouché's major-domo (as tall and broad as his master was short and slight) conducted Marjorie into the *directeur-général*'s grand office. There Marjorie was confronted by someone she described as a completely different Rouché, the charming, dignified former chief executive of a perfume empire and the benevolent sovereign of his artistic domain. 'We enjoyed your singing very much the other day, *Mademoiselle* Lawrence,' he said, 'and I am going to engage you. You must begin work with us immediately.' As Marjorie left, Rouché promised to send a contract 'shortly'.

What Rouché offered was not a position as a principal in his company, but as '*une pensionnaire*', the term used at the Opéra to describe an artist on probation and not unlike what is offered to singers today through opera companies' young artists development programs. Marjorie would work with the music staff and the production staff at the opera house, attend rehearsals of operas she might one day sing in, observe the established stars at work and understudy certain roles.

Considering how successful Marjorie had been in Monte Carlo that offer might seem like a consolation prize or even a backward step, but it should be remembered that the Paris Opéra was the flagship of French vocal art and being a *'pensionnaire'* at the Opéra was at least the equivalent of being a principal in a provincial opera house; Marjorie was more than content.

Marjorie began work at the Opéra the following week. She worked first on the role of Ortrud with Maurice Fauré, head of the music staff and the most senior of the company's team of expert repetiteurs. She also attended all the rehearsals for the current production of *Lohengrin*. Here Marjorie encountered for the first time at close range Germaine Lubin, a singer who would have a profound influence (negative as well as positive) on her future. Germaine Lubin had joined the Opéra in 1914 and quickly established herself as the company's leading dramatic soprano, a position she held until the end of the Second World War, when she was accused of collaborating with the Nazis and banned from singing.

As Marjorie watched and listened to Lubin at the rehearsals of *Lohengrin* her impressions of the great French diva could not have been other than positive. Lubin was a strikingly beautiful woman with large ice-blue eyes. Svelte and regal, she might have matched the visual ideal Wagner had in mind for roles like Elsa, Elisabeth and Isolde. Lubin had been Litvinne's most successful pupil and her expansive voice had a plangent, bell-like timbre. She was also an accomplished vocal actress, bringing originality and an attractive vulnerability to all the roles she sang. These qualities were amply demonstrated as Lubin brought Elsa to life in rehearsal, even without costume, wig and make-up. Later when Lubin became aware of Marjorie as a rival she revealed an unattractive side to her personality, but for the time being it must have been a case of admiration from the *'pensionnaire'* and indifference from the diva.

The veteran heldentenor Paul Franz sang Lohengrin with a clarion voice and the accumulated wisdom of a long career, but the contralto assigned the role of Ortrud was not in their class. It must have been frustrating to Marjorie to hear this singer struggling with the high tessitura and making heavy weather of the Invocation, knowing that she could do so much better if she were given the chance.

In the months that followed Marjorie worked on Valentine (in *Les Huguenots*), the 'Walküre' Brünnhilde and Rachel (in *La Juive*), not only with Fauré and other repetiteurs, but also with the Opéra's leading stage director Pierre Chereau. Chereau helped Marjorie to formulate her own methods for portraying the physical aspects of character and encouraged her to develop her own acting style. In later years Marjorie's acting would be described as 'plastique', 'energetic', 'convincing' and 'sincere' – legacies of a great stage director who found the time to work with her when she needed guidance most. Chereau and his American wife, the actress Abby Richardson, also became good friends of Marjorie's and she sought their advice many times about aspects of her career, especially when obstacles loomed.

The summer of 1932 passed and there was still no sign of the contract Rouché had promised and, while the contract remained unsigned, Marjorie remained unpaid. In *Interrupted Melody* Marjorie claimed that it was the malevolent influence of Germaine Lubin that delayed the contract and that the older singer feared Marjorie as a rival – the same line she took when discussing Melba. By the end of that summer Lubin would certainly have been aware of Marjorie and no doubt had heard the stories going around the opera house about the promising young dramatic soprano from Australia, so she may well have intimated to Rouché that she was his foremost priority. The real reason for the non-appearance of Marjorie's contract, however, was much simpler and much less sinister.

To appease the labour movement and protect the interests of native singers, the French Government of the time had a policy limiting the number of foreign singers permitted to sing in French opera houses. Many foreign-born singers overcame this by becoming French citizens. Others relied on being included in the small quota allowed to appear as guest artists and the even smaller number permitted to join French opera companies as full-time company members because they could sing roles no one else could.

At the time Rouché made his offer to Marjorie he had filled his current quota of foreign singers. Wanting to secure Marjorie's services, Rouché applied to the Ministry of Labour for permission to exceed his quota by one, using the argument that Marjorie could sing roles he could not cast adequately with native singers. The ministry procrastinated. Months passed. Rouché became frustrated. Marjorie became angry and disappointed.

So why did Marjorie blame Lubin when she came to write *Interrupted Melody*? Well it may have been because Lubin had become a soft target by then, vilified in the press and accused, in her own words 'of just about every crime except eating the flesh of babies'.[3] It might also have been a simple case of prima donna bitchiness on Marjorie's part, but if it was, then Lubin had given her good cause to resent her in the interim.

Working unpaid at the Opéra put another enormous strain on Marjorie's finances, until yet another of Cécile Gilly's vast network of contacts provided some relief. The impresario turned conductor Marcel Fichefet suggested that Marjorie contact the director of the opera at Nantes who desperately needed a singer to cover the role of Brünnhilde for the two performances of *Die Walküre* he was planning. The company's regular dramatic soprano, Fichefet explained, had not turned up. Marjorie pointed out that Jacques Rouché might see this as disloyalty, but Fichefet argued that as long as she was not bound by contract Marjorie was free to accept other engagements. Marjorie took Fichefet's advice, Henri Grodet phoned the theatre and Marjorie and Mimi caught a train to Nantes the next morning.

When Marjorie and Mimi arrived at the Théâtre Graslin in Nantes, a dress rehearsal for *Die Walküre* was about to begin. The missing soprano had still not arrived and a chorus member had been recruited to 'mark' the role of Brünnhilde. The director asked if Marjorie would join the rehearsal there and then. While the first act, in which Brünnhilde does not appear, was being rehearsed, Marjorie changed into her costume.[4]

The director of the Nantes opera was so delighted with Marjorie's singing that day that he regretted having given the role to another, promising that if she did not arrive Marjorie would sing both performances. If she did arrive, he added, he would insist the other singer relinquish the second performance to Marjorie. The missing soprano, Georgette Caro, turned up in time for the first performance but the outcome was happier than it had been in Monte Carlo with Nemeth and *Tosca*. Caro relinquished the second performance to Marjorie without argument and agreed to sing Sieglinde, the other soprano role in the opera that night.

On 24 October Marjorie sang Brünnhilde, the role she would be most closely associated with throughout her career, for the first time on any stage, in the ancient capital of Brittany. Her Siegmund was the Norwegian tenor from the Vienna Staatsoper, Gunnar Graarud, and Wotan was sung by Paul Cabanel, a stalwart of the Paris Opéra. Reports of this performance seem not to have survived, but an anecdote in *Interrupted Melody* hints at Marjorie's complete success. After she had sung the intensely moving closing scene of *Die Walküre* with him at the rehearsal, Cabanel put his arms around Marjorie and announced to all present: 'At last, Wotan has a daughter who looks and sounds as though she is a child of the gods'.[5]

Satisfying though this brief trip to Nantes was, Marjorie calculated that she made a profit of eight francs from it – the Nantes opera had paid her 600 francs for the performance and her expenses totalled 592 francs. To make matters worse, on her return to Paris she found there was still no sign of her contract from the Opéra. Disheartened, she returned to work there in order to keep faith with Rouché and to keep alive the now fading hope that the contract would one day arrive.

In desperation Marjorie now took a bold step. With Gilly's approval, she sought an audition at the Opéra-Comique, the rival opera house in Paris. Both theatres are state-owned and complement one another, the Opéra presenting 'grand' opera and the Opéra-Comique performing lighter works, sometimes with spoken dialogue. There was and still is, however, a lot of crossover of repertoire between the two houses (situated just 500 metres apart) and fierce competition for audiences, creating intense rivalry.[6]

Marjorie was invited to attend a general audition as she had at the Opéra. She turned up with seventy-four other singers to be heard by the director Pierre-Barthélemy Gheusi – and a team of carpenters busily (and noisily) at work on the stage. Marjorie had prepared arias from three operas she knew were in the Opéra-Comique's repertoire: Tosca's 'Vissi d'arte', Margared's aria from Lalo's *Le Roi d'Ys* and the 'Air des lettres' from *Werther*.

Marjorie's singing was so spectacular that the carpenters downed tools to listen to her sing the Lalo aria. When she finished Gheusi asked his assistants who had sent 'this great singer' to them. The assistants looked dumbfounded, so Marjorie provided the answer. 'I do not come on anyone's recommendation, *Monsieur*. I have only my voice to recommend me.' Gheusi assured her she needed no more and immediately offered Marjorie a contract to make her debut as Santuzza in *Cavalleria Rusticana* in two weeks. Marjorie accepted and Gheusi instructed his assistants to draw up a contract and post it to her.[7]

On the way home Marjorie called on Pierre Chereau and his wife to tell them the good news, but Chereau's reaction surprised Marjorie. The director, who was better informed about Rouché's negotiations with the Ministry of Labour than Marjorie was, gave her a despairing look and said she must speak to Rouché *before* she signed the contract from the Opéra-Comique. Chereau could not or would not tell her more, but Marjorie trusted him and so the next morning she tried to see Rouché, but the *directeur-général* was too busy. She tried twice the following day, on both occasions without success, so wrote a note to Rouché explaining the offer she had received from Gheusi and left it at the stage door.[8]

The next morning (a Saturday) Marjorie received a *lettre pneumatique* requesting she visit Rouché that afternoon.[9] With Mimi once again in tow, Marjorie presented herself at the *directeur-général*'s office and was whisked into Rouché's presence by the towering major-domo. Lying on Rouché's desk was Marjorie's contract.

It is unclear whether circumstances had prompted Rouché to pull some extra strings when he discovered he was about to lose a promising young singer or whether he had been sitting on the contract for some time. Marjorie never suspected him of deviousness, in fact she came to admire Rouché unreservedly and trust him completely. It is difficult, however, to accept that he had been able to accomplish in one Friday evening and one Saturday morning what he had failed to do for months. On the other hand, Marjorie's 'green card', which entitled her to sing at the Opéra, did not arrive for several more weeks, suggesting negotiations between the Opéra and the ministry were ongoing. Such considerations were of no interest to Marjorie, of course; she had her contract and thereby a regular income at last.

The contract stated that Marjorie was to continue her preparation at the Opéra, but gave no date for her debut. That, the document indicated, would occur when Rouché considered she was ready and when an appropriate role became available. The contract also specified that as an *artiste* of the Opéra, that house had exclusive rights to her services in Paris. She could apply for a *congé* if she wished to accept stage engagements in the provinces and she could appear in concert and on radio in Paris, but not in staged opera in any other theatre in the capital. Marjorie signed, Rouché kissed her in continental style on both cheeks and a dazed Marjorie tottered out into Mimi's supporting arms, whispering 'I've got it!'[10]

Mimi, Henri and the elder Grodets tried hard to match Marjorie's jubilation back at Avenue Trudaine, but they understood better than she how business worked in France. Monsieur Grodet was especially worried. He took Marjorie aside and said '*Mon enfant*, you have already made a deal with Monsieur Gheusi. What about that?' Marjorie brushed their concerns aside and, when the contract from the Opéra-Comique arrived the following Monday, she returned it unsigned with a brief note stating that she was now an *artiste* of the Opéra, and therefore no longer able to sing at the Opéra-Comique.

The Grodets had been right. A letter arrived a few days later threatening Marjorie with a writ for breach of the verbal contract she had made with Gheusi in front of witnesses. Marjorie was terrified at the prospect of legal action. She rushed to the Chereaus seeking their advice and they told her to go and see Rouché again and to take Gheusi's letter and, they suggested, Gunsbourg's contract for Monte Carlo the following year. Marjorie took their advice and laid the whole matter before Rouché. He set the Opéra's legal advisers to work and Gheusi capitulated, but Marjorie was never invited to sing at the Opéra-Comique again. Gunsbourg, for his part, took a pragmatic approach to losing his new discovery and eventually invited Marjorie back to give a concert in the Monte Carlo Opera House. As Marjorie confides in *Interrupted Melody*, with the relief of being extracted from this contractual mess came the realisation that the two great opera houses of Paris had been vying for her services. 'Even if my brother Lindsay did consider my progress slow,' she wrote, 'I thought I had done pretty well'.[11]

In the months that followed Marjorie also did pretty well in other spheres. On 8 November 1932 she took part in a 'Wagner Festival' organised by the radio station 'Porte Parisien'. For a fee of 300 francs she sang excerpts from *Tannhäuser* and *Die Walküre* accompanied by the radio station's excellent orchestra. A month later she returned to Porte Parisien's sumptuous studios on the Champs Èlysées to participate in a 'Saint-Saëns Festival', singing her old standby from her 'contralto' days, 'Softly Awakes My Heart' and an aria from Saint-Saëns's opera *L'Ancêstre*, which Felia Litvinne had first sung at the opera's premiere in Monte Carlo in 1906.

Marjorie continued to work hard at the Opéra and her diary for the autumn and winter of 1932–33 details regular coaching sessions with Maurice Fauré and Pierre Chereau. There are also many dozens of little printed notes among her papers of this period instructing her to attend rehearsals of *Die Walküre, Siegfried, Aida, Tosca, L'Africaine* and *Hérodiade*.

Marjorie also appeared as a soloist with the Lamoureux Orchestra conducted by Albert Wolff at a benefit concert and undertook several recording tests for La Compagnie Française du Gramophone, the Paris branch of 'His Master's Voice'. These tests were made over two days just before Christmas 1932 in the Salle Chopin in Pleyel's building in Rue du Faubourg Saint-Honoré, but no other details – how they came about, what Marjorie sang or how successful the tests were – have survived. Presumably nothing came of them, for almost a year would pass before Marjorie returned to the studios of Voix de son Maitre to make her first commercial recordings.

With the Opéra's approval, Marjorie also fulfilled opera engagements in Lille and again Nantes, both of which were arranged by Fichefet. She returned to Nantes for another performance of *Die Walküre* and to sing Valentine and Brunhilde in performances of *Les Huguenots* and *Sigurd* on stage for the first time. At Lille she also sang Aida, also for the first time, and repeated Brünnhilde in *Die Walküre*.

Paul Cabanel sang Wotan in *Die Walküre* in both cities and also the role of the King in *Aida* in Lille, so shared the stage with Marjorie at each of the Lille performances. Marjorie was delighted to be singing again with such an accomplished artist and commented on how comforting and stimulating it felt to be resting her head on this Wotan's mighty chest. Cabanel seems to have been experiencing similar stimulation and now had his heart set on giving Marjorie more than a public hug.

With an attractive voice, a sensitive approach to his art and a distinguished military record, Paul Cabanel, now in his early forties, was still a fine figure of a man. As photos of the day show and as Hollywood would certainly have described, he had 'sexy' eyes. Cabanel may well have been another who qualified for Marjorie's term 'a dinger of a bloke', but in his case she chose to label him 'a big, strong, slick-tongued purveyor of Gallic blarney'.[12]

The first rehearsal in Lille followed just four days after the last performance in Nantes, so Marjorie and Mimi travelled up from Nantes to Lille with Cabanel and he made his move on Marjorie during that journey. The pair left Nantes as colleagues and arrived in Lille as lovers. It was a short affair, one of those brief encounters gossip columnists would have us believe happen all the time in the world of greasepaint and celluloid and it seems not to have had a lasting effect on either party. When both returned to Lille for two more performances of *Aida* the following month, the affair was ended and for a very practical reason. The tenor singing Radames also fancied Marjorie and threatened to disrupt the performances if the baritone didn't back off.

Marjorie and Cabanel's relationship is, however, relevant to another matter. There was a rumour circulating in Australia at the time and which still occasionally surfaces that in 1933 Marjorie gave birth to an illegitimate son, fathered by someone famous. If one subscribes to that theory then Paul Cabanel would seem the most likely candidate for the child's father. However, there is no evidence to substantiate this rumour – no hints in letters, no curious entries in diaries, no unexplained documents and no long interruptions to study or work schedules – so until concrete evidence is produced to the contrary, it is fair to dismiss this claim as rumour.[13]

Marjorie freely admitted that she enjoyed sex and believed the enjoyment of it was her right as a young and healthy modern woman. This liberated attitude would have shocked her maiden aunts back in Winchelsea, but it was quite unremarkable in the sophisticated milieu of Paris during the interwar years. There is no evidence that Marjorie was ever promiscuous, but she did admit to getting carried away by male charms more often and less wisely than she should. This she attributed to having grown up without a mother's guidance.

> *Had I had the experience of loving a mother and of being loved by a mother, I'm sure my early love affairs would have been, let us say, better balanced than they were. Loving and being loved were experiences novel to me and when they did come into my life I went completely overboard.*[14]

Marjorie experienced a different kind of 'overboard' when Jacques Rouché walked into one of the rehearsal rooms at the Opéra one afternoon where Marjorie was working with Maurice Fauré. He listened for a moment then asked Fauré about Marjorie's progress. Next he asked Marjorie: 'How is Ortrud coming along? Do you have that ready yet?' Marjorie replied she certainly did and Fauré backed her up with 'Oui Maitre, elle est très bien préparée'. Rouché turned again to Marjorie and said *'Bien*, you will sing it next week'.[15]

Marjorie was elated – she was finally to have the opportunity she had dreamed of since first arriving in Paris – but with the elation came inevitable nervousness. The cast list for *Lohengrin* on Saturday evening, 25 February 1933, was posted the following day. Paul Franz and Germaine Lubin were to repeat their familiar portrayals of Lohengrin and Elsa and 'Mademoiselle M. Lawrence' was to sing Ortrud. The role of Telramund, Ortrud's ambitious husband, had been assigned to Martial Singher for the first time. Marjorie had rehearsed many times with this young baritone, just three years her senior and a former pupil of Maurice Fauré. In years to come Marjorie and Singher would appear together in North and South America and forge a lifelong friendship based on mutual respect. His presence in the cast was a comforting and steadying influence for Marjorie.

As the new members of the cast, Marjorie and Singher were given just two stage rehearsals with piano and none with the orchestra. Lubin didn't turn up to either rehearsal, which meant that the long scene between Elsa and Ortrud would have to be sung 'cold' on the evening of the performance. Not unjustifiably, Marjorie (and probably Singher) felt slighted by the prima donna not deigning to attend either of the rehearsals and failing to extend to them the professional courtesy they felt they were entitled to.

When the curtain rose on the first act of the opera that Saturday evening, the audience observed a slight, youthful figure sitting diffidently on the throne-like chair provided for Ortrud, her face made up none too convincingly to look older and evil. Many must have wondered whether she could possibly succeed in the role of the pagan sorceress – one of Wagner's most febrile creations.

Ortrud has little to do in the hour-long first act except to react to the other characters with menacing glares and join in the musical ensembles, but at the beginning of the second act she returns to the stage for two long and intensely dramatic scenes – the first with Telramund, the second with Elsa. Marjorie and Singher inspired and supported each other in their scene and this gave Marjorie time to settle down before her encounter with Lubin. Lubin glided onto the stage looking incredibly beautiful and singing like an angel – most of the time to the audience rather than to Marjorie.

By the middle of this exchange, the soprano has had two showpiece arias (one in each act), while Ortrud still awaits her opportunity to demonstrate her skill and power in a solo, but when that opportunity finally arrives, it is as if the composer were rewarding the singer for her patience. Ortrud suddenly throws off the humble guise she has been feigning and invokes her ancient gods to wreak havoc on her enemies. Settled vocally and fired up by Lubin's churlish behaviour, Marjorie launched into the passage she had sung at her audition with Rouché. She mustered all her vocal might and again hurled the top notes out into the vast auditorium, finishing this time with her arms stretched defiantly skyward.

Applause in mid-scene is discouraged at the Opéra, but the audience were not going to let this display of vocal amplitude pass unrewarded. Thunderous applause drowned the orchestra. The conductor, François Ruhlmann, kept the players going and Lubin returned to the stage and tried to deliver her next line, but the applause rather than diminishing grew. Ruhlmann and Lubin tried again, and the soprano had to sing her line three times before it was heard. As Marjorie put it, 'the fat was now in the fire and sending up clouds of blue smoke'.[16]

At this point Ortrud leaves the stage to do some plotting, which meant that Marjorie then had a break before returning at the end of the act to spit more venom at Elsa and Lohengrin. In the last act she has a third opportunity to steal the show with another passage of intense declamation which, if well delivered – as Marjorie did that evening – can focus the audience's attention on Ortrud rather than Elsa as the opera reaches its end.

When the curtain fell, the other principals and the chorus gathered around Marjorie and Singher and congratulated them, but not Lubin, and during solo bows she stood directly in front of Marjorie. As they left the stage Marjorie offered her hand to Lubin, but Lubin turned away. There were plenty of others who wanted to shake Marjorie's hand and plant kisses on her cheeks. Rouché, the Chereaus, Fauré and Ruhlmann all came to her dressing room, the latter admonishing Marjorie for prompting the interruption in the second act but assuring her he couldn't wait to conduct her in the Ring and in any other roles she was cast in.

Rouché asked Marjorie to call on him in his office the next day and at the meeting he tore up Marjorie's existing contract and gave her another with double the wage. Rouché also asked Marjorie what she would like to sing next and Brünnhilde in *Die Walküre* was agreed upon. According to Marjorie, that role became her exclusive property during her time at the Opéra – the first of her *titulaires* as they are called in France – wrested from the grasp of Germaine Lubin. Marjorie also claimed that after that evening she frequently had to step in to replace Lubin in an assortment of roles. Neither of these claims is true. Lubin continued to sing the 'Walküre' Brünnhilde occasionally and the number of times Marjorie replaced Lubin were almost equalled by the number of times Lubin replaced her.

In *Interrupted Melody* Marjorie paints Lubin as a singer whose voice and career were in decline and who resented the undoubted competition Marjorie represented. The second part of that claim is true. Whenever Marjorie and Lubin passed one another in a corridor at the Opéra, Lubin cut her dead and when Marjorie pressed the point one day and said mischievously 'Don't you recognise me, Madame?' Lubin glared at her through her lorgnette and replied that she had no recollection of her whatsoever.

After that first *Lohengrin*, Lubin also refused to appear on stage with Marjorie, although she relented three years later and allowed Marjorie to appear as her servant, Brangäne, in two performances of *Tristan und Isolde*. Like most Australians, Marjorie put great store in being sportsmanlike and giving everyone 'a fair go', so in the light of Lubin's actions it is not surprising that Marjorie's admiration for the older singer turned to contempt.

The image of Lubin as a singer in decline, however, is nothing more than a product of that contempt. Lubin had another eleven years of triumphant singing ahead of her and she might have gone on for many more had silence not been imposed on her. At forty-three she was probably not singing with the same freshness and ease that Marjorie then was and it is doubtful if she ever commanded the same brilliance and freedom above the stave that set Marjorie apart from other Wagnerian sopranos, but Lubin's qualities lay elsewhere.[17]

Although Marjorie would probably have been reluctant to admit it, she was influenced by Lubin's art. That is not surprising when one considers that Lubin was the only great Wagnerian soprano Marjorie had heard perform on stage regularly up to the time her own career commenced.[18] Consciously or not, Marjorie adopted Lubin's conception of Brünnhilde as a youthful, vibrant, even seductive 'daughter of the gods', adjectives that were often applied to them both by critics, but seldom to their Germanic or Nordic rivals. It also seems likely that Marjorie followed Lubin's example in her use of *portamento* as a grand and potent expressive device. Both singers shared this gift, both were praised for it and both criticised for it when the device was occasionally overused. Lubin and Marjorie share too a certain Gallic felicitousness in the way they enunciate Wagner's text, which is touching and apparent, whether they are singing in French or German.

There are also qualities both these singers share with Litvinne and with the great French soprano of the next generation, Régine Crespin, whom Lubin coached when she attempted the Wagner roles. Listening to this quartet of *grande dames* via recordings, it is not difficult to discern a peculiarly 'Gallic' style of Wagner singing, a style that was unique enough to differentiate Marjorie from other Wagnerian sopranos when she reached New York and earn her a niche of her own in their company.

The occasion on which Marjorie made her debut at the Opéra was another routine performance of a familiar opera and, as Martial Singher was familiar to the press from other roles and Marjorie was an unknown quantity when the curtain rose, there were few music critics in the audience. Gustave Bret was there of course, but he can hardly be considered an objective commentator. He told readers of *L'Intransigent* that Marjorie was 'one of the greatest Ortrud's in history'[19] and Pierre Ferroud, who admitted in his review in *Paris Soir* that he had never heard or heard *of* Marjorie before, concurred:

> *Mademoiselle Marjorie Lawrence's singing of the role of Ortrud for I believe the first time was a revelation. After hearing so many singers struggle with the difficult music of this part, it was a pleasure to hear a young singer who could ignore those difficulties and sing with the abandon the composer intended.*[20]

The resounding success Marjorie had scored at her Opéra debut ushered in a new, busy and rewarding phase in her career. She continued to take occasional lessons with Cécile Gilly and their relationship remained very close, but after being a student for so long Marjorie was anxious to cast off that label. There were more performances of *Lohengrin* at the Opéra with Germaine Hoerner replacing Lubin and Georges Thill taking over the title role, another *Les Huguenots* in Nantes and two performances of *Tannhäuser* in Bordeaux.

Marjorie also claimed that immediately following her debut at the Opéra she was offered engagements to sing at Covent Garden and at the Vienna Staatsoper, followed shortly after by an offer from La Scala, Milan. She turned all these offers down, she said, on Rouché's advice. There is no documentary evidence to support this claim, but interest from London and Vienna at least was probable. Scouts from other opera houses were invariably in attendance at the Opéra whenever a new singer was announced and, so spectacular was Marjorie's debut, they would not have ignored her. If Marjorie did turn down an offer to sing at Covent Garden in 1933, she must have rued that decision when later she struggled to get a foothold in the British capital.

Another consequence of Marjorie's triumph as Ortrud was her first batch of fan mail, some of which she kept all her life. *Habitueés* of the 'hen roost', where Marjorie and Archie Longden had sat through many performances, wrote to her – young females who admired her voice and her pluck and young males who admired her appearance. A small clique of stage-door 'Jeans' also assembled whenever Marjorie appeared thereafter – mostly elderly roués who pressed flowers and invitations to supper on her. Germaine Hoerner, who was just a year older than

Marjorie but who had been at the Opéra for four years, showed her how to deal with them. Hoerner also helped Marjorie negotiate the politics of life in a large opera company and, like Singher, became a valued and trusted friend.

On 9 April Marjorie sang her first Brünnhilde in *Die Walküre* at the Opéra, with Franz as Siegmund and Marcel Journet as Wotan. It was another triumph, with Pierre Ferroud telling his readers that he had witnessed the most exciting portrayal of the 'Walküre' Brünnhilde it had ever been his privilege to see and hear.[21] Robert Dézarnaux, writing in *La Liberté*, pointed out that there were both vocal and histrionic rough spots in Marjorie's assumption of the role that would need to be ironed out by experience, but concurred with his colleague that it was a very exciting and satisfying performance.[22]

Several critics commented on how athletically Marjorie acted her part in this opera. After spending her childhood leaping onto horses, climbing trees and throwing sticks, springing from stage rock to stage rock while waving her spear above her head as Wagner instructs Brünnhilde to do on her entry posed no difficulty for Marjorie, but it surprised the critics and the audience who were accustomed to more lethargic leading ladies.

Rouché offered her the part of Salomé in Massenet's *Hérodiade* next, and she did two performances of that in May. During all this activity, Marjorie continued to live with the Grodets and she was joined there for a couple of weeks in the spring by an unexpected but very welcome visitor, her brother Percy – except that he was no longer 'Percy'; he was now 'Cyril'.

During Marjorie's absence Percy Lawrence had been putting his piano-playing skills to practical use as a piano salesman in Melbourne, but was finding the insular world of Melbourne stifling and threatening. Percy was homosexual and being gay in a place like Melbourne in those days was fraught with perils. Percy longed to leave Australia and to transform himself into one of the 'beautiful' people in the sophisticated world his sister now inhabited. The only thing Percy had managed to do to effect that transformation up until the time he arrived in Paris was to discard the name Bill and Elizabeth had given him and replace it with a more exotic one. He had chosen 'Cyril', he explained, because of its association with Russian royalty. To accomplish the rest, Cyril needed his sister's help.

Marjorie had known about her brother's sexual orientation for a long time and she was way past being shocked by it. Ada Boddington, four years residence in Paris and her own exploration of sex had made Marjorie tolerant of many things she had not even heard of in Winchelsea. She also loved her brother and the bond that had been forged when they ran away from home together was still strong. Marjorie agreed to help Cyril (as she *and we* will now call him) if he came to live in Paris. As her income had begun to increase and her debts decrease, Marjorie had thought seriously about getting an apartment of her own and she promised Cyril that if he returned the following year he could share her new home.

Cyril was also able to fill Marjorie in on all the details of their father's death and the disputes that were still going on over Bill Lawrence's will, how divisions that he and she would never had thought possible had torn the family apart and how unexpected sides to characters they thought they knew had been revealed. As Cyril put it: 'It's a bloody mess, Marge'. Marjorie was now glad she was distanced from this 'mess' and had other things to occupy her. To her surprise and delight, Rouché had offered her a fantastic role in a new opera by a distinguished living composer which was about to receive its world premiere at the Opéra.

Chapter Seven
L'Étoile de l'Opéra

Marjorie's first experience as a role creator in Monte Carlo had been a disappointment. Neither audiences nor critics warmed to Gunsbourg's puerile offering and Marjorie came to realise that, rather than being favoured by being cast in *L'Escarpolette*, she had been exploited. The new opera to be presented at the Paris Opéra was in a different class, although it would also disappear quickly and be dismissed almost as ignominiously by history.

The composer was Joseph Canteloube, remembered today only for his enchanting, often-recorded arrangements of folksongs of the Auvergne. *Vercingetorix*, as the opera was titled, is Canteloube's magnum opus, a four-act grand opera celebrating the birth of French national unity. The plot concerns the struggle of the warrior chief Vercingetorix against the Roman occupation of Gaul in the first century AD. Based on history, the subject lends itself to stage action, but the libretto is static and tedious and Canteloube's predominantly slow music failed to inspire much excitement. The only memorable thing about Canteloube's score is his use of an Ondes Martenot, one of the first electronic musical instruments.[1]

The Opéra lavished all its considerable resources on presenting *Vercingetorix*. Chereau produced, Gaubert conducted and a stellar cast filled the principal roles. Georges Thill sang the title role (which the composer had written with his voice in mind) and André Pernet and Martial Singher took the other important male roles. The female roles were given to Marjorie, soprano Marthe Nespoulos and the company's principal contralto, Ketty Lapeyrette. Marjorie played the part of Keltis, a virgin priestess whose relationship to Vercingetorix must have confused him and the audience. One moment she is threatening to disembowel him, but she then falls in love with him, finally becoming his muse and a sort of allegorical figure representing 'la belle France'.

After a month of rehearsal with the composer in attendance, *Vercingetorix* was premiered on 22 June 1933, with eight more performances given before Christmas without change of cast. The critics singled out Thill, Marjorie and Lapeyrette for special praise. Pierre Lalo (son of the composer Édouard Lalo), writing in

Le Temps, described them as a magnificent trio of singers.[2] Robert Dézamaux compared Marjorie favourably with Frida Leider and Lotte Lehmann, claiming she had cause to envy neither.[3] Another critic wrote:

> At each of her appearances this young Australian moves a step closer to a brilliant career. She sings as she breathes and her voice has remarkable breadth and power. It is true and sure in attack and highly dramatic in quality. Her vivid and ardent personality gives warmth and colour to every note she sings. With the celebrated tenor, Monsieur Georges Thill as her partner, she scored a triumph.[4]

The composer of the opera was also delighted with Marjorie. He penned a catalogue of compliments on the cover of her copy of his score and presented her with a large photograph of himself inscribed (in French):

> To Mademoiselle Marjorie Lawrence, grand artist and magnificent interpreter of the difficult music of Keltis. A souvenir to remind you of the premiere of 'Vercingetorix'. With best wishes and cordial admiration – Canteloube.[5]

As evidence of Marjorie's resourcefulness and stamina, she popped down to Nimes in the south of France during the run of *Vercingetorix* to sing a role she had learned with Cécile Gilly four years earlier but had not thus far sung on stage – Sélika in Meyerbeer's *L'Africaine*. Back in Paris, she sang another role on stage for the first time – Rachel in Halevy's *La Juive* (complete with its top 'D') and two nights later Paris heard her Aida for the first time. Each appearance was praised and in the Paris performances she sang opposite tenors notable for their voices and their temperaments. Eleazor in *La Juive* was sung by the Irish tenor John O'Sullivan, nearing the end of a career that had taken him to Covent Garden, La Scala and North and South America. Radames in *Aida* was sung by the much younger José Luccioni, with whom Marjorie would sing many times. O'Sullivan struggled with his voice and Luccioni struggled with Marjorie.

Marjorie believed she had been the victim of behind-the-scenes machinations by Germaine Lubin and now she was confronted with open skulduggery by the young Corsican. In each of the scenes where Aida and Radames sing together, Luccioni deliberately held Marjorie in a vice-like embrace, restricting her breathing and making it seem as if he were in better voice than she. This had not happened at rehearsal, so it came as a very disconcerting surprise to Marjorie at the first performance. After the Nile Scene, Marjorie warned Luccioni not to hold her like that again or she would retaliate by pulling off his wig, revealing the vain tenor's receding hairline. In the Tomb Scene Luccioni grabbed Marjorie again and applied his vice-like embrace. Marjorie grabbed his long locks and yanked. The tenor was forced to let go of her to grab his wig. While Amneris intoned the final phrases of the opera, within the darkened tomb of Aida and Radames, Marjorie whispered to Luccioni. 'Well Monsieur, now you know what to expect if you try that again.' Luccioni never did.

Marjorie's burgeoning reputation as a star of the Opéra increased the demand for her services as a concert artist. She performed with the Paris Symphony Orchestra conducted by Pierre Monteux and a concert she gave with Gaubert and the conservatoire orchestra was broadcast to Britain, giving Britons their first opportunity to hear her. Offers came in from Belgium, with Marjorie subsequently singing at Liége and Antwerp and in the elegant auditoriums of the casinos at Knokke and Ostend.[6]

La Compagnie Française du Gramophone also renewed their interest in her, anxious to capitalise on her success and record her as Ortrud and the 'Walküre' Brünnhilde. On 15 September 1933, Marjorie signed a lucrative contract to make her first commercial recordings on the Voix de son Maitre label and five days later attended at the Salle Pleyel for her first professional recording session.

As a full orchestra was to be used, the company had decided to make the recordings in the spacious Salle Pleyel, rather than in their studio in the Boulevard des Italiens. The orchestra of the Concerts Pasdeloup had been engaged and the conductor was the company's music director, Piero Coppola. An eclectic musician, this small, watery-eyed Italian could turn his hand with equal ease and success to Italian, French or German music and was a notable champion of many young French composers.

It had been decided that on the first day the entire Ortrud-Elsa scene from Act Two of *Lohengrin* would be recorded on three twelve-inch sides; this was to be followed by the Ortrud-Telramund duet on two twelve-inch sides. Elsa was sung by Yvonne Brothier, a lyric soprano from the Opéra who seldom if ever sang Wagner, with Telramund sung by Martial Singher.

The Ortrud-Elsa duet is hampered by Brothier's blatant approach to the music, and her shrill tone differentiates the two characters, but does little more. The Invocation comes in the middle of this scene and, considering how Marjorie had sung it as a showpiece, one might expect it to stand out awkwardly, but it does not. It is a high point, but it is also well integrated into the scene, as it should be. Singher is a resonant Telramund in the earlier duet and his voice blends magnificently with Marjorie's in the 'Der Rache' passage.

Between these two scenes we are favoured with a substantial part of Ortrud's music (almost twenty-two minutes in total) by which to judge Marjorie's singing of it at this stage in her career – and she acquits herself magnificently. The generous number of sides allows Coppola to take an unhurried approach to the music and, combined with the spacious acoustic, allows us to hear Marjorie's voice in a way that at least approximates what the audience must have heard at her Opéra debut eight months earlier, a rich, vibrant and superb instrument under expert control, from *pianissimo* to *fortissimo*. These recordings also amply demonstrate why that audience and the critics found her portrayal of Ortrud so remarkably convincing. Each of the changes of character Ortrud undergoes is clearly mirrored in the voice, a remarkable feat of vocal acting for a relatively inexperienced performer.

Three weeks later Marjorie was back at the same venue to record excerpts from *Die Walküre*, again with the Pasdeloup orchestra and Coppola. This time she was joined by baritone Jean Claverie and eight unidentified female singers. The first excerpt recorded (on two twelve-inch sides) was the opening scene of Act Three, beginning with the 'Ride of the Valkyries', followed by Brünnhilde's arrival, and ending as Sieglinde stirs.

Probably to save money, members of the Opéra chorus were recruited to sing the other eight Valkyries in this scene and, to get them off to a good start, Marjorie sang the role of Gerhilde on the first side before relinquishing it to one of the anonymous women; on the second side she sang the role of Brünnhilde. Coppola conducts a stirring 'ride' but as soon as the Valkyries enter a comic element enters with them. Admirable though these singers may be as choristers, as soloists they make a hilarious bunch. The sopranos sound like Macbeth's witches on 'speed' and their frenetic manner infects Marjorie's singing, although she, at least, is *meant* to be frantic in this scene. This is the least successful of Marjorie's Paris recordings.

The second excerpt, recorded on one twelve-inch side is the opening of the Act Two, with Marjorie as Brünnhilde and Claverie as Wotan, roles they had sung together at the Opéra in August. Claverie is a very youthful-sounding 'war father' and if we can't *see* Marjorie leaping from rock to rock on the recording, that energy and athleticism can be heard in her singing. The Battle Cry ('*Ho-jo-to-ho*') holds no fears for her, her trill is a real trill, not just a 'shake' as some Brünnhildes resort to and her high notes have that characteristic 'ping' that already set her apart from every other Wagnerian soprano of her time.

The third excerpt (which appeared on the reverse of the previous side) was Brünnhilde's plea to Wotan: 'War es so schmählich, was ich verbrach', or in this case, 'Ai-je à ce point mérité qu'on me blame'. Apart from one uncharacteristically wobbly note that must have escaped the notice of the recording technicians, this is an expressive and eloquent reading of a passage Marjorie loved to sing.

With the lift in tessitura from Ortrud to the 'Walküre' Brünnhilde comes a complete change in the colour of Marjorie's voice. It is still unmistakably the same instrument but the dark, contralto-like tones of Ortrud have been replaced by the bright, ringing tones of the young warrior maid. That voice can be heard again, slightly darkened to suit the character's progress, when Marjorie returned to record Brünnhilde's 'Immolation Scene' from *Götterdämmerung* the following January.

By the time Marjorie came to make this last recording, she had sung the *Götterdämmerung* Brünnhilde twice at the Opéra and would sing it twice more within days of making the recording. With experience, her interpretation of the Immolation Scene would deepen and acquire subtleties it then lacked, but this is an exciting and invigorating performance. In a survey of recordings of *Götterdämmerung* in *Opera* magazine thirty years later, the distinguished British music critic Alan Blyth wrote:

> *Marjorie Lawrence is simply amazing. On this evidence she must have been one of the most exciting artists of her generation. For once a Brünnhilde really sounds as if she has been a woman totally consumed with love for Siegfried.*[7]

Coppola and the orchestra also rise to the occasion and this is the best souvenir we have of the young Marjorie as Brünnhilde.

Eight months later Voix de son Maitre paired Marjorie with José de Trevi, the Opéra's second heldentenor (one pace behind Paul Franz in the pecking order until he replaced him), to record the 'dawn' duet from *Götterdämmerung* on two twelve-inch sides, but for some now forgotten reason this disc was never issued. José de Trevi, with whom Marjorie sang frequently at the Opéra, was a highly accomplished singer, so this elusive disc sounds – at least on paper – likely to have been among the best in the series.

All these recordings are sung in French, the language dramatically changing the emphases on words within phrases, taking out some of the 'bite' of the original and occasionally upsetting the composer's carefully constructed symbiosis of text and music. Orthodox Wagnerians might dismiss them because of the language, but there is no denying the quality of Marjorie's singing – steadier than Litvinne, more invigorated than Lubin and more reliable than Crespin. These recordings sold well in France and Marjorie was invited back to make more for Voix de son Maitre, but because of the language issue, music lovers in Britain, Australia and the United States had to order them as special imports from His Master's Voice or RCA Victor.[8]

Marjorie's first appearance as Brünnhilde in *Götterdämmerung* at the Opéra was another personal triumph for her. In *Interrupted Melody* she claims that *Götterdämmerung* was revived for her by Rouché after having slipped out of the repertoire when Lubin began having difficulty with her top notes. For whatever reason, Marjorie was able to add the *Götterdämmerung* Brünnhilde to her list of '*titulaires*'.

Her success also earned Marjorie the opportunity to sing with two famous Wagnerians when they came to the Opéra as guests for two performances of *Lohengrin* in November 1934. The Czech soprano Maria Müller, who was a favourite in Berlin, Bayreuth and New York, sang Elsa and the world's leading heldentenor, Lauritz Melchior, sang the title role. Marjorie was chosen to sing Ortrud and John Brownlee to sing Telramund. As Brownlee put it: quite a coup for a couple of 'Aussies'. When Marjorie expressed her nervousness at the presence of Melchior in the cast, Brownlee produced another 'dinkum' dictum. 'Jeez, Marge,' he whispered as they waited to go on stage, 'pull yourself together and think o' Winchelsea'.[9]

Both Müller and Melchior were established stars of the Metropolitan Opera in New York and it is testament to how meteorically Marjorie's career had taken off since her Opéra debut that she was also considering an offer from the 'Met' when she sang in these gala 'Lohengrins'. The offer was the result of a chain of events, only some of which Marjorie was aware.

At this time the reigning Wagnerian dramatic soprano at the Met was Frida Leider, but she was not happy singing in New York and was in dispute over her fees, which were significantly lower than the Met management was paying some of its other leading sopranos. Finding a replacement for Leider was becoming an urgent concern for the general manger Giulio Gatti-Casazza and his deputy Edward Ziegler.

Reports of Marjorie's success at the Opéra had reached New York. Edward Zeigler contacted Erich Simon, the Met's agent in Paris, saying he had received a letter from a friend about a young Australian girl singing at the Opéra, 'with a dramatic soprano voice of such beauty, range and volume that she is destined to become the most famous Wagnerian singer' and that she has 'a splendid stage presence, is good looking and a fine actress'. Zeigler sought Simon's opinion and concluded: 'If this girl is really so extraordinary and if she is singing in Paris when I am in London, I will try to arrange to come to hear her, but only if you think it is worthwhile'.[10]

Simon wrote back to say that the report Zeigler had received was correct. It was not Zeigler, however, but Artur Bodanzky, chief conductor of the German repertoire at the Met, who came to Paris to check out the 'girl'. This stooped and bespectacled former violinist, who had played under Brahms and been Mahler's assistant at the Vienna Opera, wielded enormous power at the Met and was renowned for directing incandescent performances and taking a scalpel to composers' scores. Bodanzky asked Simon to invite Marjorie to audition for him and Marjorie agreed, although their relationship got off to a poor start.

At the audition Marjorie was introduced to the conductor before she sang. He reacted to her youthful appearance with the remark: 'A kid like you sing in the Ring? It's *ridiculous*!' delivered in a disparaging tone. Typical Aussie that she was, Marjorie was not about to let that pass unchallenged. 'You know Mr Bodanzky,' she said calmly, 'right now I don't feel like going to America at all. I have everything I could ask for right here in Paris.' With that Marjorie turned on her heel, walked out of the building and caught a taxi home.

Ten minutes after her arrival at Avenue Trudaine, the Grodets' telephone rang. It was Erich Simon. Mr Bodanzky, Simon explained, regretted if he had upset Marjorie and he assured her that his remark had been made as a compliment. One can well imagine Marjorie muttering that expressive Australian expletive 'bullshit' under her breath, but when Simon asked her to return and sing the audition as a personal favour to him and offered to pay her taxi fares, she agreed.

Back at the venue, Marjorie sang 'Dich teure Halle' from *Tannhäuser* and the 'Immolation Scene' for Bodanzky, who behaved very courteously and said he would be in touch. The following night he attended a performance of *Die Walküre* at the Opéra and watched and listened to Marjorie singing Brünnhilde. Two days later she received a contract to join the Met company for the 1934–35 season with a note from Bodanzky asking her to prepare the three Brünnhildes, Isolde, Kundry, Elsa and Ortrud – all in German.

Before signing, Marjorie sought guidance from Jacques Rouché and, while the advice the *directeur-général* gave her served his interests, it also reflected the genuine concern and growing affection he had for his young star. Rouché gently reminded Marjorie of some facts she already knew – that the Opéra was looking after her very well and helping her develop her art with new roles, good casts and a stable income. He also pointed out that the pace at the Met was more stressful than at the Opéra and that she would be expected to arrive with each of the specified roles fully prepared *in German* – an enormous task to try to accomplish in a year already filled with engagements. Further, he noted that the fee of $400 per performance the Met was offering with no guarantee of the number of performances was, as he described it, *indécent*.[11]

Fully aware of the prestige that came from singing at the Met and fearful of offending them, Marjorie delayed her decision as long as she could, mulling over the advantages and disadvantages. Simon became frustrated and impatient. Finally in December he had to report to Zeigler that he had met with Marjorie and she had decided to decline the contract and stay at the Opéra for another year of consolidation, but that she would be honoured to consider another offer from the Met at a later date.

Ziegler was bitterly disappointed and the search for a new Wagnerian soprano had to begin once again. In desperation he and Gatti-Casazza auditioned a virtually unknown Norwegian soprano called Kirsten Flagstad in a hotel in St Moritz. Unlike Marjorie, Flagstad was approaching middle age, was homely in appearance and had never sung any of the Brünnhildes. Distinctly underwhelmed by her audition, Gatti-Casazza and Ziegler nevertheless offered her a contract similar to Marjorie's – but with an even lower fee and without an option on the singer's services for subsequent seasons.

So Marjorie stayed in Paris and Flagstad went to New York and the rest is history. Completely unheralded at her debut, Flagstad created one of the greatest sensations in the Met's history and in one season obliterated memories of most of her predecessors, effortlessly filling the vacancy left by Leider. How differently things might have turned out if Marjorie had accepted that first offer from the Met and gone to New York at the end of 1934. Flagstad would not have been needed; neither auditioned nor engaged and likely would have returned to her native Norway never to be heard of again. The world would have lost one of its greatest voices and Marjorie might have succeeded to Leider's mantle.

These events were still in the future when 1934 drew to a close, and if Marjorie was suffering second thoughts about turning down the Met, she had plenty of new and challenging projects both musical and non-musical to distract her. As if affirming her loyalty to Paris, Marjorie set out in January to find the apartment she had been yearning for. With her monthly retainer from the Opéra (now 25,000 francs), fees for performances in the provinces, concerts and broadcasts, together with royalties from her recordings, Marjorie's income had never been so exalted. Furthermore, as she points out in *Interrupted Melody*, being a principal artist at the Opéra also meant that she did not have to employ a manager or spend money on self-promotion, thus saving herself expenses other singers incurred. Savings and income, Marjorie calculated, would allow her to take a roomy apartment in the vicinity of the Opéra.

The search proved long, not because apartments were scarce, but because there were so many to choose from. On occasions doubt about branching out on her own troubled Marjorie as she hiked from one address to another. Paris was suffering one of its regular periods of civil unrest and Marjorie encountered mobs of demonstrators on the major boulevards. On the day after Marjorie found her apartment, the army fired on demonstrators in Place de la Concorde and in front of the Palais Bourbon, three kilometres from her new address, but by the time Marjorie moved, the unrest had settled.

The apartment chosen by Marjorie was on the third floor of 2 Rue Baudin, just a kilometre from the Opéra and the same distance from Cécile Gilly and the Grodets. It was a beautifully appointed seven-room apartment overlooking Square de Montholon. From the balcony of her living room Marjorie had an uninterrupted view down Rue La Fayette to the Opéra and could watch the afternoon sun glinting on its gilded statues.

Marjorie packed her belongings at the Grodets and bid a tearful farewell to the aged couple who had been her proxy parents for so long. As a parting gift, the Grodets insisted Marjorie took their maid Eugenie (the successor to old Lucienne) with her, saying that Marjorie needed someone reliable to take care of her and to look after her expanding wardrobe. Marjorie employed a cook named Yvonne and these two devoted women ran her household. Marjorie also needed a piano and Pleyels came to the party with a fine instrument leased at a very reasonable rate that was manhandled up two flights of stairs and installed in the living room.

Marjorie's performing year also began with a bang – or in fact a rapid ascending run on a clarinet. In the Théâtre du Champs Elysées on 14 January, Marjorie sang the title role in a concert performance of Richard Strauss's *Salome* with the Pasdeloup Orchestra conducted by Gaubert. This was Marjorie's first opportunity to perform a role she had studied with Gilly three years earlier and to put into practice some of the vocal effects she had learned from Mary Garden.

The following month in the Salle Pleyel, Marjorie sang the title role in another concert performance – of Honegger's *Judith*, with the Colonne Orchestra conducted by Paul Paray. As with Canteloube and *Vercingetorix*, the composer was in attendance at the rehearsals and also entertained as an honoured guest in Marjorie's new apartment. A few weeks later she sang the role of Guenièvre in a broadcast of the third act of Chausson's opera *Le Roi Arthus* for Radio Paris. The Honegger and

Chausson were interesting forays into unfamiliar repertoire and nothing more, but the performance of the Strauss opera had repercussions. It heralded Marjorie's long association with her most successful and acclaimed role by a composer other than Richard Wagner.[12]

Unexpectedly, Marjorie also sang her only performance on stage of a Mozart role at the Opéra on 19 March, under the baton of the legendary Bruno Walter. Marjorie had agreed to understudy Lubin in the role of Donna Anna in *Don Giovanni* and had attended the rehearsals, keeping well clear of her rival. At four on the afternoon of that day a message came from the opera house to say that Lubin was '*souffrante*' and that Marjorie would sing the role in four hours time. There was also a summons from Walter to attend on him and his assistant Maurice Abravanel in their hotel for a hasty run-through of Donna Anna's scenes, which was followed by an equally hasty lesson from the great conductor on how to dance a minuet, so that Marjorie could acquit herself respectably in the on-stage festivities at Don Giovanni's villa.

The performance was not a triumph of the kind Marjorie had become used to. She managed Donna Anna's 'Vengeance' aria (the piece she had sung on horseback at Euse) with striking effect, but the difficult coloratura of 'Non mi dir' in the second act defeated her, even at the stately tempo Walter had set in place to accommodate Lubin. Wagnerian sopranos have and do sing Mozart with success – Lubin and Leider being prime examples – but for Marjorie, the gap between these composers was too broad to bridge. Neither she nor the audience were impressed by her one attempt at Donna Anna, but the experience did offer Marjorie a salutary and timely reminder of her limitations.

Three weeks later Marjorie received a note from Louise Hanson-Dyer's secretary telling her that James Joyce wished to meet her, adding 'Mr Joyce is so interested in your voice and has many things he wishes to tell you'. Marjorie was abuzz with curiosity and invited Joyce for afternoon tea at her apartment. The famous novelist turned up looking more like an out-of-luck bookmaker and gobbled down most of the dainty sandwiches Eugenie had prepared. He then offered Marjorie the title role in a performance of Bellini's *Norma* he was planning to mount in the old Roman amphitheatre in Orange, using Hanson-Dyer's money. Pollione was to be sung by Joyce's favourite tenor, John O'Sullivan, and the novelist assured Marjorie she would be 'superb' as Bellini's tragic priestess.

James Joyce had a genuine passion for music, but his knowledge of voices was obviously limited. No doubt with memories of 'Non mi dir' flashing through her mind, Marjorie thanked the novelist for his generous offer and pointed out that she was not a *coloratura* soprano and did not have the kind of technique that was required to sing a role like Norma. Joyce was polite but obviously put out. Later he told Ezra Pound: '*La Lawrence* did not seem to be able to manage the part'. As it turned out no one else managed it either. The project was knocked on the head by Hanson-Dyer when she discovered how much it was going to cost her.

Success was once again Marjorie's when she returned to more congenial territory in a series of performances at the Opéra of the 'other' Brunhilde in Reyer's *Sigurd*. Many famous French sopranos, including Litvinne and Lubin, had sung this role, but the critics judged Marjorie's to be the best in decades. Further triumphs came when Rouché mounted a new production of *Salome* for Marjorie, prompted by her success in the concert performance at the Théâtre du Champs Elysées. Strauss's music fitted Marjorie's voice like a glove and she had found no difficulty surmounting the great technical demands the composer places on the singer who is brave enough to tackle it, but portraying the character on stage could not be left to chance. The city that had given sanctuary to Oscar Wilde knew his erotic, teenage princess of Judea very well. Marjorie, Rouché, Chereau (who directed the new production) and Gaubert who was to conduct again, recognised that audiences would demand a credible interpretation and would expect sensation.

The quartet was also in agreement that Marjorie should perform Salome's 'Dance of the Seven Veils' rather than use a dancer substitute, which was common practice at the time. Marjorie had vivid memories of Mary Garden telling her 'You *must* do the dance yourself, my dear. It is a part of the substance of the character. Salome must feel Herod's lust *like heat on her body*'. Marjorie went on a crash diet and lost ten kilos in three weeks and the Opéra employed the dancer Surgito Majito to help her create an acceptable dance, including how to shed her veils seductively. Photos of Marjorie veiled and made up as Salome show a remarkable resemblance to super-vamp Theda Bara in her 1918 silent movie, *Salome*.

The first night of *Salome* was a triumph for all concerned. José de Trevi as Herod, Georgette Caro as Herodias and John Brownlee as Jokanaan all received praise, but the lion's share went to Marjorie. Pierre Ferrond, writing in *Comedia*, declared Marjorie had no rival in the world in this role,[13] and although Henry Malherbe writing in *Le Temps* was not impressed with Marjorie's dance, in which he said he perceived some signs of embarrassment, of her singing and acting he had no reservations.

> *All that Monsieur Strauss' music demands was delivered by Mademoiselle Lawrence. Her neat figure is ideal for the role of the whimsical, viperine, sadistic child-princess, but she needs nothing more than her incomparable soprano voice to move us and to rise to the score's full brilliance.*[14]

Malherbe also favourably compared Marjorie's voice and appearance with that of Emmy Destinn, the previous singer of the role at the Opéra, which must have been cause for comment at Rue de la Rochefoucauld.[15]

Just how phenomenally Marjorie sang the roles of Brunhilde in *Sigurd* and Salome is proven beyond doubt by the next batch of recordings she made. Voix de son Maitre were again anxious to capitalise on Marjorie's latest successes and invited her to record Brunhilde's two arias and the final scene from *Salome*. The Pasdeloup Orchestra under Coppola were again involved and the recordings were made as with the earlier ones in the Salle Pleyel. The *Sigurd* arias were recorded in one morning, each on a twelve-inch side and the *Salome* scene the same afternoon on four twelve-inch sides.

Marjorie's voice is ravishing in the *Sigurd* arias, rock-solid in the lower parts and expanding to its full, shining splendour as the music rises. The *Salome* finale sounds strange sung in French when accustomed to hearing it in German, but the softer consonants and lengthened vowels give an extra shimmer of eroticism that is not inappropriate. Having four sides at their disposal and with some minor cuts to the score, Marjorie and Coppola were able to take their time and savour the moments of stillness. Although neither Herodias nor Herod features in the recording, this was still the most complete recording of the scene made up to that time and it would be a long time before another came along to challenge its excellence. Marjorie is in glorious voice and her singing is nothing short of sensational. It is one of those recordings that stop the listener in their tracks when they first hear it and make old music lovers grumble about the present state of vocalism.

Time has only served to make this recording appear all the more astounding. When most of these Paris discs were reissued on CD in 1990, that most perceptive of writers on singing, John Steane, said in *Gramophone*, 'This Salome is wonderfully vivid in its tormented luxury: a magnificent performance and surely very close to Strauss's ideal' and the American journal *Stereo Review* contented itself with one word: 'Fabulous!'[16]

Marjorie had now made twelve recordings, preserving about eighty minutes of her singing, and although she would make other commercial recordings in America, Britain and Australia, these Paris discs (along with some 'live' performances caught on disc, which will be discussed later) stand as a great testament to her voice, which in all of them is in its joyous, youthful prime, an instrument of seemingly inexhaustible reserve and a shining silver timbre. The voice is perfectly 'placed'; chest and head registers are well integrated and display no audible gear changes as the singer moves from one to the other. In fact, around the transition point in the middle of the voice Marjorie has at her command what the French call a splendidly developed *voix mixte*, offering firm and ravishing sounds where many singers find difficulty producing resonance.

These discs also provide evidence that Marjorie was endowed with a wonderful, fluid and natural sense of rhythm, which adds to the excitement of the sounds she makes, while her commanding style belies age, as does the subtlety in the way the voice is used and how the musical line is delivered, the emotions conveyed and the text expertly enunciated without exaggeration or affectation. These are all qualities remarkable in a singer still in her mid-twenties. There is also a wonderful sense of presence in most of these recordings, as though Marjorie's voice was carrying its own opera house around with it, enhanced by Coppola's and the orchestra's contributions and the skill of the French recording engineers. The only regrets about these otherwise deeply satisfying recordings is the language in some – and the fact that there are not more of them.[17] These discs sold well, especially in France, and the large number of pressings ensured their survival after all the matrices disappeared during the Second World War.[18]

Cyril Lawrence arrived in Paris in the middle of 1934 after negotiating a passage from Melbourne to Marseilles on a freighter. He moved in with Marjorie, and sister and brother were happily reunited. For the next six years Marjorie supported Cyril while he worked hard on her behalf as her manager, arranging concert engagements, dealing with contracts, correspondence and travel arrangements. 'Big brother' also took it upon himself to manage Marjorie's private life, putting an end to her romance with Henri Grodet, whom he considered not to be 'good enough' for his famous sister. However, the impression is that if Marjorie had wanted that relationship to continue she would not have allowed Cyril to interfere. When later he tried to do the same with other men, 'Marge' told him with typical Aussie bluntness to 'bugger off', the choice of verb probably not lost on her or him.

Changes were also afoot in New York. Flagstad's popularity had led to a surge of interest in the Wagner repertoire at the Met. In the preceding decade performances of *Tristan und Isolde*, the 'Ring' and *Parsifal* played to 'respectable' houses, but with the Norwegian phenomenon on stage, during the 1934–35 season the 'house full' sign went up regularly. Not surprisingly, the board and management of the Met wanted to exploit this by scheduling more performances of Wagner in coming seasons, but this raised a problem. Flagstad would be unwilling and physically incapable of singing an endless number of Brünnhildes and Isoldes just to fill the Met's coffers. She had also discovered the lucrative concert market in the United States and was planning to spend more time giving recitals. Flagstad would sing a very generous number of performances at the Met every season for the next few years, but another Wagnerian soprano was needed to share the workload – and the Met still wanted Marjorie.

Gatti-Casazza had retired and been replaced as general manager by a former singer with the company, Herbert Witherspoon. In a memo to his board, Witherspoon said: 'I have in mind, Marjorie Lawrence, considered by Gatti, Ziegler, Bodanzky and others to be very fine and from all reports she may be as good as Flagstad only with a more brilliant voice'.[19] But before Witherspoon could translate this into action he died suddenly and was replaced by another former company singer, the tenor Edward Johnson.

Johnson and Bodanzky came to Paris in the late spring of 1935 and Erich Simon asked Marjorie if she would audition for them. Having given an audition for Bodanzky the year before and with her star now well and truly in the ascendant, Marjorie replied: 'Tell Mr Johnson I am singing at the Opéra. If he wishes to, he can come and hear me there.'[20] She probably also told Simon to remind the new general manager that she was the singer who had been offered a contract to sing at the Met before and had turned it down. What threatened to be a standoff of Marjorie's making was again resolved by Simon's diplomacy. Marjorie agreed as another personal favour to him to sing for Johnson and Bodanzky at the Salle Gaveau.

Marjorie met Johnson for the first time at the audition and took an instant liking to him. A small dapper Canadian with bright eyes and a bouncing gait, Johnson greeted Marjorie with 'Hello, Dominions!', the call sign of a radio program broadcast to both Australia and Canada.[21] Marjorie sang the same pieces she had the year before, but this time singing the *Tannhäuser* aria in German. Later Johnson wrote to Zeigler: 'Marjorie Lawrence gave an excellent audition and Bodanzky is very pleased with her. However she does not know as yet her Wagner in German. The voice will probably "get" our public even though the language may be uncertain.'[22]

A few days later a contract arrived for a five-week engagement at the Met, commencing on 16 December, to sing all the Brünnhildes and Ortrud. The contract stated that Marjorie would be required to sing not more than twice per week for a salary of $600 per week, with an extra $300 for each additional performance she agreed to. In his memo Witherspoon had stated that he believed the Met could secure Marjorie's services 'for a very small price' and it was that which Johnson was now offering. When Cyril pointed out that the fee represented less per performance than had been offered by Gatti-Casazza, Simon countered with 'Remember Mr Lawrence, the Met has Flagstad now'. Simon also pointed out that because of being salaried, Marjorie could be guaranteed $3000 for her stay in New York, about equal to what she would have earned if she had sung the previous year.

Marjorie was keen to sign. She understood what her delay in going to the Met had cost her and she was anxious to get a foot on that illustrious stage before the management lost interest in her. 'If I turn this down, Cyril, they'll never ask me again', she explained to her brother. Marjorie consulted Rouché again and he agreed with her assessment of the situation and gave his blessing to her accepting the contract. Marjorie signed. She was excited at the prospect of singing at the Met, Cyril was excited to being going to New York, Simon had earned himself a six per cent commission on Marjorie's Met earnings, and a very relieved Edward Johnson had secured his back-up Brünnhilde.

The only major concern Marjorie had was with the German-language issue. Her German lessons had faltered and she now had six months in which to relearn four operas in a new language, one of which, the *Siegfried* Brünnhilde, she had yet to sing on stage. Marjorie partly explains in *Interrupted Melody* how she overcame this problem.

> *I looked about me for a coach and decided to work with Edyth Walker, an American soprano, accepted by Europeans as an authority on German opera. At this time Edyth Walker's own singing days were over but she had sung Wagner all over Europe, enhancing her fame with numerous performances of 'Salome' and 'Elektra' under the baton of their composer, Richard Strauss.*[23]

Marjorie fails to mention that the pianist she engaged for her practice sessions also made a major contribution to her lingual transformation. For this Marjorie tracked down a forty-two-year-old German named Felix Wolfes living in Paris. Wolfes had an impeccable musical pedigree. He had studied piano with Robert Teichmüller and Hans Pfitzner, composition with Max Reger and Richard Strauss and conducting with Otto Klemperer. He had conducted all over Germany and been music director at the Dortmund opera house when forced to flee from the Nazis. Wolfes had, of course, spoken German since the cradle and as Marjorie spoke mostly of studying *interpretation* with Walker, it seems likely that it was Wolfes who showed her how to get the new language 'into' her voice and how to *sing* it – although she gives him no credit for that in *Interrupted Melody*. So swiftly and amicably did Marjorie's professional relationship with the German pianist develop, that he also became her regular accompanist when she began to give recitals. There are also hints that Wolfes might have developed a personal relationship with Cyril, further cementing his position as a member of 'the team' for many years to come.

In the months leading up to her departure for New York Marjorie was also kept busy with a heavy schedule. At the Opéra she stepped in for an ailing Ninon Vallin to sing Salomé in *Hérodiade* again, did more performances of *Sigurd*, *Die Walküre*, *Lohengrin* and Strauss's *Salome*. She also sang in the provinces, including a complete Ring Cycle under Carl Elmendorff at the opera house in Vichy. Here on 5 August, with José de Trevi in the title role, Marjorie sang the *Siegfried* Brünnhilde on stage for the first time. This visit to Vichy was not without its perils however. Marjorie had to sing Brünnhilde in French while learning it in German, and on the way back to Paris, Cyril lost control of the borrowed car he was driving and crashed into a hedgerow. He was unhurt, but Marjorie struck her face on the dashboard, breaking one of her front teeth. Back in Paris, Marjorie had the tooth seen to by a dentist who fitted a cap to it. To Marjorie's great relief (and probably Cyril's who would have borne the blame if it had), the capped tooth did not affect her voice or her singing.[24]

After a final Brünnhilde in *Die Walküre*, Marjorie bade a temporary farewell to her colleagues at the Opéra and entrusted the apartment to Eugenie and Yvonne.[25] She travelled by train to Bremen and there boarded the liner *Bremen* with Cyril, Mimi and Edyth Walker accompanying her. On 29 November, diva, entourage and a mountain of trunks embarked for New York.

Chapter Eight

Apple Pie and Horseplay

When Marjorie signed with the Metropolitan Opera, Erich Simon had suggested that she engage an American agent to manage her interests in the United States. At his suggestion she chose NBC Artists Services, a division of the National Broadcasting Company. When the *Bremen* docked at the West 46th Street Pier late on Friday 6 December, Marks Levine of NBC Artists Services was there to meet her.

Levine drove Marjorie, Cyril, Mimi and Edyth Walker through wet streets still bustling with traffic at close to midnight and dropped them at the Astor Hotel near Times Square. Next morning Marjorie got her first glimpse of the jagged New York skyline, which was dominated by the four-year-old Empire State Building and the five-year-old Chrysler Building. Impressive it certainly was, although lacking, as Mimi hastened to point out, all the elegance of the French capital.

As she had done on arriving in Paris, Marjorie insisted on first going to look at the opera house. As she, Cyril and Mimi set out along 7th Avenue, they were instantly consumed by the relentless hustle and activity of New York, which at that time had a population three times greater than Paris, and it seemed to Marjorie that most of them were out and about that morning, scurrying along to escape the snow flurries that swept down the man-made canyons or travelling in the motor cars, trucks, buses and trolley cars that jammed the roadways and clogged the air with fumes. Men with sandwich boards and touts shouted their wares above the roar of the traffic and the bleating of motor horns. On arriving at the Met Marjorie received another shock.

> *Had we gone down Broadway to the Metropolitan's front door rather than approach it from the rear, my first impression of it might not have been so shocking. But, after the rich beauty of the Paris Opéra and its picturesque surroundings, how could I have been prepared for the grimy old brick pile that met my eyes when we got to Fortieth Street?*[1]

Marjorie was not the first and would not be the last foreign singer to be disappointed by the utilitarian appearance of the old Metropolitan Opera House, nor did what she saw next fill her with confidence

> *Stacked high on the sidewalk, covered with a tarpaulin which bore evidence of the visitation of myriad pigeons, were piles of scenery, presumably to be used in forthcoming productions. I was by no means reassured to discern the words 'Walküre Act 1' on one wing from which the tarpaulin had been blown. I was scheduled to make my debut in Die Walküre.*[2]

Marjorie's spirits improved when they reached the front of the building and there found her name in large letters on posters alongside Kirsten Flagstad, Lotte Lehmann, Rosa Ponselle, Lily Pons, Grace Moore, Elisabeth Rethberg, Lauritz Melchior, Giovanni Martinelli, Friedrich Schorr, Lawrence Tibbett, Ezio Pinza, and many other famous singers. If this 'star-spangled assemblage', as she called them, could put up with the messy pigeons and the building's grubby exterior, Marjorie decided she could too.

There were eleven days between her arrival in New York and Marjorie's debut at the Met, and as it turned out much happened during that short time. Marjorie annoyingly developed a dry throat from the central heating at the Astor Hotel, describing in a telephone conversation with Edward Johnson how stifling it was. 'Oh, you'll get used to it,' Johnson said heartily, 'all American hotels are like that. Go for a walk up to Central Park and get some fresh air.'[3] Marjorie decided she needed a more satisfactory solution than that and set Cyril the task of going through the New York newspapers in search of an apartment they could rent for the five weeks. Cyril found one on 42nd Street, close to the opera house and, although it was not elegant, they decided to take it. Edyth Walker went off to stay with friends, while Marjorie, Mimi and Cyril moved into the apartment.

Erich Simon, who had also come to New York for the opera season, visited Marjorie in her new apartment and told her she must move again immediately. Had she not noticed, Simon asked incredulously, that they were living above a flea circus? Marjorie, Mimi and Cyril had noticed that the ground floor of the building housed a seedy looking amusement arcade, but had not realised the amusements included one of New York's most famous flea circuses. Happily forfeiting a week's rent, they moved again, this time into the Ansonia Hotel on Broadway, recommended by Simon.

The Ansonia was the home to many of the city's most famous musicians, including several of the Met's major stars. The management was delighted to find 'Miss Lawrence' a suite and the hotel became Marjorie and Cyril's home when they visited New York over the next few years. The Ansonia was not overheated, the windows opened and the walls were heavily soundproofed, allowing residents to practise without disturbing each other.

Marjorie discovered her near neighbours at the Ansonia included Lauritz

Melchior, whom she spotted wrapped in a tent-sized robe heading along the corridor with a towel and a cake of soap. This intrigued Marjorie as every suite in the hotel had its own private bathroom. Later she learned that no bath in the hotel was large enough to accommodate the giant Danish tenor, so he had to resort to bathing in the hotel's basement swimming pool after the other guests had retired.

Marjorie also discovered American fast food. Until they moved to the Ansonia, where their suite had a kitchen, most of Marjorie's meals had come from Horn and Hardart's coin-operated automats. Marjorie found the pre-packaged food unexpectedly good and very economical. Large slices of American-style apple pie appealed most, and Marjorie ate more of those than was wise for her figure. Later when the press began to take an interest in her, Edward Johnson sent word to Marjorie through Edyth Walker that he would prefer that his stars did not risk being recognised eating automat food, which solved the problem of Marjorie's apple pie eating binges.

The press did show interest in Marjorie from the time she appeared at the Ansonia – there were always journalists hanging about in the lobby. Requests for interviews were made and granted; Marjorie was asked about her origins, her life in Paris, her appearance and her eating habits. Photographs were taken and the articles and radio reports that resulted made reference to Marjorie's 'copper-gold hair', 'flashing, green eyes', 'shapely figure' and slight French accent.[4] Little mention was made of Marjorie's singing voice, as that was largely unknown to the New York press until she made her first appearance at the Met.

Rehearsals for Marjorie's debut as Brünnhilde in *Die Walküre* on 18 December began on the thirteenth, Marjorie singing the role in German for the first time. The rest of the cast were Elisabeth Rethberg as Sieglinde, Lauritz Melchior as Siegmund, Friedrich Schorr as Wotan, Kathryn Meisle as Fricka and Emanuel List as Hunding. The other Valkyries included Met regulars Dorothee Manski, Irra Petina and Thelma Votipka. Bodanzky was to conduct, and at the first stage rehearsal, after Marjorie had made her entrance, Bodanzky shouted to the assembly: 'You see? A Brünnhilde who can *run*.'[5]

Rethberg, Melchior and Schorr, the principals with whom Marjorie would sing most, were friendly towards her. Each was an established international star and had reached the point in their careers where they could afford to be generous to newcomers. Melchior remembered her from Paris and was very happy to have another partner to work with since Flagstad was becoming impatient with him for his irreverent manner and the childish pranks he liked to play on and off stage. Melchior was also notorious for his non-attendance at rehearsals and the very fact that he turned up at all three arranged for Marjorie demonstrates he had bestowed his approval on her even before she sang a note. As the season progressed the tenor's admiration for Marjorie grew and developed into a warm but rocky friendship that lasted until the tenor's death in 1973. At season's end he would give Marjorie a photograph of himself inscribed 'To my friend and colleague Marjorie Lawrence in remembrance of her Metropolitan Siegfried' and declare publicly that Marjorie was 'a wonderful actress' and the best Ortrud he had ever heard'.[6] Marjorie found it enormously exciting and inspiring to be matching voices with the world's leading heldentenor and with Friedrich Schorr, acknowledged as the greatest Wotan of his time. Now nearing the end of his career, Schorr insisted Marjorie call him 'Fritz' and asked if she played cards, to which he and Melchior were addicted.

Bodanzky was happy with her and so was Leopold Sachse, the stage manager responsible for mounting the opera. He perhaps more than anyone else was relieved to have a young, athletic soprano for the role of Brünnhilde. Marjorie was also relieved when she discovered she would not be performing on the sets she had seen on the sidewalk, but in brand-new sets recently commissioned from the young designer Jonel Jorgulescu.

Two nights before Marjorie made her debut, the season opened with a performance of Verdi's *La Traviata*, with Lucrezia Bori, Richard Crooks and Lawrence Tibbett singing the principal roles. Marjorie and Cyril attended and Marjorie was able to see the opera house in full operation for the first time.

> *I was dazzled by the interior splendour of the Met when I saw it in full regalia. The opulence of the Diamond Horseshoe with a king's ransom in diamonds and mink to the square foot; the devoted standees ranged all around the back of the house and the half lights playing on the brass rails and red plush of the theatre's many tiers bestowed upon it all the glamour of operatic grandness.*[7]

The 'full house' sign went up that night and again on the night of Marjorie's debut. When Sachse visited Marjorie in her dressing room just before she made her entrance, he pressed a penny into her hand saying it would bring her luck, but luck was not needed.[8] Johnson had predicted at their meeting in Paris that Marjorie would 'click' with American audiences and he was right.

The moment Marjorie appeared upstage at the beginning of the second act, wearing a white shift and a blue mantle, her long hair loose down her back and her armour, helmet and shield glinting in a spotlight, the audience welcomed her with an approving round of applause. Each time she sang Brünnhilde's battle cry, the performance had to stop while the audience applauded, and at the end of the opera when Marjorie took her solo curtain call she was showered with flowers and given a thunderous ovation, punctuated by shouts of 'Bravo!' As one critic put it, that night Marjorie sang her way straight into the hearts of the New York audience.

Among that audience were many other singers from the Met roster, curious to hear the new soprano who had been touted in the press as a rival for Flagstad. One of these was the beautiful American mezzo-soprano Gladys Swarthout. Swarthout's first impression was typical of the entire audience: 'Marjorie Lawrence had an overwhelming personality and there was a wild quality in her voice that electrified me'.[9]

Backstage after the performance Marjorie was congratulated by the other performers and photographed with a beaming Edward Johnson. Among the journalists who crowded into her dressing room was one from the Australian Press Association, who cabled news of Marjorie's latest triumph back home. When the reviews of her performance began to appear, it was clear the New York press was just as enthusiastic as the audience had been, although true to form some of the more senior writers managed to find issues for criticism.

The doyen of New York music critics, W.J. Henderson, who had reviewed every season at the Met since it opened in 1883, could judge new Wagnerian sopranos by his recollections of Lilli Lehmann, Lillian Nordica, Olive Fremstad, Johanna Gadski and Frida Leider. By the mid-1930s Henderson had a reputation for being crusty, but it hardly showed in the review he penned of Marjorie's performance for the *New York Sun*:

> *Marjorie Lawrence, a soprano from the Antipodes proved to be a singer of value and of promise. She disclosed a good voice, generally well placed, an attack almost always firm and unhampered, phrasing musically planned and commendable diction. The voice showed quite enough power for the role although the delivery of 'Ho-jo-to-ho!' was somewhat forced by reason of nerves, but in the scene with Wotan and in the 'Todesverkündigung' the true quality of the organ, rich and mellow and without impending technical faults was exhibited. It is probable this new singer will wear well and grow in the public's esteem.*[10]

Olin Downes, a less predictable critic whose reviews often disagreed with those of his colleagues, concurred with Henderson about the quality of Marjorie's voice and then went on to make some interesting and revealing observations:

> *Singing in German for the first time, Miss Lawrence displayed astonishingly clear and expressive diction, carrying each syllable of the text to the audience. Above all she most thoughtfully and consistently developed her role. When she listened to Wotan's narrative she did so with a concern, intensity and variety of expression that would have caused the audience to listen also, even without Mr Schorr's commanding eloquence. In other words, she imposed her mood, her own conception, most firmly upon the gathering. Every shade of meaning, envisaged with a beautiful plasticity and variety of gesture and facial expression, carried the part over the footlights. That Miss Lawrence is at this time, in depth of knowledge the equal of a Frieda Leider or a singer with the opulence of tone and the richly developed art of Mme. Flagstad, it is unnecessary to claim. Miss Lawrence has yet to master the variety of tone-colour needed to fully realise her interpretive intentions and yet to become a completely equipped singer, but she is a young artist tremendously in earnest, intelligent and of a consumingly dramatic temperament. Also one would say, in view of her rapid rise as an opera singer, a person with a remarkable capacity for growth.*[11]

Reviews in similar vein to these appeared in all the other New York newspapers and in *Time* magazine and other weeklies, a few days later. When Marjorie began to read them on the morning after her debut she was initially a little taken aback. She thought the reviewers nitpicking for qualifying their praise with words like 'generally', 'almost' and 'as yet', and believed, not unreasonably, that her youth was working against her. However, the telephone calls and telegrams that flowed into the Ansonia all day and the comment from Edyth Walker that she had never seen such good reviews in her years at the Met finally convinced Marjorie that by New York standards the critics had been more than generous to her.

Three days after her debut Marjorie sang again at the Met, this time as Ortrud in a matinee performance of *Lohengrin*, with Melchior in the title role, Lotte Lehmann as Elsa, Schorr as Telramund and List as King Henry, and Bodanzky again conducting. Once again the critics were generous in their praise of her, but we don't have to rely on them to judge Marjorie's singing. We can listen to it ourselves, for the whole performance is available on compact discs.[12]

Since 1931 Saturday matinee performances at the Met had been broadcast over the NBC radio network. Every Saturday afternoon in large and small communities across America people sat around their radio receivers and listened to some of the world's greatest singers free and without interruption from advertising. While these broadcasts gave pleasure and popularised opera at the time, they did an even greater service by preserving historic performances. NBC recorded each performance on acetate transcription discs and many survive, whole or in part, in that medium. Others have come down to us, thanks to the efforts of amateur opera buffs who recorded them from the broadcasts. Taken as a whole these Met broadcasts represent a priceless record of singing standards and styles in the interwar years. Many also preserve the voices of singers like Marjorie who, for one reason or another, were not always well served by commercial record companies.

Marjorie's first appearance in *Lohengrin* at the Met was the first broadcast of the 1935–36 season – and it was a cracker. The sound, it must be admitted, is pretty awful on these discs and it is no good looking for 'stereo' or anything approximating twenty-first century recording quality. Despite the efforts of modern sound engineers to improve it, the sound is boxy and sometimes badly distorted. However, once accustomed to these limitations (and the hiss and crackle of the old discs), the listener will find much to enjoy and learn from these recordings, not least being what Marjorie sounded like in full flight in a great opera house before a large audience.

Act One is hampered by Emanuel List's lame and wobbly King Henry and Marjorie's voice is barely discernible in the ensembles, but from the start of Act Two when she takes centre stage, the voltage rises. The scene between Ortrud and Telramund finds Schorr in noble voice, showing only a little strain on the upper notes and Marjorie in top form. Schorr makes us feel sorry for Telramund in a way Singher does not in Marjorie's Paris studio recording of this scene and that makes

Ortrud's mocking and manipulation of him seem even more repugnant. When Elsa enters we hear from Lehmann everything that Brothier lacked in the Paris recordings: a touching, spiritual Elsa and the perfect foil to Marjorie's unctuous, scheming Ortrud. The Invocation is delivered with the same power and brilliance Marjorie mustered at her Paris Opéra debut and was rewarded, as it was then, with a burst of spontaneous applause – the first that afternoon. When Ortrud returns to curse Elsa and Lohengrin on the steps of the church and at the end of the opera, Marjorie is in show-stopping form each time.

Marjorie need fear nothing from comparison with her more experienced and more famous colleagues in this recording, but if we compare her performance here with her Paris studio recordings of *Lohengrin* made two years earlier, a striking difference is apparent. Marjorie can still manage all Ortrud's low notes, but the voice is now much brighter. It is as if Brünnhilde had swapped her gleaming helmet and sword for Ortrud's dark spells and potions. After praising Marjorie's performance, Olin Downes was prompted to observe that she was then a better Brünnhilde than an Ortrud and that her voice was no longer dark enough to be ideal for the role. Downes was right, but this did not deter opera houses from booking Marjorie for this role or her from continuing to sing it to tremendous popular acclaim.

The language in which Marjorie sings is the other obvious difference between the Paris recordings and these CDs, which allow us to hear Marjorie singing in German for only the second time in her career, and although an expert might find details in her pronunciation to confirm that the language was not her mother tongue, in the company of German-speaking singers she sounds comfortable, confident and most importantly, harmonious.

The evening after this performance Marjorie was back on stage to appear in one of the Met's regular Sunday concerts. With the American tenor Paul Althouse, she sang the Siegmund-Sieglinde duet from the first act of *Die Walküre* and New York got its first taste of Marjorie's Sieglinde – a role she had not sung before.

Apart from one more performance of Ortrud, Marjorie was able to take a welcome break over Christmas and New Year. Felix Wolfes, who had moved to New York, joined Marjorie, Mimi and Cyril for a happy reunion on Christmas Day. On New Year's Eve, although Marjorie could barely resist joining the happy carousers who filled the streets, she and Cyril accepted invitations to three parties. They circulated between the Melchiors' suite, where the tenor's wife was a charming hostess, Lily Pons's elegant apartment and finally a restaurant where they were guests of Lawrence Tibbett for a post-midnight supper.

For the first time Marjorie got to mix socially with her hosts and with Ponselle, Bori, Moore, Martinelli, Pinza and many more of her fellow Met stars, a large number of whom would become valued friends as well as colleagues. Fond of parties since her childhood and famous for organising them in her student days in Melbourne, Marjorie entered into the celebrations with great enthusiasm. Cyril was beside himself with excitement and delight and if Marjorie ever doubted what a charming snob her brother was, their first New Year's Eve in New York put any doubts to rest.

On 3 January Marjorie sang Brünnhilde in *Siegfried* with Melchior. As Marjorie had discovered when she was learning the *Siegfried* Brünnhilde, and on the only occasion she had previously sung it (at Vichy), this is both the shortest and the most vocally taxing of the three Brünnhildes. Olin Downes described her performance as 'brave', 'intelligent' and 'competent' and if that sounds less effusive than earlier reviews it might not only have been her unfamiliarity with the role that was the cause. According to Olin Downes, Melchior was not in good voice – perhaps he was suffering the aftermath of New Year's Eve, although he had the constitution of a bear. As Brünnhilde's part in the opera is one long duet with Siegfried, an out-of-sorts tenor might have been a handicap too large to overcome.

The holiday break saw further discussion among Marjorie and her companions about a scheme they had been hatching for months. When Marjorie was studying Wagner's texts with Edyth Walker in Paris, Marjorie had pointed out that in the final scene in *Götterdämmerung* Wagner had left explicit instructions that Brünnhilde should *mount* her horse and *ride* the animal into Siegfried's funeral pyre. Marjorie asked if the older singer had ever seen or heard of a Brünnhilde doing that rather than walking the animal into the flames as was accepted practice. Walker replied that she had not and did not think any Brünnhilde had ever actually ridden their 'Grane'. 'Well,' Marjorie said, 'I'm going to be the first. When I sing *Götterdämmerung* at the Met, I'm going to ride the horse into the flames.'[13]

On their arrival in New York, Cyril suggested that since his sister hadn't sat on a horse for some time she should hire one of the hacks in Central Park – just to get the feel of a horse again. On one of the few sunny mornings of that bleak winter, Marjorie went riding in Central Park. The air was brisk, the horse was brisk and so were Marjorie's spirits, and when she reached one of the quieter riding paths, she decided that a gallop was in order. She dug her heels in and the horse responded. Horse and rider careered joyfully along, scattering other indignant riders.

Marjorie's impromptu gallop came to a sudden halt when a very large blue-uniformed NYPD officer stepped into her path and stood his ground. Marjorie reined in the horse and it stopped just inches from the policeman's barrel chest. 'That's no way to ride in the park, Ma'am,' the policeman said sternly, 'you could cause an accident. I should book you for reckless behaviour.' Marjorie apologised, told the policeman that she was a singer from the Met and was practising to ride on stage. The policeman believed her and let her go.[14]

The first rehearsal for *Götterdämmerung* was on 6 January and Marjorie announced that she intended to ride the Met's stage horse in the final scene. This caused consternation. Sachse, who was directing, immediately vetoed the idea, arguing that the risk of mishap was too great and that the slightest slip would ruin the production. Bodanzky was furious. 'No! No! No! Miss Lawrence!' he shouted from the pit, 'You have only a couple of bars before you must be off stage. These moments are too precious to be risked. They are the climax of the opera ... the climax of the *whole* Ring!' Now it was Marjorie's turn to stand her ground.

Bodanzky and Sachse appealed to Edward Johnson to order Marjorie to dismiss this 'foolish' idea. Johnson, probably envisaging the publicity sensation it would cause if Marjorie *did* ride, gave one of the non-committal chuckles he was wont to do when cornered and said 'Well, it certainly hasn't been done before'. Marjorie took that as tacit approval and, although she allowed Bodanzky and Sachse to believe they had won, she was now more determined than ever to ride Grane.

At subsequent rehearsals Marjorie dutifully led one of the Met's two former tramcar horses into Siegfried's funeral pyre and made friends with the old dappled mare, promising her a treat on the first night of the opera. Marjorie also discovered that the supers the Met employed to pad out crowd scenes – one of whom had the job of holding the horse – were all terrified of the creature. Clearly they could not be counted on to support Marjorie's venture on the night, so Cyril was willingly recruited to make his debut on the Met stage as a silent, red-wigged Gibichung, holding the horse steady as Marjorie mounted it. When the curtain went up on that performance only Marjorie and Cyril – and Edyth Walker and Mimi sitting in the stalls – knew what was afoot.

Like Marjorie's first appearance in *Lohengrin*, this *Götterdämmerung* was a matinee performance, broadcast and bequeathed to us on three CDs. All the reservations about sound noted earlier apply here, and in places the sound is even less satisfactory than on the *Lohengrin* set but, as Alan Blyth observed on their release in 1999: 'Listen through pretty atrocious sound and you can feel yourself present at a great Wagnerian event at the Met'.[15]

After a trio of fairly ordinary-sounding Norns have spun their thread, Marjorie and Melchior launch into the dawn duet and for once we hear a Brünnhilde and Siegfried who sound as if they are truly consumed by love for each other. Marjorie's voice sounds fresh, supple and easily able to slice through Wagner's busy orchestra being relentlessly driven by Bodanzky. As the duet reaches its impassioned climax, Marjorie's voice (as one commentator puts it) soars to silvery top tones with laser-like efficiency.[16]

In the scene with Waltraute (here sung by Kathryn Meisle), the sound is so poor it is difficult to make fair judgments of the singers, but it improves when the disguised Siegfried enters. In Bodanzky's experienced hands and with two such accomplished singers at his disposal, this short scene is electrifying. Melchior has the vocal resources to sound convincingly drugged and menacing, while Marjorie manages to sound both terrified and defiant, and neither resort to unmusical sounds.

In the second act we hear Marjorie as the captive Brünnhilde with Friedrich Schorr extravagantly cast as Gunther and the sonorous Hagen of Ludwig Hofmann. Marjorie mirrors every one of Brünnhilde's wide-ranging emotions as Siegfried's apparent treachery is revealed and creates a fine distinction between the character's musings and utterances. The combination of Schorr, Hofmann and Marjorie (using her middle voice to convey heart-rending sadness) in the final pages of this act is magnificent and the audience responds with thunderous applause.

The final act gives the second soprano in the cast – Manski, singing Gutrune – her opportunity to shine. Manski was a distinguished soprano with Brünnhilde and Isolde in her repertoire, but her appearance here serves only to highlight just how superior Marjorie's voice was to the soprano who might typically have sung these roles. Marjorie returns to the stage at the end of the opera for the Immolation Scene and sings it with immense authority and pathos. The voice shines defiantly above the orchestra, then relaxes momentarily for what might well be the most beautiful rendering of the line 'Ruhe! Ruhe, du Gott' ever heard on the Met stage, Marjorie using that *voix mixte* referred to earlier and with her notes taking on the velvety texture of the French horns that accompany her.

As Brünnhilde flings a burning torch onto Siegfried's funeral pyre and as the flames rise, she orders ravens to fly to Valhalla and tell the gods their reign is ending. Brünnhilde then addresses her faithful Grane – and what the audience would have seen at this point, but which we are denied as we listen to the CDs – is Cyril leading the horse to Marjorie, who gives the old mare a reassuring pat on the neck before vaulting gracefully onto its back. On the CDs we can hear a few surprised and delighted members of the audience bursting into spontaneous applause as she mounts Grane. The music continues, as Marjorie describes in *Interrupted Melody*:

> I took up the music right on the beat, noting with relief that Bodanzky had kept his head. I sang the final soaring phrases, kicked my heels into the horse's flanks and, with right arm extended towards the heavens, galloped into the flames.

There was pandemonium backstage and in the auditorium. The moment the orchestral postlude ended, the house erupted with clapping and cheering. Backstage Marjorie allowed a press photographer who had been smuggled in with the promise of a scoop to take one photograph of her on horseback before she slid to the floor with Cyril's help. Marjorie's satisfaction at having given a great performance and pulled off a dramatic coup is written on her face in that photograph.

Chorus, supers and stage hands clustered around proffering praise and congratulations, each wanting to be part of what everyone sensed was an historic moment. A beaming Leopold Sachse shepherded her to centre stage just in time for the curtain calls and when Marjorie stepped in front of the great red curtain for her first solo call, the audience went wild, clapping, cheering and shouting their approval.

The sum total of Marjorie's performance preserved on this CD set – vocal, musical and histrionic – is monumental. No other singer on record brings a greater sense of youthful impetuosity to the role of Brünnhilde than Marjorie on these discs and few sing it so excitingly. In later years Gwyneth Jones and Hildegard Behrens adopted the same 'youthful feminine' approach to the role, but neither had voices to compare with Marjorie's. Aspiring Brünnhildes might go to other recordings to learn other things, but if they wish to launch themselves on an international trajectory (as this performance did for Marjorie), they could find no better model.

The following day the press trumpeted the story of the prima donna who had ridden on the stage of the Met. Newspapers that would not normally have reported on opera or any other art form clamoured for interviews, recognising how many of their readers valued horsemanship and pluck even if they had never heard of Wagner. The serious critics mentioned the incident, but did not lose sight of their duty to report on the rest of the performance, which they did in glowing terms. Johnson was delighted with the publicity and only too happy (along with Sachse) to take his share of the credit for the innovation, and Marjorie was happy to share it with them. Back home in Australia, family, friends and supporters were also able to share in the triumph of the occasion. Not only was the performance broadcast across the United States, but it was relayed on short-wave radio across the Pacific. The live broadcast began at five in the morning in the eastern states of Australia and was rebroadcast by the ABC the following evening.

Two nights after this historic *Götterdämmerung* Marjorie returned to the role of Ortrud, this time with Kirsten Flagstad singing Elsa. Flagstad had arrived in New York not long after Marjorie, and it was considered a coup for the younger singer that Flagstad had relinquished the season's first performances of *Die Walküre* and *Götterdämmerung* to her. In the meantime Flagstad had sung Isolde and Marjorie had gone to hear her famous colleague. As with Lubin when she first heard her, Marjorie could not have been other than deeply impressed by Flagstad and was probably nervous about sharing the stage with her, where the audience and the critics could make direct comparisons between them.

Flagstad was polite and professional towards Marjorie at rehearsal and during the performance and Marjorie made no secret of her admiration for her colleague. From their first meeting on stage mutual respect developed between them which both happily acknowledged and which lasted for as long as they worked together. Such equanimity between rival sopranos singing the same repertoire in the same opera houses is not common and many observers were surprised that they did not become acrimonious rivals as Flagstad and Lehmann were, or even bitter enemies as Flagstad and Melchior were shaping up to be.

Supporters of Flagstad (of which there have never been a shortage) might say that the Norwegian soprano was willing to tolerate Marjorie because she was no threat to her supremacy. That was probably true, but it denies Flagstad the intelligence to realise that they also complemented one another. Although they sang the same music, each singer brought different and distinct qualities to it. Marjorie was the first to acknowledge that she did not command the beauty and richness of tone that was Flagstad's unique gift or possessed her ability to phrase with the breadth of a cello. Marjorie also knew that when it came to producing columns of seamless sound for page after page and performance after performance she was no match for her rival.

On the other hand, there were things that Marjorie did better (or at least differently and equally validly) than Flagstad. Though the Norwegian's singing is never cold, it is also rarely passionate and Marjorie's is passionate at all times – whether she is singing of love or hate, loyalty or betrayal. It is to Marjorie too that we look for those moments of thrilling spontaneity and vivid illumination, along with the frisson that comes from hearing a singer working their voice at its outer limits, while never slipping beyond them.[17]

There is also a distinct difference in style between the two sopranos. If we accept that Marjorie's is 'French' in approach, then Flagstad's can be classified as 'Nordic' – more expansive, glacial and godlike. Both styles suit Wagner's queens, princesses, sorceresses and warrior maidens, but Flagstad's precluded her from crossing back and forth into the French and Italian repertoire, which Marjorie could accomplish successfully at will.

That 'crossing over' also required Marjorie to have a more extended vocal range than Flagstad. Both could sing comfortably and musically from 'G' below middle 'C' up to top 'C', but for roles like Rachel and Thaïs (both of which Marjorie sang at the Met) she needed a top 'D', a note which Flagstad might once have possessed but which was long past exhibiting in public by the time she came to the Met. Flagstad would also have noted, probably before anyone else, that while she began to have difficulty with her top 'C' in the late 1930s, Marjorie's was still powering on as brilliant as ever.

Both artists knew and accepted these differences and both had the humility to 'borrow' from each other. Among the many recordings of broadcasts featuring Flagstad in subsequent years, on occasions we are startled by sounds that we have heard from Marjorie – a turn of phrase, an emphasis on a word or an incisive attack on a note – and may momentarily wonder if it is Marjorie we are listening to. More often, in her later broadcasts particularly, we hear Marjorie consciously trying to match Flagstad's beauty of sound, steadiness of emission and tranquillity of delivery and succeeding enough to raise the same question.[18]

Further proof of Flagstad's acceptance of Marjorie as a colleague came after the performance of *Lohengrin*, when she spontaneously presented Marjorie with a photograph of herself inscribed 'To Marjorie Lawrence, the splendid Ortrud from Elsa – Kirsten Flagstad'. This was the first of three inscribed photographs Flagstad would give Marjorie over the next few years. These and a couple of telegrams of congratulations from Flagstad were treasured by Marjorie and are preserved among her papers. Marjorie also proudly told a radio audience in 1976, fourteen years after Flagstad's death, how she and the Norwegian soprano would always greet each other fondly before a performance and farewell each other at the end with, on a few occasions, Flagstad adding, 'You sang better than I did tonight'.[19]

Unfortunately we can't hear that performance of *Lohengrin*, but we can hear Flagstad and Marjorie together in two performances of *Die Walküre*, one in 1937 and the other in 1940, which will be discussed in a later chapter. If any disagreement clouded their relationship, it was related to repertoire. Flagstad laid down some demarcation lines and Johnson agreed to them. While she was happy to share Brünnhilde and Sieglinde with Marjorie, as long as she remained at the Met, no other singer was allowed to sing Isolde or Kundry, two roles Marjorie sang successfully elsewhere and would have loved to have sung in New York during those years.

Marjorie made many other friends in New York that first season, including Edward Johnson, whom she would come to trust as she did Jacques Rouché and the charismatic Ezio Pinza, who told the Australian press when he was touring Australia a few months later how impressed he and all his colleagues at the Met had been with Marjorie.[20] Outside the opera house Marjorie made fast friends with a character named Betty Bee, a fashionable dressmaker with a salon on Broadway and, by all accounts a heavy drinker and the life of any party. Betty Bee made clothes for Marjorie and was accepted into the small circle of intimate friends that gathered around her when she returned in subsequent years. That circle also included Edmee Busch Greenough, a member of the powerful family who ran Anheuser-Busch Breweries (manufacturers of Budweiser beer) and who would be a staunch ally when adversity later struck.

Arthur Bodanzky also became a friendly acquaintance if not a chum and presented Marjorie with a photograph of himself inscribed 'To Miss Marjorie Lawrence, the great artist and charming woman'. The conductor also offered Marjorie a piece of advice that led her into a new romance. '*Liebchen*,' Bodanzky told her, 'your German is very good but if you want to sound like a *real* German you need to get a sleeping dictionary' – in other words a German lover. Soon after, Felix Wolfes introduced Marjorie to a young man named Heinz Friedlander, whom she decided would fit that bill perfectly. Friedlander was tall and strong with blonde hair and blue eyes and looked more like a 'Siegmund' or a 'Siegfried' than Melchior ever did on stage. He was also married, but assured Marjorie he had been separated from his wife long before they met. Marjorie and Friedlander became lovers and their love affair continued in fits and starts whenever Marjorie was in New York for several years, finally ending in a bitter break.

Marjorie's last assignment at the Met that season was in one of those crossover roles just referred to – Rachel in *La Juive*, with Martinelli as Eleazor and Pinza as Cardinal Brogni. The winter weather in New York had finally caught up with her and Marjorie had a cold on the night of the performance, but she sang, anxious to prove to New Yorkers, the management of the opera house and the critics that she was capable of distinguishing herself in music other than Wagner's. Howard Taubman, found her performance eminently satisfying. He told readers of the *New York Times*:

> *The soprano has sung this role frequently in Paris and she has a thorough command of its music and drama. Apart from some difficulty early in the opera with her top notes, due to a cold, she gave a moving performance.*[21]

Marjorie and Mimi sailed from New York for Europe on 22 January, leaving Cyril behind in the Ansonia to tidy up some loose ends before joining Marjorie in Paris. Edyth Walker had enjoyed her return to her homeland so much she had decided to stay. In Marjorie's baggage were two contracts: another from Edward Johnson for the 1936–37 season at the Met, fully signed by both parties, and one from the Teatro Colón in Buenos Aires. The Argentinean offer had come after Athos Palma, director of the Colón, had heard Marjorie sing at the Met. Enquiries were made but Marjorie was not keen to go to South America, so asked for double the fee the Met was paying her. To her surprise Palma agreed. Marjorie explained that she would need to obtain leave from the Paris Opéra if she were to accept Palma's offer, so carried the contract, unsigned, back to Paris.

Marjorie was delighted with her reception in New York, but she missed Paris. Between Christmas and the New Year she had written to Rouché to wish him a happy 1936. She said in her letter that she was very pleased with the performances she had given in New York, but that she had not forgotten all her friends at the Opéra and could not wait to be back among them.[22]

Chapter Nine
Storm Clouds Gathering

The years 1936 to 1939 were a period of consolidation for Marjorie, but unfortunately as her career consolidated the world in which she moved began to disintegrate. A few weeks after Marjorie returned to Paris, German forces marched into the Rhineland, which had been under French control since the signing of the Treaty of Versailles. Mussolini's army was in the process of conquering the African kingdom of Abyssinia and by mid-year bitter civil war would erupt in Spain.

From the safety of her apartment in Paris these events must have seemed distant to Marjorie, but France shared borders with Germany, Italy and Spain and the trickle of Jewish musicians leaving Germany for Paris, which had earlier included Felix Wolfes, had become a flood. The French were still confident that their sovereignty was inviolable and Parisians optimistic that the lights of their city would never again be dimmed, but the signs of the gathering storm were unmistakable.

Marjorie returned to the Paris Opéra and to more performances of roles she had already sung there, her reputation enhanced by her success in New York. Lubin still held sway as the pre-eminent dramatic soprano and when Rouché persuaded Marjorie to sing Brangäne to Lubin's Isolde in a series of nine performances of *Tristan und Isolde*, she must have felt some misgivings.

Marjorie did not leave us any recollections of those performances, but records show that she withdrew after the second one. That may have been because she felt the role of Brangäne lay uncomfortably low for her voice at the time, but Pierre Lalo's comments in his review of the opening night, refute that:

> Mademoiselle Lawrence possessed the fullness and richness of tone for Brangäne and her voice did wonders in the prophetic warning to the lovers from the top of the tower.[1]

It seems most likely that friction with Lubin was the cause of Marjorie's withdrawal, as she promptly took herself off for a break at the old town of Pomponne, east of Paris, and did not return until rehearsals began a month later for a series of performances of *Les Huguenots*, with Marjorie as Valentine and Georges Thill as Raoul. These performances were extraordinarily successful and Marjorie was proud to provide a pair of *deluxe* tickets for Ivor Boustead and his wife when her former teacher came on a visit to Paris.

Marjorie also continued to appear in the French provinces. As she commented in *Interrupted Melody*, many of her Paris colleagues spurned the provincial theatres after they had established themselves at the Opéra, but she did not, finding them useful places to try out roles she would later sing in Paris or abroad. The conditions were more primitive in the provinces than in the capital, however, and Marjorie had a fund of stories about mishaps on stage in places like Marseilles, Nice, Lille and Lyon.

Some of these were amusing, like Grane's tail extension falling off during the Immolation Scene in *Götterdämmerung* in Marseilles, and the occasion Marjorie was nearly immolated in the wrong opera:

> *I recall, not without anguish, a performance of* Die Walküre *at Nice for which a mobile steam-engine parked outside the theatre provided the 'magic fire' for the last act. Something or other went wrong with the mechanism, with the result that when I lay on Brünnhilde's rock, I felt more like a hamburger than a daughter of the gods. Escaping steam had made the 'rock' as hot as a gridiron and many days were to pass before I could sit with any degree of comfort.*[2]

Performances in the provinces also gave Marjorie the opportunity to sing with some distinguished artists who were not at the Opéra, including the veteran tenor Cézar Vezzani, with whom she sang *Sigurd* in Marseilles and Lyon, while another engagement took her to the old Roman amphitheatre in Orange, where James Joyce had wanted her to sing *Norma*. In this vast open-air venue Marjorie sang Brünnhilde in one of the most memorable 'Walküres' she ever took part in. At the beginning of the third act, each of the Valkyries was given a white horse to ride and so the audience was treated to a genuine 'Ride of the Valkyries' as the magnificent steeds dashed across the stage, their white coats shining in the moonlight.[3]

Soon after her return from New York, Marjorie also received an offer to sing with the Chicago City Opera Company in the late autumn. The director Paul Longone offered her performances of Brünnhilde in *Die Walküre*, Elisabeth in *Tannhäuser*, Elsa in *Lohengrin*, and two Verdi roles, Aida and Desdemona in *Otello*, at $600 per performance, the same figure Buenos Aires had agreed to. Marjorie discussed this offer and the one from the Teatro Colón with Rouché. As always the *directeur-général* was supportive of his protégé and gave his blessing to her accepting both offers. As this meant Marjorie would be away from Paris for eight months – first in South America, then Chicago, followed by New York for her second Met season – it was mutually agreed that her permanent contract with the Opéra would not be renewed and that in future when Marjorie sang at the Opéra it would be as a very welcome guest artist.

Marjorie signed the contract from Buenos Aires and mailed it back to Señor

Palma. She also contacted Longone, informing him she would be delighted to sing in *Die Walküre, Tannhäuser* and *Aida*, but declining the other roles, saying Elsa and Desdemona were no longer in her repertoire. Desdemona had of course never been in her repertoire, but Marjorie didn't mention that. Longone, who was struggling to re-establish opera in 'the windy city' following the financial collapse of the old Chicago Civic Opera, was happy to take whatever he could get.

Before embarking on this North and South American odyssey Marjorie gave a recital in Geneva, Switzerland, which was an historic turning point in her career. It was both her first solo recital and also her first lieder recital. Marjorie had begun studying German lieder as a way to improve her command of the language and had received encouragement from Lotte Lehmann, Felix Wolfes and Heinz Friedlander in New York. Over the preceding months she had built up a repertoire of about thirty songs by Schubert, Schumann, Brahms, Hugo Wolf, Richard Strauss and, at Wolfes's suggestion, Hans Pfitzner, sensibly avoiding songs which required a lighter and fleeter voice than hers and concentrating on those that allowed her to give expression to her dramatic ability. The result, as the Geneva critics observed, was a certain monotony in her program and a surfeit of 'melodrama' which was at odds with the intimacy of the *liederabend*.

Lieder became an integral part of Marjorie's concert repertoire for the rest of her career and she sang certain songs (including some very difficult ones) with appreciable authority, but some of the finer points of lieder interpretation always eluded her – as they did Flagstad and Lubin. She also developed the habit when singing lieder of dropping out of character as soon as she had sung the last note and, if she felt she had sung well, beaming at the audience, while her frustrated accompanists tried to maintain the mood of the song through the piano postlude.

Marjorie did make wonderful sounds in songs like Strauss's *Des Dichters Abendgang* and Pfitzner's *Stimme der Sehnsucht* and we have recordings to prove it. Her impeccable diction also served her well, and had she devoted herself more to the study of lieder she might have become a great lieder singer. As it was, she most often sounded like what she was – an opera singer making a conscientious and valiant attempt to make music that was at odds with her musical training and her singing style.[4]

After another short holiday in an isolated cottage twenty miles west of Fontainebleau during which she, Cyril and Mimi explored Chartres Cathedral and motored around the chateaus of the Loire Valley, the three packed their trunks for South America. From Paris they travelled to Naples via Milan and embarked on an Italian liner bound for Buenos Aires.

The Teatro Colón season was to comprise a total of twenty-seven performances and Marjorie was contracted to sing in fourteen of them. She had agreed to sing Ortrud and three roles she had not sung previously – Kundry, Senta in *Der Fliegende Holländer* and Minnie in Puccini's *La Fanciulla del West*. Ortrud required no preparation, but five years had passed since she had studied Kundry with Cécile Gilly, so Marjorie had to dust off her score of *Parsifal* and effectively relearn the long and difficult role of Kundry.

For *Der Fliegende Holländer* and *La Fanciulla del West*, Marjorie had to buy the scores and learn the roles from scratch. Like Flagstad and several other noted Wagnerians past and present, Marjorie found little about the character of Senta she could emphasise with, but the music fitted her voice comfortably. Puccini's spunky, soft-hearted saloon keeper, on the other hand, appealed enormously to Marjorie the moment she opened the score of *La Fanciulla del West*. Minnie reminded Marjorie of her own grandmother and she had no difficulty drawing parallels between wayside taverns in the Victorian gold rush and Minnie's 'Polka' saloon in California. Minnie's music – which anticipates the title role in the same composer's *Turandot* – also fitted Marjorie's voice like a glove and she hoped that Puccini's 'horse' opera, as some detractors called it, might also give her further opportunities to show off her riding skills.[5]

Other singers making their Teatro Colón debuts that season included Tiana Lemnitz, and two of Marjorie's Paris Opéra colleagues – Martial Singher and José Luccioni. Returning to Buenos Aires for the season were Hina Spani, Marcel Wittrisch, Alexander Kipnis, René Maison and Germaine Hoerner. The conductors were Ettore Panizza, principal conductor of the Italian repertoire at the Met and the revered Fritz Busch, another refugee from Nazi Germany. Busch's twenty-two-year-old son Hans was the stage director.[6]

On arrival in Buenos Aires just twelve days before she was to open in *La Fanciulla del West*, Marjorie was informed that Luccioni, who was to sing the tenor lead in the opera, was ill and the production had been cancelled. Palma offered Marjorie the role of Telaire in Rameau's *Castor et Pollux* as a substitute and as she was not about to forfeit $1800 in fees she agreed to sing the role in place of Minnie.

A greater contrast in operas or roles could hardly be imagined – Rameau's opera was written two centuries before Puccini's and the musical language belongs to a different age. Telaire is a proud, mythological princess and about as far removed from Puccini's gun-toting Minnie as it is possible to be, but Marjorie found Telaire's music fairly easy to sing and, with the help of one of the opera house's repetiteurs, she learnt the role in eight days.[7] Three days of intense rehearsal followed and *Castor et Pollux* opened the Colón season on 30 July.

Pollux was sung by Martial Singher, Hoerner sang the other female lead in the opera and Panizza conducted. To Marjorie's surprise and delight the cameo role of the 'Happy Spirit' was sung by Hina Spani, the great Argentinean-born soprano who had been a favourite at La Scala since 1914. Spani was not in the least offended and in fact amused when Marjorie told her that she was the first great soprano she had heard when she attended her first opera in Melbourne in 1928. Wearing an eighteenth-century hooped gown and a tall powdered wig, Marjorie acquitted herself well in the Rameau opera, although after this season she never had the opportunity or the desire to sing it again.

Five performances of *Lohengrin* followed, with Marjorie as Ortrud, Marcel Wittrisch and René Maison sharing the title role, Tiana Lemnitz and Germaine Hoerner sharing Elsa, and Alexander Kipnis as King Henry. Telramund was sung by a German baritone with whom Marjorie would work a great deal in future years, Fred Destal.[8] Marjorie made her stage debut as Kundry on 4 September and sang that role on three more occasions during the season, with René Maison as Parsifal, Kipnis as Gurnemanz, Singher as Amfortas, Destal as Titurel and the Austrian bass-baritone Fritz Krenn as Klingsor. Two weeks later she sang her first Senta, with Destal as the Dutchman, Kipnis as Daland and Maison as Erik. The conductor for each of these operas was Fritz Busch.

In line with a tradition – older than that of New York – several of the season's performances were recorded and broadcast over the Argentinean national broadcasting network. These included four of Marjorie's performances. Three survive and have been transferred to CD, allowing us to eavesdrop on her last performance of Ortrud on 17 September, her debut as Senta two nights later and her final Kundry three nights after that.[9]

The process used in Buenos Aires was similar to that in New York. Three fixed microphones were used, one above the orchestra and two above the stage. The signals from these microphones were captured on sixteen-inch lacquer-coated discs on a pair of turntables located in the basement of the opera house. The recording engineer could switch from one microphone to another and unfortunately did not always choose the right microphone at the right time, so occasionally a singer will sound as if they are singing in another building. The quality of the sound is, however, generally better than the broadcasts from New York, perhaps because the discs have not been played as often.

Marjorie sounds tired on the *Lohengrin* set and her performance is not nearly as exciting, vocally or histrionically, as in the Met broadcast of the previous year. This is not surprising, considering that it was the eleventh performance she had sung in nineteen days. Unfortunately, it is Maison and Hoerner we hear as Lohengrin and Elsa, rather than Wittrisch and Lemnitz. Maison's voice is glorious but his singing is unidiomatic and Hoerner is no match for Lemnitz. The glory of the set is the noble and velvet tones of Kipnis as King Henry.

Kipnis is again a tower of strength as Gurnemanz in the *Parsifal* broadcast – the earliest complete recording of this opera – and Maison is a sensitive and lyrical Parsifal. For a singer who had sung her role for the first time just a few days earlier, Marjorie's Kundry is remarkably mature and displays the full gamut of the character's emotions without distorting the musical line – even her screams are musical – and she uses her solid 'middle' register to sound sad in the first act and alluring in the second. She also manages to give Kundry a sense of mysteriousness with undercurrents of danger that is entirely appropriate and quite unlike her bold Ortrud and her forthright Senta.

Marjorie's assumption of the role of Senta is equally successful on the *Der Fliegende Holländer* discs. The chorus (singing in Italian, while the principals sing in German) sounds as if they have strayed in from a zarzuela, but the principals are uniformly excellent. Kipnis makes the most loveable of fathers and Marjorie the most youthful of daughters, singing freshly, excitingly and with rock-like steadiness. She produces some exquisite *mezzo voce* moments in Senta's ballad and throws off scintillating top notes in the long duet with Destal. It is with great expectation that the listener waits to hear this Senta launch into her final outburst at the end of the opera, but being a 'live' recording the good comes with the bad. Marjorie begins 'Wohl kenn' ich dich!' magnificently, but then gets a 'frog' in her throat and, although she gets through the final pages, fate robs us of what might have been one of the supreme moments among her recordings. However, singing three of Wagner's most difficult roles – Ortrud, Kundry and Senta – in the space of three weeks is a remarkable feat for any dramatic soprano and to do them so differently and as proficiently as we know Marjorie did from these discs is Olympian.

Fritz Busch's contribution to these broadcasts is also worth noting. He takes a much more relaxed and lyrical approach to Wagner than Bodanzky and this gives the singers more freedom, which in turn provides us with the opportunity to study Marjorie's singing a little more closely than is possible on the New York discs. There are times, however, on the Busch discs when the excitement Bodanzky conjures up is sorely missed and when Marjorie sounds as though she would like to push ahead, while the conductor holds back.

Despite not wanting to go to the Argentine capital when first asked to, Marjorie enjoyed her stay and relished singing in one of the world's most acoustically perfect and beautifully appointed opera houses. The enjoyment however, was not all musical. It will not surprise readers to learn that Marjorie acquired another ardent male admirer on this trip, and by her own admission she fell more deeply and more foolishly in love than ever before. With Heinz Friedlander in New York, the attraction had been athletic sex, but now with Pierre Delbée, it was love writ large.

Delbée was thirty-six, French, slight in build, delicately handsome and one of the leading designers at Maison Jansen, Paris's leading interior decorators and furniture manufacturers. He had joined the same ship as Marjorie, Cyril and Mimi at Naples and introduced himself to Marjorie, explaining that he also was going to Buenos Aires, where Maison Jansen had a salon. At Algiers, where the ship stopped briefly, Delbée rushed ashore and bought Marjorie a huge armful of red carnations.

On the long voyage across the South Atlantic, Delbée courted Marjorie and she succumbed rapidly to his charms, earning Cyril's approval just as rapidly with his descriptions of Maison Jansen's aristocratic and diplomatic clientele. On arrival in Buenos Aires neither were disappointed to discover that they were booked into the same hotel – the luxurious Alvear Palace, opposite the local branch of Maison Jansen.

Marjorie sent Delbée off to 'do his own thing' as we would say today, while she learned her part in the Rameau opera and prepared for her debuts as Kundry and Senta, but by the end of their ten-week stay in the Argentine capital, Delbée had proposed marriage to Marjorie and she had accepted. Cyril was happy for his sister to amuse herself with Delbée but saw the prospect of another man entering their domestic arrangements as a threat to his position, while Mimi was furious. She made no secret of the fact that she still harboured the hope that one day Marjorie would marry her brother Henri and began to make all sorts of unpleasant comparisons between her 'lovable' and 'devoted' brother and 'that slick furniture salesman', as she described Delbée.

Marjorie for her part became angry with Mimi and, when Delbée suggested she should 'ditch the Amazon', Marjorie booked a passage for Mimi on the next boat back to Europe and, by an ironic coincidence, this was the same boat Delbée was to travel home on, so it was likely an unpleasant voyage for both. Before he departed, Marjorie promised to join her fiancée in Paris after the New York season, planning to marry there in the European summer. Before leaving Buenos Aires Marjorie wrote a long letter to Henri Grodet explaining that she had found a man she truly loved and wanted to marry but that Henri would always occupy a special place in her heart as a 'brother' and a friend. After posting the letter, she went out and bought herself six pairs of shoes made from exquisitely hand-tooled Argentinean leather.[10]

As Marjorie approached her thirtieth year she began to display a number of character traits that seem at odds with her simple country upbringing and which might be said to be typical of an opera diva. Marjorie's confidence in herself, in her voice and in her ability to succeed at whatever she attempted were reaching their apex; along with that came a certain self-centredness that would not have been tolerated in Deans Marsh or Winchelsea. And yet despite this there was a lack of pretentiousness about her and a healthy pragmatism that was typically Australian. There was also an infectious sense of fun and a delight in living, as well as an ability not to take herself, her fellow human beings or life itself too seriously. Others found these characteristics endearing, with the occasional bout of self-centredness merely proving that 'Marge' was human. 'I sang about gods and I pretended to be the daughter of a god on stage, but I tried always to keep make-believe and reality separate', Marjorie told one of her students years later. It seems she succeeded – most of the time.

While at the Teatro Colón, Marjorie, Hoerner, Maison, Destal, Kipnis and Busch had been approached by Palma asking if they would consent to do one performance of *Die Walküre* at the opera house in Montevideo. All agreed. The performance took place on 29 September and was recorded and broadcast. The next day, Marjorie and Cyril sailed from Montevideo bound for New York.[11]

Before continuing on to Chicago for her next opera appearances, Marjorie gave three concerts in Carnegie Hall, appearing for the first time with the New York

Philharmonic Orchestra under the baton of John Barbirolli, making his second appearance in New York. Marjorie sang the Immolation Scene at each of these concerts, adding the great aria 'Abscheulicher!' from Beethoven's *Fidelio*. Olin Downes found her singing of the *Götterdämmerung* finale just as spectacular as it had been the previous year at the Met, but concluded that the Beethoven revealed serious flaws in her technique, not realising that this was the first time Marjorie had ever sung the piece.[12]

Marjorie dropped the Beethoven from the third concert and, throwing caution to the wind, substituted Fiordiligi's aria 'Come scoglio' from Mozart's *Cosi fan tutte*. As this is an even more technically demanding piece than either the Beethoven aria or Donna Anna's 'Non mi dir', which had brought her undone in Paris, one can only assume she tackled it for the first time, with Barbirolli's consent, just to spite the critic. The audiences at the first two concerts had applauded her singing of the Beethoven aria unreservedly and after the Mozart, a third audience recalled her to the platform three times.[13]

A few weeks later Marjorie was soloist with a much less prestigious group: the National Orchestral Association, a New York-based training orchestra. This concert was notable only because it was broadcast and from it we have the first 'live' recording of Marjorie in concert. She sings Lady Macbeth's aria 'Vieni t'affretta' from Verdi's *Macbeth*, a role she never sang on stage but which might, had she done, been a spectacular vehicle for her extraordinary voice.[14] This is the only recorded example we have of Marjorie in her prime singing Verdi.

Marjorie made her Chicago debut on 28 November as the 'Walküre' Brünnhilde with Melchior and Schorr and sang each of the other roles she had been contracted to, as well as a performance of *La Juive* with Martinelli. It was the first time Marjorie had sung Aida in America and the last time she sang Rachel anywhere. Before the year's end she had also taken part in her first studio concert in the United States, as soloist with the Detroit Symphony under José Iturbi in the *Ford Sunday Evening Concert Hour*. With this engagement Marjorie discovered how lucrative radio work could be in the United States; for fifteen minutes of singing NBC paid her $1200.

Another significant engagement at this time earned her no fee at all, but Marjorie willingly undertook it. NBC Artists Services passed a letter on to her from the White House. President and Mrs Roosevelt, the letter stated, would be honoured if Miss Lawrence would consent to sing for their guests at a dinner honouring members of the United States Supreme Court Bench at the White House. Marjorie accepted this invitation more out of curiosity than a sense of duty and to earn the prestige that NBC Artists Services assured her would come from singing at the White House. When she met the Roosevelts she was charmed by them and a few years later when she was struck down by illness, 'F.D.R.' would become Marjorie's hero and one of the major influences in the re-establishment of her career.

Marjorie returned to the Met on 8 January for the season's second performance of *Die Walküre*. Flagstad had sung Brünnhilde at the first and now agreed to sing Sieglinde with Marjorie as Brünnhilde. As Howard Taubman observed in his review in the *New York Times*:

> For Miss Lawrence this was as difficult a fashion to return to the company as could possibly be devised. In the minds of many persons in the audience must have been the thought that the Australian dramatic soprano shared the stage with the artist whose Brünnhilde had been unreservedly acclaimed. Invidious though comparisons may be, they probably suggested themselves to some listeners.[15]

Taubman then goes on to report that Marjorie gave no hint of preoccupation with anything but her job and sang with a voice that 'soared clear and free and true in the trying top notes'. Five nights later she sang Ortrud with Flagstad as Elsa, and Taubman reported their scene together in the second act was 'deeply moving'.[16]

Because she had arrived later than in the previous year, Marjorie sang less often in this Met season, but she did sing with the company outside New York for the first time, in Philadelphia as Brünnhilde in *Die Walküre*, with Flagstad again singing Sieglinde and with their regular colleagues, Melchior, Schorr and List. The splendid Swedish mezzo-soprano Kerstin Thorborg joined the company that season and sang Fricka in each of these performances of *Die Walküre*, with Marjorie and Thorborg taking an instant liking to one another and becoming firm friends.[17]

After completing her second Met season Marjorie sailed for Europe on the liner *Hansa*. Sailing across the Atlantic bound for Marseilles, she and Cyril and a group of hastily made friends celebrated Marjorie's thirtieth birthday. However, before she could return to Paris and the arms of her impatient fiancée, Marjorie had opera engagements in Marseilles and Nice and the Monte Carlo concert referred to earlier, where she sang with the opera house orchestra conducted by Dimitri Mitropoulos.

Pierre Delbée was at the Gare de Lyon to meet her, but neither Mimi nor Henri. That suited Marjorie as she had decided (encouraged by Cyril) that she would sever ties with the Grodets and most of her other Paris friends and make a new life with Delbée, who moved in wealthier and more sophisticated circles. As part of this scene change Marjorie had allowed the lease on the apartment in Rue Baudin – where her friends were in the habit of dropping in – to lapse, and she now took another apartment in a quieter and more exclusive part of Paris. The new apartment was on Avenue Junot, at the top of Montmartre, overlooking the famous windmills. There were two apartments in the building and only the back one was vacant, so Marjorie took that on the understanding that when the front apartment became free she would move there.

Avenue Junot was (and still is) one of the most desirable addresses in Paris, but it was not chic enough for Pierre Delbée. He tried to persuade Marjorie to take a spectacular apartment on the Champs Elysées at 10,000 francs per month and when Marjorie refused, they had their first tiff. As he currently lived in one of the least fashionable parts of the city and expected Marjorie to take care of the rent wherever they set up house together, we might wonder whether it had begun to dawn on Marjorie that her fiancée was planning to take advantage of her wealth as well as love her. If it did not, that may have been because Marjorie was still deeply in love with Delbée and practising for her debut as Isolde – in opera's greatest love story.

Marjorie had longed to sing Isolde for years but had wisely waited until she felt ready. As early as 1933 she had been offered the role by the Lausanne Opera and had signed a contract for two performances, but backed out.[18] Listening to Flagstad sing the role in New York and singing Brangäne to Lubin's Isolde had whetted her appetite and by 1937 Marjorie felt that the time had come for her to tackle the role. An offer came from the Lyon Opera and Marjorie grasped it, thankful for the opportunity to test the role in the provinces before, she hoped, singing it in Paris and in the United States.

Marjorie sang her first Isolde on 1 April 1937 with Victor Forti as her Tristan. The critic of *Le Petit Provincial* wrote that Marjorie was the best Isolde Lyon had ever heard or seen and lathered his review with adjectives like 'superb', 'magnificent', 'velvety' and 'scintillating'.[19] News of Marjorie's success as Isolde travelled quickly and over the next few months she sang the role in other provincial opera houses. For two performances in the casino theatre at Aix-les-Baines, Brangäne was sung by Norma Gadsden (now launched on her own career) and Kurvenal by Gadsden's future husband, Dominique Modesti.

Pierre Delbée travelled to Lyon with Marjorie for her debut as Isolde and instructed her she must immediately study Strauss's *Elektra* and Puccini's *Turandot* in preparation for singing these roles. Marjorie had occasionally considered these two roles and she was prepared to allow her future husband to manage their private life together, but the discovery that he also expected to take over her career came as a shock. Closeted away in Rue Junot, Marjorie had also missed her old friends and had sneaked back to Avenue Trudaine before leaving for Lyon to make her peace with Mimi.[20] By this time also she had become heartily sick of Delbée's aristocratic friends and their gin-swilling and boring bridge parties. In their hotel suite in Lyon after her last performance she tearfully told Delbée their marriage plans were cancelled and their romance was over.

Marjorie returned to Paris elated with her successful debut as Isolde and chastened and embarrassed about what a fool she had made of herself over the 'slick furniture salesman'.[21] The Grodets welcomed her back as their proxy daughter and Cécile Gilly was relieved that Marjorie would be able to continue her career as a free agent. Cyril was also relieved when the threat to his position as Marjorie's manager was removed, but regretted the loss of the bridge parties.

Typically of Marjorie, she did not nurse a broken heart for long. When a replacement arrived for Delbée, however, he came unexpectedly and unsought by Marjorie. During their visit to South America, Marjorie and Cyril had met a promising young Argentinean architect named Armand d'Ans, but Marjorie had been too besotted with Pierre Delbée to do more than take note that d'Ans was two metres tall and darkly handsome in a typically Latin American way. Armand d'Ans turned up at Marjorie's apartment on Montmartre one day, not long after Delbée had departed, explaining that he was in Paris to supervise the construction of the Argentine pavilion at the 1937 World's Fair and that he would like to take her out to dinner. Marjorie accepted and was soon launched on another passionate love affair, with more wedding plans.

Cynics might suggest that the best features of Heinz Friedlander and Pierre Delbée were combined in the young Argentinean. d'Ans was a giant of a man like Friedlander and just as handsome as Delbée, but he was less manipulative and more generous than either and when marriage was discussed he volunteered to give up his own career and devote himself to helping Marjorie with hers; *helping* it should be noted, not controlling as Delbée had planned to do. Marjorie respected d'Ans as much as she loved him and the only reason she did not marry him was out of consideration for the promising young architect's own career.

At around the time Armand d'Ans came into her life, Marjorie made her long-awaited and longed-for debut in Britain. Soon after her return from America, she had received a letter from the London impresario Harold Holt offering to arrange and manage a recital for her in Grotrian Hall in June.[22] Holt added that if Marjorie's debut was successful then an offer to tour the United Kingdom would follow. Marjorie saw this as an opportunity to be heard by the musical power-brokers of London and what *she* hoped would follow was an invitation to sing at Covent Garden.

Felix Wolfes was back in Paris at the time and happily agreed to accompany Marjorie. Holt had no objection to Marjorie bringing her own pianist and his publicity department put considerable effort into promoting Marjorie as 'The great Australian soprano from the Paris Opera and the Metropolitan in New York'.

On 15 June Marjorie made her British debut singing a program comprising 'Divinités du Styx', 'O don fatale', the Immolation Scene and songs by Brahms and Pfitzner, concluding with a group of English and Scottish songs.[23] Grotrian Hall was full, and among the audience were many expatriate Australians who gave Marjorie a wonderfully warm reception.

Next day the critics were generous in their praise, although discounting her experience in Paris and New York and writing about her as if she was a newcomer to opera. The critic of the Daily Telegraph wrote: 'This brilliantly gifted singer brought to her performances youthful vitality combined with confident dramatic eloquence' and *The Times* critic referred to her great brilliancy of tone, rich vitality and fine impetuosity. Both were justifiably critical of her lieder singing, but both also expressed the view that she was far short of being fully developed vocally and technically and *might, one day* become a great singer.[24] Marjorie was not impressed and in later years preferred to forget her 1937 London debut and refer to her next appearance there, in 1945, as her first.

The desired invitation to sing at Covent Garden never came. On nights before and after Marjorie sang at Grotrian Hall, Flagstad and Melchior sang *Tristan und Isolde* at Covent Garden and a week later Flagstad sang to an audience of 10,000 at the Royal Albert Hall. Frida Leider was still firmly ensconced in both the opera house and the hearts of Britons, and Germaine Lubin had also sung at Covent Garden this year, so Marjorie was forced to acknowledge that London simply did not need another 'Brünnhilde' – especially one the critics had labelled as not yet a great singer. Had war and illness not intervened, Marjorie would certainly have achieved Covent Garden eventually, most probably after Leider's retirement, but that was not to be. She was to sing on the stage of the Royal Opera House on one occasion some years later, but in recital not in opera.

Harold Holt claimed to be pleased with Marjorie after the Grotrian Hall recital but made excuses for the tour he had promised. By way of compensation he put on an extravagant farewell party for Marjorie before she returned to Paris. The party was held at the Savoy Hotel, where she, Cyril and Felix Wolfes had been staying. Among the guests was Kerstin Thorborg, singing Kundry and Fricka with both Flagstad and Leider at Covent Garden. To her new friend Marjorie confided, 'I should have stayed a bloody contralto!'[25]

Chapter Ten

Lucky Strikes and Jackboots

Sensing that her future lay there, Marjorie returned to the United States two months before her third season at the Met. She stayed on for six months, fulfilling a raft of concert engagements before, during and after her Met performances that NBC Artists Services had lined up for her. Like Flagstad and many of her other colleagues, Marjorie discovered just how lucrative concerts could be in America.[1]

She began with five recitals in Canada (Toronto, Winnipeg, Saskatoon, Vancouver and Montreal), netting $4200, and in the midst of the Met season, Marjorie made her recital debut in New York. On the afternoon of 5 January in New York Town Hall, before a capacity audience which included many of her colleagues from the Met, Marjorie sang a program similar to the one she had sung in London, with a group of French songs by Fauré, Duparc and Milhaud replacing the English numbers.

Unlike their colleagues in London, the New York critics were unreserved in their praise of Marjorie's recital performances, Howard Taubman reported that in one afternoon she established herself as a recitalist of distinction and that her singing had depth of feeling, imagination, variety and discriminating intelligence. Jerome Bohm in the *Herald-Tribune* expressed the opinion that it was the best recital heard in New York in the past five years.[2] London was forgotten and Marjorie recalled:

> From then on recitals were an important and enjoyable part of my career and I experienced new delights in 'discovering' songs and building my recital repertoire.[3]

Marjorie returned to the Met for the first two performances of *Siegfried* for the season, with a new tenor, Carl Hartmann, making his Met debut. The critics praised both Marjorie and Hartmann and several noted a greater maturity in Marjorie's singing since the previous season. Noel Strauss, writing in the *New York Times*, reported 'her art grows increasingly more significant'.[4]

A week before Christmas Marjorie sang Brünnhilde in *Die Walküre* with Kirsten Flagstad as Sieglinde. Since this was a Saturday matinee it was broadcast, recorded and later made available on CD. The sound, unfortunately, is amongst the worst on any of these 'live' sets, but even that cannot diminish the historic importance of these discs or the luxury of hearing Flagstad's and Marjorie's voices together in the same aural perspective. Marjorie enters with a stunning 'Battle Cry', the top notes shining, the treacherous leaps cleanly taken and crowned by magnificent trills. The audience bursts into spontaneous applause, but Bodanzky presses on and we are then treated to the commanding Fricka of Kerstin Thorborg berating Wotan (Friedrich Schorr). Upon Fricka's exit, Schorr and Marjorie give an object lesson in how to sing the long duet that follows. In the *Todesverkündigung* (the scene in which Brünnhilde tells Siegmund he is fated to die), if Marjorie sounds a little matter of fact, it is only by comparison with herself on the 1940 Met broadcast of the same passage, which will be discussed later; any other Brünnhilde would be proud of such an achievement, inspired by Melchior at his most sensitive.

Finally at the end of Act Two and in Act Three we hear Marjorie and Flagstad on stage together, and hearing these two great voices exchanging phrases the listener is struck by their ability to produce the same decibels with equal ease. There is no hint of a 'giant' voice and a 'pygmy' voice as often happened when Flagstad appeared on stage with other sopranos. The other surprising phenomenon this juxtaposition highlights is the different way each singer attacks their notes. Flagstad sings 'through' hers, entering, colouring the tone and diminishing as she exits – the legacy of her type of voice and the reason she preferred stately tempos. Marjorie is much quicker off the blocks, attacking each note cleanly and vigorously and then moving smartly on. Finally, it is also possible to discern a difference in the way each pronounces the German language, with Flagstad colouring some vowel sounds with a quaint Norwegian accent, while Marjorie remains 'neutral' and, therefore marginally more idiomatic.

The end of the opera, with Marjorie and Schorr generating an almost palpable poignancy, is rewarded by tumultuous applause. Milton Cross, hosting the broadcast, refers to 'Madame Flagstad, lovely Norwegian artist' and 'Marjorie Lawrence our lovely auburn-haired, Australian Brünnhilde' and Olin Downes in the *New York Times* proclaimed this 'a great performance, one that held the immense audience spellbound and communicated full measure of the wonder of Wagner's music'.[5]

Not everything was perfect that afternoon. Marjorie made what she claimed was the only language lapse of her career. After her battle cry, instead of singing 'Dir rat' ich Vater', Marjorie sang 'Alerte, o père', then realised her mistake and switched from French back to German on the next phrase. She explained later that before going on stage she had been standing in the wings conversing in *French* with Désiré Defrère, the Met's stage manager. That momentary lapse is preserved on the CDs and we can hear the prompter and another voice (probably Defrère's) 'throwing' Marjorie the next line in German. Marjorie expected that no one beyond the footlights would have noticed her momentary slip, but eagle-eared Olin Downes picked it up and couldn't resist mentioning it while praising her 'mastery of German'.[6]

For all Marjorie's success as Brünnhilde in *Die Walküre*, in *Siegfried* and later in the season in *Götterdämmerung*, an even greater success crowned her third season at the Met. Edward Johnson had told the press that he wanted to make the operas of Richard Strauss as popular in New York as those of Wagner and to do this he was planning new productions of *Salome* and *Elektra* in the 1937–38 season. Before she had left New York at the close of the previous season Johnson had offered Marjorie the title role in *Salome*, while Elektra was offered to the Hungarian soprano Rose Pauly, who had recently triumphed in that role at Salzburg. Pauly was a fine actress but no match vocally for Marjorie and Johnson hinted that if Marjorie was successful as Salome, he would cast her as Elektra the following year.[7]

Marjorie's earlier performances of *Salome* had all been sung in French, which meant that she had to relearn it in German before coming to New York, with rehearsals scheduled to begin as soon as she arrived. Felix Wolfes supported her in this, also recommending someone in New York who would assist her to reinvigorate the choreography for the 'Dance of the Seven Veils'. This was Yeichi Nimura, a dancer, choreographer and expert on Oriental dancing. On her return from Canada, Marjorie began work with Nimura.[8] She recalled:

> *I would be so tired after my dancing lessons with Nimura that when I reached the street I would have to lean up against a lamp post while I waited for a taxi.*[9]

The new production of *Salome* was by Herbert Graf and was described as more honest and less squeamish than earlier ones at the Met, meaning that the eroticism in the music was allowed to be seen on the stage, and so was the severed head of Jokanaan, which in some early productions had be covered by a cloth to appease the censors. As if to accentuate this new licence, Freddie Wittrop of the Folies-Bergère in Paris was commissioned to design new costumes. For Marjorie he created a very skimpy and slinky outfit in jewel colours – ruby red, emerald green, magenta and purple – worn over a body stocking that showed off her shapely figure and added greatly to the sensual spectacle. Wittrop produced seven filmy veils in differing shades of the same colours for the dance, which Marjorie could attach then discard in order.

At the first full dress rehearsal Marjorie rushed off stage to slip out of her costume and attach the veils behind a screen provided for this purpose. She had been practising this in her living room at the Ansonia and had memorised the sequence; however, to her dismay she found she could not differentiate between some of the colours in the gloomy backstage light. Marjorie became confused, missed her entry and the rehearsal came to a halt. Marjorie apologised to Graf, to the conductor Panizza and to rest of the cast. 'Everyone was very understanding and we all had a laugh', Marjorie later told a reporter. For future rehearsals and performances a desk lamp was provided so that Marjorie and her dresser could differentiate the colours.

That was not the end of Marjorie's woes that day. She also developed a violent ache in her one remaining natural front tooth. Cyril whisked her off to a dentist who said the tooth must come out immediately and promised to have a replacement in place in time for the first night of *Salome*. Marjorie was in so much pain she agreed.

Back at the Ansonia with a very conspicuous gap in her teeth, Marjorie tried her voice. The voice sounded almost the same, but she found inhaling deep breaths over her tender gum caused excruciating pain. Marjorie tried a handkerchief over her mouth and this stopped the 'draught' and eased the pain. At the next rehearsal she appeared with a white silk handkerchief attached to the lower part of her face, explaining her temporary predicament to her colleagues, who once again were 'understanding'. She forgot, however, to mention it to Graf, who stopped the rehearsal the moment Marjorie came on stage and shouted from the stalls: 'Miss Lawrence, aren't you overdoing things? Salome never wore such a freakish mouth piece!' The rest of the cast laughed uproariously.

Mary Garden appeared for the final dress rehearsal to offer Marjorie praise and encouragement. Garden's fame had hardly diminished since her retirement and when she attended the first performance on 4 February the press followed her, seeking her opinions and reactions. Garden was effusive in her praise of Marjorie and the critics noted she made 'excited nods of approval' throughout the performance. There had been so much hype in the press about this production that the audience was at fever pitch.

Panizza in the pit, Renée Maison and Karin Branzell playing what one critic described as 'Salome's disgusting parents', and Julius Huehn offering a young and lyrical Jokanaan, all supported Marjorie, but the evening belonged to her. The audience erupted with huge applause and shouts as the curtain fell and Marjorie took a record eleven solo curtain calls. Olin Downes described her Salome as the most original and masterly accomplishment she had so far offered New Yorkers. He went on to describe her costume as 'concealing only to reveal' and the 'evil poison that was at work in her frame'. He praised her dance as beautiful and sensual and gave a detailed account of the final scene:

> What followed was extraordinary; the demand for the head of Jokanaan, first in the light, cold, pretty voice of a cruel child; then with more and more sinister inflection, and with capricious torment of the unhappy Herod. At last came the great solo when the head is offered on a silver platter and the instruments of the orchestra howl like wild beasts. Miss Lawrence sang with the most uncommon resources of line and colour and with diction and facial expression

that corresponded to the slightest variation of the text. She never missed a single line – the despair and the pride of 'But me thou didst not see ... me, Salome, princess of Judea', the solemn invocation of the mystery of love that is greater than death and the last wild and ecstatic lament.[10]

Jerome Bohm in the *Herald-Tribune*, Oscar Thompson in *Musical America* and all the other major critics agreed with Downes's assessment. Leonard Liebling in *Musical Courier* went a step further and bestowed on Marjorie what she would have taken as the ultimate accolade: 'She was as good as Garden'.[11] There were two more performances of *Salome* in New York and one in Philadelphia, where the opera was paired with Menotti's *Amelia Goes to the Ball*. The Menotti must have seemed tame once the curtain rose on Strauss's sensual shocker.

Having created the sexiest operatic impersonation the United States had seen in years, Marjorie was accorded one of the nation's most coveted rewards – endorsement of 'Lucky Strike' cigarettes. For a fee of $1250 Marjorie gave permission for her portrait to appear on Lucky Strike advertising in a coast-to-coast campaign. Beneath the portrait a caption assured cigarette buyers that Lucky Strikes were the only cigarettes Marjorie smoked when relaxing after a performance and that she was certain they were beneficial to her throat. The caption was written by the tobacco company's advertising agency and as anyone who knew Marjorie would have testified she did not smoke Lucky Strikes or any other brand of cigarette.

Marjorie sang at five of the Metropolitan Opera's concerts this season. In one she sang part of the Nile Scene from *Aida* with George Cehanovsky as Amonasro, hoping perhaps to convince Johnson to let her sing Aida as a follow-up to her success in that role in Chicago the previous year. If that had been Marjorie's intention, then she failed. Johnson had too many good sopranos in his Italian wing (Zinka Milanov, Bruna Castagna, Gina Cigna and Dusolina Giannini) to allow Marjorie to move onto their territory. For two of these concerts, Flagstad and Marjorie teamed up to sing the Elsa-Ortrud scene from *Lohengrin*, the second being a spectacular gala to celebrate Martinelli's twenty-fifth year at the Met.

Outside the Met Marjorie did another concert with Barbirolli and the New York Philharmonic and this too was a commemorative event – the memorial concert for the American composer Henry Hadley. Marjorie sang Hadley's concert aria 'Halcyone' and most of the first act of *Die Walküre* with Charles Kullman. The Hadley serves to illustrate the interest Marjorie began to take in American composers as she built her recital repertoire.[12]

While Marjorie was in New York she took up again with Heinz Friedlander. The handsome German escorted her about town, including on a trip Marjorie had demanded to the Bronx Zoo to visit the elephants – her favourite animals. Unfortunately, they were accidentally locked in after the gates closed, Marjorie recalling:

We were just about to settle down for a very cold night filled with strange noises, huddled together in a gazebo with me wrapped in Heinz's overcoat and him shivering gallantly, when a nightwatchman with a flashlight appeared and let us out. Heinz gave him a $20 tip just in case he had recognised me and thought he could make some money from the press with his story.[13]

Shortly after this misadventure, Marjorie's relationship with Friedlander began to change as she grew suspicious of his motives. He revealed that he had always wanted to be her American agent as well as her lover and at his own initiative he set about securing engagements for her and then asking for reimbursement of his expenses. At this stage Marjorie was very happy with the services NBC Artists Services was providing and she had serious doubts about Friedlander's ability to fill the role he aspired to, but she did agree to one of the proposals he put forward.

Friedlander had approached a visiting representative of the Wagner Festival in Zoppot, Poland.[14] Friedlander presented himself as Marjorie's agent and escorted the visitor to the Met to hear her sing Salome. The Zoppot representative was impressed and asked to meet Marjorie. Initially Marjorie was angry when presented with this fait accompli, but then intrigued enough to set her objections aside. The meeting took place in the lounge of the Ansonia Hotel and after asking Marjorie many questions the Zoppot man departed without making an offer. Nothing more was heard for some weeks until a contract arrived offering Marjorie a generous fee paid in US dollars to sing in one concert and the 'Walküre' and *Siegfried* Brünnhildes during the festival's first-ever complete Ring Cycle in July.

The Wagner Festival at Zoppot was held in the outdoor 'Waldoper', a large amphitheatre surrounded by tall forest. Most of the leading German Wagner singers of the time performed there and the festival had earned the title 'The Bayreuth of the North'. Like every other Wagnerian, Marjorie hoped when conditions improved in Germany to sing at the real Bayreuth and speculated that success at Zoppot might lead to an invitation to sing there, and this prompted her to accept the offer. The only aspect of the deal that troubled her was the answer she got when she asked why there had been such a long delay before the offer was made. The Zoppot representative explained matter of factly that the management had needed the time to run an Aryan check on Marjorie to make sure she had no Jewish blood before engaging her.

Also while in New York, Marjorie received a letter from Jacques Rouché gently admonishing her for ignoring the Paris Opéra 'now you are a big star in America' and offering her guest appearances as the 'Walküre' Brünnhilde and as Ortrud in July and September. Rouché's offer arrived after the Zoppot contract had been signed. Marjorie wrote to him requesting that he arrange her performances around that commitment and Rouché was happy to oblige her.

One of Marjorie's last engagements before she left New York was to sing on the NBC's network radio program, *Magic Key of RCA*, and by coincidence it was decided to transmit this program by short-wave wave to Germany, not a rare occurrence, but not common either. Thus Germans who patronised the Zoppot Festival and might never have visited Paris were given an opportunity to hear one of the new singers engaged for the forthcoming festival. As a consequence we have our first recordings of Marjorie singing in a broadcasting studio – noble and authoritative performances of 'Divinités du Styx' and 'Dido's Lament' from Purcell's *Dido and Aeneas*.[15]

With another highly successful Met season behind her and a large sum of money in her bank account from concerts, Marjorie and Cyril sailed for Europe on 21 May on the liner *New Amsterdam*. On arrival in Paris Marjorie went straight into rehearsal for *Lohengrin* and *Die Walküre*. It had been over two years since she had sung at the Opéra, but she was welcomed back by her colleagues, the critics and the public who had taken a proprietorial interest in her success in America. For her first appearance Marjorie received the kind of reception she had at her debut and must have felt as though she had returned to her artistic and her spiritual home. No such reception greeted her in Zoppot.

Marjorie and Cyril travelled by train to Zoppot via Berlin, arriving at six on a wet evening. Marjorie claimed that when it was offered she never accepted the VIP treatment that most prima donnas demanded, but nothing was more likely to provoke prima donna behaviour in her than to find such treatment withheld. There was no welcoming committee or any friendly face on the platform at Zoppot to greet them, and Marjorie had to wait in the rain while Cyril found a dilapidated taxi to take them to the Grand Hotel-Casino. By the time she swept into the hotel foyer Marjorie was seriously displeased. 'What a dreary dump!', she wrote in her diary that night.[16]

The next morning the rain had stopped at the time Marjorie and Cyril drove out to the Waldoper, where the first rehearsal for *Die Walküre* was due to commence at eleven. There was a stir among the assembled artists and staff when she emerged from a taxi dressed in an ultra-smart Paquin suit and with a chic little Paris hat perched on her head. Marjorie was introduced to the General Intendant of the festival, Hermann Metz, and to Robert Heger, the festival's music director. Metz, whom she described as 'a dear old papa' kissed her hand, but Heger seemed very cold and merely nodded.

When she inquired about the concert which was scheduled for three days hence Marjorie was greeted by the first rude shock of a day marked by them. The festival organisers told her the program had already been advertised and she was listed to sing the Countess's aria 'Dove sono' from Mozart's *The Marriage of Figaro*. Marjorie replied as calmly as she could that 'Figaro' was not in her repertoire and that she was usually consulted about what she might sing; however, to oblige them she would sing something else. Her offer was declined and Heger told her abruptly that if she was not able to sing 'Dove sono' her services would not be required for the concert. There was much interest in this conversation from the assembled bystanders, prompting an undercurrent of whispers, most of which translated as *'Good God*, a soprano who cannot sing the Countess's arias – what *have* we let ourselves in for?' A little before eleven Marjorie was introduced to the other 'Walküre' principals – Hertha Faust, Margarete Arndt-Ober, August Seider, Hans Hermann Nissen and Sven Nilsson and they too, to varying extents, cold-shouldered her.

It transpired that the Zoppot festival had suffered from one or two other 'dolled-up' young sopranos who had arrived in a blaze of glory and departed in disgrace having sabotaged performances, and the general opinion was that Marjorie was the next in that ignoble line. Carl Hartmann was also engaged for the festival but not for *Die Walküre*, so he was not around to put his colleagues straight, and clearly none of them had heard Marjorie's broadcast recital of a few months earlier.

At the time Marjorie was unaware of the festival's past unfortunate experiences with sopranos and as she sat through the rehearsal of the first act of *Die Walküre* she became more and more incensed. She would show all these 'plump frauleins and their heel-clicking, red faced tenors and baritones'.[17] When Act Two got underway Marjorie launched into Brünnhilde's battle cry with all the brilliance and power she could muster and her voice filled the huge empty amphitheatre and the forest beyond. Heger put down his baton and shouted 'Good, good ... I wonder Wagner himself does not leave his grave to acclaim such top notes!'[18]

Marjorie continued in the same vein for the rest of the act and it gave her great satisfaction to see everyone's attitude towards her change. At the end of the rehearsal Heger challenged her with the suggestion that perhaps she would like to go through the duet from the last act of *Siegfried* while the tenor August Seider and he and the orchestra were on hand. Looking unfazed, Marjorie told the conductor she would be delighted to. The other singers quit the stage and Marjorie and Seider sang through the long and arduous duet, earning a clatter of applause from the orchestra and those assembled in the amphitheatre. Everyone now wanted to be friends with Marjorie, and Heger broached the subject of the concert again. Marjorie offered to sing the Immolation Scene, but Heger looked embarrassed and explained that if Marjorie sang that at the opening concert no one would accept the soprano who had been engaged to sing the role in the stage performance of *Götterdämmerung*. Marjorie now held all the aces and replied that it was the Immolation Scene or nothing and Heger reluctantly had to settle for nothing.

Heger told Marjorie privately that he regretted that he had not heard her before Margarete Bäumer had been engaged to sing the *Götterdämmerung* Brünnhilde. Bäumer was an accomplished singer who had been singing successfully in German theatres since the early 1920s, but Heger was right in realising she was no match for Marjorie. This was brought home to everyone when a situation arose similar to those in Monte Carlo and Lille. Bäumer was late in reaching Zoppot and absent when rehearsals began for *Götterdämmerung*. Heger came to Marjorie's hotel and asked if she would fill in for the missing soprano so the rehearsals could proceed, while promising that he would try to arrange that she, not Bäumer, sang *Götterdämmerung*.

Marjorie had grown to like the conductor, so agreed, but the day before the performance Bäumer turned up. The Zoppot organisers attempted unsuccessfully to break her contract on the grounds that she had missed the rehearsals, but the soprano produced a doctor's certificate and threatened to sue if she was denied the opportunity to sing and collect her fee. Thus, the audience at the final opera in the cycle was confronted with a different, older, stouter and smaller-voiced Brünnhilde. Marjorie noted in her diary: 'It nearly broke my heart! I think I love this role the best of all.'[19]

Marjorie had several days to fill in between rehearsals and explored the town with Cyril. Word had got around about the remarkable new soprano and wherever they went they were followed by groups of locals and tourists who quietly and discreetly honoured Marjorie. She wrote in her diary:

> *I think I was too tired and too angry to appreciate this place when we arrived. It is glorious – wonderful scenery, fine beach, masses of flowers. I am feeling a bit weary after the rehearsals, but there is not much to do and I wonder why they made me come so early – probably in the hope I'd spend lots of dollars! I'm just longing to go into the sea, but must rest. Cyril loves Zoppot and the bastard has been in the sea!*

The performances of *Die Walküre* and *Siegfried* took place on 26 and 28 July. Seider sang Siegmund, and Siegfried was sung by Gotthelf Pistor, a distinguished heldentenor remembered today for his magnificent singing of Parsifal in the famous 1928 recording of the third act of that opera. The performances delighted everyone, not least Marjorie:

> *Singing in the Waldoper was one of my most unforgettable operatic experiences. High on a mountainside, so high I felt sure as I sang that I could have reached up and plucked a star from the purple sky, the stage had been built around clumps of giant Blackwoods. These trees and the surrounding rocks are the 'scenery' for the opera and as soon as I began singing I knew the claims for the Waldoper's perfect acoustics were well founded. Down below the stage and stretching back as far as I could see, was the vast audience, beholding with religious reverence and awe what was taking place before them. During the last act of* Die Walküre *a mist descended upon the Waldoper, heightening the illusion of the final scene.*[20]

The critics, who came from all over central Europe to cover the festival, were similarly entranced. Gustave Gruber writing for the *Deutsche Allgemeine Zeitung* proclaimed that the festival had found a new star and that as Brünnhilde's character developed, so 'the voice of Fräulein Lawrence developed in strength, beauty and fullness'.[21] Carl Lange in another German-language paper wrote that Marjorie made Brünnhilde 'the most beautiful and desirable of women'.[22]

As a result of her success at Zoppot, Marjorie was re-engaged for the 1939 festival to sing all the Brünnhildes and Senta. She was also offered an engagement by the National Theatre in Prague, but turned it down because the fee was very low. Hans Hermann Nissen (who had sung Wotan in *Die Walküre* and the Wanderer in *Siegfried* at Zoppot) recommended her to Clemens Krauss, music director of the Bavarian State Opera and a generous offer arrived from Munich for Marjorie to sing there the following year. Marjorie claimed that offers came from Bayreuth and Berlin as well, and so they might have done verbally, but there is no documentary evidence of these.

Marjorie ended up enjoying her stay in Zoppot, but in her diary she wrote: 'I think I'll go straight back to Paris after *Siegfried* – I feel strangely uncomfortable here'. Marjorie had witnessed incidents that reminded her of her holiday in Mussolini's Italy and which she found deeply disturbing. The front row of seats at the Waldoper had been reserved for high-ranking Nazis and when the German National Anthem was played at least half the audience gave the Nazi salute. Several of her fellow artists and people she encountered in the hotel greeted her with 'Heil Hitler' and there were signs all over the town reading 'Juden verboten!'

Cyril had expressed interest in stopping in Berlin on the way back from Poland to undertake a business course at the university. They spent a day together in Berlin before Marjorie continued her journey alone. She admitted in her diary that it was an enjoyable day, marred only by an incident when she entered a music store and asked to buy a copy of Mahler's *Rückert Lieder*. The shop owner quizzed her on why she wanted to buy music by a Jew and then informed her he did not sell any music by Jewish composers.

When Marjorie's train crossed the border from Germany into France, French customs officials demanded to search her luggage and confiscated the spear, helmet and shield she wore as Brünnhilde, claiming they were offensive weapons. Marjorie's indignant protests and her observation that if she was intending to invade France she would not do it with a spear made out of a broom handle fell on deaf ears. The French authorities were spooked by news of German military mobilisation and the apparent inevitability of war.

Marjorie found that an anxious gloom had descended on the French capital in the short time she had been in Poland. The streets were full of French soldiers and householders buying up food to stockpile against invasion. Social life and night life continued unabated, but it was now conducted with a sense of frantic urgency and a morbid fear of the future. By the time Marjorie returned to the Opéra for three more performances of *Die Walküre*, her spear, helmet and shield had been returned to her; dumped on her doorstep in Avenue Junot early one morning without explanation or documentation.

Before she left Paris for a new round of opera and concerts in the United States, Marjorie spent as much time as she could with the Grodets, with Cécile Gilly and with the Chereaus and other friends and colleagues in Paris, sensing that it might be a long time before she saw them again. She also came to realise that whatever offers she had received to sing in Germany in 1939 were not worth the paper they were written on and she was greatly relieved when a letter arrived from Cyril to say he was embarking from Hamburg for New York and would meet Marjorie when she got there. Tearfully and with deep foreboding, Marjorie left her apartment in the care of Eugenie and Yvonne and departed on 1 October for New York on the *Ile de France*. It would be seven years before she returned to Paris.

Marjorie's fourth season at the Met was marked by successes, failures and mishaps. The successes came with more acclaimed performances of Brünnhilde and Salome; the failures came with two roles she had not sung before – Tosca and Thaïs – and which were not accounted successes by the critics. And the mishaps? Well, they were highly memorable.

Marjorie's season got underway with a performance of *Die Walküre* with Flagstad as Sieglinde, Melchior as Siegmund and Marjorie's colleague from Zoppot, Hans Hermann Nissen, making his Met debut as Wotan. All went smoothly until the first scene of the final act when Brünnhilde presents the shattered pieces of Siegfried's sword to Sieglinde. Marjorie sang the sibilant-heavy words 'schwertes stücken' and the false tooth that had been fitted the previous year shot out of her mouth like a bullet, hitting Flagstad squarely on her ample bosom. Neither singer faltered. Marjorie had a couple more bars of music to sing before Flagstad joined her with the great arching melody of 'O hehrstes Wunder!' It was the only time the great Norwegian soprano sang those noble phrases while suppressing a giggle.

Marjorie was concerned about losing the tooth. She spotted it while Flagstad was singing, sidled over to where it lay on the stage floor and kicked it into the wings with her toe, whispering to Jennie Cervini, the Met's indefatigable wardrobe mistress, who stood in the wings: '*Tooth*, Jennie, get the *tooth*! Also in the wings waiting to make his entry was Hans Hermann Nissen having a hearty chuckle. Marjorie now had a very conspicuous gap in her teeth – and the whole final scene of the opera to complete.

> *I hoped the audience wouldn't notice but when I came to that great passage 'War es so schmälich' which Brünnhilde sings without orchestral accompaniment, it came out 'War eth tho thmälith' and the audience would have to have been deaf not to have noticed.*[23]

Nissen experienced a similar dramatic incident at the next performance of *Die Walküre*. In Act Two Marjorie waved her spear about a little too vigorously and the hollow tin head flew off, striking him on the head. It was only a glancing blow and Nissen never missed a note, but Marjorie observed later: 'Hans wasn't amused that time'.[24]

A week after this incident, on 27 December 1938, Marjorie sang the title role in *Tosca* for the first time, with the Met company in Philadelphia. Gennaro Papi conducted, Cavaradossi was sung by Galliano Masini and Richard Bonelli sang Scarpia. Marjorie had waited years for the opportunity to sing Tosca and she acquitted herself respectably, but not well enough for Johnson to allow her to sing the role in New York. She sang Tosca once more in Cleveland in April the following year and then reluctantly allowed it to drop from her repertoire. On the face of it, Marjorie would seem to have been an ideal Tosca. That strong personality Swarthout referred to, Marjorie's sense of theatre and her ability to sing electrifying top notes are among the key credentials for the role; so it seems likely she suffered by comparison with others. There was no shortage of great Toscas in the Met's history so the standard would have been extremely high, and that season the role was sung in New York by Maria Caniglia, a wayward vocalist, but one with Italian *verismo* surging through her veins.

The second *Tosca* also had a farcical element. Jan Kiepura, the spitfire Polish tenor whose following among the women was more important to him than the music, was Marjorie's Cavaradossi and her good friend Lawrence Tibbett sang a splendid Scarpia. Marjorie had been warned about Kiepura. He was notorious for upstaging his colleagues – moving behind them so he could face the audience while they had to face him and *not* the audience. This had come to a head during a performance of *La Bohème* with Grace Moore as Mimi when tenor and soprano came to blows, and Marjorie was determined she was not going to be Kiepura's next victim. When they began their long duet in the first act of *Tosca* Marjorie grasped Kiepura's arm in the same powerful grip she had used on farm animals back in Winchelsea and refused to let go. Kiepura couldn't move and was furious with Marjorie, then doubly so when she did the same thing in the last act.

When Marjorie tackled the role of Thaïs for the first time on 2 March 1939 comparisons were less relevant than they had been with *Tosca*. The opera had been a vehicle for two of the Met's most glamorous stars of the past, Geraldine Farrar and Maria Jeritza, but the opera had not been seen for many years when Johnson revived it as a vehicle for Marjorie and the American soprano Helen Jepson. Marjorie was scheduled to sing the first and third of four performances and Jepson the other two, but when the premiere loomed Marjorie told Johnson she was not ready and so Jepson sang the first performance. Wilfred Pelletier conducted and both sopranos had the advantage of the rich-voiced American baritone John Charles Thomas singing Athanaël, one of his best roles.

The public loved Marjorie's portrayal of the courtesan Thaïs, but the more conservative critics did not. They found little to criticise about her French or her singing, but they brayed about her acting. After the sensual sensation Marjorie had made of Salome, she apparently felt she needed to go a step further and inadvertently overstepped the mark. She was *too* slinky and *too* sexy for the critics' taste and when she disrobed at the end of the first act, they found the display altogether 'too *French*'. Paradoxically, the same critics found Jepson tame, proving just how difficult it is to get the balance right in this musically and histrionically taxing role.

Because of her delayed debut in this role, Marjorie only sang one performance of Thaïs in New York and one on tour in Boston, after which Thaïs went the way of Tosca. Had Marjorie been more successful in these roles, she might have retained Tosca's aria 'Vissi d'arte' and Thaïs's aria 'L'amour est un vertu rare' in her concert and broadcast repertoire, but she did not and so we have no souvenirs of either of these to judge her performances for ourselves.

What we might have had from this season was a new batch of studio recordings from Marjorie, the first in five years. Marjorie's contract with the French branch of HMV had expired and their affiliate company in the United States, RCA Victor, had signed her up this year. During April and May in the RCA studios at Camden, New Jersey, Marjorie recorded multiple takes of 'O ma lyre immortelle' from Gounod's opera *Sappho*, Cézar Franck's 'La procession', songs by Pfitzner, Cook's 'Down the Burn' and the traditional song 'Danny Boy' – fifteen sides in all, of items Marjorie regularly sang in concerts and recitals. Marjorie was accompanied by Felix Wolfes and was pleased with the results, but RCA was not and none of these recordings was issued.[25]

Given the success Marjorie had been enjoying in the United States for the past three-and-a-half years it would not be unreasonable to ask why RCA Victor waited so long to record her and then did not record any of her famous roles. 'Flagstad' is the simple answer; the less simple one is that the classical music recording industry in the United States had been languishing since the beginning of the Great Depression and was taking a drubbing as a consequence of the popularity of radio. When Flagstad burst upon the American scene RCA Victor wanted its share of the bonanza and Flagstad had been whisked off to the studio to make a series of Wagner recordings in 1935 and 1937. These sold well and in the present climate, RCA Victor saw no reason to duplicate them with any other soprano.

The rejection of the recordings Marjorie did make is all the more inexplicable by the quality of the singing we can hear on taped broadcasts made just before she went to Camden. From two NBC 'Magic Key' broadcasts (one conducted by Eugene Goossens) we can hear Marjorie doing a fine job of three songs by Hugo Wolf in the orchestrated versions by Liszt, Cleopatra's aria, 'Piangerò la sorte mia' from Handel's *Guilio Cesare*, Strauss's song 'Zueigning' and one of the songs she had recorded for Victor, 'Down the Burn'.

Before she quit America this time Marjorie sang again at the White House. On this occasion she was invited by the Roosevelts to give a full recital, accompanied by Arped Sandor, and with the pianist Erno Balogh as supporting artist. Marjorie also made her debut in St Louis, singing *Die Walküre* with Melchior, Irene Jessner and Fred Destal and this performance produced another of those farcical mishaps to which Marjorie seemed prone this year.

As this was the inaugural performance by a newly formed company, the Mayor of St Louis came on stage between the second and third acts and made a speech, talking for even longer than Thorold Waters had at the Sun Aria competition – so long that the third act of the opera didn't get under way until 10.30. Marjorie and Cyril were booked on the midnight train back to New York and when Marjorie finally got off stage it was 11.45. Cyril had a taxi waiting and still in costume she arrived at St Louis's Union Station just as the train was disappearing into the distance. To the amazement of those waiting on the platform, 'Brünnhilde' and brother tore back out to the street and into another cab, giving the driver instructions to chase the train to the next station. That proved to be in the small town of Collinsville, almost twenty miles from St Louis, but they made it. Marjorie – still in costume – and Cyril dashed on board, only to discover they were in the wrong car. Marjorie had to make her way down almost the entire length of the moving train. The reactions from her fellow travellers to a spear-wielding warrior maiden covered in greasepaint were mixed. Some thought it a joke; some thought she was a lunatic escaped from an asylum; others thought it was some kinky kind of hold-up.

Marjorie and Cyril left the United States in May, but not to cross the Atlantic to Europe. This time they were heading in the opposite direction – across the Pacific for Marjorie's first homecoming concert tour of Australia.

Chapter Eleven

Homecoming

There had been speculation in the Australian press since 1936 about Marjorie returning to her homeland for a concert tour, fuelled by comments Marjorie made whenever she was interviewed by correspondents from Australian newspapers. 'I am longing to come home to sing to my countrymen and women and I will do so just as soon as I can', she had said many times, sentiments supported by reports from Ivor Boustead and Thorold Waters and quoted in *Australian Musical News*. Letters between Marjorie and family members also mention plans in 1937 and 1938; disappointment inevitably followed when those plans were shelved.

The delays resulted partly from Marjorie's very full schedule, but also because the Australian concert industry had undergone a dramatic upheaval during the years of her absence. Since the 1890s private entrepreneurs had risked their own money bringing distinguished artists to Australia and firms like J.&N. Tait and J.C. Williamsons had earned enviable reputations for their efficiency and their acumen. The entire landscape was then reshaped in the early 1930s when the federal government established the Australian Broadcasting Commission and a process which detractors referred to as 'nationalisation' of the concert industry began. The ABC established new symphony orchestras in each state and set itself up as concert promoters using taxpayers' money.

NBC Artists Services was one of the agencies the ABC negotiated with to secure artists for Australia and Marjorie's name had been mentioned as early as 1936, but the American agents encouraged the ABC to take artists who would earn them the maximum in commissions and Marjorie was not one of these. It has been suggested that, in an attempt to discourage the ABC, NBC Artists Services advised them Marjorie really did *not* want to go to Australia, while advising her she would be wise to spend her time consolidating her position in America instead of wasting it in Australia.[1]

The ABC brought Pinza, Rethberg, the Australian pianist Eileen Joyce and the British conductor Malcolm Sargent to Australia in 1936, and Lotte Lehmann, violinist Bronislaw Huberman and the Australian contralto Essie Ackland in 1937.[2] The following year Flagstad, Kipnis and Richard Tauber headed the ABC's roster and the inclusion of Flagstad angered some Australians, who wrote indignant letters to the press asking why our own Wagnerian star had not been engaged first. All of these artists were well received in Australia but Lotte Lehmann's visit was considered by the ABC to be the most successful, so negotiations were commenced for her to return in 1939.

In the meantime the ABC's chief musical adviser and conductor of its Melbourne orchestra, Bernard Heinze, had attended one of Marjorie's performances of *Salome* at the Met and cabled the ABC, suggesting that, as Lehmann had not yet signed, Marjorie should be engaged immediately. Negotiations began, but when NBC Artists Services insisted the ABC pay Marjorie the same fee they had offered Lehmann, the ABC demurred, expecting to be able to secure Australian artists more cheaply than their foreign counterparts. Negotiations collapsed. Lehmann signed and both the ABC and NBC Artists Services felt they had got the better deal. The ABC believed that Australians would not support concerts by two sopranos singing the German repertoire in the same season and that if Miss Lawrence wished to be considered as one of their celebrity artists for the 1940 season she should now acknowledge that she would accept the lower fee they had offered.

Marjorie was furious, but she had a trump card to play of which neither the ABC nor NBC Artists Services were aware. In the summer of 1938 she had received an offer to tour Australia from a private entrepreneur. Her friend from her student days, Archie Longden, had realised his dream and had managed successful recital tours of Australia for John Brownlee and that other distinguished Australian Wagnerian soprano, Florence Austral. At their meeting in Paris he offered to do the same for Marjorie the following year – during the southern hemisphere winter, when concert activity was at its peak in Australia. Marjorie liked and trusted Longden but she equivocated. Negotiations were still under way with the ABC at this time and Ivor Boustead had impressed on her when he was in Paris how powerful the ABC had become. Longden countered with the fact that the Taits and Williamsons were still prospering despite opposition from the ABC and that, as they spoke, Marjorie's friend from the Met, Lawrence Tibbett, was playing to packed houses in Australia under the Tait banner.

When negotiations broke down with the ABC, Marjorie contacted 'Archie' and said she would take up his offer. Longden proudly announced to the Australian press that he was to have the privilege of managing her first homecoming tour, commencing in June 1939, the month after Lehmann departed Australia. The deal Longden had offered Marjorie was far more attractive than the ABC's. She was to receive seventy-five per cent of the net profit from each of thirty scheduled recitals and broadcast fees were added to this when Longden persuaded the ABC to transmit seven of Marjorie's recitals. The ABC also offered to make their Sydney and Melbourne orchestras available for concerts with Marjorie – for a suitable fee – if Longden required them.

In the lead-up to this tour Longden had flooded the Australian press with stories of Marjorie's triumphs in Europe and North and South America, and her fans, family and friends in Australia were impatient for her arrival. Marjorie and Cyril were excited at the prospect of going home and, when they and Felix Wolfes (who had agreed to accompany Marjorie on the tour) set off from San Francisco on the *Monterey* on 24 May 1939, all things seemed in place for an artistic and commercial triumph. But as Robert Burns wrote, the best laid plans are apt to 'gang' astray and Marjorie's would prove that adage true.

Before leaving New York Marjorie had had an enormous row with Heinz Friedlander as a result of his ongoing demands for 'expense' money and an incident on the Zoppot trip he had organised. During their first stopover in Berlin, Friedlander's mother had met Marjorie and Cyril and confided to them her son's plans to divorce his wife, marry Marjorie and take control of her career. Marjorie described *Mutter* Friedlander as sweet, but found her revelations decidedly galling. And on board the *Monterey* there was much discussion about Friedlander, with Felix Wolfes inadvertently letting slip that Friedlander had paid him $300 for the introduction to Marjorie back in 1936. Had it been at all possible, Wolfes would have found himself out of a job and, as Marjorie put it, 'dumped on a desert island to rot', but there was no handy island, so Wolfes stayed.

Encouraged by Cyril, Marjorie had forgiven Wolfes by the time the ship reached Sydney, but there the situation flared up again. A cable was waiting for Marjorie at her hotel. It was from Friedlander informing her that his divorce had finally come through and *wunderbar* she could now marry him. Marjorie cabled straight back telling Friedlander he was sacked as her self-appointed manager and that henceforth they were strangers. Privately she expressed relief that she was 10,000 miles away when the hot-headed German received her cable.

What, if any, marriage plans Marjorie had became one of the most often-asked questions from the Australian media over the next few weeks. Marjorie remained non-committal and answered with a deliberate twinkle in her eyes that she hoped to settle down some day, perhaps with an Australian husband on 'a nice little property somewhere'. She had grown tired, she said of European men. Fortunately for Marjorie, the press never got wind of the Friedlander fracas.

The tour was to begin in Victoria, so Marjorie, Cyril, Wolfes and Longden (who had come on board the *Monterey* from the pilot boat via a rope ladder) stayed in Sydney for one night only, travelling the following evening on the overnight train to Melbourne. At Melbourne's Spencer Street railway station they were greeted by a crowd of 700, including all the school children from Deans Marsh and Winchelsea, who had been given the day off to form a Melbourne guard of honour for Marjorie. There was also a large contingent of Lawrences, including sister Lena and brothers Lindsay, Ted and Alan. Ivor Boustead and Thorold Waters were nearby, as were two new acquaintances – Alfredo Luizzi, young baritone pupil of Boustead's who had won the 1938 Ballarat Sun Aria and who would be

Marjorie's assisting artist on the tour, and the equally young Charles Buttrose, whom Longden had engaged to travel with the artists on the Victorian leg of their tour. There was also a massive press contingent and Marjorie was photographed with her brothers and sister, her right arm around Lena's shoulders and her left around Lindsay's. The photograph shows a happy and united group and it seems that in the excitement of reunion, differences had been genuinely, albeit temporarily, set aside. Marjorie reported later:

> *I had more or less adjusted differences with Lindsay, who was nevertheless still adamant about me repaying the £500 to the estate, i.e. himself. I refused and left without doing it.*[3]

That afternoon Marjorie hosted a tea party for her nieces and nephews at her Melbourne hotel and shared cakes, jelly, cream buns and lemonade with this awestruck group, one of whom had been named in her honour and none of whom had ever met their famous aunt before. Marjorie explained to the children (all dressed up in their best clothes and with faces scrubbed until they shone) how 'not a mile from here' she had worked endless hours sewing buttons onto frocks. The press reported:

> *People who met Miss Lawrence found her little different in manner and temperament from 'Marge', the happy-go-lucky youngster who went away in search of fame. We are pleased to report that success has not spoiled her.*[4]

Marjorie kept her promise to her father to begin the tour with a concert in the Globe Theatre in Winchelsea. She, Cyril, Wolfes, Longden and a cavalcade of newsmen and photographers progressed down to her hometown the following day and an even more remarkable welcome awaited them there. Led by a family friend carrying a large Australian flag, one hundred of the district's citizens, all mounted on horses of various shapes and sizes, met them on the outskirts of town and escorted them to the Shire Hall, where the rest of the local population was assembled for a civic reception.

> *The old bluestone building had been bedecked for the occasion with finery from half a dozen nearby drawing rooms. There were speeches galore, more kissing, weeping and, being an Australian bush gathering, much concentrated eating of home-made delicacies washed down with oceans of thick, strong tea.*[5]

Marjorie was presented with an illuminated address and the event was filmed by Movietone News and broadcast 'live' by an outside broadcast unit from radio 3LO. That evening a ball was held in her honour at the Globe Theatre. Marjorie re-met many old friends that day and evening, including Pat Considine with whom she danced twice and who whispered in her ear that she was still the best looking 'bird' he'd ever seen.

Marjorie and her party stayed with Ada Boddington for the five nights of their visit to Winchelsea. Marjorie remarked that Felix Wolfes's European nobility was put to the test by staying in an unheated Australian farmhouse in mid-winter and having to cope with the intricacies and discomforts of an outdoor toilet. 'Boddie' presented Marjorie with a magnificent concert gown she had made for her over the preceding months and Marjorie described it as being 'as exquisite as that of any celebrated French couturier'.[6]

On the night after the ball Marjorie gave her concert at the Globe Theatre. The best piano in the district (a Steinway belonging to a local family) was removed to the theatre for Wolfes to play and 300 people crammed inside, with twice that number outside listening through the fortunately flimsy walls. The concert was broadcast nationally by the ABC, which meant that hundreds of thousands of Australians heard Marjorie sing songs by Schubert, Rachmaninov and Mussorgsky. These were followed by traditional songs, with the triumphant climax being the Immolation Scene from *Götterdämmerung*.

The next morning Marjorie and her party drove to Deans Marsh and Marjorie sang during the Sunday service at St Paul's church. Lindsay, Ted, Cyril and Alan resumed their old places in the choir. It was just like old times, the only missing figure being Alex Pearce, who had died a few years earlier. Other visits included afternoon tea with aunt Emma Smith, now eighty and the most consistent letter writer of Marjorie's family.[7]

Ted Lawrence drove Marjorie and Cyril out to see the Lawrence farm at Winchelsea, which had been sold and was now sadly rundown, and to visit their parents' graves at Bambra cemetery. The absence of her father from all these events had been the one note of deep sadness for Marjorie. At his graveside she spoke to him, telling him 'Well, I made it Dad' and that she had fulfilled her promise to sing in the Globe.

The press discreetly absented themselves from this last trip but they were on hand for two important photo opportunities before Marjorie returned to Melbourne. Decked out in a tweed jacket, jodhpurs and boots, Marjorie went riding, and photographs of her galloping over the paddocks were published in newspapers across Australia. The second opportunity involved another celebrity. On arriving in Melbourne Marjorie had told the press that she enjoyed bicycle riding but had not been able to bring her 'bike' with her to Australia. The Melbourne-based cycle manufacturers Malvern Star became aware of this and despatched one of their directors to Winchelsea with a brand new Malvern Star ladies' roadster for Marjorie. The director and presenter of the bicycle was the legendary Australian cyclist Hubert Opperman and the press had a field day photographing 'Oppy' and 'Marge' together. Marjorie proudly told Opperman and the press that she had been on the finishing line for the Brest to Paris endurance race that Opperman had won in 1931, cheering her heart out but too shy to approach him after the race.

Marjorie's recitals in Melbourne and provincial centres in Victoria were widely successful, despite strong opposition from the ABC. On the evenings between Marjorie's appearances in the Melbourne Town Hall, the ABC presented the great German pianist Artur Schnabel in the same venue. Thus Melbournians were treated to six major recitals in seven days, more, Longden told the press, than he thought a city the size of Melbourne could support. Longden also accused the ABC of trying to elbow him and all private impresarios from the field and of being unpatriotic by engaging Lehmann in preference to Marjorie. The General Manager of the ABC, Charles Moses, countered in the press by claiming that Marjorie had been offered a tour in 1940 but had turned it down, that they had agreed to broadcast her recitals and had amended their orchestra dates for her appearances to suit her.

An average attendance of 2800 at Marjorie's Melbourne recitals more than equalled Schnabel's and, while connoisseurs might have preferred to hear the legendary pianist, the general public flocked to hear Marjorie singing Wagner showpieces and songs they knew, including 'My Ain Folk', where in the final stanza she substituted 'dear Aus-tra-lia' for 'dear old Scotland'.[8]

Vast armfuls of flowers were presented to Marjorie at her every appearance and she particularly delighted in the small posies of daphne which filled her hotel suite with their exquisite perfume. Hundreds of people queued to meet Marjorie after each recital and to present her with chocolates, cakes and even a basket full of sand crabs and a home-made rabbit pie. A small toy kangaroo was passed up to her on stage at the end of one recital and at another a small toy platypus.[9]

Marjorie and Wolfes both caught colds in Melbourne and one recital had to be cancelled, but if Marjorie and Longden felt they had done it tough in the Victorian capital they had a rude shock in store when they began their Sydney season. Fewer than 1000 people turned up for Marjorie's first recital in the Sydney Town Hall, and even fewer for the second and third. Marjorie complained that more people had turned up to see her in tiny Winchelsea than in Australia's largest city and herein lies the key to this apparently incomprehensible situation. Reviews of Marjorie's concerts were unsparing in their praise and there was no competition with the likes of Schnabel as there had been in Melbourne. Perhaps Sydneysiders stayed away because Marjorie was a Melbournian? There had always been intense rivalry between Australia's two largest cities and all the hype about 'Victoria's golden haired beauty' and 'Melbourne's gift to the Paris Opéra and to the Metropolitan' probably ruffled feathers in Sydney. Marjorie cancelled a fourth recital and that stirred the press into a campaign in support of her. The Sydney papers berated their readers for their shabby treatment of a great singer and speculated on the damage their action (or inaction) would do to the city's cultural reputation.

A committee of socialites headed by Lady Gowrie, wife the Governor of New South Wales, rallied support and at her fifth recital Marjorie finally sang to a respectably sized audience, but when she appeared five nights later with the ABC's Sydney Symphony Orchestra conducted by Wolfes, numbers had dropped off again. Longden suggested that prices might have affected ticket sales so Marjorie agreed to do a series of short recitals in the State Theatre, the city's most palatial cinema where tickets were cheaper. Here, she finally sang to full houses, but no one could be sure whether Marjorie's resplendent singing of opera arias or Bing Crosby's crooning of half a dozen songs in the film *East Side of Heaven*, which followed each recital, was the drawcard. While in Sydney, Marjorie also looked up Emily Skyring, who had helped her with money in Paris nine years earlier. Skyring now lived there and reluctantly accepted repayment of the money along with a pair of complimentary tickets to Marjorie's final recital at the State Theatre.

Anxious to quit a city where she felt unwanted, Marjorie, Cyril, Wolfes and Longden headed off for packed-out recitals in Canberra, followed by Brisbane. Marjorie experienced flying for the first time on the journey south from Brisbane and found the experience exhilarating, prompting her to praise the efficiency and convenience of air travel to the press. After another round of recitals in Victorian country towns, the group returned to Melbourne on Sunday 3 September to prepare for two final concerts. That evening Marjorie, Cyril, Wolfes and Longden gathered around the radio in Marjorie's hotel suite to listen to a speech by Robert Menzies, recently elected prime minister of Australia. Menzies announced that as Germany had failed to meet a deadline set by Britain a state of war now existed between Britain and Germany and, therefore, between Australia and Germany. The storm that had been gathering for years had finally broken. Marjorie's first act was to hug Felix Wolfes, who was in tears, and over the next few days she was preoccupied with thoughts of Mimi, Henri, Monsieur and Madame Grodet, Cécile Gilly and all her colleagues and friends in Paris.

Alfredo Luizzi (Australian, despite his Italian name) had not contributed much to the tour, but what he had done had been done well, so Marjorie had willingly agreed to sing at a testimonial concert organised for him in the Melbourne Town Hall. On the advice of his colleagues the young baritone had decided to travel to America and further his studies there, Europe now being effectively off limits. Also taking part in the concert was a delightful and prodigiously talented twelve-year-old pianist from Adelaide, Allison Nelson, who would unexpectedly reappear in Marjorie's career decades later.

At this concert Marjorie sang two songs by Australian composers: Percy Grainger's 'Willow, Willow' and Linda Phillips's 'The Charioteers'. The latter was dedicated to Marjorie and written by a young composer of more than average talent who became a lifelong friend and who eventually succeeded Thorold Waters as music critic of *The Sun*. Marjorie had met Grainger in America and the two had discovered they were not only compatriots but kindred free spirits. Marjorie would later include several songs by him and other Australian composers in her recital repertoire, adding an antipodean element to an already eclectic mix and giving exposure to works by composers who struggled to be heard. At the suggestion of Thorold Waters, around this time Marjorie established the 'Marjorie Lawrence Prize' of ten guineas, to be awarded to a young Australian singer annually, in conjunction with the Ballarat Sun Aria.[10]

Another distinctly Australian incident on this tour, this time with a slightly absurd element to it, was a story in the press which was probably true. It concerned Marjorie being approached by a local film company who were planning to make a movie of the life of Dame Nellie Melba. Marjorie Lawrence, they were reported as saying, would be ideal for acting and singing the role of Melba. When the press questioned Marjorie about this she was very diplomatic and said she believed it a great honour to be considered for the role, avoiding having to mention that her voice and her repertoire were nothing like Melba's by explaining that she had already been approached by Hollywood to appear in films, which was probably also true.

The final concert of the tour took place on 13 September with the ABC's Melbourne Symphony Orchestra, conducted by Bernard Heinze. Marjorie had wanted to sing the *Salome* finale and the Immolation Scene, but Heinze vetoed the Strauss on the grounds that the performance would earn a royalty for a living enemy composer. Privately, the conductor was afraid the audience might react violently to two German opera excerpts on the same program. The Wagner was considered a reasonable risk, but the Strauss was replaced by a group of arias by French composers – Australia's allies in the war – and Marjorie announced after singing the Wagner that she was donating her 250-pound earnings from the concert to the Red Cross.

Among the string players in the Melbourne Symphony at that time was Isabelle Moresby, who a few years later would write a book about music in Australia. We are indebted to Moresby for what is the most intimate portrait of Marjorie during this tour.

> *There was something so natural and spontaneous about her that she had most of her fellow Australians at her feet. Rehearsing with the orchestra – two thirds of whose string players were women – Marjorie beamed and dimpled at us, as if she were a sister to us all – with a quaint wisp of a hat nodding on top of her golden curls. 'But why on earth must she wear such a funny little hat?' queried one puzzled admirer. 'What does it matter?' was the whispered rejoinder, 'If I were as pretty as she is, I wouldn't care what I wore on my head!'* [11]

Marjorie, Cyril and Wolfes left Sydney to return to the United States two days after the final concert in Melbourne. Archie Longden stayed behind in Australia and volunteered for the Royal Australian Air Force.[12] In the Fijian capital Suva, Marjorie fulfilled a commitment made on the outbound journey to give a concert for the local Red Cross. Most of the British, Indian and American communities on the island crammed into the Suva Town Hall to listen to Marjorie singing Gluck,

Schubert, Mussorgsky and Wagner as giant punkahs swung to and fro above their heads stirring the hot, moisture-laden air.

Marjorie also gave a concert in the McKinlay Auditorium in Honolulu and she, Cyril and Wolfes were photographed in tropical attire, Marjorie and Cyril holding a pineapple and Wolfes holding a ukulele. Marjorie was also photographed by the press sitting on Waikiki Beach with the ubiquitous ukulele and the score of *Die Walküre* propped up in front of her. She was not attempting to play Wagner on the ukulele (as a glance at the photos might suggest), but in fact learning a new role – Sieglinde, which she was contracted to sing for the San Francisco Opera on their arrival back in the United States.

Having become one of the two or three leading Brünnhildes in the world, it may seem strange that Marjorie would have bothered with the lighter soprano role in *Die Walküre*, but the request for Marjorie and Flagstad to alternate in these roles had come from both Gaetano Merola (head of the San Francisco Opera) and Edward Johnson. Both impresarios had recognised the publicity value of what neither would have admitted was a stunt.

The 'stunt' nearly didn't come off when word reached both companies that Flagstad was having difficulty getting a passage from war-torn Europe to America. Marjorie received a cable in Hawaii from Johnson's assistant Edward Zeigler saying she should hold herself ready to take over all the Wagner dramatic soprano roles at the Met in the coming winter season if Flagstad arrived late or not at all.[13] As it turned out Flagstad reached the United States in time for the first performance of *Die Walküre* at the San Francisco Opera, in which she sang Sieglinde and Marjorie sang Brünnhilde. A week later on 24 October 1939, Marjorie sang Sieglinde for the first time, with Flagstad as Brünnhilde.

Three of the four performances of *Die Walküre* given by the San Francisco Opera that season were conducted by Erich Leinsdorf, Bodanzky's dynamic new assistant in the German wing at the Met, and the fourth by Flagstad's tame and obedient protégée Edwin McArthur. Marjorie was unlucky to have McArthur in the pit on the night she tackled Sieglinde for the first time. McArthur had never conducted the opera before and Leinsdorf had cornered all the rehearsal time, so when McArthur stood before the orchestra to conduct the prologue it was for the first time. A pedestrian performance resulted, redeemed only by the voices of Flagstad, Marjorie and Melchior.[14] The critics praised Marjorie, although some expressed the opinion that she was a better Brünnhilde than a Sieglinde. Olin Downes attended and wrote in the *New York Times* that Marjorie brought a spontaneity and abandon to her singing of the part which made plausible Siegmund's apostrophe to the Spring and the blossoming of the Walsung blood.[15]

Marjorie and Melchior next met up for a performance of *Siegfried* in St Louis, which was followed by a series of joint recitals in Chicago, Detroit and Toronto, further cementing their friendship and treating audiences to mouth-watering programs of Wagner, including the dawn duet from *Götterdämmerung* and the Siegmund-Sieglinde duet from *Die Walküre*.

While in Montreal Marjorie also gave a joint recital with Ezio Pinza and, while Cyril was driving them back to their hotel after the recital, the Italian *basso* tried to seduce Marjorie.

> *Pinza clutched my hand and fervently declared he had adored me since the first time he saw me. He lamented that because Cyril was with us, he could not talk freely but, he panted, there were many things he yearned to tell me. He would come to my room directly we got to the hotel and relate them he said. I laughingly told Signor Pinza that I did not think anything he might have to say would stale if it remained unsaid until the following morning when we were less tired, but it had to be tonight, he said. When we reached the hotel Cyril did a magnificent job of running interference and I was able to escape to my room, but Pinza would not be put off. Just as I was getting ready for bed he arrived outside my door. He sang, he shouted, he hammered and he threatened to break down the door until a hotel official attracted by the din arrived and led off my gifted, warm-hearted colleague.*[16]

Pinza was an adored matinee idol and a handsome man who exuded tremendous virility and charm and Marjorie must have been tempted to succumb to his passion, but no doubt his reputation as a womaniser deterred her and the prospect of being another of his much vaunted conquests did not appeal to her. Rejection did not affect Pinza's friendship with Marjorie and when he married the daughter of a Larchmont dentist (less than half his age) the following year he sent most of the women he had successfully or unsuccessfully tried to seduce, including Marjorie, invitations to his wedding.

Back in New York, Marjorie and Cyril settled into the Ansonia as Marjorie prepared for her next season at the Met as well as for opera and concert engagements across the length and breadth of the nation that fate had destined would now be her new home. Early on, there were a couple of events which consolidated her recent renewed association with her homeland. Marjorie joined John Brownlee in providing the entertainment for the inaugural dinner of the Australian Association of New York, of which they, Percy Grainger and about one hundred other Australians living in the city were founder members. On this occasion Marjorie sang Grainger's powerful and moving song 'Shallow Brown', impressing the composer so much he sent her a note a month later saying her singing still lingered in his memory.

Marjorie and Grainger were also elected executive members of the ANZAC War Relief Fund, an organisation established to raise money to buy personal items for Australian and New Zealand troops then being committed to the war in Europe, and towards the end of 1940 they also collaborated on a fund-raising concert at Carnegie Hall.

This was organised by Marjorie and billed as a 'Dominions Night Concert', featuring Marjorie, Grainger and assisting artists, with the proceeds going to 'Bundles for Britain', a British charity set up to assist Britons on the home front suffering nightly bombing raids from the Luftwaffe. In the preceding months Grainger and Marjorie had met several times and corresponded to discuss which of Grainger's songs and arrangements Marjorie would sing in the second half of the program, which was devoted entirely to the Australian composer's work. Eventually they settled on 'Hubby and Wifey', 'Rule Britannia', 'Willow, Willow', 'The Old Woman at the Christening' and 'Shallow Brown' with Grainger and the American composer Henry Cowell playing the guitar and piano parts and a string ensemble led by cellist Willem Durieux.

Plans for the concert went smoothly until a day or so before the concert was to be held, when Lord Lothian, the British ambassador to the United States died. The British charity felt obliged to withdraw out of respect for their ambassador, announcing that the concert had been cancelled. Marjorie hastily assembled the press and informed them the concert was back on and she was taking over full responsibility for it, believing, she said, that no Briton (least of all a representative of His Majesty the King) would want to deny the suffering population of Britain the comforts the money raised by the concert could provide. Privately Marjorie was furious. So much work had been put into the event by so many people she considered it immoral that it should be cancelled because of the death of an individual who had refused medical treatment on religious grounds.

As well as the Grainger items Marjorie sang songs by Brahms, Fauré, Duparc and Canteloube, an English group and a new song ('Miranda') by the American composer Richard Hageman. Marjorie dedicated the 'Four Serious Songs' of Brahms to the memory of Lothian and in a speech she quoted what she said had been the ambassador's final words: 'Before the judgement seat of God each must answer for his own actions', which must have stirred mixed reaction from those who knew the circumstances of his death. Noel Strauss reported in *The New York Times* that Marjorie and Grainger received 'a series of overwhelming ovations by the large and patriotic audience, including many Australians, who set up their native "*Coo-ee*" call'.[17]

On the train back to his home in White Plains the following day Grainger wrote to Marjorie. Referring to the concert he noted with numerous underlinings and several Graingerisms:

> It is the only time that I have heard my songs <u>perfectly</u> done – *with glorious sincerity and exquisite differentiation of mood, warm emotionality and crystal clear diction. No other singer I know would have had the courage to present these songs as they should be – in a <u>drastic</u> way – a thoroughly <u>Australian</u> way.*

Your great artistry is a match for your thrilling voice. I also want to say how much I admired the way you and your brother stuck to your guns and put the concert through. That again is truly <u>Australian</u>.[18]

Grainger's words are a timely reminder that, even at the height of her career and long after she adopted the United States as her home and became an American citizen, at heart Marjorie was and would always remain an Aussie.

Chapter Twelve

The Glory Years

With hindsight Marjorie would look back on the period between her return to the United States after her first Australian tour and June 1941 when a horrendous misfortune befell her in Mexico City as the high point of her career. It was certainly the period where her services were most in demand, when she commanded the highest fees and when her popularity was greater than it had ever been.[1] At the time, however, Marjorie saw these two years accomplishments as nothing more than an increase in the pace towards a summit that was not yet in sight.

> *My career was surging on to the topmost levels of vocal achievement, and because I was young, strong and healthy, I derived the last ounce of joy and triumph that came my way.*[2]

A month into her next Met season, Marjorie celebrated her thirty-third birthday, an age at which many dramatic sopranos are only beginning to experiment with the arduous roles she was already famous for and, given the excellent state of her voice, which seemed to be getting better and stronger, she could reasonably expect to have another twenty years in which to refine her art and enjoy that 'joy and triumph' at the top of her profession.

The increasing strength and responsiveness of Marjorie's voice was due in part to the influence of an elderly American named Louis Bachner. Bachner made himself known to Marjorie on her return from Australia and offered his services as a vocal adviser – an expert Marjorie could consult on all matters pertaining to her voice, her singing and her repertoire – and Marjorie accepted. Bachner had an impressive CV, having held the post of Professor of Singing at the Berlin Hochschule für Musik for twenty-six years, teaching Karin Branzell, Lily Djamel and Ria Ginster and acting as vocal adviser to Leider, Heinrich Schlusnus, Sigrid Onegin and Michael Bohnen.

Marjorie believed that Bachner helped her (in her own words) 'to loosen up my voice' and to correct a few unfortunate vocal habits she had developed since leaving Cécile Gilly's studio. In fact it was not so much 'the voice' Bachner worked on with Marjorie as her muscles and her breathing apparatus. A tightness that was giving some of her notes a pinched quality and causing pitch problems had been creeping into Marjorie's singing in recent times and with Bachner's help this was replaced by a new (or new-found) relaxation, which helped her voice considerably, heralding a new blossoming in the beauty, richness and surety of Marjorie's singing, which is clearly evident in broadcasts of her performances in 1940. It also permitted those moments referred to earlier where Marjorie could (when she chose) emulate Flagstad's noble sound. All this was accomplished after a few short weeks of working together and was testament to his knowledge and her willingness to experiment and improve.[3] The New York critics noticed the difference. Olin Downes reported: 'Marjorie Lawrence is singing better this season than ever before' and Francis Perkins in the *Herald Tribune* commented that this period marked a new stage in her evolution as a great singer.[4]

There were also substantial changes at the Met when Marjorie returned on 6 December 1939 to sing the first of nine performances of *Die Walküre*. Not for the first time during this turbulent decade, the organisation was in serious financial trouble and a 'Save the Met' fund had been established to raise enough capital to rescue both theatre and company. Artur Bodanzky was dead – dying suddenly four days before the season commenced. Erich Leinsdorf was now in charge of the German wing and Felix Wolfes had obtained an engagement as an assistant conductor.[5] Melchior and Flagstad had called a temporary truce to their squabbling and joined forces to oppose musical changes Leinsdorf was making, including his restoration of the cuts Bodanzky had made to the Wagner operas. The tenor was now feuding openly with Leinsdorf over the conductor's demands that he attend all rehearsals and Flagstad was simmering with resentment over Edward Johnson's reluctance to engage Edwin McArthur. Both publicly questioned Leinsdorf's fitness to succeed Bodanzky – a concern, incidentally, Marjorie did not share. Another formidably voiced Wagnerian dramatic soprano had also joined the roster this season: Helen Traubel – eight years older than Marjorie and with no international reputation and limited stage experience. Circumstances would later catapult Traubel into stardom, but at the time neither Flagstad nor Marjorie would have seen the homely looking, unassuming soprano from St Louis as a threat to their respective positions.

Leopold Sachse had also decided to introduce some innovations in the staging of the Ring this season and Marjorie was involved in one of the least successful. To exploit the public's continuing fascination with Marjorie's equestrian skills, Sachse decided that Brünnhilde should hold Grane by the bridle throughout the *Götterdämmerung* dawn duet and that Siegfried would then lead the horse off stage. A suggestion made at rehearsal that Siegfried should mount the horse and ride it off stage was greeted with derision by Melchior and alarm by the horse, which was not much bigger than the tenor.

Marjorie agreed to hold the horse and Melchior to leading it off, and it was further evidence of Marjorie's skill as a horsewoman and her cool-headedness that she kept the animal under control for almost ten minutes without missing a note as she and Melchior sang the demanding duet. In performance the presence of the horse so close to the footlights proved too much of a distraction for the audience and to everyone's relief that 'inspired' idea was scrapped after one performance.

That devoted old horse also figured in another remarkable occurrence during the final performance of *Götterdämmerung* this season. Each time the animal was on stage and each time Marjorie sang, the creature whinnied in distress, the final pages of the opera becoming a bizarre duet between horse and soprano. At the time no one could account for the animal's uncharacteristic behaviour, but with hindsight Marjorie wondered if it had sensed what she could not have known at the time – that this was the last time they would appear on stage together and the last time Marjorie would ride this or any other horse into Siegfried's funeral pyre.

Two of Marjorie's performances from this season were broadcast and are available on CD – both of *Die Walküre*. The first comes from New York and preserves Marjorie's second appearance in the house as Sieglinde – on her birthday – with Flagstad singing Brünnhilde. The second comes from the spring tour and captures a performance in the Boston Opera House with Marjorie as Brünnhilde and Lotte Lehmann as Sieglinde. Both are conducted by Leinsdorf and both also provide remarkably vivid sound, at least equal to what radio listeners would have heard at the time.

Marjorie's Sieglinde is no wilting violet. She sounds (as she should) like a wife who is prepared to drug her husband to save the man she loves, but she is more youthful than Lehmann and more vulnerable than Flagstad. The first act of the New York performance is a dramatic and vocal tour de force. Melchior is in tremendous voice. He holds onto the words 'Walse, Walse' for about a dozen beats instead of the required three, which may have been his revenge on Leinsdorf, but it is hard to criticise him when he pours out such golden, trumpet-like tone, with Marjorie matching him measure for measure.

Marjorie proves in the second act just what a consummate vocal actress she had become. She conveys every ounce of Sieglinde's guilt, confusion and fear without ever disturbing the musical line. This is followed by Flagstad singing with an other-worldly beauty of tone, and the contrast between the two soprano roles (fallible woman and daughter of the gods) is for once fully realised and made explicit to the spellbound audience.

The scene between Brünnhilde and Sieglinde in the final act is also a revelation. After Flagstad demonstrates her vocal superiority over the other Valkyries, Marjorie sings Sieglinde's part with her newfound radiance. It is as if she were saying to Flagstad: 'See, I can sing just as beautifully as you when I want to' and the combination of these two remarkable sopranos creates a kind of vocal plenitude that has no equal in this age of puny voices.

Six weeks separate the New York and Boston broadcasts and in the interim Melchior had celebrated his fiftieth birthday. Marjorie sent him a huge floral arrangement and received a card in return signed 'love from Lauritz'. The Boston performance was close to the end of the spring tour and finds the artists sounding a little tired in places. Melchior seems less involved than in the earlier broadcast and so does Marjorie, this time singing Brünnhilde. Then, in the second scene of Act Two (perhaps inspired by Thorborg's splendidly telling Fricka in the previous scene), she suddenly seems to pull herself together and the long exchange with Wotan (Schorr) comes brilliantly to life. The superior sound and Leinsdorf's clean textures allow us to hear these two consummate artists inspiring one another and with their sincerity and conviction imprinting phrase after phrase on our memory. The magic continues with Melchior in the *Todesverkündigung* and here Marjorie finds that extra depth and understanding that eluded her in past years. Wagner singing does not get much better than this. Marjorie, Schorr and Leinsdorf bring the opera to a close with heart-rending intensity, and the Boston audience, knowing they have witnessed something special, roar their approval when the curtain falls.

When Marjorie makes her first solo curtain call, wolf whistles are added to the cacophony. Broadcast host Milton Cross in his concluding remarks mentions that 'our lovely Brünnhilde this afternoon' eschews such titles as 'Madame', 'diva' or 'prima donna', preferring to be called simply 'Marjorie Lawrence', and that she hails from Deans Marsh in Australia. No doubt most of the population of Deans Marsh were listening and gladdened to hear their little town mentioned, for this broadcast was also transmitted to Australia. In response to an interval appeal for the 'Save the Met Fund', the Lawrence family passed the hat around and gathered five pounds, which was duly sent to New York.

Not long after her return from Australia, Marjorie had received an offer from the opera company in St Louis to sing a role she had not sung before, one she and they thought would suit her and which might prove to be as popular as her Salome. A week after the Met spring tour ended in Dallas, Marjorie hastened to St Louis to begin rehearsals for her debut in the title role of Bizet's *Carmen*. Marjorie's old sparring partner from Cleveland, Jan Kiepura, was to sing Don José and Ezio Pinza was the dashing toreador Escamillo.

True to form, Kiepura set out to cause trouble at rehearsal, putting his knee on Marjorie's throat, then throwing her so far across the stage that she almost slid into the orchestra pit. Breathless and having missed her next cue, Marjorie called a halt to the rehearsal and marched up to Kiepura, who was standing centre stage looking innocent and unconcerned.

> *I told him in no uncertain terms that if he ever did that to me again I would kick him in the balls so hard he wouldn't be able to sing Don José or anything else for a very long time.*[6]

Marjorie walked out on the rehearsal and left it to the company management to sort out the problem. As the whole enterprise had been developed around her assumption of a new, popular role and Kiepura was running out of opera houses that would tolerate his antics, it didn't take much persuasion to convince the tenor to behave himself, and the first performance, on 25 April 1940, went off without incident.

The St Louis public liked Marjorie's glamorous interpretation of Carmen, but the critics did not. Many famous divas have found themselves adrift trying to understand the gypsy girl's complex character and instil her music with the right mix of insouciance and nobility, and on the evidence of her debut performance it seems likely that Marjorie would join their ranks. Marjorie would sing Carmen a few times more and might have grown into the part as she had so many others, but time ran out before she had that chance.

The whole of Act Two from a San Francisco performance the following October is available on CD and it reveals the essential ingredient Marjorie failed to deliver. She sings accurately and her French is better than that of the rest of the cast, but her character does not reach across the footlights – everything is generalised and all too reliant (one imagines) on her facial expression, her costumes, her acting and her much publicised dancing.

It is encouraging to know that the most severe critic of her Carmen was Marjorie herself. After the first performance in St Louis she wrote in her diary 'Not so good' underlining the first word. The San Francisco performances were also sung by default rather than choice. Marjorie had been engaged to sing Minnie in *La Fanciulla del West* but, as in Buenos Aires in 1936, another cast member fell sick and the management begged her to sing Carmen instead. After these performances Marjorie wrote in her diary 'Still not so hot'.[7]

Evidence that Marjorie was singing well at the time of these Carmen performances can be found on a group of studio recordings she made for RCA Victor in May – the most successful batch since Paris. Over three days and accompanied by Felix Wolfes, Marjorie recorded multiple takes of eleven songs, including some she had unsuccessfully recorded the year before. Six of these were released on 78s and two more found their way onto an LP years later. These included three songs by Pfitzner, who was still living in Germany but out of favour with the Nazis. Both singer and pianist give carefully considered and beautifully controlled performances of these difficult songs. Perhaps the most difficult, 'Stimme der Sehnsucht', is the most successful – full of atmosphere, sombre colour and dramatic fervour. Marjorie's diction is excellent in these songs and why her lovely singing and Wolfes splendid playing of Pfitzner's 'Die Einsame' had to wait for the LP era to be released is a mystery.

There are also thrilling performances of Strauss's 'Lied an meinen Sohn' and 'Des Dichters Abendgang', where the placement of the voice is sure and Marjorie's rich tone is matched by Wolfes's at the piano, both artists achieving a truly 'Straussian' sweep. Experts will still find aspects of Marjorie's lieder singing to criticise when comparisons are made with the greatest, but these are recordings no open-minded student of great singing would wish to be without.

The same applies to Marjorie singing some of the traditional English and Scottish songs recorded during these sessions. Curiously, it is Melba that the listener might be reminded of when hearing Marjorie sing 'Danny Boy', 'Annie Laurie', 'My Ain Folk' and 'Down the Burn'. She brings the same kind of affecting simplicity her older compatriot brought to her recordings of such songs – 'John Anderson, My Jo', for example. Verbal acuity, strong, well-placed tone and avoidance of sentimentality, plus excellent work from Wolfes, lend these recordings a timeless distinction.[8]

Days after Marjorie made these recordings, the Germans occupied Paris and propaganda film of German troops marching up the Champs Elysées and Hitler ogling the Arc de Triomphe and the Eiffel Tower were shown in cinemas across America. Marjorie was deeply distressed by the news and concerned for the fate of the Grodets, Cécile Gilly, her employees in Rue Junot and her friends and colleagues at the Opéra. Cyril wrote numerous letters to Paris on Marjorie's behalf, but it was months before any reply was received.

Two letters finally arrived, which, far from reassuring Marjorie, added to her distress. The first came from Henri Grodet reporting that he, Mimi and their parents were safe, but Marjorie's apartment in Rue Junot had been looted by the Germans and the whereabouts of Yvonne and Eugenie were unknown. The second letter came from Sam Waagenaar, one of Cécile Gilly's few male pupils. He now lived in California and had received a letter from Gilly in which she requested he share her news with Marjorie. Madame had fled Paris before the Germans arrived and was living in her villa at Euse. Her son Max was a prisoner of war in Germany and her daughter Yvonne had recently died of blood poisoning, leaving Cécile to care for her three children, including a four-month-old baby. Another daughter, Paulette, had entrusted the care of her twins to her mother and so had Renée Gilly, who had one child. 'Thus,' Waagenaar reported, 'Madame Gilly is heartbroken and left to care for six children without any help'.[9]

The effects of the war in Europe were spreading rapidly around the globe, shrinking the sphere of activity for singers now domiciled in the United States to little more than North, South and Central America. Because of this, Marjorie changed agents this year, leaving the international-focused NBC Artists Services for the domestic-focused Vincent Attractions of West 57th Street, New York. J.J. Vincent and his assistant Henry Phohl managed to secure her lucrative opera and concert engagements from Boston to San Diego and Seattle to Miami and Marjorie was also offered another contract to sing at the Teatro Colón in Buenos Aires from August to October 1940. She was reluctant to accept this last offer, not because of artistic considerations, but because there were many Nazi sympathisers there and word had got around that Buenos Aires was a dangerous place for British subjects. In the end Marjorie decided the benefits outweighed the risk and she signed.

The new director of the Colón, Fiore Ugarte, offered her $US8400 in cash to sing six performances of Brünnhilde, two of Salome and five of a role Marjorie had been longing to sing again – Kundry in *Parsifal*. While the figure was not large for so many performances, Ugarte also agreed to pay all Marjorie and Cyril's expenses, including first class passage to and from Buenos Aires and three months occupancy of a luxury suite at the Alvear Palace.

Marjorie and Cyril travelled from New York to Buenos Aires (via Barbados) on the cruise liner *Uruguay*, on which the passengers were entertained by the All American Youth Orchestra conducted by Leopold Stokowski. Marjorie had become used to the fast Atlantic liners and found this cruise ship tiresomely tedious. 'I'm bored to death on this boat – it's too slow', she noted in her diary. Eventually they reached their destination and a limousine provided by Ugarte whisked Marjorie and Cyril off to the Alvear Palace.

Marjorie's first appearance at the Colón this season (in *Die Walküre*), was broadcast and has been released on CD. The sound is variable: sometimes good, more often distorted and muddy. In places extraneous noises intrude. In Act One, for example, what sounds like a small revolution seems to be taking place in the background, with some very unmusical sounds. The rest of the cast sing impressively but offer no real competition to their counterparts in New York and, although Marjorie is in splendid voice, this performance adds little to what we already know about her 'Walküre' Brünnhilde.

It does, however, confirm how consistently brilliantly and effortlessly she now sings and acts the role and provides more of those memorable moments where she emulates Flagstad's sepulchral tone. It is also interesting to hear her adapting herself to the direction of a third fine conductor with his own views on how the score should go. In this case it is Erich Kleiber who manages to combine Bodanzky's feverish tension with Leinsdorf's clarity, putting strain on most of the cast but not on Marjorie, who seems indefatigable. Apart from the single act of Carmen from San Francisco, this is the last 'live' recording we have of Marjorie before her illness and it is further proof of the heights to which she had climbed – and an indication of what she would lose.

The audience that night was captivated by Marjorie and so were the local music critics, the *Buenos Aires Herald* pronouncing her 'the world's greatest Brünnhilde'.[10] Herbert Janssen (singing Wotan) became ill during the run of *Die Walküre* and as no replacement was available, two performances had to be cancelled. The audience was compensated with an extra performance tacked onto the end of the season. By then the good folks of Buenos Aires had also witnessed Marjorie's Salome for the first time and renewed their acquaintance with her Kundry. Marjorie's vivid assumption of the Strauss role had bowled them over much as it had audiences in New York and Chicago, prompting the *Buenos Aires Herald* to go a step further and bestow on her the title 'World's greatest dramatic soprano'.[11] The five performances of Kundry in ten days that followed must have taxed the whole cast, but Marjorie came through with flying colours. This time the critic of the Buenos Aires Herald found her 'convincing', 'mysterious', 'terrifying' and 'seductive'.[12]

Ugarte was so impressed with his new prima donna that he offered her Isolde, the *Götterdämmerung* Brünnhilde and Senta for the next season and asked if she might consider donating the helmet, spear and shield she had used in *Die Walküre* to the Colón Museum. Marjorie was happy to oblige and also to accede to a request from the British ambassador to Argentina to sing a benefit concert in Buenos Aires for the Lord Mayor of London's Air Raid Appeal.

While in Buenos Aires Marjorie received a daily flood of fan mail from local music lovers and from rich cattle ranchers and sugar planters who offered her much more than admiration. Among these were a clutch of passionate cables: 'Je t'aime, cherie', 'Vie impossible sans toi' and 'T'adore, t'adore' etc. These came from Armand D'Ans who had been waiting for Marjorie when she arrived in Buenos Aires and proposed marriage again just before she left. Marjorie was happy to be escorted about town by the handsome Argentinean, and tempted to accept his offer, but again declined. D'Ans now had a successful architect's practice in the city he loved and where his extended family lived. All this he was prepared to throw away for her before moving to the United States, but the sacrifice was too much for Marjorie's conscience.

After the 'slow boat to Argentina' on the outward journey, Marjorie and Cyril decided to fly back to the US. D'Ans was at the airport to farewell them on what was to be a marathon flight – Buenos Aires to Santiago, then Lima, Cali, San Cristóbel, Guatemala, Mexico City, Los Angeles and finally San Francisco, where news of the cancellation of *La Fanciulla del West* and her second attempt at *Carmen* awaited her.

In the third act of the Bizet opera, Carmen and her companions try to read what the future holds for them in the dramatic card scene. Carmen's companions see untold riches and marriage to noble and distinguished men, while Carmen discovers she is being stalked by death. If Marjorie had been superstitious (which she was not), she might have seen her own future in the combined readings of all three characters, for she was about to be courted by a prince, turn him down for a better man and come close to losing her life, all in the next few months.

The prince was a dashing fifty-year-old Russian named Serge Obolensky Neledinsky Meletzky who could trace his lineage back to the ninth century. Despite having at least one saint on his family tree, Obolensky (he dropped the last two names when he moved to the US) was anything but a saint. He had been twice married and twice divorced, first to Grand Duchess Catherine Romanov, then to the American heiress Alice Astor. By the time Marjorie met him he was considered one of the world's most famous playboys, maintaining that reputation long after he disappeared from her life, with one of his last conquests being (according to Hollywood gossip) the young Marilyn Monroe.[13]

Obolensky saw Marjorie singing Carmen and apparently decided he wanted a much closer look. He opened his campaign by sending her huge bunches, baskets and urns of exotic flowers, sometimes twice a day, with charming cards embossed with his family crest, each addressed to 'My little princess' and expressing his admiration in ever more ardent terms.

> Serge had a flair for the composition of these billets-doux. His stock of heart-fluttering phrases, all, to the best of my knowledge and experience, original, was endless. And, thoroughly normal woman that I am, the 'princess' idea was not without appeal.[14]

Obolensky moved to the next phase in his conquest of Marjorie by giving her expensive gifts and escorting her to some of the most exclusive restaurants and night clubs in New York. Soon he was whispering marriage proposals in her ear and the 'princess' idea seemed to be moving towards a concrete possibility. Marjorie's agent, J.J. Vincent, was all in favour of the idea. He could see 'Princess Marjorie' on billboards across the country and Cyril was over the moon, probably wondering whether Obolensky's relations could manage a small title for him as well.

Obolensky followed Marjorie to Chicago, where she sang more performances of *Carmen* and *Salome*, to Minneapolis where she gave concerts with the Minneapolis Symphony and attended a fund-raising event in New York, at which she met the legendary pianist Jan Paderewski. Obolensky also agreed to be one of the patrons for another war charity concert Marjorie was planning to give in Carnegie Hall and she had almost made up her mind to accept his offer of marriage when she returned to the Met for the 1940–41 season.[15]

Marjorie embarked on her sixth season at the Met in a buoyant frame of mind, thanks to Obolensky and the prospect of performing the title role in an opera that had not been seen at the Met before. This was Gluck's *Alceste*, the first complete opera Marjorie had studied with Cécile Gilly ten years earlier and which she had not yet sung – and on this occasion she almost missed out as well.

In the spring of 1940 when the current season was being planned, Edward Johnson decided that he should capitalise on the success of a new production of Gluck's *Orfeo ed Euridice* two seasons earlier by mounting the Met's first production of *Alceste*, 173 years after its premiere in Vienna.[16] Marjorie made it known that she knew the role and Johnson promised to consider her for it. Later she learned that he had decided to bring a new singer into the company to sing Alceste – none other than her Paris rival, Germaine Lubin.

Marjorie was disappointed and resentful about the role going to Lubin, but Johnson's choice was logical, since Lubin had sung *Alceste* to great acclaim in Paris and London and was arguably its greatest living exponent. As the US had not yet entered the war, it was hoped that the German authorities in Paris would give their favoured soprano a visa to travel outside France and, although Lubin kept her destination a secret from them, in the end the Germans declined her request. Just two weeks before rehearsals commenced, Johnson had to come, 'cap in hand', and ask Marjorie if she would take over the role.

Marjorie's first instinct may have been to refuse Johnson's request, but she knew that if she declined it would be given to the up-and-coming American soprano Rose Bampton, who had agreed to understudy Lubin. Marjorie also realised that being asked to perform in a Met premiere is not an everyday occurrence, since it ensures the singer a unique place in the company's history. She agreed, and rehearsals got under way with the producer Herbert Graf, the conductor Ettore Panizza and the rest of the cast, which included René Maison as Admetus and the young Leonard Warren as the High Priest of Apollo.

On the night of the premiere – 24 January 1941 – Marjorie received notes and cables from many of her fellow artists wishing her well, including Helen Traubel, who had sung Sieglinde with her the previous season. The public enjoyed the performance and gave the singers a warm reception, but the critics were not impressed. Graf's production relied very heavily on spectacle and it seems that he and Johnson had concerns that Gluck's sombre work might send their patrons to sleep if they didn't overload it with visual effects. The critics revelled in pointing out aspects of the production that were out of keeping with the score, the story and the period in which it is set.

The same critics praised Marjorie's noble singing of 'Divinités du Styx', but reported that she seemed to make tough going of the rest of score. Pitch problems and shortness of breath were mentioned, criticisms that had never been levelled at Marjorie before and which seem at odds with her recent performances in New York, Boston and Buenos Aires. As Olin Downes pointed out, Graf may have been partly responsible for this, as he made the singers sing much of their music while standing in uncomfortable, static poses simulating figures on a classical frieze.[17]

For a singer who threw herself physically as well as vocally into her roles, this must have been an enormous encumbrance – and to make matters worse Marjorie was suffering a debilitating, but thankfully, temporary malady which was affecting her emotionally and physically. She managed to get through the first two performances, but had to relinquish the third and fourth to Bampton, returning to the role for the final performance in March.[18]

Criticism of this kind was absent when Marjorie's Wagner performances this season were reviewed, but these were plagued by political considerations. With German atrocities in Europe reported daily in the American press, Johnson feared a backlash from the public to German operas. He therefore scheduled fewer performances of Wagner at the beginning of the season until he could gauge the public's mood. To everyone's relief there were no complaints or protests, so the German wing was allowed to move into full swing by the fifth week. This meant that Marjorie's appearance (and those of her regular colleagues) was delayed and apart from *Alceste*, Marjorie sang only two performances of *Die Walküre* (alternating as Sieglinde and Brünnhilde with Flagstad), two of *Götterdämmerung*, one of *Siegfried* and two of *Lohengrin*.

Marjorie's first appearance on 2 January was also a red-letter day in her personal life. The man who would supplant all her previous boyfriends and lovers, marry her within three months and spend the next forty years at her side walked into Marjorie's life that day – and if he was not a prince he would soon prove himself princely. Tom King (as he called himself) was a lanky young man with undistinguished features, a cheeky grin, bright eyes and an accent that betrayed his upbringing in a southern state of the union. He was also the antithesis of the exotic and romantic men Marjorie had previously been attracted to. Marjorie described their first meeting in *Interrupted Melody*:

> *There was no fanfare; no rumble from the drums to warn me of his approach. I had just finished singing Brünnhilde in* Die Walküre *and my dressing room was filled with friends and well-wishers. Out of the chattering throng about me he suddenly emerged, shook my hand, congratulated me and said: 'My, but you must be tired. Why don't you sit down?' And reaching back through the crowd he dragged out a chair for me. The thought flashed through my mind that here was an extraordinarily considerate young man and I would have liked to go on talking with him, but in the melee there was no chance.*[19]

A few nights later Marjorie was surprised to see the same young man at a party given by Edmee Busch Greenough. This mutual friend introduced him as Doctor Thomas King, a promising GP with a burgeoning practice located near Carnegie Hall. Marjorie recalled that they chatted briefly that evening, but she still didn't learn much about this young man whom she found attractive, despite the fact that she was still in love with Serge Obolensky.

The next step in their association was a strange one. Marjorie received a letter from Tom saying he had seen her leaving the Met the previous night and had noticed she was not wearing a hat, despite the cold wind and steady snow fall. In his professional opinion (he wrote), that was extremely foolish and a great risk to her health. A woman with the intellect to memorise the Ring, he concluded, should have better sense.

This curious epistle both angered and intrigued Marjorie. For years she had become accustomed to slavish praise not criticism from people outside the music profession. Tom's address was on the letter so she decided to ring him up and 'give him a piece of her mind'.

> *But I learned it is extremely difficult to rebuke an American southerner. I attempted to castigate him but he replied to my opening tirade in his unruffled, even-measured drawl, and as I waited for him to round out his long, deliberate sentences, my annoyance evaporated.*

The upshot of that phone call was that Marjorie agreed to attend a cocktail party with Tom the following night, but they never made it to the party. Tom arrived to collect Marjorie at six and as Cyril was out for the evening she invited him in. They ended up spending the whole evening talking.

I liked his quiet assertiveness, his provocative ideas, his capacity for sober discussion and the manner in which he took it for granted that the male is the boss.

Marjorie found out a great deal about Tom that evening. First she learned that he was just six weeks older than she, having been born on New Year's Day in the same year. She also discovered that his middle name was Michael, but King was not his family name. He was the second son of Oscar and Mabel Boggs, struggling sharecroppers of Madison County, Indiana, at the time of Tom's birth. Tom related how his family had moved to St Augustine, Florida, soon after his arrival and how his father had found work there as a cook in a humble café, later moving on to Miami and to a similar post in a large hotel. His loving parents (Tom told Marjorie) had worked hard and made many sacrifices to send him to medical school and on his graduation gave their blessing to him changing his name. 'Tom Boggs' he had decided did not sound prepossessing enough for a young doctor, so he became 'Dr Thomas King' legally adopting his mother's family name.

Marjorie found Tom's pride in his humble beginnings endearing and as he prepared to leave that evening, she suggested he accompany her to hear Grace Moore in a much-publicised revival of Montemezzi's opera *L'Amour Dei Tre Rei* at the Met a couple of nights later. Marjorie reported:

That night did it. Serge was still sending me flowers and love notes and seeing me quite often, but after my first night out with Tom King, Serge was out of the race.

Serge Obolensky didn't quit the field until after a confrontation between the two men. This occurred during Marjorie's second performance in *Lohengrin* on 28 February. At her first performance (a month earlier) she had permitted Obolensky to keep her company in her dressing room during the long wait before Ortrud reappears at the end of the opera.[20] At the second performance Obolensky performed the same service and it was while he was sitting holding Marjorie's hand and cooing in her ear that the confrontation occurred.

Suddenly there was a tap on the door and in strode Tom. Smilingly phlegmatic as usual, he very possessively kissed me on the cheek and shook hands with Serge. Serge was beside himself. His eyes narrowed to two steely points of light. Spots of high colour glowed on his cheeks. That another man should visit me at a time he believed sacrosanct to him was outrage enough, but that the interloper should presume to kiss me ... If Tom had any idea of the fire of resentment he set ablaze (and I am positive he did), he gave no hint. He did not even laugh, as I nearly did, when Serge made a sudden dramatic exit, but bade him good-bye with good-natured formality. He did it so perfectly I nearly kissed him there and then. Instead, I patted him on the shoulder, told him to wait and went on stage to finish the opera.

Marjorie and Tom's romance now moved forward like whirlwind, but like a whirlwind it was turbulent and for a while highly unpredictable. Many times they went for long walks along Riverside Drive, rugged up against the cold, arm in arm and totally preoccupied with each other. On one of these walks Tom suddenly detached himself from Marjorie and threw himself onto his back in the snow, then proceeded to flail the snow with his outstretched arms. A bemused and slightly alarmed Marjorie didn't recognise one of the favourite pastimes of American kids in winter. Tom was 'making an angel' and when he stood up there it was – the deep crisp outline of a tall angel with outstretched wings impressed into the fresh snow. From that day forward Marjorie called Tom her 'Angel'. That affectionate name stuck for forty years and Tom reciprocated by calling Marjorie his 'Angel' and, as anyone who knew them later in life might testify, 'angels' flew about in alarming profusion whenever they conversed.

Marriage was proposed and accepted before either party gave thought to the practicalities of their union. Arguments then flared, mostly over one of the character traits Marjorie had first admired in Tom – his assertion that a husband must be 'the boss' – and especially over money. Marjorie decided she would let her fiancée have his way on the first issue and act dutifully until after they were married, subsequently (as she admits in *Interrupted Melody*) showing him who was really boss. Marjorie's candour about this suggests she planned to do this with consideration for Tom's feelings, but there were no such considerations from either party when they argued over money. Tom had no income outside his medical practice and that was not large or very profitable. Marjorie on the other hand had declared an annual income for the previous year of just over $34,000 – a vast sum at a time when the basic wage in the US was about $2000. Marjorie proudly told Tom that her income would allow him to give up the drudgery of his present life and share the luxury of hers. Tom exploded and insisted he was not giving up his career to become 'Mr Lawrence' or traipse around the country with her like a lapdog, and if that was a condition of their marriage, Marjorie would have to find another prospective husband. After one particularly acrimonious argument along these lines, Tom walked out on Marjorie.

> *I was dumbfounded. I wanted to shout to him to come back. But I could not. I just sat there, my hand over my mouth, unable to believe what had happened. I had offered this man everything I had and everything I was. And he, the stupid ungrateful fool, had walked out on me. No man had ever done that to me before. I was angry, hurt and humiliated.*

During the ghastly week (Marjorie's description) that followed, Marjorie heard nothing from Tom and she was so upset she made herself ill. This was the mystery malady that forced her to withdraw from *Alceste* and with hindsight it is possible to speculate that the turmoil in her private life was also a factor in her lack of success in that role.

A reconciliation was brokered by a mutual friend and Tom came back to the Ansonia bearing a modest bunch of flowers. Marjorie was desperately relieved to see him, but her pride was too damaged to allow her to let him off the hook too soon. She admonished him for walking out on her and as she was speaking he spied a bunch of long-stemmed roses on the table. Assuming – wrongly as it turned out – that they were from Serge Obolensky, Tom seized them and hurled them out of a window, where they fell on the heads of passers-by on Broadway. The pair argued until they were quite exhausted, finally collapsing tearfully into each other's arms at midnight, with both agreeing that nothing mattered but their being together and that everything else could be sorted later.

And Marjorie wasn't only arguing with Tom during this time. Cyril was aghast at the prospect of his sister rejecting a prince in favour of, as he put it, 'a dollar chaser looking for a meal ticket' and even more distraught to see his position as the main man in her life supplanted. In *Interrupted Melody* Marjorie claims that Cyril threatened to have Tom 'bumped off' if she didn't give him up, but Cyril denied that to his dying day. Years later Tom put paid to Marjorie's claim by saying it had been her way of getting back at Cyril for having made a pass at Tom himself.

Marjorie and Tom were married on 29 March 1941. Marjorie spent the previous two days in hiding (she says from Cyril, but more likely from the press) in a Brooklyn Heights hotel, although on the night before the wedding she was soloist in a concert with the New York Philharmonic. The ceremony was held in the historic Plymouth Church of the Pilgrims in Brooklyn and conducted by the pastor, Dr Stanley Durkee, a friend of Tom's. Before leaving the Ansonia, Marjorie had left a note for Cyril telling him where and when the ceremony was to take place and asking him to be there. Marjorie, Tom, Betty Bee, Henry Phohl and another friend of Tom's, Bob Hilton, were all assembled on the steps of the church and the organist had struck up the Bridal March from *Lohengrin* when a taxi screeched to a halt and out leapt Cyril. Marjorie braced herself for a scene, but instead her brother embraced her, shook Tom's hand and wished them both good luck and happiness.

After the ceremony the party emerged to find a crowd of journalists and photographers, tipped off by a publicity-keen church secretary. The photographs taken show Marjorie wearing one of her distinctive hats, clutching an armful of American Beauty roses and looking adoringly at her new husband. Tom looks equally smitten and we can see the tiny sprig of wattle someone had provided for him to wear as a buttonhole in tribute to Marjorie's homeland.

During the service Tom had made a vow to love and care for Marjorie in sickness and in health. Although neither had any inkling of it as they strolled arm in arm back to the Brooklyn Hotel, where a small wedding breakfast awaited them, that vow would be severely tested in a very short time.

Chapter Thirteen

'Was ich liebe, muss ich verlassen'

As soon as a date for their marriage had been decided, Marjorie and Tom had set about finding a place to live afterwards. Tom made it clear that he had no intention of living at the Ansonia (that 'hothouse of egos' as he called it) and Marjorie refused to move into his pokey apartment near Carnegie Hall. Instead they took out a bank loan and purchased a spacious apartment on the second floor of 1609 West 73rd Street, near Verdi Square. They also leased a modest beach house at Long Beach, intending to spend their summers there. It was at the beach house the couple enjoyed the first idyllic two weeks of their honeymoon.

> The gentle surf sang us to sleep at nights and in the mornings the sea mist swept through our open windows. We defied the cold and swam nearly every day. Tom hired a couple of bikes and we rode all over the countryside. Other days we forsook our bikes and walked for miles along the hard, pebbly beach.[1]

Marjorie also indulged in bouts of wishful thinking at this time, writing across the April pages of her diary 'Going to France with Husband to have a Baby', and across the month of May (which had not yet arrived), the single word 'Germany' – by which she meant singing in Bayreuth, Berlin or Munich. Had the war not intervened, Marjorie might well have been taking Tom back to Paris to show him off to her French friends and going on to sing Wagner in that composer's homeland.

There was nothing fanciful about the cable – and which Marjorie might have considered the perfect wedding present from the Met – she received while at Long Beach from Edward Johnson:

> Flagstad not likely available us next season. Hold yourself ready sing Isolde and Kundry as well as other roles. Regards Johnson.[2]

Flagstad, it transpired, had advised Johnson through an intermediary that she intended returning to German-occupied Norway and sitting out the rest of the war at the side of her businessman husband Henry Johansen. As Johansen was a member of the Quisling Party in Norway and a supplier of lumber to the occupying forces, the German Embassy in Washington issued her with a German passport and she had promptly departed, leaving the Met minus its biggest drawcard.[3]

For Marjorie everything was now falling into place. She was married to a good man she loved and who loved her in return and her career was about to soar to new heights. When she returned to the Met in November she would no longer be singing in Flagstad's shadow and would be rightfully acknowledged as the company's leading dramatic soprano. The torch was about to be passed and she knew she was ready, physically and vocally to seize it and carry it aloft.

After receiving the cable and replying to Johnson that she was ready to meet whatever challenges the next Met season offered, Marjorie and Tom set out to spend the second half of their honeymoon in Mexico. Marjorie had a contract to fulfil there and despite his refusal to traipse around after Marjorie, Tom had agreed to treat this journey as their official honeymoon trip. They first visited a colleague of Tom's in New York who administered their regulation smallpox 'shots', Tom taking his in the arm and Marjorie hers in her right leg. Marjorie and Tom took twelve days to cover the 2000-odd miles from New York to Mexico City, driving a rented car at a leisurely pace and taking in the sights along the way.[4] Meanwhile, Cyril (who was still officially Marjorie's manager) flew to Mexico City to make arrangements for the arrival of his sister and brother-in-law.

According to the contract signed in January Marjorie was to appear as the principal guest artist in the inaugural season of the Mexican National Opera. This was a state-sponsored organisation charged with establishing a permanent opera company and producing regular seasons in the Mexican capital. Marjorie had agreed to sing Brünnhilde in *Die Walküre*, Salome and Carmen. Mostly local singers were to fill the supporting roles and the musical director was Karl Alwin, another refugee from Nazism. The performances were to be given in the beautiful, 3500-seat Palacio de Belles Artes, famous for its Tiffany stage curtain studded with millions of opalescent crystals. Marjorie had been offered $US5000 for seven performances and paid an advance of $600. That advance would later be a bone of great contention between Marjorie and the company when she was unable to fulfil her contract.

Light-hearted and perfectly healthy during the journey, Marjorie began to experience severe and persistent headaches accompanied by back pain on arrival in Mexico City. These she and Tom put down to the stress caused by the weight of responsibility Marjorie carried for the success of the opera season. Never one to shirk her duty, Marjorie swallowed aspirin, tried to ignore the pain and, with both Tom and Cyril keeping watchful eyes on her, got on with the round of social engagements, publicity appearances and other commitments that are incidental to any opera season.

Marjorie was to open the season in *Die Walküre* and when she left her hotel to attend the final dress rehearsal, she admitted to Tom that she was feeling sicker than she ever had before. On arriving at the theatre she donned her costume and sat out the first act, waiting for her entry in the second. In the excitement of listening to the opera taking shape on stage and warming up her voice, Marjorie forgot the pain. She sailed out onto the stage confidently, but when she began to sing the pain returned with redoubled violence. It felt, she later recalled, as though the top of her head was lifting off each time she took one of the high notes in Brünnhilde's Battle Cry.

Interrupted Melody contains a fictionalised version of what happened next, with Marjorie collapsing dramatically on stage, awakening to find her legs paralysed and being carried from the theatre with Tom in tears and her colleagues looking shocked and frightened. The testimony of others present and Marjorie's own notes show that in fact she managed to complete Act Two, despite suddenly and unexpectedly losing control over her right knee. The joint wobbled threateningly when she put any weight on it and Marjorie found she was unable to rise from a kneeling position unaided. Feeling unwell and alarmed at the behaviour of her knee, Marjorie appealed to Maestro Alwin, who stopped the rehearsal. Marjorie apologised to him and the rest of the cast, explaining she felt too ill to continue.

Marjorie's colleagues clustered around her making solicitous noises and, if they looked frightened as *Interrupted Melody* suggests, it may have been out of concern for their own fate should the company's prima donna not be recovered in time for the beginning of the season the following night. Tom and Cyril bundled Marjorie into a taxi and whisked her back to their hotel, where she immediately took to her bed. A doctor on the staff of the theatre arrived soon after and examined her. His diagnosis was that Marjorie was suffering from altitude sickness and that if she rested, her body would soon acclimatise and her symptoms disappear. Tom was not satisfied with that. His medical knowledge and experience told him there was something more seriously wrong with his wife, whose condition was worsening rapidly. He tried to get a neurologist to come to the hotel, but discovered that medical specialists in Mexico (as in most places) don't like making house calls.

During the night Marjorie's condition continued to deteriorate. Her body was wracked with pain, her temperature soared and she vomited continuously. She also slipped in and out of consciousness and in her waking moments was delirious, imagining that Christ's Apostles were gathered around her bed waiting to take her on a long journey. Later she recalled with lingering dread:

> *I know I should have died that night and my apostolic imaginings could have been linked to my subconscious acceptance of that fact. In what few rational moments I did have that terrible night, I would have welcomed death; better death than unrelenting agony.*[5]

Marjorie's body also began to be overtaken by paralysis, beginning in her legs. After more frantic calls from Tom, the neurologist attended Marjorie at four the next morning. He examined her and admitted he was not sure what was wrong with her, suggesting it was 'inflammation of the nerves' possibly brought on by a reaction to the smallpox immunisation she had had, or possibly that most dreaded of diseases at the time – poliomyelitis. The neurologist suggested transferring Marjorie to the American Hospital in another part of the city where he could conduct tests to try to pinpoint the cause. Marjorie was taken by ambulance to the hospital and Tom reported:

> *Marjorie was in agony and she was completely paralysed from the neck down. The hospital doctors told me that they believed she had polio and that it was one of the most virulent cases of the disease they had seen. If she lived, they said, she would never walk again – or sing again. I insisted they kept their diagnosis a secret from Marjorie for the time being and I tried to comfort her by letting her think that whatever she had she would slough off in a few weeks.*[6]

Meanwhile the opera company was in turmoil. On the day the season was to have commenced, it was announced in the press that there would be a two-week postponement and that the management hoped their star would be completely recovered by then and able to take her place at the head of the company. Based on advice from Cyril, who liaised with the opera management, substitute singers were hastily lined up in case Marjorie did not recover in time. Rose Pauly agreed to sing Salome and Carmen and Dorothee Manski, to sing Brünnhilde. Both artists stood by to fly south if they were needed.[7]

Marjorie remained in the American Hospital as the days ticked by, receiving as much help as the medical staff could provide. Her condition improved slightly, but the pain and the paralysis remained. Diathermy (the application of electric current to produce heat in the deeper tissues of the body) was the only therapy they could offer, but Tom was wary of the Mexican doctors' ability to apply that treatment safely.

Poliomyelitis – or 'Infantile Paralysis' as it was commonly called because of the large number of children afflicted by the disease and its most obvious symptom – was not well understood by the medical profession at that time and the treatments offered (such as diathermy) were largely experimental. There was no cure and the most that victims of the disease could hope for was amelioration of some of their symptoms and mechanical support for the now paralysed bodily functions. Tom was distraught and frustrated:

> *Marjorie's utter helplessness nearly killed* me *because I knew how she loathed being served and handled. The pain continued and I soon realised that the Mexican doctors were unable to help her. I went to the head doctor and demanded to know what else he planned to do for her. He shrugged and admitted there was nothing more they could do or were equipped to do.*[8]

Cyril meanwhile had returned to New York to arrange for the cancellation of all Marjorie's immediate engagements. News of her illness had been cabled to the

US and there was much speculation in the major newspapers about her future, so Cyril issued a statement saying that his sister's illness was the result of an adverse reaction to her smallpox immunisation and that she was 'not suffering too much' and had regained a little movement in her left leg. She hoped, Cyril said, to be back on her feet and able to resume her career in a few weeks.

Cyril did not mention polio in his statement and several possible reasons suggest themselves for that omission. Firstly, Tom might have kept Cyril in the dark about the diagnosis the doctors at the American Hospital in Mexico City had made, or he might have decided on his own initiative that it was in his sister's best interests for the American public to believe her illness was something more transient. Another possible reason is that Cyril's assessment was correct and that the cause of Marjorie's condition was not poliomyelitis at all.

In later years both Marjorie and Tom were adamant that Marjorie was a polio victim. By then they had become involved in the national crusade against the disease and were using Marjorie's case for its publicity value, so it would have suited them to conceal any doubts they might once have had. However, not all characteristics of Marjorie's case support that claim. Based on the limited records we have of her illness and drawing on the greater knowledge the medical profession now has about both poliomyelitis and reactions to immunisation, questions arise – questions worthy of our interest, but which at this distance in time we cannot hope to answer confidently.

A good case could be made for poliomyelitis. Some of Marjorie's symptoms were typical of that disease: headache, fever, paralysis (tending to greater severity in the legs than the arms) and so on, but others, such as loss of consciousness and sporadic loss of vision (which Marjorie claims she suffered) would not be expected. These and other characteristics of Marjorie's case suggest she might have suffered an immunological reaction to the smallpox vaccination, triggering a combination of acute disseminated encephalomyelitis and an acute inflammatory polyradiculopathy. Had Marjorie suffered her illness today she would have been subjected to sophisticated neurological tests and a positive diagnosis made rapidly, but that was not possible in 1941. The truth about the nature of Marjorie's illness, therefore, remains a mystery.

Although undoubtedly at the time Tom speculated about the nature of his wife's illness, her suffering would have been foremost in his mind. He decided Marjorie needed to be taken back to the United States where, he hoped, she could receive more sophisticated care and treatment. Reluctantly he left Marjorie to fly back to New York to consult with what he hoped were more knowledgeable specialists, although he received little comfort from this four-day trip, except a suggestion to get Marjorie to Hot Springs, Arkansas, where the therapeutic waters might alleviate her pain. Otherwise the prognosis was the same from each expert he spoke to. If Marjorie had polio, they said, there was little they could do for her. Deeply disheartened, Tom flew back to Mexico City.

Marjorie was overjoyed to have Tom at her side again, but her condition remained unchanged. She was (as Cyril had reported) able to move her left leg very slightly, but the pain that wracked her body and intensified whenever she was moved, showed no signs of abating. Tom contacted the US ambassador to Mexico, Josephus Daniels, who had been planning a reception for Marjorie at the embassy, and asked for his help to get Marjorie out of Mexico. While Daniels persuaded Pan American Airways to remove seats from one of their US-bound aircraft to accommodate a stretcher, Tom obtained a certificate from one of the Mexican doctors authorising Marjorie's transfer to Saint Joseph's Hospital, Hot Springs. Marjorie was relieved to be going back to the United States but terrified of the journey.

> *To my mind, almost unhinged by pain and the partial realization of what was happening to me, the prospect of the long journey was terrifying. I was prepared to give up the ghost. I begged Tom to let me remain where I was. I was going to die. Why inflict new tortures on me? My poor husband was not far from the end of his own tether, but with superhuman patience and gentleness, he told me that once we got to Hot Springs, something would be done to relieve my suffering ... there were facilities there, too, for the treatment that would put me back on my feet, he told me, and didn't I want to be fit for the Metropolitan season?*[9]

On 4 July – Independence Day in the United States – Marjorie and Tom set out on the first stage of their journey to Hot Springs on a Douglas DC3, bound for Brownsville, Texas. Marjorie was carried onto the plane, swathed in blankets and groggy from pain killers, but with her face still carefully made up and putting on a brave smile for the pack of Mexican press photographers who had come to 'snap' her ignoble departure from their city.

The flight was accomplished without incident, Marjorie lapsing in and out of sleep, reassured by Tom each time she woke that they were 'nearly there'. An ambulance was waiting at Brownsville, which took them to the Catholic Hospital. There the sisters cared for Marjorie while Tom planned the next stage of their journey. Without an ambassador's influence, he was unable to persuade any airline to fly them the remaining 500 miles to Hot Springs, but the Missouri Pacific Railway agreed to carry them to Benton, the nearest station to Hot Springs. Tom reluctantly broke the news to Marjorie that she now had a two-and-a-half-day train journey to endure.

> *Again my courage deserted me. Again I begged to be left where I was. But again too, Tom rallied my waning spirits and we set off. The journey seemed to take an eternity. The train crew had been told I was aboard and the driver glided the locomotive into every stop and eased it off on every start with amazing smoothness. Even so, my unhappy body was in such a state that it was never free from torment. I cursed my moments of awareness and yearned for the merciful fog of unconsciousness to envelop me.*[10]

Another ambulance was waiting when they finally disembarked at Benton and Marjorie and Tom were driven the last twenty-five miles into Hot Springs, where Dr George Fletcher and the staff of St Joseph's Hospital were waiting to receive them.

Marjorie was in such a poor state after the journey that Fletcher advised three days complete rest before she began thermal water treatment. On the fourth day a bath was placed beside Marjorie's bed and she was rolled into the heated, mineral-rich water. This procedure was followed several times daily and as soon as Marjorie was strong enough the treatment was transferred to the Maurice Bathhouse on Bathhouse Row, which specialised in patients with paralysis. Massage was not part of Dr Fletcher's treatment plan for Marjorie, so Tom secretly massaged her arms and legs at night, and these combined treatments eventually began to alleviate Marjorie's pain.

Dr Fletcher had wide experience of polio and, when he concurred with the Mexican doctors' diagnosis, Tom decided it was time to tell Marjorie the truth as he saw it – that she was a victim of polio and if she recovered, even partially, it would take many months and maybe years. Marjorie was devastated.

> *As the pain ebbed my mind began to take in the full scope of my tragedy. Would I ever walk again? Would the paralysis affect my voice? Would I get to sing Isolde and Kundry at the Met? Was my career at an end? Even worse, was I condemned to spend the rest of my life in a hospital bed? Terror and foreboding overpowered me and I wept for days. My depression was accentuated by the hospital atmosphere, the constant handling as though I was a piece of meat, by being cooped up in one room and knowing there were sick and suffering people all around me. The nursing staff were the soul of goodness, consideration and efficiency, but I was forced to tell Tom that if he didn't get me out of that place and quickly, I would go mad.*[11]

Tom was occupying the room next to Marjorie's and paying a patient's fee for the privilege, adding to the pile of bills that was rapidly accumulating, so he was also keen to move out of St Joseph's. Dr Fletcher gave his approval for Tom and Marjorie to live outside the hospital and return for her treatment every second day, but when Tom went house hunting it proved more difficult than he expected.

It was high season in Hot Springs and tourists filled most of the rental accommodation. Tom had almost despaired of finding anywhere when the driver of the ambulance that ferried Marjorie between the hospital and the bath house mentioned that he knew of a place that might suit them. At his suggestion he drove Tom down Highway 7 South and, twelve miles out of Hot Springs, turned into the gateway of a property called 'Villa Rustica'. A long, flower-lined driveway led to a spacious, stone house that blended perfectly with the landscape.

The taxi driver introduced Tom to the owner, a Mrs Mary Hedrick, whom Tom later described to Marjorie as 'a fine Southern lady'. Mrs Hedrick showed

Tom over the house and the garden and he was enchanted by all he saw. Mrs Hedrick's late husband had designed and built the house in the 1920s. The architectural style of the building – which still stands – is original, but 'Pueblo' influence is apparent in its sharp lines and flat roof. Two small streams teeming with fish flowed down the rocky, wooded hill behind the house and two large ponds (which Marjorie later insisted on calling 'lakes') fringed with pines and willows formed a backdrop to the garden.

The house was actually three residences in one, each occupying a separate wing and each with its own entrance. Mrs Hedrick explained that she was having difficulty maintaining the twenty-room building on the limited profits the surrounding farmlands earned and had decided to rent out one wing to, as she put it, 'nice folks'. When Tom explained who he and Marjorie were and Marjorie's situation, Mrs Hedrick decided they were more than 'nice' enough and a deal was struck there and then. Marjorie and Tom acquired a peaceful, comfortable, private, five-room, ground-level home with free run of the rest of the house and the garden for a fraction of the cost of two hospital rooms. They also acquired a devoted friend in Mary Hedrick and she two new friends who became generous employers when Marjorie and Tom bought the property two years later and kept her on as farm manager.

When Tom told Marjorie about his find and described Villa Rustica, she was as delighted by the place and its chatelaine as Tom had been.

> *Directly we moved to 'Villa Rustica' my morale improved. Part of every day I spent out of doors in the sunshine. And I know no Australian, young or old, robust or feeble who is not better off for a few hours in the sun. Helpless though I was, and unable to move, I began to feel a little pleasure again in life as I lay on a stretcher in the warmth and colour of Mrs Hedrick's flower-filled garden.*[12]

Marjorie's mood improved and her pain receded, but the paralysis remained and as the weeks passed Tom became ever more anxious to find some treatment that would prevent that from becoming a permanent state. Marjorie was only thirty-four and could confidently look forward to another forty years of life, but the prospect of her spending all that time lying rigid on her back was more than he or she could bear.

A further stimulus to action came in a succession of cables from Edward Johnson and Edward Ziegler making ever more urgent inquiries about Marjorie's health. Losing Flagstad had been a terrible blow for the Met, but the prospect of losing its other leading female Wagnerian at the same time was a disaster. Marjorie asked Dr Fletcher to write to Ziegler and explain her condition and, perhaps at her request, Fletcher put an optimistic spin on his account of her illness and her progress, but wisely did not make any predictions about when she might be well enough to resume her career. That letter must have encouraged Johnson and Ziegler, but likely did little to put their minds at rest.[13]

Tom decided their best option lay in contacting Sister Kenny, an Australian nurse working at the University of Minnesota Hospital in Minneapolis. Elizabeth Kenny was a formidable, out-spoken sixty-year-old Australian with very little formal medical training who had been achieving good results in treating the effects of polio. Kenny's theories about the disease and her methods of treating it were unconventional and had put her at odds with the mainstream medical profession for most of her career, but the results she produced spoke for themselves.

Tom wrote to Sister Kenny who replied promptly saying that, if he brought Marjorie to Minneapolis, she would do all she could to help. Marjorie was loaded onto a train at Benton and Sister Kenny was waiting with an ambulance when they reached Minneapolis on 26 August. Immediately on arrival at the university hospital, Kenny submitted Marjorie to a rigorous examination.

Dear Sister Kenny was a big, powerful Amazon and where it had taken two or three people to lift me in Hot Springs, she picked me up like a baby then proceeded to bend, stretch and squeeze my arms and legs brutally. At Hot Springs the doctors had treated me like I was made of glass, not even touching my limbs for fear of hurting me and doing more damage. Kenny first lay me facedown grasped both my ankles and bent my legs as far they would go. Next she rolled me over and endeavoured to push my legs up until my big toes nearly touched my forehead, then set to work on my arms and my shoulders and neck. The 'examination', if you could call it that, was so terrifying I could hardly speak for three days.[14]

Sister Kenny told Tom that she had no doubt that Marjorie had polio, and in an advanced stage. Kenny also explained that her best results were achieved when she was able to commence treatment within a few days of the patient contracting the disease. She therefore had doubts about how useful her procedures might be with a patient who was now in the third month of their illness. 'But, rest assured Dr King,' she said, 'I will do my *best*.'[15]

Tom moved into the university faculty club just a block from the hospital and Kenny, her adopted daughter Mary, and a small team of assistants commenced Marjorie's treatment the following day. To Marjorie's relief this proved less brutal than the examination and consisted of heat packs applied to all the affected parts of her body, primarily to stop muscular spasms, intramuscular injections of Vitamin E and what Sister Kenny called 'muscle re-education' – the coaxing back into life of wasted muscles. This was done by massage, passive movement (manipulation) and the encouragement of active movement by the patient herself.

During the first month, Marjorie's body began, as she put it, to slowly 'awaken'. Almost imperceptibly she began to twitch her toes and move her fingers, then lift first one shoulder then the other. As she developed strength in her upper body, she was able her sit up in bed supported by pillows, and by late September she could write and knit – to strengthen her fingers. For the first time the press were admitted to Marjorie's hospital room, where she and Tom tried to answer questions to which neither knew the answers. Photographs were taken, with Tom looking dapper and Marjorie looking brave, her hair carefully brushed, nails painted and lipstick applied; both their faces showing the determination that had carried them through thus far.

Every attainment, no matter how small, was a cause for celebration, but progress was frustratingly slow. Cables kept arriving from the Met and Marjorie slipped back into periods of deep depression as she realised her great opportunity was slipping away. Reluctantly she wrote to Edward Johnson to inform him that, barring a miracle, she would not be able to rejoin the company for the 1941–42 season. Johnson wrote a touching letter in reply, addressing Marjorie by the name he had adopted for her when she first came to New York.

My dear Margie:

Thank you for your kind letter and I can never tell you with what a heavy heart I announced to the press at our meeting a few days ago that you would be unable to take over your roles at the beginning of the coming season. However, I did hold out to them the ray of hope which you conveyed to me, by the reference to your 'Aussie pep', that you might resume your work with us for the second half of the season.

You will never know how our hearts go out to you in this very difficult moment and how our devout wishes are continually reaching out in your behalf. We will miss you more than I have words to tell but will live in the hope that the miracle of which you speak will return you to us sooner than anyone anticipates.

Please keep us informed of your condition and if there is anything we can do please do not hesitate to write. God bless you and keep your chin up.

Affectionately yours,
Edward Johnson.[16]

Letters, cards and cables from colleagues, friends, fans and acquaintances from all over the world had arrived in Mexico City, Hot Springs and Minneapolis. Typical was one from Irene Jessner who was singing in Buenos Aires and had collected the signatures of most of the artists at the Colón that season, including Erich Kleiber, Herbert Janssen and the team of Valkyries whom Marjorie would have been leading had fate not intervened.[17] Vincent Attractions wrote or cabled regularly, detailing the dozens of offers of engagements they had received from all over the United States for Marjorie to replace Flagstad. Encouraging though the news and kind wishes were, they also brought home to Marjorie the magnitude of her loss.

To assist her mentally, Tom sought Sister Kenny's permission for them to live away from hospital again and for Marjorie to attend as an outpatient. Kenny agreed, but only on condition they took a small apartment that was vacant in the building where she and her daughter lived, so they could come to Marjorie's aid at any time. A bond deeper than common nationality was developing between Marjorie and Kenny, each recognising the other's strength and courage, with Kenny (not unreasonably) devoting extra time and attention to a high-profile patient whose recovery would boost her own reputation. Tom was also deeply impressed by Kenny and began to attend the classes she ran for medical professionals who wanted to learn her methods. He reasoned that this knowledge and skill would enable him to take over some and eventually all of Marjorie's treatment and treat other polio victims if he returned to his medical practice. The desire to fill his days with activity and keep despair at bay was another motive.

The move into an apartment brought some temporary relief to the drain Marjorie's illness was having on their finances. Marjorie had earned much but saved little, anticipating that her income would grow and never imagining it would dry up. Funds she had in France had been confiscated by the Germans and some of the profit from her Australian tour which she had been forced to leave behind in Australia was now frozen under government wartime regulations. Tom's savings were as modest as his earnings, but at least they were unencumbered. Using their available funds he had paid Marjorie's medical bills in Mexico City and Hot Springs but cash was running low. Sister Kenny did not charge any of her patients, but the vitamin injections she prescribed for Marjorie were costly and so were the University Hospital fees. So far Marjorie's illness had cost somewhere in the region of $10,000 and no respite from bills was in sight. Mortgage payments also had to be found for the unoccupied apartment in New York and rent for the house in Long Beach.

As soon as Marjorie was settled into the Minneapolis apartment, a maid engaged to look after her and reassurances received from the Kennys, Tom drove back to New York. He found a tenant for the 73rd Street apartment, whose rental payments would cover the mortgage repayments, and managed to terminate the lease on the beach house. He then set about disposing of as many of his and Marjorie's possessions as he could before packing their clothes, personal items and Marjorie's scores and costumes for shipping to Minneapolis.

Disposing of his own possessions was easy enough, but when it came to making decisions about his wife's, Tom found that taxing. When the time came to consider the fate of Marjorie's bicycle – the one Hubert Opperman had given her in Australia – Tom's courage deserted him and he cabled her: 'Precious Angel, confirm OK to sell bike? Tom'. Two hours later a reply came back: 'Refuse sell bicycle. Am not dead yet. Dismount handles pedals & store. Love Marjorie.' In years to come, Tom would say that he knew Marjorie was going to make it through her long and cruel ordeal from the moment he received that cable. Chuckling to himself for the first time in months, he dutifully dismantled the bike and packed it away for the day Marjorie might ride it again.

Marjorie's father, William Lawrence, photographed in Geelong, Victoria, around the time of his marriage to Marjorie's mother, 1898.

Marjorie singing at radio station 3LO, Melbourne, June 1928.

Ivor Boustead, Marjorie's singing teacher in Melbourne.

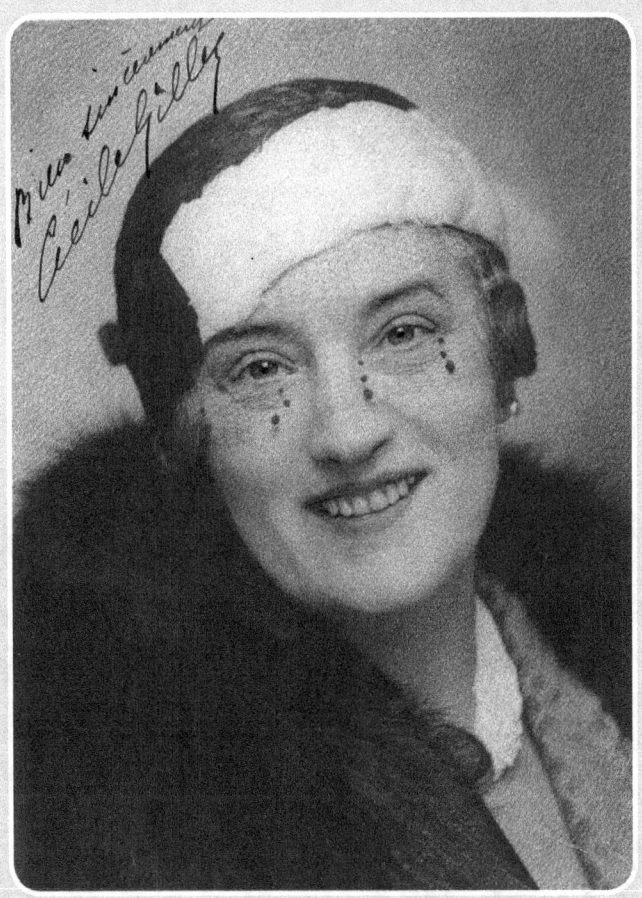

Cécile Gilly, Marjorie's singing teacher in Paris.

Marjorie (centre, holding handbag) with family and friends on the deck of S.S. *Jervis Bay* at Port Melbourne on the day she departed for Paris, 23 October 1928. Her father stands on her left.

Marjorie (centre) posing with Gladys Petrie and Marguerite Palustre (with parasol) at the auberge in Euse, Midi-Pyrénées, June 1929. This photograph was taken by fellow Australian Rita Miller.

Marjorie as Brünnhilde at the time that she sang this role in *Die Walküre* at Lille, January 1933.

Marjorie in various roles: (*from top*) as Ortrud in Wagner's *Lohengrin* at her Paris Opéra debut, 25 February 1933; in *Die Walküre*, Paris Opéra, April 1933; as Keltis in Canteloube's *Vercingetorix*, a role she created at the Paris Opéra, 22 June 1933.

Marjorie as Brünnhilde in *Die Walküre* at the time of her Metropolitan Opera debut, New York, December 1935. Later Marjorie would comment that it was prophetic that this, the most widely published of the photographs taken at her New York debut, should have shown her seated.

An elated Marjorie backstage after she had ridden this stage horse into Siegfried's funeral pyre at the conclusion of *Götterdämmerung* at the Metropolitan Opera, New York, 11 January 1936.

Marjorie in the suite she lived in at the Ansonia Hotel, New York, 1936.

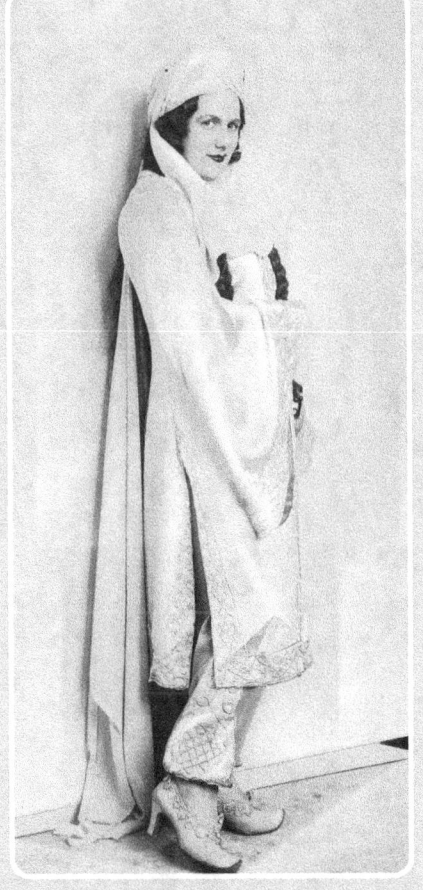

Elegance: Marjorie as Rachel in Halévy's *La Juive*, Metropolitan Opera, New York, January 1936; Cyril (Percy) Lawrence, New York, December 1938. Cyril always wanted to belong to the beautiful set.

Marjorie in the title role of Strauss's *Salome*, Metropolitan Opera, New York, February 1938. She wears the famous costume designed for her by Freddie Wittop of Folies-Bergère fame.

A studio portrait New York, 1939.

Riding at Deans Marsh, Victoria, during her 1939 Australian tour.

Cyril Lawrence, Marjorie and Felix Wolfes in Hawaii, September 1939.

Studio portrait, 1941.

With Lauritz Melchior after a joint recital they gave in Toronto, 25 November 1939.

In the title role of Gluck's *Alceste*: dress rehearsal for the first production at the Metropolitan Opera, January 1941.

As Bizet's *Carmen*, at the time she first sang this role in St Louis, April 1940.

Marjorie and Tom on their wedding day, Plymouth Church of the Pilgrims, Brooklyn, 29 March 1941.

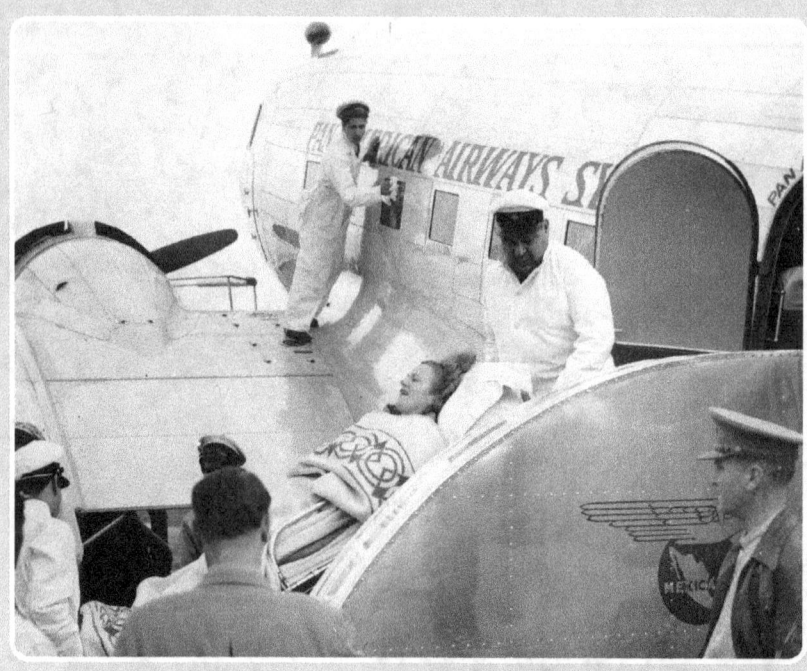

Marjorie leaving Mexico City on a Pan American flight bound for Brownsville, Texas, 4 July 1941; four weeks after she was stricken with polio.

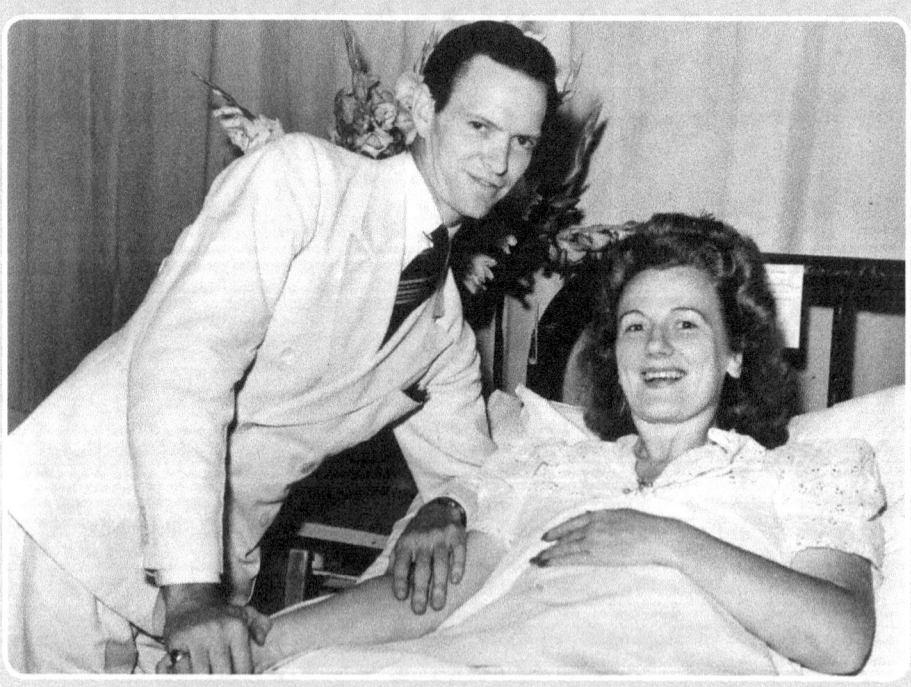

Tom and Marjorie at Minneapolis University Hospital where she received treatment from fellow Australian, Sister Elizabeth Kenny, August 1941.

Marjorie surrounded by admiring fans after her New York Town Hall 'comeback' concert, 29 November 1942.

Singing Venus in the Venusberg scene from Wagner's *Tannhäuser* with Lauritz Melchior as Tannhäuser during the tribute concert to benefit Marjorie at the Metropolitan Opera, 27 December 1942 – Marjorie's first opera appearance after her illness.

Marjorie at a luncheon in the State Dining Room of the White House to celebrate President Roosevelt's 61st birthday. *Left to right:* Eleanor Roosevelt and movie stars Dennis Morgan, Roy Rogers and Loretta Young, 30 January 1943.

With conductor Sir Thomas Beecham after Marjorie had sung Isolde in Montreal, 27 May 1943, Beecham told the press that in his opinion Marjorie was the finest dramatic soprano in the world.

Act 1 of *Tristan und Isolde* at the Metropolitan Opera, New York, 14 March 1944. Marjorie (*centre*) singing Isolde, Lauritz Melchior as Tristan and Kerstin Thorborg as Brangäne.

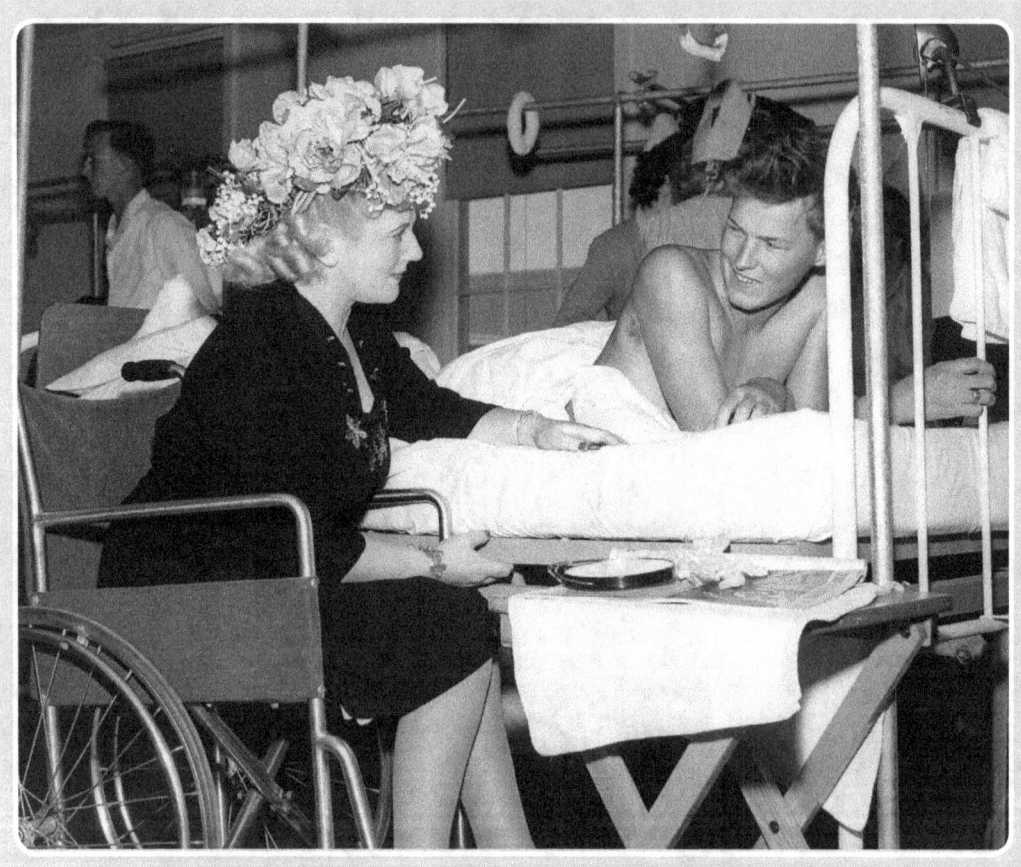
Marjorie with Private First Class Lawrence Barr, one of hundreds of patients at American military hospitals that Marjorie visited in the early 1940s.

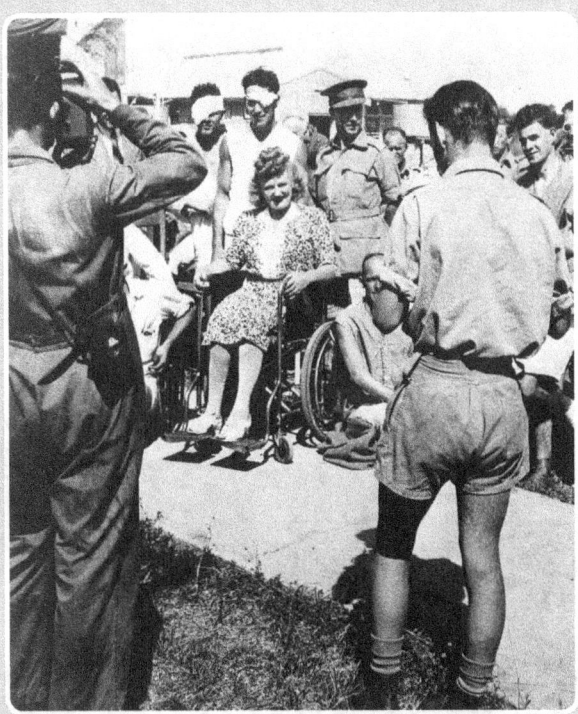

Marjorie with patients and staff at one of the military hospitals that she visited in the Northern Territory, Australia, in July 1944.

Marjorie, Tom, Amy Featherstone and RAF Flying Officer Templar (in shirt sleeves) beside one of the crematorium ovens at Belsen Concentration Camp, Germany, 20 July 1945.

Her Majesty Queen Elizabeth and their Royal Highnesses Princess Elizabeth and Princess Margaret chatting with Marjorie and Tom after Marjorie performed at Buckingham Palace, 1 August 1945.

The homestead at 'Harmony Hills' near Hot Springs, Arkansas – Marjorie and Tom's home from 1943 to 1975 and the venue for Marjorie's annual summer opera workshops.

With one of their devoted German Shepherds at 'Harmony Hills', 1946. Marjorie's wheelchair is parked in the shadows while she supports herself on the gate.

Marjorie singing with L'Orchestre National de Paris at the 'Penicillin' Gala, Théatre National de Chaillot, Paris, 16 October 1946.

Marjorie with the commanding officers of the occupying forces in Berlin after a historic concert in the Titania Palast, 30 December 1946, at which Marjorie performed with the Berlin Philharmonic. *Left to right*: Brigadier-General Charles Gailey (US Army), General Aleksandr Kotikov (Soviet Army), Major-General Frank Keating (US Army), Sir Brian Robertson (British Army), General Lucius D. Clay (US Army) and General Charles Noiret (French Army).

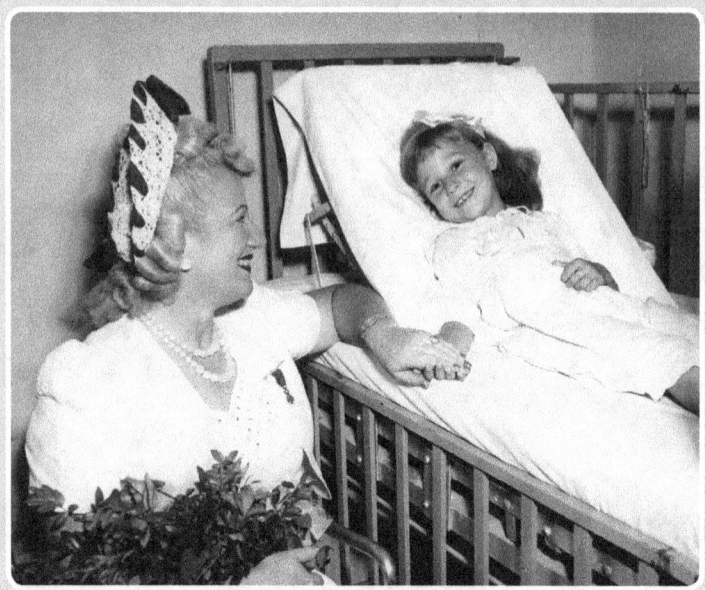

Marjorie visits another polio victim. Marjorie wears the miniature version of her Légion d'honneur award, presented to her by colleagues at the Paris Opéra in 1946.

Marjorie signing copies of the Australian edition of her autobiography *Interrupted Melody* during her 1949 Australian tour.

Marjorie as Amneris with her 'slaves' ready for their entrance at a performance of Verdi's *Aida* at the Princess Theatre, Melbourne, 1951.

Marjorie as the guest of honour on the NBC television program 'This is Your Life', Hollywood, 17 May 1955. *Left to right:* Ralph Edwards (creator and host of the program), Lawrence Tibbett, Mimi Grodet, Wynn Rocamura, Tom, Lauritz Melchior, Edward Johnson and Marjorie's brothers Ted and Cyril.

Marjorie and Tom with Eleanor Parker who played Marjorie in the film *Interrupted Melody*, on the set of 'This is Your Life'.

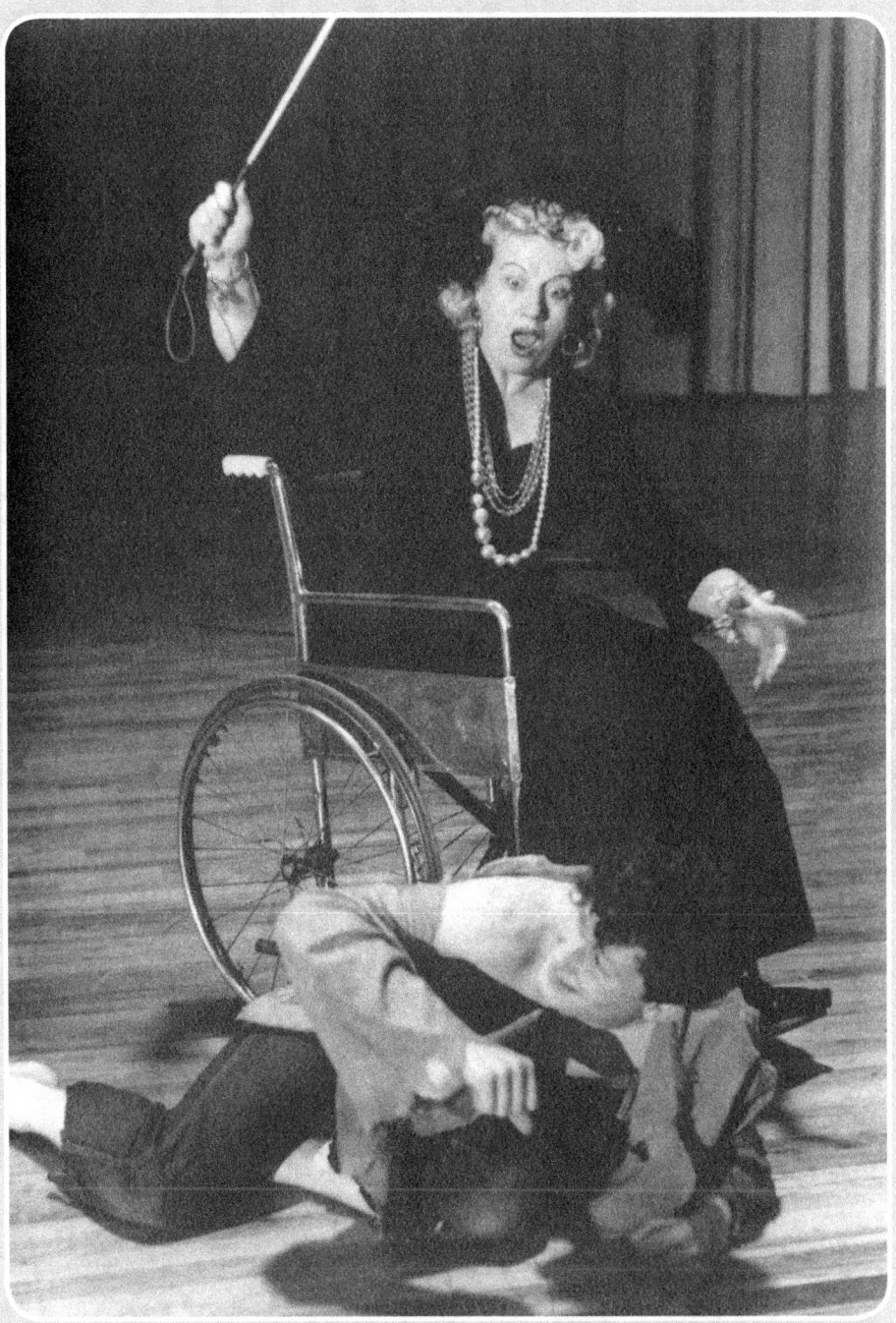

Marjorie singing the role of Madame Flora in her student production of Menotti's *The Medium*, Southern Illinois University, Carbondale, February 1966, with Gary Carlson as 'Toby'.

Marjorie rehearsing a group of her students at Southern Illinois University, 1960s.

Marjorie and Tom being shown over the construction site of the Sydney Opera House, 15 March 1966.

One of the last photographs of Marjorie singing; at a recital in Shryock Auditorium, University of Southern Illinois, Carbondale, in the late 1960s.

On his return to Minneapolis Tom found Marjorie was now able to sit in a wheelchair and move her upper body freely. Her legs were still paralysed and, until she gained more strength, a retaining strap was required to prevent her from sliding out of the chair, but this was an achievement and it meant that Marjorie was no longer confined to bed. Tom decided it was time Marjorie had her first real outing in months – a trip to the movies. Before telling Marjorie his plans, Tom investigated the fifteen-block route to the theatre and found that by taking side streets and back alleys, obstacles could be avoided.[18] The trip to the movies was a great success. Marjorie admitted that she hated being stared at, but getting out into the world again was a tonic for her. 'I wouldn't mind going to a footie match next time', she told Tom and he hastily arranged that as well, travelling to and from the stadium by taxi. With Marjorie's chair perched on an aisle at the top of a grandstand and both rugged up against the cold, they watched the Minnesota Golden Gophers thrash a visiting team from Michigan.

Marjorie managed to get through both these adventures without being recognised or mobbed by fans, but when Tom suggested they go to a concert by the Minneapolis Symphony, with whom Marjorie had sung in the past, both knew it would be a different experience. 'And I've got nothing I can wear in this *bloody* chair!' Marjorie protested. Tom fixed that. He went out and bought Marjorie a magnificent white satin evening gown. The gown had a full skirt that would drape gracefully over her legs which Marjorie now believed were unsightly. Marjorie was delighted with the dress and Tom couldn't bring himself to admit that it had come from a charity shop and had cost just $25. The maid, Marie, altered it slightly, at the same time concealing a slight stain on the hem of the skirt.

The concert was held at the huge Northrop Auditorium and the orchestra was conducted by Dimitri Mitropoulos, with whom Marjorie had sung in Monte Carlo and Boston. Tom waited until most of the audience were in their seats then wheeled Marjorie into the auditorium. If this was an attempt to avoid notice it failed. Marjorie was recognised immediately and her name whispered throughout the auditorium. The whole assembly rose to their feet and applauded. The orchestra joined in, string players tapping their instruments with their bows. As Marjorie couldn't make it backstage, Mitropoulos came to her in the interval and kissed her hands. Marjorie was not 'back', but it almost felt as if she was, and the warmth of the audience that night gave her the courage to do something the next day she had been avoiding – to give her voice a proper try-out.

Marjorie had kept the score of *Tristan und Isolde* beside her bed in the Minneapolis apartment and over the past weeks when Tom was at his classes and Marie out shopping, Marjorie had attempted to sing a few phrases *sotto voce*, too afraid to sing in full voice in case she discovered she could not. After the Minneapolis concert she threw fate to the wind and tried singing a few of Isolde's phrases in full voice. To her immense relief and joy she found the voice was still there. The paralysis had affected her breathing and she could not manage the deep breaths required to sustain long phrases, but the sound itself was intact.

When Tom got home from the hospital at lunch time that day an overjoyed Marjorie told him he must get her a piano – she wanted to sing again. The ever-faithful Tom immediately went out and bought a second-hand upright piano they could probably not afford. It was delivered the same afternoon.

> *I was able to use my voice only for about five or six minutes at the first attempt, before it and I tired, but I was back at the piano the next day and every day thereafter, singing for longer periods.*[19]

Experimentation and sheer hard work slowly restored Marjorie's vocal strength. By using her arms to pull herself up until her back was straight and moving her body until her weight was supported entirely on her buttocks, Marjorie found that she could control her diaphragm without restriction. She also discovered that if she drew her lower abdominal wall in and up in this position, she could achieve the physical sensation of standing – at least from the waist up – and her immobile legs could be forgotten. In this position Marjorie was able to achieve the kind of physical and vocal freedom she needed to make rapid progress. Within three weeks she was going through Isolde's part in whole acts of *Tristan und Isolde* at one sitting and, according to Tom, startling their neighbours up to three blocks away.[20]

While the knowledge that she still had her voice and devising new and efficient ways to sing were enormously encouraging, the prospect of not being able to put her voice to good use was equally distressing and discouraging. What possible value could there be in a singer stuck in a wheelchair, Marjorie pondered, and who would want to listen to a cripple sing? Friends and acquaintances passing through Minneapolis, including some of her former colleagues, didn't help either. They found it impossible to disguise their distress at Marjorie's predicament and invariably exclaimed things like 'To think this should have happened to *you* of all people ... you were always so lively' and 'Whatever are you going to do now, dear?', the assumption being that Marjorie's professional prospects were now almost nil.

It was only to Tom that Marjorie could unburden herself and express her fears. When one day she said (probably for the umpteenth time) 'What will I do, Angel?', Tom surprised Marjorie by suggesting they put their trust in God and simply wait to see what He had in store for them. Neither Marjorie nor Tom was particularly religious. Marjorie had not attended church regularly since singing in Alex Pearce's choir in Deans Marsh and Tom had let his attendance slip since moving from Florida to New York. Together they set about reviving their faith and, as so many people in *extremis* do, found unexpected peace and strength.

Tom and I prayed; prayed not so much that I should be cured, but that we should be given courage and hope to continue our lives ... to bear our crosses with patience and fortitude. From the day we acknowledged God's part in our lives and turned to Him, there was a miraculous change in my mental outlook. Faith exorcised my fears. The will to fight my way back and the will to succeed was restored to me.[21]

The words at the beginning of this chapter are spoken by Wotan to Brünnhilde in Act Two of *Die Walküre* and translate as 'I must abandon what I love most'. This poignant phrase might have occurred to Marjorie many times in the preceding months. If it had, then it now seemed she could add 'or maybe not'.

Chapter Fourteen

'Master of my fate and captain of my soul'

By the end of October Tom was proficient enough in the Kenny method to take over Marjorie's treatment and, as winter snow began to blanket Minneapolis, he suggested a move to a warmer climate, where Marjorie could benefit from sunshine, as she had at Villa Rustica. Hot Springs was far from hot at this time of year, so Miami – the city where Tom had grown up and where his parents still lived – was the obvious choice.[1]

Marjorie and Tom set out in Tom's small and aged Oldsmobile, which he had driven back from New York in September. They travelled via New York so that Tom could put his medical practice on the market and raise some urgently needed capital.[2] To avoid publicity they stayed at a hotel in White Plains just outside New York City and from there Tom wrote a long and moving letter to Sister Kenny thanking her for all the help she had given them.[3] He also wrote to Reverend Dr Everett Smith, pastor of the Miami church he had attended as a boy. Tom told Smith that he and Marjorie were on their way to Miami and offered Marjorie's services to sing at Smith's Christmas Service.[4] In *Interrupted Melody* this episode is presented as a conspiracy cooked up between Tom and Smith after they arrived in Miami and without Marjorie's knowledge, but once again, that appears to have been an invention. Whether Tom told Marjorie he was engineering her first public singing engagement since her illness *before* he got a positive response from Miami is unclear. In all probability he waited and then presented Marjorie with a fait accompli, reasoning that to be the best way to get her to 'take the plunge'.

Tom and Marjorie spent the second night of their journey to Miami at Alexandria, just south of Washington. There they learned the news that had stunned all America that day and thrown Washington into chaos – the surprise attack by the Japanese on the American Fleet at Pearl Harbor. The United States, which had become the safe haven of millions fleeing the war in Europe, was now itself at war.

On arriving in Miami Tom and Marjorie rented a modest, three-room bungalow near the Hialeah Park horse-racing track. Among the redirected mail awaiting them was a letter from Cyril which gives a clear indication that his behaviour at Tom and Marjorie's wedding and in Mexico had been an armistice not a peace. Over the following weeks there were more letters from him, criticising Marjorie for dispensing with the services of MacMillan, whom he seems to have had more faith in than anyone else, and encouraging her to relinquish Vincent Attractions. Cyril also writes in one letter that he is looking for a job so that he can support Marjorie when she is abandoned by Tom. He finishes each letter by urging his sister to try harder to get well.[5] Marjorie was justifiably angry. She ignored Cyril's letters for a few weeks, finally writing back and beginning her reply with 'How dare you?' and ending with 'Go bag your head!', the paragraphs in between liberally spiced with Aussie expletives.[6]

Marjorie hardly needed a manager at that time and when her career resumed, Tom filled the role at least as efficiently as Cyril had. Nor could Marjorie now afford to support Cyril or bear to have him around her on any kind of permanent basis. Their relationship never fully recovered, although they remained on speaking terms and age softened their differences. For years after, Cyril pinned his hopes on Tom breaking under the strain and rebelling at being Marjorie's full-time carer at which time he, Cyril, would heroically step in and save his little sister. That, of course, never eventuated and as the years passed Cyril floated from one dead-end job to another, drank heavily and became embroiled in homosexual love affairs of ever more sordid natures. He also penned numerous frankly awful songs, which he tried to foist on Marjorie and other singers.[7] Eventually he ended up playing dame roles in drag with amateur theatrical companies in New York and his sad life came to an end shortly before Marjorie's.

At this time Marjorie was also in touch with the firm of Blake & Riggall, solicitors, of Melbourne whom she hoped would help her avoid paying the income tax bill the Australian Government had presented her with following the 'homecoming' tour, persuade the Commonwealth Bank of Australia to bend wartime rules and forward her 2500 pounds which was sitting in a fixed deposit in Melbourne, and extricate her from the ongoing battle over her father's will. Despite pleas based on Marjorie's health and financial distress, Blake & Riggall reported that they had been unsuccessful in all three endeavours, commenting about the will, 'You brother Lindsay's position has not changed'.[8]

If Marjorie seemed to be losing one family, she gained another in Florida. Tom took her to visit his parents, Mabel and Oscar, and his 'kid-sister' Doris, who lived in an apartment in midtown Miami. Heaven knows what these simple folk must have thought when they had learned their 'Tommy' was going to marry an opera star – a breed entirely alien to their world of corn stalks, prayer meetings and steamy hotel kitchens – and they must have been even more nervous of meeting their daughter-in-law than she was of meeting them, and with everyone's discomfort intensified by Marjorie's condition.

The Boggs family immediately fell for Marjorie and she for them. Mabel and

Oscar might have hailed from Deans Marsh had their accents been different, and they were enormously relieved to find their son's new wife was a country girl at heart, able to shed the airs and graces of a prima donna like an overcoat. Marjorie was immediately adopted by the Boggs family as she had once been by the Grodets, and Mabel and Oscar referred to her as 'our new daughter' for the rest of their lives.

The Boggs were present when Marjorie sang at the Christmas Service at Dr Smith's First Christian Church. That was another red-letter day in Marjorie's life and one she would never forget. Three days earlier Tom had taken her to Dr Smith's house to meet the pastor and the choirmaster and organist, George Slack. Smith's daughter accompanied Marjorie at the piano as they tried out several pieces, deciding finally on Malotte's setting of 'The Lord's Prayer', the Bach-Gounod *Ave Maria* and the Christmas carol 'Silent Night'. Marjorie also agreed to sing a wordless descant to the choir's singing of a curious piece entitled 'The Christmas Story', which Slack had arranged using themes from Sibelius's *Finlandia*. There was a rehearsal with the choir in the church the following day, before which the logistics of Marjorie's appearance in her wheelchair were carefully worked out by Tom.

On the evening of the service over a thousand people crammed into the church and microphones were set up to broadcast the proceedings on a local radio station. Marjorie felt enormously self-conscious as Tom wheeled her in from the vestry and placed her chair in front of the choir, facing a sea of curious faces. She had expected the first musical number to begin as soon as she appeared, but instead Dr Smith climbed into the pulpit and made a long speech of welcome, extolling Marjorie's courage and unintentionally adding to the pressure Marjorie was already feeling. Smith then led the assembly in a prayer for Marjorie's recovery and, finally, Slack played the opening bars of 'The Lord's Prayer'. For the first time in her singing career, Marjorie's eyes filled with tears and emotion constricted her throat, but the moment passed.

> *After the first phrase I forgot about how I looked, forgot the sea of faces, forgot everything but the music and just sang my heart out.*[9]

Applause was not permitted during services in Dr Smith's church, but when Marjorie sang the final 'Amen', her voice matching the majestic peal of the organ, the pastor and the entire congregation burst into spontaneous applause, which was repeated each time Marjorie sang. The respect and admiration that crowd of strangers offered Marjorie was like the soothing balsam Kundry brings in *Parsifal*; it soothed her cares and fears and proved beyond doubt that people still wanted to hear her sing.[10]

That was not the only balm offered that evening. After the service dozens of people pressed around Marjorie to shake her hand and thank her for singing and one lady pressed a small jar into Marjorie's hand, saying 'Do try this, my dear, I just *know* it will help you'. There were other small gifts and as she received them, Marjorie passed them over to Tom. It was not until the next morning that they discovered the jar contained snake oil, according to the label, a remedy for all aches and pains.

Tom drove Marjorie to the beach most days for 'swimming' and encouraged her to try crawling on her hands and knees on the sand. On the first day she managed only about six feet; a month later she could manage sixty feet and get herself in and out of the sea. Mabel and Oscar often joined them at the beach, Oscar bringing hampers of delicious food he had prepared himself.

Progress was slow, but it was not for want of encouragement or determination. Marjorie's left leg strengthened and she was able to move it a little more, but her right remained leaden and unresponsive. Her right buttock also became dangerously wasted and flabby. Tom reported this to Sister Kenny and she requested a photograph of Marjorie's posterior so she could better judge what was happening. Tom was a keen amateur photographer and decided the best image could be produced if the photo was taken outdoors in sunlight. The womenfolk from the neighbouring houses were recruited to help and on the chosen morning Tom placed Marjorie over their small garden table, face down. The helpful neighbours then moved in, holding bed sheets to make a screen, Tom flipped Marjorie's dressing gown up over her back and snapped what must have been one of the most remarkable photos ever taken of a prima donna.

While Marjorie was submitting to having her bottom immortalised on film and learning to crawl again under the bright Miami sun, back in cold New York, the 1941–42 season at the Met was in full swing. As was to be expected, the absence of both Flagstad and Marjorie was grievously felt in the German wing. Johnson had desperately sought replacements and not always in the right places. He had high hopes for the Icelandic soprano Maria Barkan, but Barkan came and went after singing just one role, showing a vocal scattiness neither the public nor the critics found acceptable. The young Astrid Varnay was another. She would develop into one of the best Wagnerians of the next generation, but at twenty-three she had a lot to learn before she could even begin to approach the standards set in previous seasons by Flagstad and Marjorie. One or two older singers bravely stepped in to help. Elisabeth Rethberg, for example, took on the *Siegfried* Brünnhilde for the first time, but found experience was no substitute for power.

Johnson reluctantly entrusted the bulk of the Wagnerian soprano roles in this and coming seasons to the forty-two-year-old Helen Traubel. Traubel became a highly valued, respected and influential member of the company, and she endeared herself to the American public, but she was no rival for either Flagstad or Marjorie. Traubel had an enormous voice and an endless capacity to sing, but her voice and singing lacked the beauty of Flagstad's and the excitement of Marjorie's – and her top notes were sometimes unreliable. She was also one of the least romantic figures ever to stride the boards of the Metropolitan Opera and it would be hard to imagine a less romantic looking pair of stage lovers than Traubel and Melchior.[11] Marjorie kept in touch with the Met management (and Ugarte and Busch in Buenos Aires, who were facing the same dilemma as Johnson), but if either they or she still clung to the hope that one day she would again spring from rock to rock, flourish her spear and leap onto Grane's back, those hopes were fast fading.

Once again Tom managed to conjure up a piano from somewhere to enable Marjorie to work on her voice in Miami. Years later he recalled with amusement how, when there was a big race meeting on at Hialeah Park, cars would stop in the street to listen to Marjorie singing and that he always feared her voice might spook the horses. With time on his hands, Tom also set about canvassing the medical profession across the United States to identify any physician, surgeon or therapist who might be able to speed up Marjorie's recovery or restore enough mobility to allow her to return to the stage. Dozens of letters were written and a mixed bag of responses received. The best prospect seemed to be two doctors in California – Doctors Harreveld and Billig, who offered a surgical treatment for paralysis.

Harreveld and Billig declined to make any kind of prognosis about what their treatment might or might not be able to do for Marjorie until they examined her, so Marjorie and Tom set about making plans to travel to Pasadena. Tom scraped together enough money to trade in his old Oldsmobile on a larger and more comfortable Cadillac and for the fifth time in nine months they began repacking their bags. As these preparations were being made, the couple had their first piece of really good news in months – Marjorie was going to have a baby.

Marjorie's initial fears that her condition might affect the pregnancy or that her unborn child might already be afflicted with her illness were quickly dispelled by Tom and confirmed by a gynaecologist consulted in Miami. Unlike her parents in Australia back in 1909, Marjorie and Tom left the doctor's rooms with a positive message and lighter in spirit than they had been in months. A letter was hastily sent to inform Harreveld and Billig and they reassured Tom that their surgical procedure was not likely to affect the pregnancy.

The 2000-mile journey from the Atlantic coast to the Pacific coast took two weeks. Marjorie rode in the back for comfort and shared her space with a puppy she had been given by the Miami Police Department and which she would not part with. The trip was arduous and made more so by the constant stops that had to be made so the puppy could pee. Heat, dust, punctures and uncomfortable beds in auto parks (forerunners of highway motels), where they stayed for convenience and economy, added to their discomfort.

On arrival in Pasadena Marjorie was admitted to the Huntington Memorial Hospital and underwent a surgical procedure at the hands of Doctors Harreveld and Billig – a procedure which was experimental and crude by modern medical standards and which, in the long-term, would prove of no benefit to her, although everyone nursed high hopes at the time. Long incisions were made at the back and front of each of Marjorie's thighs. Nerve endings were then located and destroyed by crushing, in the belief that new, vigorous nerves would regrow in greater numbers, restoring vitality to her leg muscles. Marjorie was given a general anaesthetic (probably ether or chloroform) and Tom was told the procedure would take approximately one hour. By the time it was completed and the incisions secured with sixty stitches, Marjorie had been unconscious for four hours.

Marjorie remained in hospital for a week, which was followed by another two in a nursing facility. The healing process was slow and Marjorie experienced great difficulty sleeping because of pain in her thighs. She and Tom filled in long waking hours by making plans for their future. At this stage they were hopeful that the surgery would improve Marjorie's mobility and that in late August they would have a strong, healthy son or daughter, but money problems cast a dark shadow over their plans. Every day they remained in Pasadena the medical bills kept mounting, the Mexican Opera Company was threatening to sue Marjorie over the $600 advance, restrictions in Australia had not been lifted and neither Marjorie nor Tom had earned a cent in months.[12] Some of Marjorie's friends had suggested she consider building a new career as a singing radio star, a field where her disability was irrelevant. Past experience had shown how lucrative radio work could be, so the decision was made to go to New York as soon as Marjorie was well enough and, after the birth of their child, lay siege to the radio networks.

The journey east was a nightmare, exceeded in pain and suffering only by the trip from Mexico City to Hot Springs. On the day before they departed Marjorie's puppy became ill and had to be left behind at a veterinary clinic, where it died of distemper. Marjorie began haemorrhaging in Oklahoma and their car broke down outside Knoxville in Tennessee and had to be towed into town. The haemorrhaging stopped, but at this point both she and Tom were on the point of collapse from exhaustion. As soon as their car was repaired they made a desperate phone call to Mary Hedrick and then backtracked to Arkansas, heading for the peace and tranquillity of Villa Rustica.

Doctor Fletcher cared for Marjorie and also kept a watchful eye on Tom while they recovered enough strength to resume their journey. They stayed several days and before leaving asked Mary Hedrick to let them know if she ever decided to sell her property. As they drove out the long driveway, they both felt that one day they would return and that this beautiful place that had offered them welcome shelter twice would become a permanent part of their lives.

In preparation for their return to New York, Tom cabled a statement to Vincent Attractions for release to the press. It appeared in newspapers in the United States and Australia and stated that Marjorie was continuing to improve slowly and that every effort was being made to speed up her recovery so that she could return to the Met. 'Miss Lawrence's voice' the statement proclaimed, 'is lovelier and more powerful than ever'. The punch line came last. 'Dr King also proudly announces that his wife is expecting a baby in the fall and says he is exceedingly happy to share this news with Miss Lawrence's fans and admirers'.[13]

It was late June before they reached New York and moved into the 73rd Street apartment, recently vacated by the tenant. As Marjorie was now in the seventh month of her pregnancy, Tom made a reservation for her at the Columbia Presbyterian Medical Centre. In the course of a routine examination by doctors there, concerns were expressed about the pregnancy and a series of X-rays taken. These showed Marjorie's baby was dead and had been for some time. It is likely that Marjorie had suffered what is called a 'missed abortion', with the foetus dying while Marjorie was under anaesthetic for so long in Pasadena.[14]

Marjorie and Tom were grief-stricken. Marjorie entered the Columbia centre so the aftermath of the pregnancy could be dealt with and Tom issued a second, much briefer statement to the press, saying he regretted to announce that he and his wife had lost their baby and that Marjorie was recovering.[15] As family, friends, colleagues and fans read this news – coming so soon after the good news – most must have wondered what other misfortune could possibly befall this unfortunate couple.

Marjorie never had another child, but there is a clue that she and Tom might have wanted and tried hard for another. Over the next few years Tom kept exact records of Marjorie's periods of menstruation. This may have been for purely practical reasons, but as most of Marjorie's engagements were booked well in advance and the dates could not be easily changed, it seems more likely that they were predicting when Marjorie would be ovulating, thus increasing the chances of conception. It is a pity Marjorie and Tom didn't have a child since they would have been excellent parents.

A favourite saying of Bill Lawrence's had been 'When you're down the only way is up' and Marjorie had quoted that to herself during tough times in Paris, always hearing her Dad's sturdy mellow voice echoing in her memory. Marjorie recognised that the loss of her child was the low point in her life to date and that it was time to heed these words, to muster her courage and move onwards and upwards to the next phase in their plan – if not for herself, then for the proud, independent man who had proven his devotion a thousandfold over and who had sacrificed everything for her.

When Vincent Attractions informed the radio networks that Marjorie was available to sing in studio broadcasts they were not swamped with offers as they and Marjorie had hoped. Apart from the congregation of the First Christian Church in Miami and those eavesdroppers who had listened to her practising, no one had heard Marjorie's voice since the onset of her illness, so their caution is understandable. For fifteen months the press had been rife with speculation about the effect the illness might have had on Marjorie's voice and no radio station executive wanted to take the risk of his network being associated with an embarrassing fiasco.

A friend of Marjorie's finally made a direct approach to the conductor of the WABC Network's *Coca Cola Hour*, Andre Kostelanetz. Kostelanetz and his wife

Lily Pons were also friends of Marjorie's, but the conductor was too conscientious a musician to offer her an engagement without auditioning her first. Marjorie's initial reaction, as she relates in *Interrupted Melody*, was to tell Kostelanetz to take his orchestra and the Coca Cola company and jump into the Hudson with them, but when she calmed down she realised that in a similar situation she would probably have done exactly the same. At Marjorie's invitation, Kostelanetz and a clutch of WABC executives visited the apartment and, while Marjorie sang, the conductor played the new grand piano Knabe & Co. had given her on perpetual loan.

After Marjorie sang Strauss's song 'Zueignung', Kostelanetz winked at her and said 'Well there's nothing wrong with that voice. But what will you sing for us?' [16] Marjorie suggested Wagner, but Kostelanetz wanted lighter pieces as the broadcast was being transmitted to American troops in Australia. They decided on the Strauss song (sung in English) and 'Annie Laurie'. When Kostelanetz also asked for anything typically Australian, Marjorie produced her vocal score of 'Waltzing Matilda' and when she sang that iconic piece, Kostelanetz was overjoyed, immediately requesting the score so he could arrange it for orchestra.[17]

The weekly *Coca Cola Hour* was broadcast from Liederkranz Hall in Manhattan each Sunday afternoon and Marjorie's reappearance on the program took place on 6 September 1942. Kostelanetz conducted the forty-five piece orchestra; the violinist Albert Spalding was the other soloist. While there was no audience, about fifty people, including a large press contingent and some of Marjorie's friends, found their way into the hall. Marjorie was photographed looking vibrant and excited, a large corsage of orchids pinned to the lapel of her jacket and with Tom in the place he would occupy in hundreds of press photos over the coming years – firmly grasping the handles of her wheelchair and smiling a little self-consciously at the camera.

Marjorie might have looked confident but she was nervous, as is evident in her singing of the Strauss song in the recording made of the program. However, she rallied with 'Annie Laurie' and sang with her accustomed surety. Kostelanetz's sparkling arrangement of 'Waltzing Matilda' displays rapid key and rhythm changes and culminates with a stirring march tempo and Marjorie threw this final piece off with joyous élan. Spalding introduced Marjorie's items and when she did the same for him, she began by saying: 'This is Marjorie Lawrence. I cannot tell you what a thrill it is to be singing again!' The sincerity behind those words leaps across the seventy years since the recording was made. After fifteen months in the wilderness of hospitals, massage tables and therapeutic pools, Marjorie really was 'back'.

The next day a flood of cables arrived from friends and colleagues who had listened anxiously to the broadcast, and their expressions of joy seem to indicate they had been as nervous as Marjorie, although none knew better than she that the step she had taken (metaphorically) was only a small one. Singing on radio where the listening audience could not see her was all very well, but to appear before a 'live' paying audience where her disability could not be disguised was another matter entirely. Always proud of her glamorous appearance and the grace of her movements, Marjorie dreaded having to appear in a wheelchair before an audience and dreaded even more their pity and embarrassment at the spectacle – a little of which she had already experienced in Miami. By the time she sang on the *Coca Cola Hour*, however, a date had been fixed for that test and Marjorie had little time left to dwell on her fears.

The impetus to appear before a 'live' audience in New York had come from the organisers of a benefit concert for crippled children, predominantly young polio victims. When the request was made, Marjorie felt she couldn't refuse and hadn't wanted to, reasoning that the sooner she took the plunge, the sooner she would know for sure how a broad audience would react to her. Tom eased the situation by suggesting that Marjorie sing while seated on a settee, which she was now strong enough to do without risk. He proposed that he transfer her from her wheelchair to a settee behind a screen on stage or before the curtain was raised, removing the screen or raising the curtain when Marjorie was ready to sing. The procedure was practised and timed and found to work smoothly. This became the method used for most of her appearances over the following few years.

A building with a musical history had been chosen as the venue for this concert – the Hammerstein Ballroom in the Manhattan Centre on West 34th Street. In former times this had been the Manhattan Opera House, where Oscar Hammerstein had presented seasons of opera in opposition to the Met. When she sang on that historic stage on 9 September, Marjorie was singing where Melba, Garden and Nordica had sung and she received an ovation as large as any of them might have received. When the curtains parted Marjorie was revealed sitting on a rose and gold settee, looking regal in a long white gown that covered her legs and feet.[18] She acknowledged the applause by nodding her head after she sang Gluck, Strauss and, appropriately, a song called 'This Day is Mine' by the American composer Harriet Ware. Thunderous applause accompanied the lowering of the curtain.

Two weeks later Marjorie sang at a war benefit gala on the New Jersey estate of a member of the Metropolitan Opera Guild. In one sense this was a greater test than the Manhattan concert, because Edward Johnson and many singers from the Met were among the guests. Ten days on and Marjorie sang again for the Guild at a luncheon in the Waldorf Astoria Hotel in New York. Before Marjorie sang this time, the formidable founder of the Guild, Mrs August Belmont insisted on reciting Henley's poem *Invictus*[19] in Marjorie's honour. At the end of the evening event Bruno Walter said to her 'Your voice is as wonderful as ever, but greater still is the spirit behind it'.[20]

Encouraged by her successes, Marjorie allowed herself to be persuaded to plan a solo recital in New York Town Hall when the city's regular concert season got underway. Once committed to the idea, she questioned the ability of Vincent Attractions to promote the event with the flair the enterprise would need and went in search of a new agent. Before her illness Marjorie had been courted by Lawrence Evans of the powerful Columbia Artists Management who wanted to add her to his stable of famous singers. Evans had been desperate to sign Marjorie up then, but now he procrastinated and made excuses. As Marjorie's voice and art were unchanged, she assumed it was her disability that was the cause of Evans's change of heart. In fact that was probably not the case. Evans was an ethical and just man, but also a shrewd business operator and he had just invested a great deal of money promoting Helen Traubel as 'America's leading Wagnerian soprano' and the successor to Kirsten Flagstad. It is understandable, therefore, that he would not have been keen to undermine his own campaign. In the meantime a new player in the field, Austin Wilder approached Marjorie. She and Tom were impressed by Wilder, who was full of bright, fresh ideas. Marjorie signed with him and Wilder proceeded to promote the recital with tremendous enthusiasm.[21]

The Town Hall was packed on the night – 29 November 1942 – and Marjorie's' success mirrored what she had already achieved, but with one important additional element: New York's leading music critics were present and their reports provide us with the first objective accounts of Marjorie singing a major program since her illness. Noel Straus, who knew Marjorie's work well and had always admired her, described her reappearance as a triumph, informing his readers in the *New York Times* that he had never heard her sing with 'such absolute firmness of tone', 'imposing effect' and 'depth of human feeling'. As a final encore she sang the Immolation Scene and Straus noted she was tiring just a little by then. She still managed, he reported, 'fine singing', 'keen insight' and 'immense grandeur of line'.[22]

An entirely objective viewpoint was offered by the composer Virgil Thompson, recently appointed as music critic of the *Herald Tribune*. He wrote:

> *It happened not to have been my pleasure to hear Miss Lawrence at the opera. Persons familiar with her work tell me, however, that the enforced repose has freshened her voice and solidified her mastery of it. Certainly her singing last night was secure, resonant and masterful.*[23]

Marjorie's Town Hall triumph caused stirrings at the Met. With the support of several other singers, John Brownlee approached Johnson with the suggestion that the Met mount a gala benefit in her honour. So many of the company's artists offered their services that much diplomacy was needed to keep the program down to a reasonable length. Johnson was adamant, however, that the one singer who *must* appear was Marjorie herself.

Johnson suggested Marjorie sing the Venusburg scene from *Tannhäuser* with Melchior. The Met's current production of that opera provided Venus with a high-backed divan looking vaguely like a giant scallop shell liberally cushioned and draped. Other singers had reclined on the couch before stalking Tannhäuser. Johnson argued that Marjorie could sing the whole scene from the couch and Melchior could move around her. It would work splendidly, he assured her, adding (according to Marjorie): 'Our audiences haven't heard a first class Venus since Fremstad!'[24]

Marjorie's first reaction was to refuse. Part of her wanted to seize the opportunity, but another part counselled caution. She had by her own admission been trying to avoid the inevitable thoughts of a return to opera; she had been focusing on the idea of a future as a recitalist, believing that the sooner she accepted that her stage career was over the better. Furthermore, she did not know the role of Venus, having always sung Elisabeth in the opera since her debut in Monte Carlo; however, Venus is a short and not particularly taxing role and Marjorie had proven herself time and time again a fast learner. Under pressure from all parties, including Tom, Marjorie agreed and from the moment she did, the excitement of the challenge consumed her.

Edyth Walker and Louis Bachner were recruited to help Marjorie learn the role and by the time she attended the rehearsals she was word and note perfect.[25] Betty Bee was enlisted to create her costume and went to work with a bolt of pale pink voile and a box of paste gems. Queues formed down Broadway towards Times Square when tickets went on sale and an audience of 3800, led by Eleanor Roosevelt and the Mayor of New York, Fiorello La Guardia (a long-time fan and friend of Marjorie's), filled the Met on Sunday evening 27 December, for what was billed as 'A Tribute and Benefit Concert to Marjorie Lawrence'.

Sir Thomas Beecham was at the Met that season and he conducted the first part of the program – an overture, which was followed by the Saint Sulpice scene from Massenet's *Manon* with Jarmila Novotná and Charles Kullman. Later in the evening Brownlee sang Papageno in a scene from Mozart's *Die Zauberflöte* and Licia Albanese and Lawrence Tibbett offered a scene from Verdi's *La Traviata*. During scenery changes, Lily Pons, Ezio Pinza and Frederick Jagel sang arias, but it was Marjorie and the extended *Tannhäuser* segment the audience had come to hear. Graphic, first-hand accounts of what happened backstage survive in a series of excellent photographs taken by a *Time* magazine photographer and articles written by the press.

> Behind the curtain, stage-hands, satyrs, angels, graces and nymphs fluttered, pirouetted or stood in whispering groups. Then a hush fell on the cavernous, dim lit setting for the opening scene of 'Tannhäuser'. A wheel chair came on stage from the right. Désiré Defrère, the voluble stage director, a prompter and dungareed scene shifters cleared way for it in the extraordinary quiet. The chair

was pushed gently beside Venus' divan. Tenderly the director, stage hands, and a giant medieval huntsman lifted Marjorie Lawrence from her chair. Lauritz Melchior, red-wigged Tannhäuser, hovered over her.[26]

Marjorie settled herself in the golden pillows. Tom checked that she was comfortable while Betty Bee plied her with a glass of water and Jennie Cervini helped her adjust her costume. There was no time, nor was this the place for emotional outbursts. Before they quit the stage, Tom whispered '*Merde*' into Marjorie's ear – the amusing salutation French singers exchange when they are about to go on stage – and she smiled back.

Orange and blue spotlights high in the flies blazed and burned in her wide bracelets and in the jewelled girdle that held her diaphanous robes. Around her baccantes danced, satyrs leaped and she smiled upon them. One old stagehand told another 'She's got something, she has. She's got guts.' A taller one nodded and said 'I'll say, she has'.[27]

Lauritz Melchior kissed Marjorie's hand then draped himself cumbersomely at the base of the divan. Frances Alda, the New Zealand-born soprano who had grown up in Australia and become one of the Met's most durable stars of the previous generation, was standing in the wings swathed in furs. She whispered, '*Toi, toi*, Marjorie', which means something like 'good luck'. The idling huntsmen, the satyrs, the nymphs, the monks and every one else backstage took up the call, the refrain subsiding only as the great golden curtain rose.

In the dim half light the chorus sang, sweetly subdued, then Melchior 'awakened' at Venus' feet. Finally it was Venus' cue. Again a hush fell on the house. Then Venus sang. The notes soared and softened. They poured from the singer's lips, liquid and soothing but steady as a rock. Miss Lawrence's arms extended towards Tannhäuser. Song poured forth from her and it was rich and beautiful. She fondled the knight's hair and the music flowed.[28]

At the end of the scene the curtain fell as the audience exploded with applause, shouts of 'bravo' and the kind of cheering and stamping Met audiences don't often indulge in. Melchior shared the first bow, after which he thoughtfully left the stage, leaving Marjorie to bask in her triumph. In the wings Jenny Cervini whispered triumphantly: 'Tell Mr Johnson, not all the great sopranos are in Europe' but Johnson was only steps away, heading onto the stage to congratulate Marjorie. 'From now on Margie,' he said, 'everyone who sings Venus in this house will want to do it sitting down!'[29]

Next day the press were as ecstatic as the audience had been. Jerome Bohm's words in the *Herald Tribune* summed up the general feeling:

> *How sorely opera-goers have missed Miss Lawrence's art was proved by the tremendous ovation she received for her performance of Venus, which has not been equalled here since the days of Olive Fremstad.*[30]

Two days later a cable arrived from Johnson offering Marjorie three complete performances of *Tannhäuser* – two in New York and one during the spring tour in Chicago – at $250 per performance. By mail came a cheque for $3571.50, the proceeds of the testimonial gala. John Brownlee also turned up at Marjorie's apartment bearing a gift from her fellow artists: a large autograph book signed by ninety-three singers, dancers and conductors, Met stars of the past, the present and the future.[31]

As the New Year of 1943 dawned, Marjorie could banish her fear that she had joined those stars of the 'past'. She was still disabled and likely to remain so and the world was still embroiled in a terrible conflict, but Marjorie's courage and Tom's support had given her back a 'present' and a 'future'.

Chapter Fifteen
Chin-up Girl

As soon as Marjorie's life returned to normality – albeit an altered one – she began looking about for ways to help others. Altruism had not figured large in Marjorie's philosophy during the first thirty or so years of her life, but that was changing. The process had begun with the Bundles for Britain concert, when in 1939 she was touched by the plight of Australians and Britons at war. Thereafter the transformation gained momentum. Marjorie's brush with death, the experience of learning to rely on others, a new-found faith and Tom's benevolent influence all combined to make Marjorie a more humble, less egocentric person, with these qualities remaining with her for the rest of her life. She would never lose her feistiness or her determination, but henceforth these would be balanced by the compassion and serenity that is characteristic of many people living with a disability.

One obvious group Marjorie could assist were the victims of polio, and the concert at the Hammerstein Ballroom was the first step in that direction. There Marjorie had made the acquaintance of Basil O'Connor, President of the National Foundation for Infantile Paralysis. O'Connor was a shrewd middle-aged lawyer and the architect of the successful 'March of Dimes' campaign which funded support for victims and research for a polio vaccine. O'Connor recognised a kindred fighting spirit in Marjorie and appreciated the enormous publicity value she might offer his cause.[1]

O'Connor had once been Franklin Delano Roosevelt's partner in a law firm and was still an intimate friend of the President and Mrs Roosevelt. He was also privy to a fact many Americans were unaware of at the time – that the reason why 'FDR' always appeared in public seated was because his legs were partially paralysed, the result of poliomyelitis contracted in 1921.[2] Possibly at O'Connor's suggestion, Marjorie and Tom were invited to the President's sixty-first birthday luncheon at the White House on 30 January 1943.

As noted earlier, Marjorie had sung at the White House on two previous occasions and Mrs Roosevelt had been happy to acknowledge their acquaintance whenever their paths crossed. She had also gone backstage to congratulate Marjorie after the Met testimonial concert, but this was the first time Marjorie and Tom had been invited to the White House in a social capacity and they were delighted to accept. Tom and the Boggs family were staunch Democrats and the little Marjorie had observed of American politics had led her to support the same party, over and above her personal admiration for the Roosevelts.

That day Marjorie and Tom joined Robert Young, James Cagney, Dennis Morgan, Edgar Bergen, Loretta Young, Al Jolsen, Jack Benny, Roy Rodgers and other luminaries of the American stage and screen to partake of a surprisingly frugal lunch in the State Dining Room. Eleanor Roosevelt was a gracious hostess to all her guests, taking a particular interest in Marjorie. Conspicuous by his absence, however, was the President who was in Casablanca in North Africa at a secret meeting with Winston Churchill.

Two weeks later the Australian Association of New York hosted a 'Victory' dinner for Marjorie to celebrate her thirty-sixth birthday and her return to her profession. Two hundred people turned up, including Basil O'Connor. After the meal, O'Connor rose to his feet and said he had a letter he wished to read to the assembly. He removed a long white envelope from the breast pocket of his dinner jacket, opened it, carefully unfolded the single sheet it contained, adjusted his glasses, and then read in a voice that had commanded attention in the nation's great courts of law.

Dear Miss Lawrence:

I am asking my old friend Basil O'Connor, President of the National Foundation for Infantile Paralysis, to bring you a message at the Victory Dinner, so appropriately tendered to you at the Town Hall Club in New York City.

Your courage and faith and determination in overcoming the after-effects of infantile paralysis and thereby restoring to the public the opportunity of enjoying your beautiful art – all result in a victory – your victory – which is an inspiration to everyone at any time.

But today when all we love and cherish is jeopardized by those who take their rules of life from the brutality of barbarism and preach and practise that all but the physically perfect should be summarily liquidated, your victory exposes with the light of truth the godlessness of the lie they teach.

In the days ahead, while we fight for life itself, those whose trials and sorrows may be many and heavy will courageously carry on in the spirit you have so nobly exhibited.

Mirrored in your great victory for many years to come, those beset with burdens and harassed with handicaps will see the glory and the satisfaction of the good fight well won.

From an old veteran to a young recruit my message to you is 'Carry on'.

Cordially yours...

As Marjorie recalled in *Interrupted Melody*, Basil O'Connor paused at that point and had deliberately held the letter where she, seated beside him, could not see the White House crest or the signature while he read it. When he announced the signatory's name – Franklin Delano Roosevelt – carefully refolded the letter, placed it back in its envelope and presented it to Marjorie, she unashamedly burst into tears as the rest of the gathering erupted into spontaneous applause.[3]

If Marjorie had needed any further persuasion to throw in her lot with O'Connor's group, that letter – a singular honour for an Australian – provided it. Thereafter she took part in numerous fund-raising concerts for the foundation and visited polio victims wherever her travels took her. Shortly before his death in 1972 Basil O'Connor cited Marjorie as among those who worked unceasingly to destigmatise the disease and bring comfort and encouragement to its sufferers.

Marjorie also began to set aside complimentary tickets at each of her performances to be used by polio victims. She did this for the first time when she sang the first of her complete performances of *Tannhäuser* at the Met and the Kennys brought along two charming little girls aged eight and ten. Both were wheelchair-bound and both probably enjoyed the sodas and doughnuts Marjorie offered them in her dressing room after the performance rather more than the long and confusing opera.

Those performances of *Tannhäuser* set the seal on Marjorie's return to professional music-making. After the first, the normally hard-to-please Olin Downes made no secret of his admiration for her performance:

> *Physical obstacles have in no sense lessened Miss Lawrence's interpretative powers. The limited scope of her acting in no way limited her presentation of the part. Her gestures were admirably planned and composed. She carried the scene. But the burden must be carried by the voice and Miss Lawrence's was fresh and dramatic, the tones skilfully coloured. Because of this, all aspects of the Venus music were fully communicated. The sensuous, sustained song of 'Geliebter, komm!' was as convincing as the fire and majesty of Venus's outburst, 'Zieh hin' and 'Kehrst du mir nicht zurück'. In sum this was an exceptional, complete revelation of the passage, done so eloquently that the audience interrupted the performance with applause. There are singers in full possessions of their physical resources who have not accomplished nearly as much as Miss Lawrence did.*[4]

At the Chicago performance, which took place on Marjorie and Tom's second wedding anniversary, the audience was so enthusiastic that Lawrence Tibbett (singing Wolfram) jokingly asked if Marjorie had brought her own cheer squad.

'Yep, Larry, all four thousand of 'em', she replied and the exuberant baritone roared with laughter and whacked her soundly on the back. Claudia Cassidy, the much-feared music critic of the *Chicago Tribune* added her voice to the approbation, telling her readers Marjorie sang 'radiantly' and 'magnificently' with a voice that had taken on 'a new and lovely lustre'.[5]

Marjorie's success as Venus prompted the Met to consider other roles she might sing either seated or carried on stage. Several (including Ortrud) were informally discussed but no decisions made.[6] The role Marjorie most longed to sing there – Isolde – was not among them. Marjorie was therefore doubly delighted when her new agent cabled to say that Beecham wanted her to sing two performances of *Tristan und Isolde* at the Montreal Arts Festival in May.

Marjorie assumed these would be concert performances and cabled back accepting the offer and asking for details. No reply was received, until a few weeks later when Wilder rang to say there would be only one performance and that Beecham and Herbert Graf wished to call on her that afternoon to discuss it. The conductor, director and agent duly arrived and Marjorie learned the performance was to be fully staged. Beecham laughed off her objections and said that Graf had worked out all the production details – Marjorie would remain on Isolde's shipboard couch during the first act, be seated on stage when the curtain rose on Act Two and be carried on by Kurvenal in Act Three.

The other singers engaged for the performance were all happy to cooperate. Tristan was assigned to Arthur Carron, an English dramatic tenor with a robust voice who had been at the Met for several seasons without making much impact or challenging Melchior's supremacy in the roles they shared. Elizabeth Wysor, then at the beginning of a distinguished career, was prepared to be an unusually mobile Brangäne, circling about her mistress, and the young Julius Huehn, with whom Marjorie had sung many times in New York, was ideally built to carry Isolde on stage in the last act.

Marjorie's last performance of Isolde had been six years earlier in Lyon and sung in French. She had matured greatly in the interval, both vocally and emotionally. Beecham had seen she was ready to give something extraordinary and that she had the vocal resources to surmount the technical difficulties of the role in a way Flagstad could no longer manage, and Traubel probably was never able. Beecham pushed her hard, making no concessions and she did not disappoint the faith he had in her. There are, tragically, no recordings known to exist of that performance, but there are ecstatic reviews.

Montreal Herald readers who had been foolish enough to miss the event learned the next morning:

> *Miss Lawrence's Isolde was like a dream come to life. She went through the whole opera radiantly, singing with sunshine in her voice and reaching heights of tragedy in the last act the like of which it has never been our privilege to witness before.*[7]

The conductor was also sincerely impressed by his star's performance. Sir Thomas was a master of hyperbole, but one gets the impression that a statement he made to the press was unexaggerated and came straight from the heart. It was, after all, made *after* the performance when he had nothing to gain from it. 'You can quote me gentlemen', he said. 'The finest and most imposing dramatic soprano today is Marjorie Lawrence. No other Wagnerian soprano can equal her, except perhaps Flagstad, and in my opinion Miss Lawrence is the fresher of the two. Montreal has heard the best sung Isolde anyone is likely to hear anywhere in the world today.'[8]

News of Marjorie's triumphant Isolde in Montreal reached New York the same evening and demands that she be given the role at the Met flooded the press and the opera house over the following weeks. It also raised the hackles of a couple of singers and brought to a head a controversy that had been brewing since Marjorie's return.

Traubel pre-empted any move of Johnson's by informing him that if he allowed Marjorie to sing Isolde, then Marjorie could also sing all the Brünnhildes for him as well, because she, Traubel, would not. This formidable woman, who towered over Johnson, also reminded him that she had come to the Met's rescue when they had lost both Flagstad and Marjorie and expected their loyalty in return.[9] Melchior was also getting tired of playing second fiddle to Marjorie and unlike Tibbett he did not find the public adulation of her amusing. In the first draft of *Interrupted Melody* there is a paragraph which was later edited out. It is published here for the first time:

> *I was told that Melchior resented the enthusiasm with which audiences greeted me and my work and joined in a plot because he felt having me in a cast detracted attention from his singing. I was sickened that fellow artists could be capable of such shabbiness towards me – especially those who had taken part in my testimonial concert. I came to realise that some of them had imagined the concert would be my operatic swan song; that once it was ended I would go my way doing a little radio and concert singing and leaving the glories of the Met to them.*[10]

Just who (apart from Traubel and Melchior) Marjorie was referring to is unclear. Some who did *not* join 'the plot' can be at least identified. These included Schorr, who had recently retired from the Met but who was delighted to appear in concert with Marjorie in Carnegie Hall that year, and Tibbett, Brownlee and Thorborg, all of whom remained staunch allies.

Other forces were at work against Marjorie as well. Traubel informed Johnson that she thought the performance of *Tannhäuser* she had attended as an audience member was tasteless in the extreme and unworthy of the company.[11] Traubel was partisan, but her sentiments echoed those of some of the Met's most influential subscribers. Some of these accused Johnson of turning *their* opera house into a freak show. Others accused him of exploiting Marjorie's disability and a few more accused Johnson of pandering to Marjorie's desire to exploit her own situation. There were even rumours that Marjorie was not really disabled at all, that she had made a full recovery and was now feigning paralysis as a publicity stunt.

Johnson found himself in a dilemma. He wanted to help Marjorie out of affection for her and he wanted his patrons to be able to experience the exceptional work she was still capable of. On the other hand, he could not afford to alienate Traubel, Melchior or the less sympathetic of his influential subscribers. Reluctantly, he offered her more performances of Venus in the next season, but, for the time being, nothing more. The pro-Marjorie faction kept up their pressure on Johnson to let them hear 'the best sung Isolde anyone is likely to hear' and Tom added his dime's worth by referring to the anti-Marjorie faction as 'cowardly dogs' and pestering Johnson to give Marjorie the opportunity he knew (and believed Johnson knew) she deserved.

If the Met felt constrained in their dealings with Marjorie, concert promoters did not. Wilder booked Marjorie for concerts with the nation's leading orchestras and conductors all over the United States and beyond – to Canada and Cuba. It must be said that a large part of Marjorie's appeal was her personal history and the massive publicity surrounding her disability guaranteed full houses, but if patrons expected a freak show they were disappointed. Marjorie gave performance after performance of the highest artistic standard and musical snobs could hardly complain when she sang 'Annie Laurie' or 'Danny Boy' as an encore after she just sung magnificent performances of the Immolation Scene or Isolde's *Liebestod*.

Marjorie's standard fee for a concert appearance was now $1500 and for a solo recital $2000. Few artists got larger fees and few got so many engagements. To facilitate ease of travel, Tom acquired a folding wheelchair for her, designed by the part-time inventor Aaron Stein, better known to readers of crime fiction as the author, George Bagby. This chair had removable wheels and armrests, a leather sling seat and folding footrests and could be easily carried on the aeroplanes Marjorie now favoured for long-distance travel.

A return to financial stability and the discharge of their debts allowed Marjorie and Tom to invest some money in their personal comfort. They rented out the 73rd Street apartment again and took a lease on a penthouse on top of 310 West 106th Street. The building had a high-speed elevator and no steps, and the glass-lined apartment had magnificent views over Riverside Park and the Hudson. Marjorie and Tom adored their new home, but the cook–housekeeper they had employed while at 73rd Street was less enthusiastic. Clara Weekes was her name and she was a generously proportioned African-American woman whose demeanour and manners suggested she might have stepped straight out of *Gone With the Wind*. She was completely devoted to Tom and Marjorie and there was no question of her abandoning them, but when she first entered the penthouse she exclaimed 'Glory be, Mrs King, are you sure there's gonna be enough oxygen for us all up here?'

Just a month after they moved to the penthouse, an even bigger change to their domestic arrangements unexpectedly materialised. A letter arrived from Mary Hedrick at Hot Springs. She was no longer able to maintain Villa Rustica and was now forced to put it on the market and, in accordance with the promise made to them, was offering Marjorie and Tom first option on its purchase. The market value of the property was somewhere in the vicinity of $40,000, but Mrs Hedrick was as keen for it to pass to Marjorie and Tom as they were to secure it, so she made it clear that she was prepared to strike a deal which suited them as well as her.

Marjorie and Tom now had a dilemma of their own. They both yearned to own the Arkansas property and establish a permanent base there that would serve them for the rest of their lives and they recognised if they failed to secure it at that point, the opportunity would likely never come again. On the other hand, they were still smarting from being flat broke and in debt just a few months earlier and were acutely aware of the risks involved in raising such a large sum. Having seen how quickly bubbles burst and lives shatter, reason told them to go cautiously, but their hearts were set on owning what Marjorie later called 'our bit of Paradise'.

Tom drove down to Hot Springs to explore options with Mary Hedrick. Both put their cards on the table and approached the negotiations in a spirit of friendship and trust. The result was a deal that suited everyone. Mrs Hedrick agreed to accept $25,000 for the property in easy instalments over the next ten years on the condition that she could continue to live in her part of the house rent-free for as long as she wished. Tom agreed to invest some borrowed capital in turning the property back into a profitable working farm, reasoning that the income from the farm would cover the repayments to Mrs Hedrick. She agreed to manage the property, under Tom and Marjorie's instructions for a small remuneration, giving her a modest income. On 17 April 1943, Marjorie and Tom made their first payment of $2000 and the property passed into their hands, along with six horses, fifty-one head of cattle, 500 chickens and a flock of ducks. On 1 June, Villa Rustica was renamed 'Harmony Hills Ranch'.

At the first opportunity Marjorie and Tom moved base to Harmony Hills, retaining the West 106th Street penthouse as their New York pied à terre. Hot Springs was abuzz to have a new celebrity resident and every time Marjorie and Tom drove into town in the big Cadillac to shop or for Marjorie to use the thermal baths, it caused interest and excitement. One of Tom's first jobs at Harmony Hills was to have two parallel bars constructed in the garden to enable Marjorie to 'walk' holding onto them. At first she could manage only one or two steps but later would spend half an hour each morning, laboriously pushing her still leaden limbs back and forth along the full length of the bars.

Marjorie was also fitted with leg braces at this time; a full brace on her weaker right leg and a half brace on her left. She also experimented with walking on crutches, but neither braces not crutches appealed to her vanity and she was never seen in public with either if she could avoid it. Marjorie also returned to Doctors Harreveld and Billig for a second operation, showing remarkable pragmatism considering the pair's actions had probably caused the death of her unborn baby. The second procedure was similar to the first and equally fruitless. Marjorie had not yet given up hope of walking one day, but for the time being had exhausted all the options available to help her achieve that goal.

Simply being at Harmony Hills and knowing that the property was theirs was a tonic to Marjorie. With the help of a couple of the farm hands, she was lifted onto the back of one of the horses and rode for the first time since her illness, trotting around the property looking at the livestock, the crops and the scenery and experiencing a freedom reminiscent of times that now seemed to belong to a different lifetime. She also spent a great deal of time in the garden, Tom wheeling her out to a flower bed, lifting her onto a rug on the ground, then leaving her to attack weeds with trowel and hand fork. Marjorie enjoyed this work in the garden and on one memorable afternoon when their local senator called unexpectedly, an immobilised Marjorie had to greet him from the rug, covered with soil and reeking of fertiliser.[12]

Tom also acquired a black and tan German Shepherd dog, whose name has been lost to history, and a pure white one, named 'Snow King'. These were superseded in later years by another pair of white German Shepherds, appropriately named 'Tristan' and 'Isolde'. These creatures were devoted to their owners, and especially to Marjorie, whom they protected ferociously. No one arriving at Harmony Hills could leave their car until either Tom or Marjorie called the dogs to heel.

The 'other' Tristan and Isolde was still a bone of contention. Marjorie was now singing Isolde's Narrative and Curse and the *Liebestod* in concert regularly, and performances with the New York Philharmonic under Fritz Reiner, in Seattle with Beecham, and in Philadelphia, Boston and Chicago provoked widespread interest in hearing her perform the whole opera again. Karl Alwin, in charge of the Miami Symphony, offered Marjorie two complete performances in concert, but she had to decline, as the dates clashed with previous commitments. Marjorie also sang the *Liebestod* on radio twice during the summer and fall of 1943 and on both occasions there were calls asking why she was not singing the role at the Met. Beecham was also now vociferously advocating that Marjorie should take over the role at the Met, having suffered agonies (his words) in the pit while Traubel dodged Isolde's top notes.

Edward Johnson finally found the solution. Traubel was contracted to sing the five scheduled performances of *Tristan und Isolde* during the 1943–44 season, while Marjorie had been allocated Venus in each of the eight performances of *Tannhäuser* – five in New York and one each in Milwaukee, Chicago and Cleveland. Between the third and fourth performances of *Tannhäuser*, Johnson rang and asked: 'How would you like to sing Isolde for us on March fourteenth?' Marjorie admitted that the question took her so much by surprise that she almost dropped the telephone and had difficulty containing her excitement as she answered, as calmly as she could, that she would be delighted to.

The performance on 14 March was a matinee and not part of the regular subscription season at the Met; it was one of the benefit performances the company gave most years for charity. On this occasion the charity involved was the Grenfell Missionary Association, the president of which was a great fan of Marjorie's. He had suggested the opera and the singer, giving Johnson an excuse should Traubel or anyone else object. As it was for charity, Melchior had not objected when asked to sing Tristan and soon entered into the spirit of the event without any of the pettiness he had recently displayed. Kerstin Thorborg was delighted to sing Brangäne with her friend, Julius Huehn was again the strong-armed Kurvenal, Emanuel List sang King Marke and Beecham conducted. The *mise en scène* devised for Montreal was adapted to the Met stage and worked almost as well as it had there. The only mishap arose when Melchior found he did not have sufficient space in which to 'die' and had to move twice, *after* he had supposedly expired, to get into a comfortable enough position to last out the remainder of the opera. But nothing could detract from Marjorie's triumph.

As had been the case with Marjorie's first Venus, massive public interest had prompted the press to send along photographers to make a visual record of her first Isolde at the Met. The result is a series of candid photographs taken at rehearsal and during the performance. One of these in particular is, as the saying goes, a picture worth a thousand words. We see Isolde gesturing to Brangäne to prepare the goblet of poisoned wine, while Tristan stands self-consciously with his back turned to her. The essence of Marjorie's Isolde is distilled into that gesture – nobility, pride, determination and scorn are reflected on her upturned face and are echoed by her imperiously stretched arm and the thrust of her fluttering fingers. So potent is the image that it is almost possible to hear Marjorie's voice upbraiding her servant, and then coercing Tristan into drinking the poison.

We also have a clutch of reviews, more detailed and more scholarly than those that were written in Montreal. Jerome Bohm in the *New York Tribune* reported:

> *One scarcely missed Miss Lawrence's ability to move about, so strong was the lure of her personality and so apposite her gestures and her facial play. Her identification with the aggrieved Irish princess was complete. In the first act, her singing was profoundly stirring in its realization of the impassioned music, subtly coloured to suggest its shifting moods from the brooding, through the ironic to the tempestuous. It is many years since New York has heard so veracious an account of this portion of the score. The raging Isolde of the first act gave way to a meltingly tender and womanly impersonation in the second act.*[13]

Bohm noted, as did most of the other critics, that Marjorie seemed a little tired by the end of the long love duet, understandable considering how much she had already given and the enormous stress the occasion must have inflicted upon her. But she rallied for the *Liebestod*. Oscar Thompson told readers of the *New York Sun*:

> *Miss Lawrence was Isolde, because she sang Isolde's music as it should be sung, knowingly and with amplitude of tone. In the second act she sang the high Cs which we have not heard since Kirsten Flagstad began to ignore them in her last years here. These, with the climactic Bs in the first act were projected into the house with all the characteristic energy and power of this soprano before her illness.*[14]

Thompson predicted that Marjorie's Isolde would become a fixture at the Met like her Venus and would be heard for many seasons to come. He was wrong. Chicago demanded to hear Marjorie as Isolde during the spring tour and she gave her final performance of the role with the Met company in that city a month later.[15] What may seem inexplicable is not really hard to explain. Traubel stood by her ultimatum and Johnson gave in. It was better to have a mediocre Isolde who could also appear as Brünnhilde, than no Ring Cycle at all – and Johnson was still being accused of mounting 'freak shows'.

As with the Montreal performance, we have no recordings of either the New York or the Chicago *Tristan und Isolde* – their lack being all the more regrettable because of the superiority of the Met cast. We do, however, have a complete *Tannhäuser* taken from a broadcast of Marjorie's third performance of the season, about a month before her Isolde. Melchior sings the title role, Astrid Varnay sings Elisabeth, Wolfram is sung by Huehn and Kipnis is the sonorous Landgrave, with Paul Breisach conducting. Wagner's 'goddess of love' is a cardboard character and offers only a fraction of the vocal and dramatic opportunities of Isolde, but when we hear how Marjorie sings certain phrases in this broadcast we get an inkling of what her Isolde must have been like.

Sonically this is not one of the better Met broadcasts, but it is of enormous historical importance, preserving one of the most publicised assumptions of any role in the company's history. Through the crackle and distortion we can hear the 'sensuous, sustained song of *Geliebter, komm!*' referred to by Downes in his review of the testimonial gala. The warmth of Marjorie's middle voice, which had made her Salome so sexy, served Venus equally well. On this occasion the audience does not interrupt the performance when Venus curses Tannhäuser, but we can hear why this occurred elsewhere. It is also a pleasure to hear broad sensuous phrasing and top notes taken with ease, where most Venuses struggle and lose momentum. Listening to the young and vocally insecure Astrid Varnay doing her best as Elisabeth in the subsequent acts also highlights just how splendid Marjorie's voice still was and how accomplished her singing remained.

This recorded performance was also not without its offstage drama. After the Venusberg scene the curtain was raised so Marjorie and Melchior could take a bow together. The applause continued after the curtain fell again, but before it was raised a second time, Désiré Defrère hurried Melchior off stage so Marjorie could take a solo bow. The applause doubled and Defrère ordered that the curtain remain up for almost five minutes. Melchior stood in the wings for a while, fuming, then stormed off to his dressing room. So angry was he that he refused to take a solo bow after the next act.[16]

While petty battles raged at the Met, much larger and deadlier were those being fought in the Pacific, South-East Asia, Europe and North Africa. Marjorie, like everyone else in the United States, had followed the course of the war through newspapers and was appalled at the wholesale slaughter of Allied troops, horrified at the treatment of civilian populations and the atrocities committed on prisoners of war by the Axis forces. In the spirit of 'helping others' Marjorie and Tom both longed to make a contribution in whatever way they could to the Allied war effort.

As soon as she had become established once again, Marjorie offered her services to the United Services Organisations (USO) – a branch of the United Sates military that presented camp shows at home and abroad. Marjorie was welcomed onto the USO's huge roster of artists, which already included Bob Hope, Bing Crosby, Frank Sinatra, Judy Garland, Marlene Dietrich and Lily Pons. Marjorie's first assignment was a concert at Fort Hancock, which formed part of the key defences of New York Harbour. For this and any subsequent camp concerts, she was advised to sing 'lighter' music, but Marjorie rebelled at that and in the end was proven right.

What ridiculous impulse was it that made some people, and people in authority, too, think that because men had been put into uniforms their taste had suffered some strange metamorphosis enabling them to appreciate only the flippant and the trivial? Before I had finished my concerts in war areas, I had sung to hundreds of thousands of fighting men of all nationalities and it was a rare occurrence for me to give a concert without having many of the men come to me afterwards and thank me for having sung good music to them.[17]

Seated on a settee and wearing one of her most glamorous gowns, Marjorie sang 'The Lord's Prayer' (by way of introduction); this was followed by Purcell, Brahms, Schubert and Wagner, with the evening rounded off by English, Scottish and American songs. A small chamber orchestra accompanied her, and the troops at Fort Hancock loved the concert. In her diary that night Marjorie wrote 'Thank God, the boys like me. I'm so happy I could cry!'[18]

Marjorie returned for an annual concert at Fort Hancock for the remainder of the war, and for several years after she was adopted as part of the establishment's honorary personnel. Her first appearance at Fort Hancock, which took place after her return to the Met, prompted the camp to produce a handbill with a drawing of a very nubile young woman reclining seductively on a couch, her nakedness barely disguised by a diaphanous drape. Beneath the drawing was the caption 'Marjorie Lawrence as Venus, the Goddess of Love – A rare treat. Don't miss it!' Marjorie was amused and flattered by the drawing, but a few in the audience were probably disappointed when a fully robed Marjorie, carrying a few more pounds than she once had, appeared before them and opened her program with 'The Lord's Prayer'.

Between her regular engagements, Marjorie appeared at camps and military hospitals all over the United States. Her visits to hospitals (in her wheelchair) were an enormous morale booster for injured and sick men. She would sing for them and then mingle and chat with them about their experiences, their families and their hopes for the future. Many had no future, but Marjorie maintained her composure and her cheerfulness and a few minutes spent with her was often their last pleasant memory. At one of these hospital concerts, a spokesperson for the patients asked if they might adopt Marjorie as their 'Chin-up Girl'. 'We have plenty of *pin*-up girls', he explained, 'but we need a *chin*-up girl'. Marjorie was deeply touched and thereafter the USO billed her as 'The US Army's favourite chin-up girl'.

Marjorie also appeared at dozens of War Bonds rallies, was invited to launch a Liberty Ship[19] and made recordings of some songs for Columbia which were packaged in an album with the title *Marjorie Lawrence's Records for Fighting Men*.[20] Making these generous efforts on the home front was satisfying, but Marjorie wanted to emulate other entertainers who were being sent by the USO to the battlefields of the Pacific and South-East Asia to entertain the troops.

> *I wanted to get nearer the thick of things. At first the army was very reluctant to send me and my wheelchair to the battlefronts, saying I could expect no special consideration if I did go abroad. And I was told very bluntly that the authorities were not prepared to accept responsibility for what might happen to me and my health. But I could not be fobbed off! Whenever I got close enough to anyone with influence – American, Australian, English – I submitted them to what Australians call an earbashing and begged them to pull whatever strings needed pulling to get me overseas.*[21]

An invitation duly arrived from the Australian Government for Marjorie to tour army bases and military hospitals in northern Australia, singing for Australian, American, British, Indian and Dutch troops stationed there. Austin Wilder wrote to Sir Frank Tait (head of J. & N. Tait) suggesting that a public recital tour of the southern states of Australia under the Tait banner might be combined with the camp and hospital tour. Tait showed interest, but knowing how keen Marjorie was to sing for the troops in Australia, offered very paltry fees as an opening gambit. Austin Wilder took this up with Tait's agent in New York, Dorothy Stewart, and a better deal was struck. Wilder also began negotiations with the ABC for Marjorie to sing with their orchestras in Australia – without telling them about the arrangements already made with Tait. This resulted in yet another clash between Marjorie and the Australian Broadcasting Commission. Meanwhile Tom went into battle with the military authorities, trying desperately (and in the end unsuccessfully) to persuade them to lift the ban on civilians flying across the Pacific.

Between 15 and 19 May, Marjorie made a short propaganda film for the Australian Red Cross, to be shown during her forthcoming visit, before returning to Montreal for another performance of *Tristan und Isolde*. The following week the US military bestowed the honorary ranks of 'major' on Marjorie and 'captain' on Tom – to allow them entry to militarised zones and the use of officers' messes on their tour. It was also, as the officer who delivered their uniforms put it, 'Just a bit of insurance, ma'am, in case you should fall into enemy hands'. Marjorie doubted the Japanese would be overly intimidated by a major in a wheelchair or a captain who had been exempted from military service because of an old leg injury, but she was proud to wear the smart uniform and thought her oak leaf cluster looked rather nice pinned to her concert gowns. Fiorello la Guardia (who admitted he was envious of Marjorie for organising her way to the front) gave her and Tom a send-off at City Hall and they embarked from the airfield that now bears his name, on what would prove to be a trying, humbling and ultimately, deeply satisfying new adventure.

Chapter Sixteen
Off to War

When Marjorie and Tom embarked from Los Angeles on the small freighter *Parakoola*, only the ship's senior officers knew their exact destination. The passengers (nine in all, including Marjorie and Tom) had been told only that they were headed for an undisclosed port, somewhere in Australia. Although the *Parakoola* was registered in neutral Sweden, it was carrying armaments bound for General MacArthur's 'push' towards Tokyo. The ship's hold was crammed with tanks, guns and ammunition, and four brand new PT Boats were lashed to its deck. At night the ship was blacked out but in daylight it was a sitting target for Japanese aircraft and submarines. Many times on the twenty-four-day voyage, the captain had to order a change of course and zigzag to avoid detection or attack.

On board Marjorie discovered why Tom had tried so desperately to arrange for them to fly to Australia.

> *It had not entered my head that the hero I had married might be a poor sailor, but he was that and more. Two days out, poor Tom was wretched and vomiting continuously. And I discovered how helpless I was without him. I had gotten so used to him doing everything for me, it was frightening to see him so sick he couldn't get out of his bunk and me sitting in my wheelchair not being able to help him or myself.*[1]

There was one stewardess on board but she was not strong enough to lift Marjorie, so the burly second mate, Gunnar, offered his services and told Marjorie 'You want go somewhere? Just holler "Gunnar" and I come.' Marjorie hollered 'Gunnar' many times during the journey and the giant Swede carried her effortlessly from her cabin onto the deck, into the small saloon or the dining room and back again. There were other services Marjorie felt uncomfortable asking the seaman to perform, so a young Australian couple on board also came to her aid.

By one of those strange coincidences that occur when least expected, the couple came from Birregurra where Marjorie's aunt and uncle Prime had lived and where her mother had died. Yvonne Nicholls was suffering terribly from seasickness, but her husband Frank, like Marjorie, seemed immune to the illness. With instructions from Tom, Frank Nichols helped Marjorie shower and dress and carried out the daily massage treatment that was required to stop her legs aching.

> *Poor Frank. I really strained the friendship with him! As soon as he had his wife bedded down he'd come to help us and I asked him to do things I could never have asked a stranger to do, but then I never saw other Australians as 'strangers', rather as members of the same big family.*[2]

The *Parakoola* reached Sydney safely on 11 July and Marjorie found a very different city from the one she had left five years earlier. Huge guns and anti-submarine nets guarded the harbour entrance. Allied warships of all sizes were anchored in the harbour and dockside buildings were smeared with camouflage paint.

> *I was in a mood to be sad, when I looked down on the dock and saw an Australian 'digger', his cocked-up hat jauntily perched on his head as he walked with fixed bayonet along the dock. He looked up too and saw me sitting in my chair. 'Marge Lawrence!' he shouted, 'What the* hell *are you doing here?' That was better; that soldier's informal shout was Australian enough for me. This was home all right.*[3]

Marjorie had anticipated spending a week in Sydney to rest and recuperate and to rehearse with Raymond Lambert, her accompanist for the tour, but that was not to be.[4] Just hours after they settled into their hotel, two Australian Army officers arrived. One carried a large box of flowers from General Sir Thomas Blamey, Commander-in-Chief of the Australian Military Forces, and the other the news that the *Parakoola* had docked five days later than anticipated and, as soon as Marjorie's official permit to enter the Northern Territory (classified as a military zone) arrived, they were expected to commence the tour. Tom was still decidedly unwell, and both were relieved that the permit took two days to arrive.

On the afternoon of 14 July Marjorie, Tom, Lambert and a Lieutenant Kelly who had been assigned to travel with them were driven to Rose Bay on the southern shore of the harbour, where they boarded a Catalina flying boat bound for Townsville, two thousand kilometres north in tropical Queensland. The flight cheered Tom enormously. He wrote in his diary when they reached their destination:

> *We had the rear cabin to ourselves and we expected to spend the night at Gladstone, but Captain Denny flew on, reaching Townsville at 10.30 pm after fuel stops in Brisbane and Gladstone. Wonderfully smooth trip up the coast and incredibly I am not sick – ate a full lunch, dinner and snacks. Australian Army has a flat here (really half a house) for us overlooking the harbour and Magnetic Island.*[5]

Orme Denny's flying skills (he was one of Qantas's most-respected pilots) had earned Marjorie and Tom the luxury of a morning on the beach in Townsville and a drive in a staff car to view some of the beauty spots in the hinterland before Marjorie's first concert the following night. Townsville was full of American, Australian and other British Commonwealth troops and Marjorie commented in *Interrupted Melody* that she felt for the first time that indefinable 'war atmosphere' that pervaded the city, even though the nearest fighting was another 1500 kilometres to the north. That first concert – in the Wintergarden Theatre – almost prompted a riot. Hundreds of civilians claimed seats before the concert began and were then herded out by military police. As it was, only half of the 4000 soldiers who turned up could be accommodated in the theatre, but those who made it in rewarded Marjorie with a tremendous reception that included a chorus of wolf whistles.

Once again Marjorie refused to compromise on what she sang at this or any of the subsequent concerts on this tour. She opened with 'The Lord's Prayer', then offered excerpts from Wagner and German lieder, introducing these with a brief explanation of the story of the opera or the text of the song. The concert ended with English, Scottish, American and Australian songs. As well as accompanying Marjorie, Lambert played solo brackets of Bach, Beethoven, Brahms, Chopin and Debussy. The audiences lapped up the fare.

A celebratory supper organised by one of the Australian officers responsible for the defence of Townsville followed the first concert, but bright and early the next morning they boarded a huge Douglas C-47 transport plane, bound for Darwin. This time they had to share the accommodation with a hundred five-gallon cans of paint remover. Unfortunately during the first part of the journey one of the cans ruptured and the acrid fluid seeped along the floor of the fuselage. When they landed to refuel at Cloncurry in western Queensland, airfield staff used petrol to clean out the paint remover and when the passengers reboarded the aircraft they had another unpleasant smell to contend with. Next stop was Fenton Drome, a strategic airfield on a remote cattle station in the heart of the Northern Territory and home base for a squadron of American Liberator bombers.

On landing in Darwin they were met by a Major Paterson, in charge of amenities for the Australian army's Northern Territory Force, whom Tom described as 'a swell guy'. Paterson explained that Darwin's exposure to Japanese bombing raids meant that most of the force was stationed inland at Adelaide River. 'It's just down the road a bit', he explained as he bundled Marjorie, Tom, Lambert and Lieutenant Kelly into a staff car. The 'bit' turned out to be 130 kilometres through arid and dusty bushland. Between the fumes in the aircraft and the thick dust on the road to Adelaide River, Marjorie wondered if she would have any voice left. Major Paterson reassured his passengers that he had a crate of beer on ice awaiting their arrival, and although Marjorie didn't often drink beer, she spent much of the journey imagining how welcoming that cool and refreshing drink would be. It was late when they arrived at Adelaide River and as Marjorie was being placed in her wheelchair an agitated corporal approached Paterson and whispered something to him which seemed to distress the Major. A dinner of thick locally bred and butchered steak was waiting for them, but Paterson had to explain sorrowfully that he had bad news – some 'blighter' had 'pinched' the beer.

The following evening Marjorie and Lambert gave a concert in what was euphemistically called 'The Adelaide River Theatre' – a huge open-air amphitheatre with a crudely built stage constructed of scrounged timber, galvanised iron and hessian. The commanding officer, General George 'Tubby' Alan owned the only settee on the base and was happy to lend it to Marjorie. During the afternoon, 10,000 American, Australian, Dutch, English and Indian troops began arriving from airfields, anti-aircraft posts, camps, hospitals and naval stations within a 200-kilometre radius, and when a staff car came to convey Marjorie, Tom and Lambert to the venue they became caught in a traffic jam so dense that it took almost an hour to cover a kilometre. Finally the concert got underway – but the delays were not quite over.

In the utter silence of the bush night Raymond Lambert began the introduction to 'The Lord's Prayer'. Hushed and attentive the vast audience waited. I filled my lungs with air and opened my mouth to sing when the funny little locomotive that drags a weekly train from Central Australia to Darwin let out a piercing peep to announce its departure from Adelaide River. I stopped dead, my mouth agape. There was a roar of laughter from the assembled soldiery followed by a shout from a typically Australian voice, 'Come on Marge, give it a go!'

I nodded to Raymond. He played the introduction again and I 'gave it a go'. Raymond and I played and sang for an hour and half. If I never achieved more with my singing than I did that night, my career has been worthwhile. As the concert ended the commanding officer came on stage and made a speech. He wound up saying, 'And now boys, let's give three cheers for Marjorie Lawrence'. That moment I shall remember forever: ten thousand troops standing in the darkness beneath a star-smothered sky and cheering me. I was very proud because I had been able to bring them brief surcease from the horrible business of war.[6]

The next morning Marjorie held a press conference for war correspondents based at Adelaide River and visited the military hospital, again capturing the hearts and touching the souls of the wounded troops. To a soldier in a wheelchair, Marjorie said cheerfully 'I hope we'll both be out of our jeeps soon'. Tom reported that the hospital was nothing more than a vast collection of huts and tents in clearings cut out of the bush, but the patients were expertly and lovingly cared for. The vegetable farm at the base also impressed him and he wrote in his diary: 'It's a forest of tomatoes, vegies, pineapples and watermelons that grow like wildfire in this climate'.[7]

That afternoon the party were driven back to Darwin and they dined with the general officer commanding the city, while the following day was spent relaxing and feasting on chilled watermelon from a giant crate of produce that had been delivered to them as an offering from the Adelaide River farm unit. That evening they gave a concert in the Darwin Theatre – another makeshift venue completed just an hour before they arrived for the performance. Tom described the event as 'another thrilling concert before many thousands of cheering, appreciative troops' and noted that small green frogs hopped all over the stage during the performance.[8]

This Darwin concert was to have been the final one of the troop tour, but the following morning Marjorie was approached by senior staff of the Australian General Hospital and the US Camp Hospital in Darwin asking if she would sing for their patients. Only a few hours remained before their scheduled departure, but Marjorie could not refuse. At the American hospital she was rewarded with the first glass of her favourite drink – Coca Cola – since leaving America and the gratitude and admiration of some of the most seriously wounded soldiers she had so far encountered.

That afternoon Marjorie and her party flew from Darwin to Katherine, where she gave another impromptu concert at the local military hospital there, then on to Adelaide via Alice Springs, in time to catch the Adelaide to Melbourne Express. Tom estimated that in a week and a half Marjorie had sung to 22,000 soldiers and won the hearts of most of them. A few days after they reached Melbourne a letter arrived from General Blamey saying how much he appreciated what Marjorie had done, but it was the responses that came from ordinary soldiers that touched her most. One soldier told her that she reminded him of the blonde barmaid in his home town who was a 'real corker', as was Marjorie. A sergeant of the Ninth Docks Operations Company based in Darwin wrote to say that she had put new life into many a sad heart and that he felt she must be telepathic. When he attended Marjorie's concert, he explained, he had done so with the vague hope that she might sing one of his two favourite songs – 'Danny Boy' and the Bach-Gounod 'Ave Maria' – and she had sung both. 'I feel sure I will never hear them sung so beautifully again. May God forever bless you', he wrote.[9]

In the weeks leading up to this tour and while Marjorie and Tom were in northern Australia, the Allied thrust against the Japanese had seen the retaking of most of New Guinea and a rapid advance towards the Philippines. Much of this action was in evidence when Marjorie and her party had arrived in Townsville and Darwin, with reconnaissance planes taking off and landing non-stop, flotillas of fighting ships and supply ships being loaded and vast squadrons of planes setting out for the battle zone. Marjorie found this satisfying not only because it meant the tide of war was turning against the Japanese, but for a personal reason as well. Before leaving the United States, she had decided that after completing the northern Australian leg of her tour she would try to get permission to travel to

New Guinea and entertain the front line troops there. Given the current situation, this plan now seemed practical. The office of the United Services Organisations in Australia was happy to arrange the trip and General MacArthur's headquarters said they had no objection, but pointed out that, as New Guinea was now under the operational control of the Australians, she would need their permission as well. To Marjorie's dismay General Blamey's headquarters flatly refused to let her go. Marjorie immediately went over Blamey's head and applied to the Australian Government.

As she awaited a response from the government Marjorie visited her family in Victoria and toured military hospitals and military bases in the southern states. Her answer finally arrived in a cable from Frank Forde, Deputy Prime Minister and Minister for the Army, and supported Blamey's decision. In *Interrupted Melody*, Marjorie claims that the reason for their blunt refusal was that the Australian authorities considered her too great a security risk – that she might 'blab' about what she saw in New Guinea and put their military efforts in jeopardy – but that was wrong. The true reason was that there were still pockets of Japanese resistance in New Guinea and the surrounding islands, and neither the general nor the politician wanted to be blamed if such a high-profile and popular Australian as Marjorie Lawrence fell victim to desperate enemy fire.[10] It would not be long before Marjorie was back giving concerts to grateful troops, but in the meantime she had to content herself with her public recitals under the Tait banner and concerts for the ABC.

Marjorie and Tom stayed for a couple of days with Lena and her husband Nelson Batson on their small farm at Wallington, west of Geelong. Marjorie was photographed by the press in her wheelchair nursing a lamb, feeding a calf from a bottle and scattering grain for the 'chooks'. For one memorable photo she also hoisted herself up into a standing position, holding onto a gate while she fed chaff to two friendly plough horses. Tom was introduced to the simple pleasures of country life in Australia and commented to the press that he hadn't seen meat, butter and cream of such quality or quantity in the United States since before the war. The tour continued with Marjorie's triumphant return to Winchelsea on the back of a farm cart and splendid civic receptions organised for her in Melbourne, Geelong, Ballarat and Sydney.

Marjorie's recitals were a resounding success – artistically and commercially. There were no problems with attendance this time. Marjorie sang well, Lambert played well and capacity audiences cheered them enthusiastically. The doyen of British critics, Neville Cardus, who spent the war years in Australia, penned a laudatory and perceptive review of her third Sydney recital that gives a more accurate assessment of her as a recitalist than most of those written in the United States.

The superb range of Marjorie Lawrence's voice never ends in mere abnormality. Always there is the touch of nature in it, so, unlike many opera singers, she is

> *not removed from intimate poetry. She is an artist in all she gives us. There is unselfconscious pathos woven into her singing. She sings Rachmaninov's* Floods of Spring *with the utmost gush of lyricism and from its almost banal melody she distils a rapture that is as near to tears as happiness. She even makes something engaging and rhythmically enchanting out of* Waltzing Matilda.[11]

Through Cardus we also learn that Marjorie has (too late) found the key to singing Carmen and how she coped with pieces like the *Liebestod* from *Tristan und Isolde* with only a piano to support her.

> *With hardly a gesture and using her expressive eyes and a voice that acted, she sang the 'Seguidilla' from Carmen as vividly as I have heard it for years … and she began the* Liebestod *with the softest and most raptly phrased singing. Later, though the surge to the climax was rich in vocal splendour, no doubt she would have given it greater 'throb' and exultation had she been singing with an orchestra.*[12]

At her final recital in Melbourne, on 29 August, Marjorie took the opportunity to celebrate some news that had just reached Australia – the liberation of her beloved Paris after four grim years of German occupation. The audience rose to its feet as Marjorie sang first the *Marseillaise*, then *Rule Britannia*. Pride turned to relief when a postcard arrived a few weeks later from Madame Grodet, the first communication Marjorie had from her adopted French family for three years. In a spidery hand that betrayed how little vision she had left, Marie Grodet explained that 'Monsieur' had died a year earlier, that she and Mimi were well and living in a tiny apartment just a block down the hill from Avenue Trudaine and that they both hoped Marjorie's career was prospering.[13]

While in Brisbane to give recitals, Marjorie agreed to audition a young singer with a fine tenor voice. The young man was Harold Blair, an Australian Aborigine who had grown up on a mission station and who currently worked as a sugar cane cutter. At that time he was completely unknown. Wearing borrowed clothes and the first hat he had ever owned, Blair came to Marjorie's suite at Lennon's Hotel in Brisbane, desperately intimidated by his surroundings and the task before him. Tom wheeled Marjorie to a piano and she asked the young man to sing some scales, as others had asked of her years before. By his own admission, until that time the only 'scales' Blair had heard of were attached to fish, so Marjorie had to improvise.[14] Eventually she had him singing excellent top Cs and giving a reasonable account of himself in her stand-by, 'The Lord's Prayer'.

Marjorie liked Blair and he was fascinated by her. Through Marjorie's efforts the press began to take an interest in him and she recommended he start taking singing lessons with a view to making a career as a singer. Eventually he did have a short career (including a tour of the United States and a recital at Carnegie Hall) but, as the few records Blair made prove, he was not quite good enough as a singer to make the grade. Instead, he became a modestly successful businessman and a highly respected activist for the advancement of Aboriginal people in Australia. How Blair's singing career ended was a disappointment to Marjorie, but it always pleased her to recall that she had given encouragement to the first Indigenous Australian to at least attempt a career as a classical singer.

Controversy surrounded the concerts Marjorie gave with the ABC's symphony orchestras on this visit. The conductor of the Philadelphia Orchestra, Eugene Ormandy, was appearing in Australia at the time – the first conductor of note to venture 'down under' since Beecham in 1940 – and the public wanted to hear Ormandy and Marjorie together. Marjorie had sung under Ormandy's baton in America and they shared a mutual regard and respect for one another. Ormandy would have been delighted to have had Marjorie as soloist at his concerts and told her so when he called on her in her Sydney hotel.

A rash of letters appeared in the newspapers, demanding the ABC bow to the public's desire to hear them together and the ABC responded with a statement that joint appearances by the singer and the conductor were not possible because Marjorie's troop tour of northern Australia had disrupted their concert schedule. This was clearly not the case and it is more likely that the ABC was simply considering the financial implications of a joint appearance and that combining these two major celebrities squandered their individual drawing power. At the time another explanation was widely canvassed among the players in the orchestras which may also have had some credence. The Machiavellian Bernard Heinze, now senior among Australia's resident maestros, was set on conducting any and all concerts Marjorie might give with the ABC orchestras and was not averse to using his power to achieve that. In the end she gave only two concerts – with the Sydney Symphony Orchestra and the Melbourne-based Victorian Symphony Orchestra, both conducted by Heinz.

While in Sydney Marjorie also made a small group of recordings for the Australian branch of Columbia, with Raymond Lambert accompanying. Two discs were issued. The first featured 'Rule Britannia', backed by Alfred Hill's arrangement of 'Haere Ra' (the 'Maori Song of Farewell'), which 2000 Australian troops about to embark for the front had sung to Marjorie at Keswick Barracks near Adelaide. The second disc offered the local patriotic song 'God Bless Australia' and Marjorie's now famous rendition of 'Waltzing Matilda'. Popular though these discs proved with the Australian buying public, they contribute little to our knowledge or enjoyment of Marjorie's singing. Her diction is, as always, exemplary but the voice sounds tired and the singing uncharacteristically tentative.[15]

Before she departed from Australia, Marjorie gave one of her Lilly Daché hats (her 'pepper-uppers' as she called them) to be auctioned for charity. The wife of the president of the Footscray Football Club secured the hat for fifty pounds, less than it had cost Marjorie in New York. She also handed over to the *Argus* newspaper in Melbourne the pair of crutches she had used occasionally in private during this tour with instructions that they be given to someone deserving. Eventually they were presented to a female patient at the Alfred Hospital who had fractured both legs in a riding accident.

This time Marjorie left Australia with more than had arrived with her, including all her earnings. She also took with her seeds of various native Australian plants for the garden at Harmony Hills, an odd-looking hat trimmed with gum nuts, gum blossom and two felt kangaroos (the gift of a patriotic milliner) and a masseuse named Amy Featherstone, whom Marjorie had employed in Australia and who had served Marjorie so well during the latter part of the tour that she was asked to accompany them back to the United States to double as masseuse and personal maid. 'Feathers', as Marjorie called her, stayed on as part of Marjorie's team for some years.

Marjorie, Tom and Feathers took passage again on the *Parakoola*, bound for Vancouver and reached ice-bound New York in time to round off this tropical Australian adventure with a New Year's Eve concert for Australian servicemen. Here Marjorie was joined on the platform by another Australian, Flying Officer Kenneth Neate of the Royal Canadian Air Force, who would have a distinguished career as a tenor in London and Germany after the war.

Marjorie immediately got back into the swing of performing life in the United States doing concerts with the major orchestras, including with Eugene Ormandy, this time with the conductor's own orchestra in Philadelphia. She contacted Edward Johnson to let him know she was available, but there was no interest from the Met, then or in the future. *Tannhäuser* was not performed during the 1944–45 season and when it returned to the repertoire, a new star, Blanche Thebom, sang Venus. Traubel meantime had regained her hold on Isolde and dominated that role at the Met until she abandoned opera a few years later in favour of nightclubs and Broadway.

Marjorie also renewed her acquaintance with the Roosevelts. She sang 'The Star Spangled Banner' at the opening of the President's fourth inauguration dinner in Washington, although the President himself was too busy to attend. Perhaps it was well that Roosevelt did not, for Marjorie inadvertently almost turned the dinner into a strip show. As Tom was dressing her in an anteroom, the long zip in the back of her gown broke and she had no other with her to wear. A member of the Woman's Army Auxiliary Corp volunteered to sew Marjorie into the gown, but as Marjorie sang the stitches popped out one by one. By the end of the song only will power and the back rest of her wheelchair were holding the gown up.

The next morning Marjorie and Tom joined the crowd assembled on the snow-covered lawn below the south portico of the White House to witness a frail and exhausted FDR being sworn in for his fourth term. There was a bank of newsreel cameras lined up to record the historic event and the *United News* crew took a panning shot across the front of the crowd. Marjorie can be seen clearly, sitting in her wheelchair, rugged up against the bitter cold and with Tom standing in his accustomed position behind her. That afternoon Marjorie and Tom returned to the White House for afternoon tea with Mrs Roosevelt, along with 3000 other guests.

> *We entered the White House through the President's own private entrance and elevator. The butler said 'Tell me your names for Mrs Roosevelt' and Marjorie said 'I think she'll know me'. Then Eleanor turned around and greeted us saying 'I think you'd like to see the President, wouldn't you?' She left for a moment, returning almost immediately to say it was arranged. On the way to the study, the President's old coloured [sic] manservant said to Marjorie: 'But ma'am, you're such a pretty lady. I didn't think anybody like you would ever be in a wheelchair!' We were pounding with excitement when we were shown into the President's study. We found him poring over a huge file marked 'Confidential'. He knew but we didn't, that he was leaving the next day for the Yalta conference that would decide the fate of the post-war world. He greeted us courteously and cheerfully and he and Marjorie talked about their conditions. 'My doctor tells me we get better until we're seventy, so I've at least got that to look forward to', he said. Marjorie mentioned that her knees gave her trouble and the President agreed saying 'What a pity it gets us all in the knees!'* [16]

Few people saw President Roosevelt that day and Marjorie rated her private audience with him as one of the highlights of her life. She was so proud to have been singled out for this honour that she couldn't resist boasting about it to the taxi driver who drove them from the White House back to their hotel.

Three months later Marjorie returned to Washington to give a recital in Constitution Hall. She took a nap during the afternoon and was woken by Tom to say that it had just been announced over the radio that President Roosevelt had died. Marjorie cancelled her recital and sent all the flowers she had been given to the White House. Just as Marjorie was an inspiration to so many others, Franklin Delano Roosevelt had inspired her.

As the world slowly emerged from darkness and the defeat of Germany and Japan became a probability rather than a possibility, there were moves to re-establish opera in the capitals of Europe. In London the Royal Opera House had been used as a dance hall since 1939, but now a committee appointed by the Arts Council was making plans to resume performances of opera and ballet. A member of that committee, Ralph Hawkes (a partner in the music publishing company Boosey & Hawkes) visited New York in January 1945 and one of the singers he approached was Marjorie, possibly at the suggestion of Sir Thomas Beecham. There were discussions about what Marjorie might sing in the inaugural post-war season at Covent Garden and interest centred on Isolde. Marjorie was elated. She had not sung in London since the brief and disappointing tour of 1937 and she was keen to make a fresh start.

Marjorie had changed agents again, replacing Austin Wilder with J. Colstan Leigh, and Ralph Hawkes confirmed that he would commence negotiations with

Leigh as soon as he arrived back in London.[17] To Marjorie's dismay the negotiations never even began. *Tristan und Isolde* was not included in the repertoire for the first post-war season at Covent Garden and by the time it was given (in the second season) Flagstad was back in circulation and sang each of the ten performances.

Marjorie received a consolation prize, however, in the form of an invitation from ENSA (Entertainments National Service Association), which organised entertainment for British troops, to tour Britain the following summer. In mid-May ENSA invited Marjorie to extend her tour to include concerts for the Allied occupation forces in Germany for, by then, the war in Europe, which had dragged on for six ghastly years, was over.

Chapter Seventeen
Twilight of the Gods

Marjorie, Tom and Feathers embarked for Europe aboard the *Queen Mary* on 5 June 1945. The great Cunard liner had served as a troop carrier for the previous six years and still wore its shabby, field-grey wartime uniform, with defensive guns mounted where elegant couples had once promenaded. There were 1200 other civilians on board and most, like Marjorie, were returning to Europe for the first time since the war, excited and apprehensive in equal measure about what they might find on arrival.

Disembarkation was at the Scottish port of Gourock. An ENSA bus was waiting to drive Marjorie, Tom and Feathers to Glasgow and before they flew south to London, Marjorie asked if she could be taken to see Loch Lomond, claiming she had often sung about that famous stretch of water. In fact, Marjorie's recital programs and radio broadcasts show that she seldom sang 'Loch Lomond', but no one could blame any musician for wanting to catch a glimpse of its sun-bright waters and bonnie banks. In the end a glimpse was all they got. The car they were taken in broke down near Dumbarton and when they finally arrived at the loch it was enveloped in a heavy mist.

In London they were met by the young Joan Ingpen, later founder of an influential artists' management company, artistic administrator of Covent Garden and consultant to the Met. Ingpen drove them to the Savoy, where a suite had been reserved for them. There they also met the other members of their tour concert party: Valda Aveling, a young Australian pianist who was to be the supporting artist and accompanists Norah Newby and Hubert Greenslade, the latter doubling as musical director and tour manager.[1]

Marjorie was impressed by her colleagues' friendliness and professionalism, but found the tour itinerary and the arrangements for their concerts disappointing and disorganised. There were excuses – hostilities had just ceased, military mopping-up was still in progress, millions of displaced people had to be dealt with and the Allies were still learning by trial and error how to be effective occupying forces – but none of these impressed Marjorie. No concerts had been organised in London, even though the city was teaming with military personnel and concert life was beginning to return to normal. Marjorie and Tom were told to sit and wait and when the authorities could use them, they would. It was not an encouraging start.

Marjorie and Tom put this spare time to good use, scheduling meetings with Ralph Hawkes, Harold Holt and Walter Legge. Legge was then attached to ENSA, but Marjorie was more interested in the influence he had over the Gramophone Company and the London concert business through the new orchestra – the Philharmonia – he was forming. They also attended a performance of Benjamin Britten's new opera *Peter Grimes* at Sadler's Wells and Ralph Hawkes introduced Marjorie and Tom to the composer. Later Tom wrote in his diary:

> *Some fantastic music, singing and scenery. Britten young and unassuming. Ralph Hawkes interested in him doing something with Marjorie.*[2]

Nothing came of that interest and the musicians seem on paper unlikely collaborators, but who knows what such a mix might have produced: we might have had a piece like Britten's *Phaedra* thirty years earlier if Hawkes had pressed on. As it is, there is no record of Marjorie ever singing anything of Britten's, apart from one or two of his folk song arrangements. For her 'English' opera meant Purcell, and English song ended with the generation before Britten.

ENSA finally managed to organise one concert for Marjorie in London – in a workers' club in Walthamstow, before she and the rest of the concert party departed for the continent. The first stop was Brussels, where they went sight-seeing (Marjorie and Tom photographed one another beside *Le mannikan pis*.) No concert had been arranged in Brussels but, as it was American Independence Day, Marjorie agreed to an impromptu lunchtime concert for 400 American engineers, bored and frustrated at their posting.

Marjorie's loosely planned itinerary covered cities and towns in the British Occupation Zone, stretching across northern Germany from the Belgian border to the Baltic. From Brussels they flew to Lübeck, Tom noting in his diary how they passed over hundreds of burnt-out aircraft on the ground and airfields, bridges and towns destroyed by bombs. When the plane landed for refuelling in Hamburg they made their descent over block after block of blackened ruins, and Marjorie wrote in her diary that the once great city looked like a ghost town.

On arriving at Lübeck they were told they were neither expected nor wanted there. The local head of ENSA whom Tom described as 'a pompous ass', claimed he did not know they were coming and said he could not possibly arrange a concert without several days notice. Someone in the Baltic port must have been aware of their arrival, however, for Marjorie and Tom found a *char-à-banc* waiting for them at their hotel. With the vehicle came a friendly 'Tommy', named Sergeant Bill Marshall, who introduced himself and said he and his vehicle had been put at the concert party's disposal for the tour.

The large, grey-painted *char-à-banc*, which had probably been a civilian bus in England before the war, had been fitted out with comfortable seating for eight, sleeping compartments for four, a toilet, a kerosene stove and a sink. Marjorie inspected the vehicle and gave it her approval; 'very comfortable', she wrote in her diary. Bill Marshall, indomitably cheerful and a skilled driver, proved his worth and so did the *char-à-banc* as they travelled over roads pitted with bomb craters and rickety temporary bridges and through areas where the hotels had been requisitioned by the military and restaurants had no food.

In Lübeck Marjorie and Tom once again filled in time sightseeing and watched children scrambling for loose potatoes as a truck was unloaded, while adults scrambled for cigarette butts discarded by soldiers. They drove to the resort town of Travemünde and witnessed German families trying to enjoy themselves on the beach. Marjorie reported that they encountered no antagonism, just intense indifference from these undernourished and careworn members of 'the master race'. The pompous ass in Lübeck finally organised a concert for Marjorie in the White Knight Theatre. In the audience at this and each of the concerts Marjorie gave in Germany were British and Commonwealth military personnel; German civilians were not permitted to attend. Many tried, however, gathering in the street outside each venue, sitting on the pavement to hear what they could not see and joining in the applause.

> *Inevitably, I suppose, because of the place and the prevailing mood, I found myself singing more German music. I sang the Immolation Scene at almost every concert and sometimes Isolde's Narrative and Curse or the* Liebestod, *plus a lot of Brahms and Schubert. Hubert Greenslade and Norah Newby were both very intelligent and sensitive musicians and coped well with the music and the battered pianos they had to play. Many of these instruments had notes that stuck and pedals that had to be pumped. I usually started, as I had on the Australian troop tour, with 'The Lord's Prayer' and now finished with 'Rule Britannia'. Amazingly, the Germans outside seemed to get caught up in the fervour of this last piece as much as the British audiences inside and applauded it as much as they did their own music.*[3]

After complaints from Greenslade about the treatment Marjorie was receiving, the ENSA people in Hamburg organised a concert there for Royal Air Force personnel. As Marjorie, Tom and their companions drove into Hamburg their earlier impressions of the great German port were confirmed, with Tom reporting that they drove for miles through streets lined with rubble and wreckage, beneath which lay thousands of bodies yet to be retrieved. After the concert the RAF officers put on a supper of poached eggs and baked beans washed down with whisky and cognac for their guests in an undamaged house requisitioned from a German doctor.

Subsequent concerts were given at Cuxhaven, Hesedorf, Verden, Lüneburg and Celle, all relatively inconsequential places forced into unwanted prominence by the presence of large occupation forces. At Detmold and Bad Oeynhausen they had the luxury of performing in opera houses, patched up and dusted off for the occasion. At Lüneberg they visited Johanniskirche, where Bach had once been organist, and the house where the poet Heine had lived, and at Cuxhaven they watched Allied minesweepers clearing the port. At Hesedorf when Tom admired a high-powered German rifle a Canadian major had 'souvenired', the friendly officer insisted on making Tom a gift of it.[4]

At Celle a RAF Flight Officer asked if Marjorie and Tom would like to visit Belsen Concentration Camp, a few kilometres away. Belsen had been liberated just thirteen weeks earlier and the officer warned that it was not a place for the faint-hearted. Prompted by curiosity, the uniqueness of the opportunity and an indefinable sense of duty, Marjorie, Tom, Feathers and Sergeant Marshall accepted.

The dead had been buried and many of the buildings at Belsen burned to prevent the spread of typhus, but a miasma of terror, privation, suffering and death still hung over the camp. Michael Bentine (of 'Goons Show' fame), who had visited a few weeks earlier, described Belsen as 'the ultimate blasphemy', and Marjorie, Tom, Amy Featherstone and Bill Marshall would have agreed. Marjorie wrote in her diary:

> This can't be possible. The stench of the dead is overpowering. I will never forget that odour. A mud-stained Hebrew Testament was fluttering on top of one of the mass graves where 5000 people are buried and further on, a French Bible. There are bones and shoes and old clothing everywhere, barbed wire and smashed searchlights. It is just unbelievably awful and I will never, ever forget this place.[5]

Bill Marshall used Tom's camera to take some 'snaps' at Belsen. One of the most moving shows a grim-faced Marjorie with Tom, Feathers and the RAF Flying Officer beside one of the crematorium ovens. Marjorie gave a concert in Celle that evening and was invited to a chicken and champagne supper afterwards. Truth to tell, she was not in the mood for frivolity or food, but accepted the supper invitation because she desperately needed to hear the sounds of men living and laughing again.

While staying at Bad Salzuflen, the location of the British Occupation Forces headquarters, a signal came from London that dispelled any lingering emotions Marjorie may have been feeling about Nazi efficiency and ENSA's lack of it. A full colonel from General Montgomery's staff presented himself at their quarters, saluted and handed Marjorie an envelope. Inside was a message from Buckingham Palace, requesting that Marjorie sing for Her Majesty Queen Elizabeth (the mother of the present monarch) at the palace on 1 August – one week hence. Marjorie was surprised and delighted. Tom was delighted, but not surprised, for he had engineered the invitation without informing Marjorie.

Back in June, Tom had written from the Savoy Hotel to the palace saying that his wife would be honoured and gratified to be given the opportunity to sing for

King George VI and Queen Elizabeth, should their majesties wish it. At the time, the queen was looking for a way to reward the female staff of Buckingham Palace and Windsor Castle who had voluntarily joined her weekly knitting and sewing bees throughout the war years. Tom's offer prompted the idea of a concert in the Music Room at Buckingham Palace, to which these 200 loyal women would be invited to hear Marjorie sing, with Her Majesty present. Walter Legge had liaised with the palace and the signal that arrived at Bad Salzuflen was the culmination of the pair's endeavours.

Before returning to London, Marjorie had two more concerts to give on the continent, not for ENSA, but for the American United Services Organisations – for American troops. One was at the Théâtre Monnaie in Brussels and the other in the Théâtre Marigny in Paris. It was a pleasure for Marjorie to sing in the great opera house of Brussels, but a joy beyond expression to be returning to her beloved Paris.

The historic Théâtre Marigny, where Offenbach had once been director, was filled to capacity on the night of the concert, which was intended for American military personnel only, but a few of Marjorie's old friends and colleagues bribed their way in. None of the Grodets were present, but Mimi had been waiting for Marjorie in the lobby of the Hotel Favart when they first arrived and after the concert, Marjorie took Tom to the Grodets' little apartment for supper. Madame Grodet was now so frail she looked as if a puff of wind might blow her away, but she was still the gracious aristocrat, offering a wizened hand for Tom to kiss. Henri was there too, desperately gaunt and still recovering from a period of imprisonment by the Germans. Mimi looked twenty years older, but treated Marjorie with the same sisterly affection she always had. There were many tears, with Marjorie distressed at the state of her friends and they at seeing her for the first time trapped in a wheelchair.

According to Marjorie, when they returned to London Tom phoned the palace and spoke to Lady Katherine Seymour (future Lady-in-Waiting to Queen Elizabeth II) about the concert. When he explained how Marjorie usually made her appearances, Lady Katherine suggested he come to the palace and oversee the arrangements. Tom's solo visit to the palace daunted him and amused Marjorie.

> *Imagine my angel, a small town American doctor, going through the palace looking for a suitable settee with attendants nonplussed at his rejecting this one and that one because of the height or the angle of the back or the colour. Finally Tom selected a beautiful one that would not clash with the gown I had chosen (the gown was embroidered with golden Australian wattle flowers) and located the right platform to go under it and a screen for when he transferred me from my chair to the settee.*[6]

On the great day Marjorie, Tom and Norah Newby (who was to accompany Marjorie) arrived early at the palace to set up the screen and prepare Marjorie for the 4 pm recital. Their understanding was that the guests would arrive, after which the Queen would enter, talk to the guests and then greet Marjorie, but before Marjorie was ready one of the Queen's Ladies-in-Waiting rushed up and said: 'The Queen is coming and will see Miss Lawrence first'.

The Queen arrived followed closely by the Princesses Elizabeth and Margaret. Norah Newby whispered under her breath: 'My God, there're *three* of them. I'll have to curtsy three times!'[7] Marjorie had practised an elaborate bow in lieu of a curtsy, but Tom caught her looking upwards during her bows, her face gleaming with excitement.

> *I couldn't believe that it was me – Marge Lawrence from Dean's Marsh – being greeted by the Queen and about to sing for her. At that moment I felt I was not only doing something wonderful for myself but for my country as well. I was struck by how beautiful, natural and gracious the Queen was and I understood in that moment why everyone loved her so much.*[8]

The palace had approved the program Marjorie had submitted. She had particularly asked if it would be acceptable for her to sing some lieder in German and the answer had come back that Her Majesty had no objection. In honour of the Queen's Scottish heritage, Marjorie also included 'Annie Laurie' and 'Doun the Burn', but quite unexpectedly the highlight of the concert came when Marjorie sang the Seguidilla from *Carmen*. Two of the royal corgis had also joined the party, trotting in and settling at Her Majesty's feet. When Marjorie threw off the final top note, one of the dogs ('Crackers' by name) leapt to his feet and barked furiously. The audience laughed and so did Marjorie. She addressed the Queen: 'Your Majesty, I don't think your little dog likes me' and the Queen replied: 'On the contrary Miss Lawrence, he is showing his appreciation … he is Welsh and all the Welsh are music lovers'.[9]

Despite this canine interjection, the recital went very well, Her Majesty leading the applause and inviting Marjorie, Tom and Newby to take tea with her and the princesses at its conclusion. Marjorie noted with pride that the sandwiches served were thinly buttered and sparsely filled and that the Royal Family shared the privations of food rationing along with their people.

> *The Queen chatted to me for about twenty minutes and asked many questions about the ENSA tour I had just done and my troop tour of Australia. She seemed genuinely interested in every detail. The princesses, Elizabeth and Margaret Rose, stayed in the background shyly, until Tom suggested they join the conversation.*[10]

Sixty-six years later, Her Majesty Queen Elizabeth II still remembers that afternoon and how beautifully Marjorie sang.[11] If Marjorie was alive today, no doubt she would be as proud to be remembered by the present sovereign as she was to sing in her presence on that memorable afternoon in 1945. The day after the concert Marjorie received a memento in the form of an inscribed photograph from the Queen.

Before leaving London, Marjorie signed a contract with Harold Holt to return to Britain for a recital and concert tour the following winter. During the voyage back to New York, news arrived that the Japanese had surrendered and peace had finally been restored to both sides of the globe. Back in New York Marjorie was asked to write an article for *The Musical Digest* about her wartime musical experiences and she took the opportunity for some rare and profound philosophising:

> *Although bombs and guns can destroy lives and cities there are things they cannot destroy. Music is one. No amount of destruction can wipe out the music of the great masters. Physical destruction of scores, instruments and even musicians can and has occurred, but the music itself remains. Music can make us forget the horrors of the past and it can foster tolerance among us as we enter the future. Out of the chaos and destruction of this war has come a new soberness of thought and understanding, and appreciation of classical music will grow as a result. It is up to us to foster and preserve the things we fought for and music has always been and always will be part of what makes us civilised.*[12]

In November, Marjorie and Tom were back in Britain and preparing for Marjorie's post-war public debut in London as soloist with the BBC Symphony Orchestra conducted by Sir Adrian Boult in the Royal Albert Hall. They found London much changed in three months and not for the better, as they had expected. Evening concerts began at six because of desperate fuel shortages; people in the street, now divested of their uniforms, looked shabbily dressed. Food rationing was stricter than ever and when Marjorie asked for eggs and bacon at the Savoy, the waiter replied: 'Did you bring them with you, madam?'[13]

As noted earlier, in later years when Marjorie discussed her career she chose to overlook her 1937 concert in London and refer to the one she gave with Boult in the Royal Albert Hall on 14 November 1945 as her debut in the British capital. This is understandable in light of the differences between the two occasions and the concomitantly different responses each drew from London critics. Marjorie was in top form and *The Times* reported:

> *Marjorie Lawrence, who comes to us from Australia by way of Paris and New York, is endowed with a voice that is generous in tone and in range and solid and brilliant in quality. She sang 'Divinités du Styx' from Gluck's* Alceste *and finished with the closing scene from Strauss'* Salome, *which revealed the full extent of her dramatic powers. In both she sang to the scale of the music, and that in* Salome, *means riding triumphant above the tumultuous seas of Strauss' orchestration.*[14]

The critic of *The Star* commented that Marjorie 'astonished and shocked' the vast audience in the Royal Albert Hall and released 'a pent up thunderstorm of sound' in the Strauss scene. 'Vast notes left her throat as if it were a trumpet and the audience cheered her.'[15] The *Daily Mail* reported that her singing placed Marjorie 'among the greatest singers of our time'.[16] Four nights later she returned to the Royal Albert Hall, this time to sing the Immolation Scene with the London Symphony Orchestra conducted by Beecham. Walter Legge attended both concerts and wrote to Marjorie:

> *Wagnerian sopranos are the capital ships of the operatic fleet, universally admired but rare and precious. Your launching here has been a most auspicious one. I owe you a resplendent meal for the delight of hearing the* Salome *and* Götterdämmerung *scenes again after so long.*[17]

Legge was right. Marjorie's two appearances had afforded Londoners their first hearing of these pieces since before the war and, although that novelty element may have contributed to her success, there can be no doubt that Marjorie deserved the praise she received *and* that she could feel vindicated after the 1937 debacle. The critic of the *Musical Times* had likened her wheelchair to a conqueror's chariot and Marjorie was feeling like a conqueror when she headed off for a one-month recital tour that took her all over England, Wales and Scotland.

Such was Marjorie's success in Britain this time that she was engaged to return the following spring to fulfil two more contracts. The first was with the London Symphony Orchestra, who had booked a trio of artists from the United States for concerts in London and the provinces. Under the batons of Erich Leinsdorf and the young Leonard Bernstein, Marjorie was the featured soloist in seven concerts, singing her familiar Wagner scenes and adding two new arias to her repertoire: Tatiana's letter scene from Tchaikovsky's *Eugen Onegin* and 'Adieu forêts' from the same composer's *The Maid of Orleans*, each sung in credible Russian.[18] With Bernstein also including works by American composers not heard in Britain before, including Copeland's *Appalachian Spring*, the series of concerts was rated an outstanding success. The second contract was with the BBC and Marjorie sang Isolde's Narrative and Curse and the *Liebestod* with the BBC Symphony Orchestra conducted by Beecham in another memorable, sold-out concert in the Royal Albert Hall.

While in London on this occasion Marjorie made a number of recordings in Kingsway Hall for the Decca company. Two were with organ accompaniment and one of Britain's leading piano accompanists, Ivor Newton, joined her for the others. Nine songs were recorded and seven of them issued. The best are three songs by Brahms issued on one disc. To 'Der Schmied' and 'So willst du des Armen' she brings vigour and an attractive fullness of tone that suits the songs, but 'Nicht mehr zu dir zu geben' is overloaded with what one critic called 'hothouse languor'. The best seller among these discs was a coupling of Grieg's 'I Love Thee' and Rachmaninov's 'Floods of Spring'. In these two songs we can hear an echo of those 'vast trumpet-like notes' capable of 'riding triumphantly above tumultuous seas', about which the London critics had commented. The Rachmaninov is an engaging performance, but the Grieg is spoiled by a surfeit of sentiment which also derails Marjorie's normally reliable technique in a couple of places.

A tantalising recording project was proposed by Decca shortly after these discs were made. Richard Strauss had been invited to London by Beecham to attend a series of performances of his music and it seemed likely the composer would accept, if for no other reason than to collect the large royalties owed to him which had been frozen by Britain during the war. Would Marjorie, Decca asked, be prepared to record the *Salome* finale with a London orchestra if they could arrange for the composer to conduct it during his visit? Marjorie could hardly contain her enthusiasm, but in the end nothing came of this. Strauss came in September the following year; Beecham conducted several concerts and Strauss conducted one. If Decca's proposal did reach him it is unclear why Strauss declined. The explanation given to Marjorie was that the eighty-two-year-old composer was still recovering from an appendix operation from the previous year. What might have been a recording of paramount historical importance and which would have kept Marjorie's voice permanently in circulation, thus turned out to be another of those monumental might-have-beens which haunted her career.

After a brief return to the United States Marjorie was back in Europe again in the autumn, this time to stay five months and to sing in Britain, France and Germany. The French Ministry of National Education and the French Press Federation had joined forces to mount a gala concert in Paris for the benefit of Des Centres Français de la Pénicilline. Penicillin was revolutionising the treatment of infection, and funds from the concert were to be used to build up stocks of the drug in French hospitals. By general agreement it was felt that Marjorie would be the ideal soloist for this important event and when the offer came she had been happy to volunteer. Such was the demand for tickets that the venue had to be changed from the Opéra to the giant Théâtre National du Chaillot near the Eiffel Tower. The change of venue was a disappointment to Marjorie, but singing to 6000 Parisians with the National Orchestra of Paris conducted by Albert Wolff was a prospect that excited and delighted her.

As fate would have it, Marjorie was unwell for this concert on the evening of 16 October. She noted in her diary that morning: 'Did not sleep all night, awoke feeling lousy, sore throat and bad cold'.[19] Had it been a less prestigious event, she would have cancelled. Instead she went ahead, making a short speech in excellent French explaining her condition and apologising to the audience for the state of her voice before she sang. She then offered a long and demanding program comprising *Divinités du Styx*, Dido's Lament, Liszt's orchestrated version of Schubert's 'Erlkönig', Tatiana's letter scene and 'O ma lyre immortelle' from Gounod's *Sappho*. An interesting and rare item was 'Orpheus's Invocation' from Jacopo Peri's *Euridice*, in which she was accompanied by an ensemble of seven harps led by Lily Laskene; the final item was the Immolation Scene. The concert was recorded in its entirety and parts of it have been available in various forms over the years. In truth, it is a sad document. Marjorie sounds blocked up with her cold and her top notes are excruciating. The Purcell, nevertheless, is nobly sung and the audience (led by the President of the Provisional Government) leave no doubt about their appreciation of the return of one of their favourite singers. As a memento, the organisers of the concert presented Marjorie with a copy of the program bound in white calfskin and including a letter from Alexander Fleming (the discoverer of penicillin) thanking her for taking part.

If the penicillin gala concert was the centrepiece of Marjorie's short visit to Paris, it was by no means the only memorable event. On the day before the concert, her former colleagues at the Opéra organised a reception for her in the grand foyer of the opera house. Pierre and Abby Chereau were there, along with Germaine Hoerner, who had befriended Marjorie when she first joined the company. Marissa Ferrer, who had sung Sieglinde to Marjorie's Brünnhilde many times, hugged her affectionately. Paul Cabanel (former lover as well as colleague) was there, as charming and urbane as ever. So was François Ruhlmann who had conducted her debut in the house and André Pernet, who had been present when she auditioned for Jacques Rouché. Poor Pernet was so overcome by emotion at seeing his friend and colleague in a wheelchair he could not bring himself to approach her and had to be led to Marjorie by Hoerner. Rouché's successor, Georges Hirsch, made a speech of welcome and then, to Marjorie's delight, invited her to return to the Opéra for a guest appearance the following season.

On the day after the gala concert Marjorie was awarded the Legion d'Honnuer for her services to French music, becoming a 'Chevalier' in that noble order. The presentation was made in the Assemblée Nationale in the presence of the French Cabinet. The elegant white and green badge with its red ribbon was pinned onto Marjorie's jacket by the wife of the President of the Provisional Government, and when she was next in Paris, Marjorie's colleagues at the Opéra presented her with a diamond, emerald and ruby miniature of her Legion d'Honnuer insignia. That became her favourite piece of jewellery, proudly worn on all her concert gowns.

After Paris Marjorie and Tom travelled to London, where Marjorie was to sing in two complete broadcasts of *Tristan und Isolde* for the BBC. The initiative for this project came from Sir Thomas Beecham and the broadcasts were of historical importance. It was the first opportunity the British had had to hear this opera 'live' since Beecham conducted it at Covent Garden with Lubin and Melchior in 1939 and quite probably the first presentation of a German opera on British radio since the end of the war.

Arthur Carron was engaged to sing Tristan and other younger British singers filled the other roles. Beecham conducted with the BBC Chorus and the BBC Symphony Orchestra. There were two rehearsals, followed by two performances four days apart, transmitted on the BBC Third Program, While the Wagner-starved public who tuned in appreciated the performances, the critics were reserved in their praise, describing the singing as adequate but no more. Some individual listeners were more impressed. The Australian composer John Antill happened to be in London and he rated the broadcasts and Marjorie as 'magnificent', and when John Culshaw came to write his book, *Ring Resounding*, he recalled how fine these broadcasts were, although it was probably Beecham's contribution that he remembered most vividly.[20]

Two weeks after the second broadcast of *Tristan und Isolde* Marjorie finally achieved her ambition to sing on the stage of the Royal Opera House – in recital, with Gerald Moore at the piano. The critic of *The Times* praised Marjorie's singing, saying that she proved she was more than a great Wagnerian, but rebuked her for singing 'The Day is Mine' and 'Annie Laurie' –'Not at Covent Garden, *please*, Miss Lawrence!'[21] That prompted Marjorie to write in her diary: 'Pompous bugger – the Queen liked Annie Laurie'.[22]

Marjorie then embarked on another short recital tour of England and Scotland. In Dundee she received a telegram from Sir Harry Lauder saying he regretted not being able to attend her recital but wished her 'Joy be with you always'. Also at that recital in Dundee she encountered a young pianist who later made a career in Australia – Isador Goodman. Goodman was terrified by the prospect of meeting his first diva, but Marjorie put him at ease by saying: 'For goodness sake, love, call me Marge! Down in Australia they all know me as "Marge"'. Goodman never forgot this prima donna's humility or her friendly laugh.[23]

Ten days after this Dundee recital Marjorie recorded two Schubert songs, 'Erlkönig' and 'Der Lindenbaum', for Decca with Hubert Greenslade accompanying. 'Erlkönig' is given a dramatically charged performance which lieder experts might insist was too operatic, but which is enticingly grand in conception and execution. 'Der Lindenbaum' (from the cycle *Winterreise*) is given a beautifully controlled performance, although taken a little slower than the composer requests. Neither recording was issued and on the evidence of tapes made from the matrices that seems inexplicable. A clue exists in the recording company's notes on these recordings. Greenslade is listed under the pseudonym 'H. Grunstadt', suggesting that perhaps contractual problems relating to him meant that Decca was forced to withhold what would have been an attractive disc.

As Marjorie and Tom were packing to return to the United States after their fourth visit to Europe and making plans to spend the Christmas of 1946 relaxing at Harmony Hills, an unexpected cable arrived. It was from General Lucius Clay, Commander in Chief of the United States Occupation Forces in Berlin, who asked if Marjorie would return to Germany for a series of five concerts with German orchestras over the Christmas-New Year period. Marjorie's first reaction was to refuse, but changed her mind when a member of the US Embassy staff in London called to explain that not only were these concerts planned to boost the morale of US troops, they were also part of a strategy by the Pentagon to foster *détente* between the individual occupying forces (American, English, French and Russian) and between the collective occupying forces and the German civilian population. Under the circumstances, Marjorie felt she could hardly refuse.

The first concert was given at Wiesbaden with that city's orchestra under the baton of Technical Sergeant Gibson Morrisey of the American Army, former head of music for the special services division in North Africa. A West Virginian in his twenties, Morrisey had been assigned to conduct all but one of these concerts. What the German players thought of him is unrecorded, but Marjorie's feelings are expressed in her diary. After the first concert she wrote: 'I shall never forget this one. I had to conduct it myself!'[24] By the second concert – with the Berlin Philharmonic – it seems young Morrisey had pulled himself together sufficiently to remove the need for Marjorie to beat time as well as sing. At the third concert, in Bremerhaven on Christmas Day, 6000 American troops turned up and took the opportunity to protest at being stuck in a bleak German port instead of at home in the United States with their families. One-half of the assembled crowd cheered Marjorie, while the other booed the senior officers sitting in the front row. The situation became so volatile that Marjorie stopped the concert. Tom came onto the platform (wearing his American lieutenant's uniform) and was also loudly booed as he wheeled Marjorie off the platform.

The final concert in Berlin more than compensated for the dismal event in Bremerhaven. On this occasion the Berlin Philharmonic's own conductor, the dynamic Sergiu Celibidache, was permitted to conduct and drew from Marjorie and the players a performance which she rated as amongst her finest. In the audience as guests of General Clay were Russian General Kotikov, French General Noiret and English General Robertson, along with their starred-and-striped entourages. Also sitting silently and applauding discreetly were 1200 handpicked Berliners, the first group to be permitted to attend a public concert since the end of the war. For the Russians Marjorie sang Tatiana's Letter Scene and Kotikov shouted 'Bravo' at the end, followed by the *Liebestod*, and finally the Immolation Scene. That performance of the final scene from *Götterdämmerung* Marjorie believed was the finest she had ever sung. It was as if her voice was truly announcing the passing of corrupt gods and the cleansing of the world by fire. After Celibidache put down his baton there were tears streaming down his face and the concert master of the orchestra, Gerhard Taschner, made an unprecedented gesture. He rose from his seat, stepped across to Marjorie and kissed her hands, whispering 'Das passiert nur einmal im leben' ('This only happens once in a lifetime').[25]

After the concert General Clay hosted what Marjorie called a 'glorious' party and she was photographed surrounded by six generals, beaming happily and clutching a bedraggled sheath of ferns and winter flowers.

By a sad coincidence on that night, 30 December 1946, while Marjorie was singing with this great orchestra and conductor in Berlin and being feted by the mightiest military moguls in Europe, in Paris Madame Grodet died in Mimi's arms.

Chapter Eighteen
Interrupted Melody

While Marjorie was forging a new career in Britain and participating in history on the continent, she was not neglecting her career in the United States. Between trips to Europe there were memorable concerts and recitals in America, and two new opera roles to sing – Strauss's Elektra and Amneris in Verdi's *Aida*. There were also private moments worthy of recounting, such as the time Marjorie was accompanied at the piano by the great violinist Fritz Kreisler and sang 'Auld Lang Syne' as a duet with the legendary Maria Jeritza at a New Year's Eve party arranged by Edmee Bush Greenough – occasions which people lucky enough to have been present would sit and proudly describe to their grandchildren in decades to come.

Before she left for Australia in 1944, Marjorie had promised the conductor of the Detroit Symphony, Karl Kreuger, that she would sing Elektra in a concert performance of the opera with his orchestra on her return. She had taken the score with her to Australia and studied it when time permitted, but her European commitments had forced several postponements. A date was finally fixed and on 31 January 1946 in Detroit Marjorie made her debut in a part that has been described as a voice killer.

Elektra had been one of the roles Pierre Delbée had tried to foist on Marjorie during their troubled romance, and Marjorie had toyed with the idea of singing it ever since Edward Johnson mentioned it in 1938, but she had wisely waited until she was sure she was ready. Kreuger mustered a formidable cast around her, including Herbert Janssen in the crucial role of Elektra's brother, Oreste. The concert was a resounding triumph for all concerned, with the press's only regret being the circumstances that prevented its being a staged performance. Marjorie noted in her diary that evening: 'OK, but *what* a work!'[1]

Marjorie again sang *Elektra* in concert in Chicago (twice) and in Melbourne and Sydney. The only recording we have of her singing part of this score comes from a short Pathé-Warner newsreel film reporting on her first performance in Chicago. We hear (and see) Marjorie singing bars 53 to 59 from Elektra's monologue, ending with the phrase 'rings um dein Grab' and a top B. That performance, on 11 December 1947, was widely reported, not because of Marjorie's singing, but because she stood to sing.

Marjorie had made progress with her crutches, her leg braces and the parallel bars at Harmony Hills, but by 1947 it had become apparent that she would never walk unaided again. She could stand unaided, however, which prompted Tom to consider the idea of having a singing platform made for her, similar to a conductor's podium. He then joined forces with Keefes, the New York manufacturers of wheelchairs, to plan the perfect device.

Many versions were drawn up and ultimately scrapped, including a motorised one which Marjorie refused to consider. The final version consisted of a base about sixty centimetres square with hollow, cylindrical uprights on each corner and a railing around three sides, one metre above the base. Constructed of thick aluminium, the platform had four small sturdy wheels fitted underneath to enable it to be rolled about. Weighing only a few kilograms, the platform could be easily dis-assembled and packed into a canvas carrying bag.[2]

Marjorie tried the platform and felt comfortable on it, but found that she faced a similar dilemma to that she had experienced in Minneapolis in 1942, when she had been forced to learn to sing sitting down; now she had to reaccustom herself to singing standing. She practised over many months, mostly at Harmony Hills, while Tom, Mary Hedrick, the farm workers and Clara Weekes offered constant encouragement. As the date for the first *Elektra* in Chicago approached, Marjorie decided this would be the occasion on which she would return to the concert platform standing.

Marjorie had changed agents again and was now represented by Jack Adams. She had also employed her first publicist, Ethel Sipperly, and between them these two ensured the media knew there was a big story in the offing. Tom speculated that there were as many reporters, photographers and newsreel cameramen in attendance that night as there had been for Al Capone's trial. In the Pathé-Warner newsreel we see Tom propelling Marjorie through the ranks of the Chicago Symphony Orchestra, then the snippet of her singing, and finally Tom drawing her backwards off the platform at the end of the opera, the audience giving her a standing ovation and Marjorie beaming, waving and ducking her head as she disappears through the artists' entrance. It's not much, but it is the only record we have of Marjorie singing one of the most challenging roles in her repertoire.[3]

Amneris in Verdi's *Aida* proved a more durable role and the initiative for suggesting that Marjorie sing it came from Tony Stivanello, stage director of the Cincinnati Zoo Opera. Stivanello phoned Marjorie in April 1945 just as she and Tom were packing for their third visit to Britain. Would she, he asked, be prepared to sing Amneris for his company on their return? Stivanello also explained that he and Oscar Hild, the company's music director, had worked out a logical *mise en scène* in which Amneris would be carried on and off stage in a palanquin.

Having already sung the soprano title role in this opera, Marjorie was a little taken aback at being asked to sing the mezzo-soprano role of Aida's rival, but Stivanello persuaded her when he explained that he and Hild were tired of listening to contraltos struggling to reach the high notes in the part; they were convinced that Marjorie would triumph as the Egyptian princess.

Marjorie made her debut as Amneris in Cincinnati on 31 July 1946. Among the other cast members was the baritone Angelo Pilotti singing Amonasro, not a particularly distinguished or famous singer, but one who brought back memories from Marjorie's distant past. In Melbourne in 1928 when Marjorie had heard Toti dal Monte sing the title role in *Lucia di Lammermoor*, a very young Pilotti had sung Lucia's brother, Enrico.

Marjorie enjoyed the experience of singing Amneris and exploited all the considerable vocal and histrionic opportunities the role offers. The critics and the public in Cincinnati gave her an enthusiastic reception and she returned to repeat the role the following season and also to sing Venus in *Tannhäuser*. Marjorie also sang Amneris in Montreal, Miami and Greenville, South Carolina, where Radames was sung by Ramon Vinay and Amonasro by the young George London.[4] Later she also sang it in Melbourne, and it was with this role that she fulfilled her invitation from Georges Hirsch.

On 14 December 1946, Marjorie made a triumphant return to the Paris Opéra as Amneris, with Hoerner singing Aida. Radames was sung by José Lucciano, with whom Marjorie had appeared in this opera in 1933 (and whose wig she had tugged). Other former colleagues filled the remaining roles and François Ruhlmann conducted, but these other artists received little recognition. The press advertising carried just seven words: 'Aida – Mdme. Marjorie Lawrence will sing Amneris' in capital letters and large type. The house was filled with friends, former colleagues and an army of pre-war fans, many of whom had not entered the Opéra during the years of occupation.

When the curtain fell, Marjorie was carried on stage in her palanquin to take her bows with the other principals and then several solo curtain calls. Tom lifted her into her wheelchair and wheeled Marjorie off stage, but still the audience didn't leave, with shouts for 'Loh-ronce', 'Loh-ronce' filling the auditorium. Hoerner and Luccioni wheeled Marjorie back on stage, then retired, leaving her immobile on the vast stage. The audience continued to roar their approval and, seeing Marjorie becoming distressed, Pierre Chereau walked on and took her hand, saying: 'Weep, *mon enfant*. It will do you good. We all understand what kind of tears they are.'[5] Marjorie said it took her three days to recover.[6]

Conspicuous by her absence from this event and the earlier penicillin gala was Cécile Gilly, who was too ill to attend either. Marjorie took Tom to meet Madame a couple of days after her performance at the Opéra. *Maîtresse* and *pupille* spent a sentimental afternoon together reminiscing about the past and trying to block out the tragedies of recent years. Gilly died seven weeks later on 6 February 1947, although Marjorie did not learn of her death until Renée called her in New York five months later.

Despite Marjorie's continuing success, the Met showed no interest in re-employing her. She applied to Johnson for both the 1947–48 and 1948–49 seasons but was told each time that he had nothing to offer her. Marjorie's visits to Australia and Europe had allowed the dust to settle at the Met and clearly Johnson was not prepared to stir it up again by bringing her back into the company. Marjorie did however sing on one further occasion on the stage of the Met – at a benefit concert in 1949 with the New York Philharmonic Orchestra. Sharing the program with her were Salvatore Baccaloni and Giuseppe de Stefano, the famous buffo bass in the autumn of his illustrious career and de Stefano (the great white hope among lyric tenors of the post-war years) at the beginning of his. Marjorie sang Isolde's Narrative and Curse and the Immolation Scene, and her colleagues sang arias from their repertoires. It would be gratifying to think that Baccaloni and de Stefano joined forces with Marjorie (individually or collectively) in an encore or two, but there is no record of that happening and it is hard to imagine this odd trio finding common musical ground, even if they had wished to.

Marjorie was paid 10,000 francs for her performance at the Paris Opéra and $3000 each for her appearances as Elektra in Chicago. Cincinnati paid $500 each time she sang Amneris, but smaller opera companies could only manage about half that figure. Marjorie could still command good fees for concerts and recitals in major centres in the United States, but for similar appearances in Britain the fee averaged only about 150 pounds. The unpaid work Marjorie had been doing for the military and for numerous charities meant that her annual income had begun to taper off quite soon after it peaked in 1943. Marjorie and Tom then began searching for other ways to capitalise on the publicity bandwagon that had accompanied her illness and the fame she now enjoyed among people who had never before attended opera.

The idea of an autobiography surfaced, its source unknown. It may have been Marjorie's own idea, or Tom's, a friend's or an agent's. It could also have been a publisher's or it might have been the brainchild of the man who came to ghost-write the book – Charles Buttrose. Buttrose had travelled around Victoria as Marjorie's road manager during the 1939 homecoming tour of Australia, later moving to the United States to work in the Australian Government's News and Information Bureau. In February 1944, Buttrose approached Marjorie in New York to do a story about her life for the *Sydney Morning Herald* and Marjorie invited him to attend her performance of *Tristan und Isolde* at the Met. A bond was re-established.

Whether the biography was discussed at this time or later is unclear, but eventually Buttrose was contracted to ghost-write the book and this was one of the wisest decisions Marjorie ever made. By her own admission she was not scholarly and while she had an extraordinary capacity to express other people's words in song, her ability to express her own thoughts on paper was limited. Buttrose, on the other hand, combined a talent for words, the practical judgment of a journalist and a sound knowledge of opera. The result was a much better book than Marjorie could possibly have written herself and one of the most engaging 'autobiographies' of any singer. The work would earn Marjorie substantial sums in royalties and boost her career enormously, but did little for Buttrose's bank balance or his reputation. Marjorie offered and Buttrose accepted a flat fee for writing the book and was, quite reasonably, chagrined when it hit best-seller lists on three continents.

When the book was published Buttrose's name did not appear on any edition. It is believed that his employer at the time, the newspaper magnate Ezra Norton, forbade this, but the level of secrecy Marjorie demanded from Buttrose and employed for the rest of her life about his part in creating *Interrupted Melody* suggests she was keen to take all the credit.[7] It might be said that Marjorie treated the journalist unfairly but equally true to say that she could never have predicted the scale of the book's success when she signed up Buttrose. He tended to laugh it off philosophically. In his own autobiography he comments wryly that he has since learned about contracts.[8]

The process adopted to create the book was simple. Marjorie and Tom jotted down their reminiscences, Tom typed them up and these sheets were passed on to Buttrose. He then did more than simply turn the notes into prose; he used the facts they contained to create passages of strong narrative and dramatic impact, retaining the first person singular to convince the reader that it is Marjorie they are listening to. How well the process worked and how effectively the individuals worked together is demonstrated by the results, but the process was prone to inaccuracies and to 'embroidery'. If Buttrose is to be accused of occasionally getting 'carried away', however, it must be remembered that Marjorie and Tom approved everything he wrote.

It is also unclear who suggested the very apposite title *Interrupted Melody*, but it was likely Buttrose, for when the manuscript was finished on 16 October 1948 the title page already carried those words. As part of the deal with Buttrose, publishing rights for Australia were committed to Invincible Press, a Sydney-based publishing company which belonged to Ezra Norton. The New York literary agent Maurice Crain took on the task of finding publishers in other countries and Appleton-Century in New York and Falcon Press in London snapped it up.[9] The Australian edition came out first, in May 1949. The initial print run of 10,000 copies sold out in three weeks and caught Invincible Press off guard. There was a short hiatus, during which Marjorie complained bitterly about sales being lost before a second printing of 20,000 copies was made in late June, all of these events coinciding with Marjorie's third concert and recital tour of her homeland, again under the Tait banner and with Raymond Lambert providing expert support.

On her journey to Australia Marjorie gave three sold-out recitals in Hawaii. (Some excellent photographs of her singing on her new platform were taken in

Honolulu.) Marjorie charmed the Hawaiians and also the captain of the plane that carried her from Honolulu to Sydney. On landing he paid a Sydney florist to arrange for a corsage of orchids to be delivered to Marjorie on every day of her Australian recitals. Twenty-two in all were delivered, all carrying the message: 'With admiration for a gracious passenger'.

In the tradition established on earlier visits, Marjorie gave her first recital in the Globe Theatre in Winchelsea, now the property of the local shire council. The reunions with family and old friends, which should have been joyful affairs, were marred by the ongoing bitterness between Marjorie and her brother Lindsay – any amicability there might have been between them was shattered when he read *Interrupted Melody* and exacerbated by the exchange of odious letters in the press. Others were happy to pay tribute to Marjorie without reservation. After part of the first recital was broadcast on radio an anonymous former soldier wrote to Marjorie:

> *Dear Miss Marjorie Lawrence. Here is a tribute to your bravery after I listened to you on the radio last night. Good luck and God bless you. You have triumphed over difficulties.*

It was signed 'A Digger' and enclosed with the note were the anonymous soldier's service medals: the 1939–45 Star, the 1939–45 War Medal and the Pacific Star, complete with their ribbons.[10]

Recitals followed in Melbourne, Sydney, Canberra, Brisbane and provincial centres, with Marjorie commended by local composers for including a number of their songs in her programs, but criticised in the press for other aspects of her programming. Like *The Times* critic in 1946, snobbish Australian reviewers berated her for leaping from 'Brünnhilde' to 'Matilda' and gave her little credit for including songs most Australians had never heard before, by Stravinsky, Poulenc and Joaquin Nin. For the first time in her now twenty-year-long career Marjorie was also occasionally criticised for the quality of her singing, the reviewers' favourite complaint being that her top notes had become 'unreliable' since her last visit and sometimes sounded 'squally'.

The quality of musical criticism in Australia in 1949 was not high, but on Marjorie's return to the United States (where the critics were also fallible but had greater experience) she continued to receive adverse comments about her voice and as the years passed, the comments intensified. We must therefore conclude that, rather than being a temporary aberration, this period marks the beginning of a decline in Marjorie's vocal powers, which may be attributable to several factors. Firstly, Marjorie was in her forty-third year and, although that is no great age for a dramatic soprano, seven years of confinement to a wheelchair must have had some effect on her physically. Photos show her figure spreading and muscular wastage. She may also have begun to experience menopause. Tom's careful notes about her menstrual cycles cease at this time and if Marjorie's body was undergoing physiological changes they would have affected her voice. Marjorie's eclectic repertoire might also have been a contributing factor. In former times she was able to move comfortably between soprano and mezzo-soprano roles – Thaïs and Carmen, as examples – but alternating between such diverse roles as Elektra and Amneris might have taken its toll. Some might argue that singing Elektra alone would have exacted a vocal price, but the brief newsreel film of her singing that role in Chicago dispels any doubts about her capacity to do justice to it just eighteen months before the criticism starts.

That newsreel film clip also provides evidence of the most likely cause of the problems now besetting Marjorie. After her illness she had resorted to using the muscles of her upper body to aid in producing the volume of air required to sing. As she sings the high B in the *Elektra* clip we can see the muscles of her neck and throat engaged and straining, then disengaging almost painfully when the note is ended. Any competent singing teacher would reprimand a student for using those muscles, remind them of the importance of 'relaxed throats' and direct their efforts to the muscles of the lower abdomen – the able-bodied singer's powerhouse. But the output of Marjorie's 'powerhouse' was restricted and for seven years she had been forced to use a singing technique which Cécile Gilly, Ivor Boustead or Louis Bachner would have told her courted disaster. Marjorie probably realised this danger when she recommenced singing and had decided to take a calculated risk; to sing well for a few years and if necessary pay the price later. The top note we hear on that film clip is as resplendent as ever, but cut short and the work required to produce it shows that a reckoning was approaching.

Marjorie had several years of professional singing ahead of her in 1949 and she was far too accomplished a vocalist to ever allow herself to be seriously compromised in public by the failings of her voice, but the days when she could dispense top Bs and Cs like starbursts belonged to the past. The secure 'middle' of Marjorie's voice and her lower notes stayed intact and as beautiful as ever and drew praise sufficient to offset the criticism. There were also occasions, as there often are with singers entering their decline, where the years seemed to drop away and Marjorie would give a recital or a concert performance with her old brilliance, but as the years went by these 'miracles' became rarer. She also remained a soprano to the end, the voice firmly anchored in the dramatic soprano range and with a soprano 'sound', although others would mistakenly claim that she turned into a contralto because she chose to sing pieces in lower keys and because of the absence of high notes.

The Australian Government also gave Marjorie a difficult time at the end of her Australian tour, insisting she leave a large part of her earnings behind when she left. Tom appealed to politician Arthur Calwell, pointing out that Marjorie had been permitted to take all her earnings back to the United States in 1944. Calwell brought the matter to the attention of Prime Minister Ben Chifley, and a compromise was reached. Marjorie had to leave 500 pounds behind in an Australian bank account. This was only one sixth of her earnings, but it was money she could have used as she waited for the royalties from *Interrupted Melody* to flow in over subsequent years.

From Sydney Marjorie moved on to New Zealand, but the fourteen recitals she gave there attracted mixed houses – some full, many almost empty. To add to their woes, when they got home Marjorie was served with a law suit by a masseuse who had worked for them after Amy Featherstone's departure and who claimed Marjorie had agreed to endorse her 'treatments' for polio. The woman sought $109,200 in damages, but in the end common sense prevailed and the claim was dismissed in court. Engaging lawyers to fight this added further strain to Marjorie and Tom's finances and they found themselves reluctantly having to appeal for help. That ever-faithful friend, Edmee Bush Greenough, now almost eighty, made a gift of $3000 to each – to tide them over. Despite the success of the Australian edition of *Interrupted Melody* and being named 'Arkansas Woman of the Year' in what was now her home state, 1949 had been a bad year for Marjorie. Fortunately the first year of the 1950s promised to be better.

Marjorie was one of the non-singing guests on the stage of the Met when a farewell gala was mounted in February 1950 for the retiring Edward Johnson and in April she sang two performances of *Tristan und Isolde* with the Pittsburgh Opera, the second of these proving to be the last time she sang a Wagner role on stage. The same month Marjorie also sang in two performances of Mendelssohn's *Elijah* – her only appearances in oratorio during her career – one in New Jersey and one in New York Town Hall. These were not particularly distinguished performances and the only reason Marjorie agreed to learn the principal soprano part was because her old friend and colleague Martial Singher was singing the title role. Marjorie's singing of 'He ye Israel' was considered the highlight of both evenings.

The American edition of *Interrupted Melody* had been launched at Christmas and between her musical engagements, Marjorie took part in the promotional campaign devised by Appleton which continued into the New Year. There were interviews for radio, newspapers and magazines and her first appearance on television as a guest on America's first daytime chat show, *The Dorothy Doan Show*. Marjorie undertook a little self-promotion as well, sending inscribed copies of the book to a long list of celebrities, including Eleanor Roosevelt, General Clay, Elsa Maxwell, most of the leading New York music critics and the new general manager of the Met, Rudolf Bing.

Marjorie also sent a copy to Ida Koverman, executive assistant and confidante of Louis B. Mayer at MGM Studios. That copy prompted a reply in which Koverman said she thought the book had film potential and that she hoped 'something would come of it' in the future. Encouraged by this, Marjorie sent a copy to her favourite actress, Greer Garson, stating that if a film was ever made, she hoped that Garson would be cast in the leading role. The ever gracious Garson wrote back to say she was touched and honoured that Marjorie wanted her to play the lead in any film about her life and that she would write to MGM in support of the idea.[11] Garson seems to have taken up this idea with some enthusiasm, seeing Marjorie's story as a vehicle to revive her own career, which had been flagging since her great, wartime hits *Random Harvest*, *Mrs Miniver* and *Madame Curie*.

Maurice Crain entrusted the promotion of the book as a film to an associate: the motion picture agent Annie Laurie Williams, whose given names seemed a propitious omen to Marjorie. Williams brokered an agreement between Marjorie and the independent screen writer Leo Katcher, who would make a screen adaptation of the book. Under the terms of the agreement Katcher would then have a ten-month option to sell the script to a film studio and, if he was successful, each party was to receive half the sum realised by the sale.

While Katcher set to work on *Interrupted Melody*, Marjorie and Tom flew back to Australia for Marjorie's Melbourne performances of Amneris. These took place in the grand old Princess Theatre with the National Theatre Opera Company of Melbourne. The company's director was Gertrude Johnson, a former Melba protégée who was now working tirelessly to establish a permanent opera company in her homeland. These six performances in March 1951 were Marjorie's only appearances in staged opera in her homeland, and for the fledgling company and the young Australian singers who shared the stage with her (including John Shaw singing his first Amonasro), they were of great moment.[12]

Marjorie also appeared in recitals and concerts for the ABC. In Melbourne on May Day she sang the title role in the first performance of Strauss's *Elektra* in Australia with local artists and the Victorian Symphony Orchestra conducted by Eugene Goossens. A concert performance of *Salome* a few days later had to be cancelled when Marjorie contracted a chill, but later concert performances of both operas were given in Sydney, also conducted by Goossens and with the young Ronald Dowd singing Herod in *Salome*. As it was the fiftieth anniversary of Australia's Federation, Marjorie also agreed to sing in jubilee concerts in Melbourne and Canberra, where her fellow artists included Harold Blair and the veteran Australian baritone Peter Dawson. Also in Canberra, she sang the National Anthem on the steps of Parliament House at the opening of parliament – a singular honour last accorded to Melba at the opening of the building in 1927.

Many members of Marjorie's family and old friends from the Western District attended her performances in Melbourne. Lena took Alan's daughter June along to hear 'Auntie Marge' in *Aida* and the fourteen-year-old was also taken to a recital, after which she attended a supper party at Marjorie and Tom's hotel. June, who was delighted to be in the presence of her famous aunt, was equally taken by her gallant and suave American uncle.[13]

Leo Katcher in the meantime had completed a fifty-page film script based on *Interrupted Melody* and touted it around the Hollywood film studios.[14] The asking price he, Marjorie and Williams had agreed on was $50,000, but when interest was shown, that figure proved overly optimistic. While Marjorie was in Melbourne a cable arrived from Williams saying MGM had offered $31,000.

Williams recommended that Marjorie accept the offer on the grounds that a film made by MGM was likely to be better than one made by any other film company and there were no other offers.[15] Tom phoned Williams in New York to suggest she and Katcher urge MGM for a bit more money and discovered that Western Union had made a typographic error on the original cable and MGM's offer was actually $21,000. Williams still recommended acceptance and pointed out that, if Marjorie was engaged to sing on the soundtrack of the film (which it had always been assumed she would), then at least another $10,000 might be earned from that. With the present state of their finances still perilous, Tom and Marjorie decided to accept the offer, with Tom cabling Williams to this effect and requesting an immediate cash advance from MGM.[16]

A long reply from Williams explained that as soon as the contract was prepared she would send it on but that MGM would not advance any money in the meantime. Williams also explained that she had been in discussion with Jack Cummings, the producer of the film, and that he had assured her he would try to engage either Greer Garson or Deborah Kerr to play Marjorie in the film. Cummings had also told Williams that, subject to satisfactory sound tests, Marjorie would sing the opera sequences and songs for the soundtrack. Williams closed by recommending that on her way back from Australia Marjorie stop in Los Angeles to meet MGM executives.[17] Marjorie alerted the Australian press, following which all the dailies carried stories with headlines like 'Our Marge to sing in Hollywood film about her life'. It was fantastic publicity and boosted ticket sales for the remaining recitals and concerts of the tour.

Marjorie and Tom broke their journey in Los Angeles and in Hollywood they were introduced to Dore Schary (Mayer's successor as head of the studios), Jack Cummings and composer Saul Chaplin, who would be in charge of the music. Marjorie and Tom were given red-carpet treatment and it was agreed that when Marjorie returned to Los Angeles in a few months for a scheduled concert with the Los Angeles Philharmonic, she would take part in a series of sound tests on one of the studio's sound stages. Happy with their reception in Hollywood and the prospect that lay ahead, Marjorie and Tom headed for Harmony Hills and a much deserved summer break. Two important tasks, however, remained to be carried out before Marjorie and Tom could relax. The first was to cancel a recital tour of Scandinavia.

Planning for that tour had begun in 1946 when Marjorie had run into Einar Johansen in Paris. The young Dane, who had helped her settle in at the Grodets in 1928 and now a respected concert pianist in his homeland, was also involved in concert promotion. He suggested a tour of Denmark, Sweden, Norway and Finland for her in 1948 or 1949. Marjorie was attracted to the idea and when Johansen returned to Copenhagen he set about making the arrangements. Harold Holt became involved, as did Marcel de Valmalète, Marjorie's agent in Paris, while Jack Adams in New York liaised with all three. Much work was done, but with mixed results. De Valmalète pulled out, claiming a lack of interest in France and Johansen had difficulty juggling dates. Finally in 1950 Johansen managed to organise the tour, but it was now reduced to two weeks. Following the offer of a five-month tour of Australia and New Zealand during the same period Marjorie requested a postponement of the Scandinavian tour, which was granted. After her meeting with MGM, however, she felt she needed to hold herself at the studio's disposal, so from Harmony Hills she wired Adams to cancel the Scandinavian tour. Coming on top of the postponement, Adams and Johansen were anything but pleased. Adams felt Marjorie had compromised his reputation so badly that when his contract came up for renewal he declined to enter into a new one. As for Johansen, Marjorie never heard from him again.

The second task Marjorie set herself at Harmony Hills was organising the large batch of release forms provided by MGM to be signed by family members, friends and colleagues. In these forms the signatories gave the studio permission to use actors to represent them in the film and to put words in their characters' mouths they perhaps had never spoken. Most of those Marjorie sent the forms to were flattered at the prospect that they might appear as a character in the film, but three at least felt flattery was insufficient reward.

Brother Lindsay in Australia sent his form back unsigned. As a consequence there is no 'Lindsay Lawrence' in the film and that probably pleased Marjorie as much as it did him. Cyril made a fool of himself by insisting that he would only sign if MGM included in the film's soundtrack one or two of the songs he had written. His was a critical character in the story, but the studio laughed at Cyril's demand, entrusting Marjorie with the task of talking sense into her brother. What finally made Cyril capitulate was news that he was going to be played in the film by the young and debonair Roger Moore. When he later saw the script and realised his character had been written less sympathetically than he believed it should, he complained bitterly, but by then it was too late. Leopold Sachse, the old stage manager at the Met who had given Marjorie all those pennies was the third who refused to sign. Instead, he proposed that he play himself in the film. When the studio learned he had once been an actor they agreed, believing his presence in the cast would add credibility to the film.

Other wheels were turning in Hollywood that summer and MGM was following the path of most large film studios in those days (some still do). Having gained the rights to a good story, they set about changing everything they didn't think spelled big dollars. First of all they scrapped Leo Katcher's screenplay and commissioned William Ludwig and Sonya Levien to write a new one. Ludwig and Levien took even greater liberties with the content of the book than Katcher had, but produced a more dramatically compelling screenplay.

When the provisional cast list was announced, Lana Turner was listed to play Marjorie with Glenn Ford as Tom, Moore as Cyril, Ann Codee as Cécile Gilly and the veteran Australian actor Cecil Kellaway as Bill Lawrence. Turner's name disappeared when Cummings (according to Williams) decided that she was too 'lightweight' for the role. Greer Garson was now back in the frame and Cummings arranged for singer and actress to meet at a resort in Hawaii. Marjorie was told that this was so that she could be certain that she wanted Garson to play her, but in fact it was to enable Garson to study Marjorie at close range. Marjorie and Tom were happy to accept a few days in a luxury hotel in Hawaii at the studio's expense and Marjorie and Garson hit it off immediately, each delighted with the prospect of merging personalities.

In August Marjorie and Tom flew to Los Angeles. Marjorie sang her concert in the Hollywood Bowl and as a courtesy sent complimentary tickets to Cummings and Chaplin. A week later Marjorie spent three days at the MGM studios making test recordings of arias which were likely to feature in the film.[18] Chaplin, the conductor Adolph Deutsch and Walter Ducloux (Head of the Opera School at South California University who had been employed as a consultant) all appeared satisfied and Marjorie departed confident that she had passed what she believed were merely technical tests.

Marjorie went home to study a new operatic role – Madame Flora in Menotti's *The Medium*. The opera was being produced by a semi-professional company in Little Rock and the stage director had decided that a Flora in a wheelchair was not alien to the plot. For Marjorie it was a long way from singing Brünnhilde or Isolde at the Met but she gave the role her all and Ray Edelstein, playing the mute Toby, claimed that he was terrified by Marjorie's portrayal and swore that she actually made the medium's table levitate by the power of her concentration.

A week later Marjorie received a cable from MGM to say the studio had decided to postpone the film temporarily and that Marjorie was released from any obligation to sing in it when production resumed. The first piece of news was bad enough, but the second was devastating for Marjorie. Tom phoned Douglas Field, Marjorie's latest agent, who happened to be based in Hollywood and Field did some quick checking. He reported back that Dore Schary had pulled the plug on the production because it was already over budget and that the studio had decided a different singer would be used for the soundtrack. Marjorie was furious. She cabled the studio using all her prima donna prowess:

> Have received your shocking and vicious telegram telling me that you are not going to use my singing voice in 'Interrupted Melody', with no explanation. I do and shall violently protest this unjust and unreasonable decision after leading me to believe for over a year that I would do the singing, especially after my test recordings were declared highly satisfactory. I would never have sold my story to MGM if I had thought for one moment that you would not use my singing voice. If you now persist in unjustly using another singer in a film of my life it would be far better that the picture never be made, for surely you realize it would ruin my career and my life.

Williams followed up with a letter quoting the clause in Marjorie's contract which stated that she had agreed 'to sing a musical program to be dubbed into the film'. The studio wrote back reminding Williams that the clause also mentioned 'subject to satisfactory tests' and that they deemed the tests Marjorie had made to be unsatisfactory. Therefore, they argued, the clause was redundant. Since Marjorie had no legal grounds on which to challenge the studio, she resorted to a direct appeal to Schary for the opportunity to undertake another set of tests. If Schary agreed, she assured him, she would prove that she could sing better than she had in the first tests. The canny head of the studio knew that Marjorie could scuttle the film by publicly denouncing it, so for that reason only, he granted her request.

When production of the film finally resumed in the middle of 1954, Marjorie went back to Hollywood and made her second set of tests, but she and Tom alone among all those involved seemed to be unaware that this was merely to satisfy her vanity. The studio provided the same orchestra they had for the first tests (players from the Los Angeles Philharmonic) and Marjorie recorded 'Un bel dì' from Puccini's *Madama Butterfly*, two versions of 'Mon coeur s'ouvre á ta voix' from *Samson et Dalila* (one in French and one in English), the *Salome* finale, 'Annie Laurie' and Kostelanetz's arrangement of 'Waltzing Matilda'.[19]

These recordings survive and demonstrate why MGM decided to use another singer. They preserve some splendid singing (especially the two versions of Dalila's aria and the *Salome* scene, where it is a bonus to hear Marjorie singing this in German), but the voice is that of a great *mature* singer. To have dubbed that voice to an actress playing the young Marjorie would have produced a glaring anomaly, which audiences and certainly the critics would have found unacceptable. When news came that the studio had not changed its mind, Marjorie was forced to accept their decision, with a cheque for $3000 in compensation for 'inconvenience' softening the blow.

MGM employed the American soprano Eileen Farrell to record the opera and song sequences for the film. Farrell was a distinguished singer, just thirteen years Marjorie's junior; with a fresher voice but with none of the vocal charisma Marjorie had exhibited in her prime. In her own autobiography Farrell acknowledges that Marjorie's was one of the great voices of her time and that she did not attempt to emulate its size or sound. Farrell did as good a job as any singer could under the circumstances and, out of courtesy to Marjorie, Farrell's name did not appear in the film credits. Audiences who were unfamiliar with Marjorie's voice assumed it was she they were listening to, although the illusion was shattered when the soundtrack was issued on LP with Farrell's name and portrait on the sleeve.

Marjorie's other great wish also remained unfulfilled. By the time production had resumed, Greer Garson had left MGM and the role was assigned to Eleanor Parker. Parker had been in Hollywood for many years and had a reputation for being highly decorative, but too mild-mannered for big dramatic roles. Recognising its potential, Parker threw herself into the part as she had done no other, creating a spirited cinematic character which caught much of Marjorie's vibrancy and youthful impetuosity. She also mimed very well to Farrell's voice and if she overacted when miming that was probably the fault of the larger-than-life Russian tenor Vladimir Rosing, who supervised the opera sequences. Parker (in her ninetieth year at the time of writing) has been quoted as saying that *Interrupted Melody* was her favourite film, and it earned her an Oscar nomination. Glenn Forde made a credible and likable 'Tom' and Roger Moore managed to make Cyril's character both petty and charming.[20]

The film remains an excellent example of mid-twentieth-century Hollywood movie-making and arguably the best film up to that time on an operatic subject. Scenes like Marjorie riding Grane into the funeral pyre at the Met and singing for wounded soldiers are brought vividly to life. But if the goal is an accurate portrayal of Marjorie's life, then words like 'travesty' and 'fantasy' spring to mind. The inventions in the screenplay are too numerous to list, but a couple of examples will suffice to show the extent of their fabrication. In the film Marjorie meets Tom in Monte Carlo after she makes her debut as Musetta in *La Bohème* and in Miami we see her attempting suicide by overdosing with sleeping pills, of which there is certainly no record.

Marjorie's brush with Hollywood had proved frustrating, demoralising, embarrassing and not nearly as lucrative as she had hoped. She must have regretted cancelling that tour of Scandinavia and, at the lowest ebb, probably rued having become involved with 'tinsel town'. When the film was released and proved an even bigger success than her book, however, the rewards finally came.

Chapter Nineteen
Professor Lawrence

The filming of *Interrupted Melody* was finally completed in November 1954 – in brilliant 'Technicolor' and using the new wide-screen process 'Cinemascope' – exactly five years after Ida Koverman had first expressed interest in the subject. The following February it was ready for the public, a large number of whom had followed the trials of its gestation in popular movie magazines. The studio executives invited Marjorie and Tom to a preview screening, flew them out to Hollywood, put them up in five-star hotel and made sure the press didn't get close enough to report their comments until they were sure of Marjorie's reaction. Marjorie admitted that she liked the film and the way she was portrayed on screen by Eleanor Parker. She knew a good show when she saw one and appreciated what the film could do to boost her career.

So sure were the studio executives that the film would be an international box office success they decided against holding the world premiere or the US premiere in New York or another major American city. The honour of hosting the world premiere on 20 April 1955 went to the Metro Theatre in Collins Street, Melbourne, and as a mark of respect to Marjorie, the US premiere was held at the Malco Theatre in Hot Springs. The latter was as huge an event as Hot Springs had ever witnessed. The Governor of Arkansas proclaimed 30 June 'Marjorie Lawrence Day' and Marjorie and Tom were limousined into the town from Harmony Hills. Movie and music celebrities flew in from all over the country and entered the theatre along a red carpet under the glare of floodlights and popping flashbulbs. Before the film Marjorie appeared on stage and sang 'Mon coeur s'ouvre á ta voix', 'The Lord's Prayer' and a hymn 'I'll Never Walk Alone'. Proceeds from the gala were shared between the National Polio Foundation and the Arkansas Crippled Children Centre, and amid all that hype the film itself made a powerful and indelible impact on its first American audience as it would on others worldwide.

Cyril made one of his rare visits to Harmony Hills to attend the US premiere and Ted Lawrence accepted an offer to travel from Australia at Marjorie's expense to be there as well. Both brothers also took part in the filming of an episode of the television program *This Is Your Life*, honouring Marjorie.[1] The creator and host of that program, Ralph Edwards, had contacted Tom some months earlier and, believing that Marjorie would approve of the honour, Tom had been liaising with Edwards and his team since. As still occurs on the program, the guest is manoeuvred into a place at a time where the host can surprise them. Marjorie was told that her agent required her in Hollywood to do an important television interview and went along happily, but when the evening arrived disaster threatened. Marjorie was feeling a little 'under the weather' and announced she was not going to the studio and that the interview would have to be rescheduled to a time when she felt better. Tom tried to cajole her into going, but Marjorie would not budge. Finally, he had no choice but to tell her that the program she was to appear on was to honour her, omitting only the program's name. Marjorie made a spontaneous recovery, got ready in record time and sailed off to the NBC studio, where Edwards duly 'surprised' her. Being the fine actress she was, Marjorie had no difficulty feigning amazement, and her delight was genuine.

As well as Cyril, Ted and Tom, a succession of other guests appeared on the program including Lauritz Melchior, Lawrence Tibbett, Edward Johnson and Eleanor Parker; Mimi Grodet was flown over from Paris and looked chic but slightly bewildered. Marjorie was in her element, accepting tributes graciously, beaming with pleasure and dominating the proceedings as only a great prima donna can.

Appearing on television held no fears for Marjorie, for in recent months she had hosted her own weekly television program – *The Marjorie Lawrence Show* – on KRTV, Little Rock. During the hour-long program, sponsored by the Arkansas Power and Light Company, Marjorie chatted to the television audience and sang for them, scheduling many songs by Australian composers. Marjorie was supported by local singers and young dancers from local studios and, while the production standards and some of the performances bordered on the amateurish, an undemanding viewing audience loved the program and flooded the studio with fan mail. *The Marjorie Lawrence Show* first went to air in September 1953 and ceased production at Marjorie's request in 1955.

The success of the film *Interrupted Melody* and the associated publicity gave a temporary boost to Marjorie's concert and recital career. If the major orchestras in New York, Chicago, Boston and Philadelphia no longer showed interest in her, she was still a drawcard in places like Cincinnati, Minneapolis and St Louis and there were plenty of less prestigious groups in the Midwest and the South who were happy to engage her as a celebrity guest. Wynn Rocamura, manager of the Hollywood Bowl and a personal friend, engaged Marjorie to appear in the 'Symphony Under the Stars' concerts with the Hollywood Bowl Symphony Orchestra several times during the 1950s, but slowly and inevitably as the decade advanced and Marjorie's face and voice aged, her career as a singer contracted and drew to a close.[2]

In late 1958 Marjorie entered into the last musical collaboration of her career, with the accomplished duo pianists Nelson and Neal. Harry Neal came from Paris, Tennessee, and his wife, Allison Nelson, was the little Australian girl who had played at Alfredo Luizzi's benefit concert in the Melbourne Town Hall in 1939. Before Marjorie set out to tour with the Neals, she also appeared on their *This is Your Life* program. Between 1959 and 1961, the trio sang and played their way through the Deep South and the Midwest.

Allison Nelson has a fund of reminiscences about Marjorie and their work together to enlighten us about Marjorie in the final years of her singing career. She recalls that the Immolation Scene was always the *piece de résistance* of their recitals, performed in a new transcription by a friend of the Neals. Harry and Allison would play their parts in this with the lids of both pianos fully raised and producing a torrent of sound, but Marjorie would still demand 'More support ... I need more support'. Marjorie would also turn up for a concert and change the program at the last minute. Allison remembers with amusement the evening when they performed at a Catholic college in Miami and Marjorie thrust the score of 'Danny Boy' into her hands, saying 'Let's sing this for the nuns'. To her alarm Allison found the middle page missing. 'Don't worry, dear, just make it up', Marjorie said calmly, at the same time requesting that Allison transpose it. That was too much even for this accomplished pianist, who finally rebelled. Allison Nelson also felt like rebelling on another occasion when Marjorie bought her small son John a pet – a baby South American Caiman (a relative of the alligator), which had to be kept in the kitchen sink of the mobile home she, Harry and their three children toured in.[3]

Photographs taken at their joint recitals confirm that Marjorie always dressed 'like a star' for every appearance she made in public right up to the end of her career and that she exuded charm and *bonhomie*, captivating audiences and earning praise that her laboured singing probably no longer deserved. Her gowns were always showy, her hair carefully dyed to hide any traces of grey, paste diamonds dripped from her ears, neck and wrists, and generous amounts of make-up covered her wrinkles. It seemed that in appearance as the years went by Marjorie almost became a caricature of herself. The scarlet-painted lips were just a little too bold and a little too bright, and the hard hairstyles and the painted eyebrows reminiscent of the 1940s.

Psychologists might read all sorts of things into Marjorie's appearance in middle age – compensation for her disability and fear of aging – but in truth it was probably no more than a combination of ingrained habits and her commitment to what she believed was every star's duty to her public – to be one size larger than life and to *shine*. Inevitably too, Marjorie's personality also changed as she grew older, the hard knocks she had suffered probably leaving internal as well as external scars. In private she must inevitably have felt bitter about the hand fate had dealt her, but something of that impetuous, strong-willed and pragmatic young woman from

Winchelsea with a larrikin streak remained and sustained her. No doubt too, as hundreds of people still living, including Allison Nelson will testify, she was also great fun to be around to the very end of her days.

With her singing career coming to an end, Marjorie needed to find other ways to occupy herself. She had never (she claimed) considered becoming a teacher until the young woman who would be her first pupil phoned her at Harmony Hills in the fall of 1953. The caller was Imogene Gunther, daughter of the local gas station manager. According to Marjorie, Gunther said 'I want to become a singer and you're a famous singer so will you help me?' Marjorie explained to the ambitious young woman that she was not a teacher and didn't intend becoming one. A few days later a letter arrived from Gunther claiming that she was very disappointed by Marjorie's refusal and that she believed established singers like Marjorie had an obligation to help newcomers. In the end, recognising that the young woman probably had a point, Marjorie phoned and invited her to the ranch. When Gunther sang for Marjorie she revealed an attractive coloratura soprano voice. 'I will try to teach you as Madame Gilly taught me in Paris,' Marjorie told Gunther, 'but you must agree to enter as many singing competitions as you can, just like I did, as soon as I think you are ready'.[4]

Lessons began, Gunther made progress, word got out and other students followed in her footsteps. By year's end Marjorie had at least three more – two tenors and baritone. One of these, a cherubic-faced tenor named Robert Bivens, was good enough to sing the love duet from *Tosca* with Marjorie at the annual fund-raising concert she gave for the Army and Navy Hospital in Hot Springs in January 1954.

Exactly what and how Marjorie taught this first group of private students is unclear. Her statement about emulating Madame Gilly suggests that she probably taught them some vocal technique, but later students confirm that her specialties were interpretation of operatic roles, arias and songs and stagecraft. Marjorie's own technique was rock-solid up until her illness, but how much of that had been achieved by doing as she was instructed by Boustead, Gilly and later Louis Bachner, and how much came from her own knowledge of the science of singing is unclear. There must also be some doubt about Marjorie's ability to pass such knowledge on to others. Being the fortunate possessor of a robust set of vocal cords and never having to worry too much about risk of damage even when singing arduous roles in her prime also raises a question about her suitability as a trainer of immature voices of more fragile calibre.

There is no evidence, however, that whatever Marjorie taught those first students did them any harm and, in the case of Imogene Gunther, her instruction helped the young soprano win the first vocal competition she entered, at Tulane University in New Orleans in January 1956. Marjorie and Tom travelled down to the colourful metropolis at the mouth of the Mississippi to support Gunther during the competition and told the press that they were considering moving there so Marjorie could expand her teaching. When this news reached the department of music at Tulane and after Gunther had given a show-stopping vocal display in Zerbinetta's aria from Strauss's *Ariadne auf Naxos* during the competition, Peter Hansen, head of the department, wrote to Marjorie to sound her out about the possibility of her joining his faculty.

Marjorie was flattered by the offer, returning to New Orleans and meeting with the Dean of Newcomb College, where the music department was then located, and a deal was quickly struck. Marjorie would be given the title 'Professor of Voice' and the college would provide her with a studio and a piano, collect the students' fees, retain ten per cent and pay the rest to Marjorie. The hours were flexible and Marjorie could take leave when she had performance commitments. She could also choose her own students and there would be no limit to their number.[5] Essentially, it was like running her own teaching practice, except that the college took care of all the administration, leaving Marjorie free to concentrate on her classes.[6]

At that point Marjorie and Tom made a decision they soon came to regret – they put Harmony Hills on the market. The property they had paid $25,000 for in 1943 was now valued at $80,000 and the agents listed it as 'a picturesque and wholesome hideout from hypertension'. Marjorie and Tom also offered to exchange the property for one of like value in or near New Orleans. Despite the desirability of Harmony Hills, there was no rush of offers, and as the days and weeks passed they both began to regret their decision. Tom wondered how he would cope without walking under the pines in the cool of evening, feeding the wild deer that came to the lake to drink and driving up into the hills in the farm jeep to what he described as his 'private place' – a small pond surrounded by mossy rocks and fed by a tinkling waterfall – where he could ponder problems, muse on the strange course his life had taken and find solace. Marjorie (still a farm girl at heart) knew she would miss the animals, the peace and quiet, the open spaces, and above all her garden, which was guaranteed of taking out a prize in every local competition she entered.[7]

In the end Harmony Hills was withdrawn from sale and Tom and Marjorie rented a modest apartment in Calhoun Street, New Orleans (beside the neighbouring Loyola University), in time for Marjorie to take up her appointment in September 1956. Another critical reason for retaining Harmony Hills also presented itself during Marjorie's second year at Tulane. Under the auspices of the university, Marjorie decided to hold a summer workshop for aspiring young opera singers at Harmony Hills. These workshops, which soon became an institution and continued for seventeen years, were run over six weeks from mid-June, during the university's summer vacation, with students coming from all over the United States to participate.

Initially the twenty or so students who were accepted to take part each year paid a fee of $75 (the amount later increasing) and donations were sought and received from Arkansas businesses and institutions to offset costs.[8] 'The Harmony Hills

Music Foundation Incorporated' was established, with Tom as executive director to administer the funds, and accompanists employed, mostly from among senior music students at Henderson State University in nearby Arkadelphia. Female students were accommodated in one of the outer wings of the homestead and given the use of the kitchen in the central wing. Just occasionally, a special student would be honoured with an invitation to coffee in Marjorie and Tom's 'private' wing and all were invited to dinner with Marjorie and Tom, just once, towards the end of the six weeks and to a 'farewell' picnic by the lake, to which they would all contribute dishes.[9] Male students had to find their own accommodation in and around Hot Springs. Many students (male and female) brought their families with them and proud mothers, fathers and siblings took a vacation in the thermal spa while their 'prodigies' attended the workshop.

The students were allowed to relax, boat and fish in the lakes at Harmony Hills in their spare time and were expected to take part in group physical exercises each morning before lessons began, giving the whole venture a holiday camp atmosphere. For many it was both their first encounter with 'a real live prima donna' and with country life. The German Shepherds were too protective of Marjorie and Tom to be petted or played with and had to be kept locked up, but Marjorie's Australian sulphur-crested cockatoo Salome and pink-crested parrot Pinky would squawk merrily, perform tricks and chatter to the students. Many a city boy or city girl would listen contentedly to the sounds of country life for the first time and watch with fascination as the local fauna gathered timidly and silently at the lake at sunset.

In reality there was not much time for such extracurricular pursuits. Marjorie was determined that each student would get their money's worth and leave feeling as if they had achieved something special. She would work with each individual on arias or songs that suited their voices, giving sound and practical advice based on her own experience. She made them work hard, but in reality it was simply being in Marjorie's presence that the students found most inspiring. One of those students at a later workshop, mezzo-soprano Suzetta Glenn, now Lecturer in Applied Voice at Ouachita Baptist University, in Arkadelphia, remembers:

> *Miss Lawrence was musically inspiring, but also an inspiration to the soul. To see the reality of her having to live every minute of her life in that wheelchair – getting in it, getting out of it, manoeuvring it through rooms – and still being 'Marjorie Lawrence' was a tremendous example of an indomitable spirit.*[10]

Participants have a wealth of anecdotes about these summer workshops illustrating that Marjorie was both a benevolent and, when necessary, *stern* task master. One of the most revealing found its way into the newspapers:

> *Once a student, obviously seeking attention, complained that she could not continue singing in a group rehearsing a scene from a Verdi opera, because she*

was not feeling well. Miss Lawrence told her to go and lie down in an anteroom and instructed another student to sing her part so the rehearsal could continue. No sooner had the second student begun to sing, than the first exploded back into the room demanding, 'What is she doing singing my music?' There was a deathly pause while Miss Lawrence wheeled herself to the centre of the room. Addressing the first student she said quietly but in steely tones: 'First, I would like to say that Verdi did not write the music for you'. A glint then appeared in her eyes and she added, 'And while we're on this subject I should like to point out that on many occasions at the Metropolitan Opera, Madame Kirsten Flagstad would stand in the wings while I was on, ready to step in should it be necessary and I performed the same service for her'. She then wheeled around to the pianist. 'Take it from the top, please.'[11]

The rehearsal referred to would have been for one of the two concerts the participants at the summer workshops gave in Hot Springs – a concert of sacred music midway through, and a concert of operatic excerpts at the end. The term 'sacred' was applied fairly loosely and the program included items such as the 'Miserere' from *Il Trovatore* and the 'Easter Hymn' from *Cavalleria Rusticana*. This first concert was given in a Hot Springs church, while the ballroom of the elegant Arlington Hotel was used for the opera concert. For many of the young singers taking part, this valuable performing experience was the culmination of six enlightening weeks. These concerts became welcome fixtures on the Hot Springs social calendar and gave families staying in the area an opportunity to feel part of the event.

In 1959 Marjorie was approached by the Elwood Emerick Agency in New York to join their stable of celebrity lecturers. One of the engagements booked for Marjorie was at Southern Illinois University (SIU) in Carbondale. Marjorie delivered her lecture (entitled 'Keep busy, keep talking') in a venue on campus where she had given a public recital in 1945. After the lecture she was approached by Fred Denker, acting head of the School of Music at SIU. Dr Denker explained that he, Dean Shryock, and Assistant Dean Phil Olsson of the Faculty of Communications and Fine Arts were keen to develop new performing arts programs at SIU, in particular an opera school. If Marjorie ever wished to leave Tulane, Denker said, there would be a place for her at SIU to develop and head the new opera school.

At the time Marjorie explained to Denker that she was happy at Tulane, but within hours of leaving Carbondale the challenge of creating a new opera school began to fire her imagination and stir that part of her that had always relished a challenge. The other great attraction at Southern Illinois University was the venue in which Marjorie had delivered her lecture and which Denker had told her would be available to the new opera school. This was a free-standing building next door to the school of music, opened in 1917 and named in honour of Dean Shryock's father. Since Shryock Auditorium boasts comfortable seating for over a 1000, raked stalls and balcony, a generous stage, full proscenium arch, orchestra pit, backstage equipment and facilities, spacious foyers and elegant art deco decoration, Marjorie would, in reality, have her own opera house to command. She envisaged full-scale student productions of opera on the Shryock stage, concerts and maybe an occasional recital of her own. These alone were prospects too appealing to ignore.

Marjorie also realised that establishing a new opera school from scratch and attracting new students carried a risk. She therefore informed SIU that she would accept the post on condition that Tulane was willing to give her indefinite leave to do so, reasoning that she could return to New Orleans if the Illinois project failed. Tulane University was most accommodating, even when two of their students announced that if Marjorie went north they would follow. A deal was struck similar to that Marjorie had with Tulane and possibly because of her continuing association with the New Orleans university, SIU gave her the title 'Research Professor'.[12]

Tom and Marjorie rented a small house in South State Street, Carbondale, and Marjorie joined the faculty at SIU at the beginning of the fall semester of 1960. Thus began a thirteen-year association with Southern Illinois University which gave Marjorie stimulating occupation, stability of income, the respect of a whole new generation of young singers and an enormous amount of personal satisfaction. Her presence also brought international attention, credibility and honour to the university's school of music. Marjorie would rapidly become and remain one of the university's great characters – beloved, respected and occasionally a little feared by her students and her colleagues.

It was tough in the beginning. Marjorie began her opera school with just three students, including the two who moved with her from Tulane. One of these was Bonnieray Elsie, a lirico-spinto soprano from Tulsa, Oklahoma, who would later go on to have a successful career in the United States and Europe under the name Rosanna Rocco. These were joined by tenor Thomas Page, Marjorie's first new recruit at SIU. By the end of the second or third semester, three had become thirty, with most of her students working towards a Bachelor of Arts or Master of Arts degree with singing as their principal subject.

Marjorie was allocated a studio in the Altgeld Building, home of the School of Music. 'Miss Lawrence' wheeling herself at high speed around the corridors became a familiar sight and the sound of her laughter rang through the building. Both here and at Tulane, Marjorie fitted remarkably well into academic life, especially considering she had never received a tertiary education and had no academic qualifications. Just occasionally she encountered resentment from the stuffiest of her colleagues, but for every one who resented her presence there were many more who revered her. When Dean Shryock retired, he wrote to Marjorie saying, 'You are doing a perfectly wonderful job and everyone loves you dearly'.[13] After having weathered the barbs of newspaper criticism, Marjorie found it easy enough to laugh off the occasional negative jibe or innuendo. Of one tetchy colleague, she commented, 'He's got more letters after his name than a crossword ... but, can he *sing?*'

Marjorie did sing in concerts and gave the occasional recital in the Shryock Auditorium during her first years at SIU, accompanied by either Dr Denker or his successor Robert Mueller. With the Southern Illinois Symphony (made up of teachers and students from the School of Music supplemented by other local musicians) she trotted out some of her old standbys, including the Immolation Scene. She also narrated Benjamin Britten's *Young Person's Guide to the Orchestra* when the orchestra performed that work.[14]

A year after arriving in Carbondale, Marjorie undertook her last new operatic role – Dido in Purcell's *Dido and Aeneas* with a semi-professional group at Edwardsville, Illinois. Dido had also been Flagstad's last role, sung in London in 1951. Marjorie did not have Maggie Teyte, Thomas Hemsley and Geraint Jones to support her as Flagstad had, and the Alton High School Auditorium in Edwardsville was not the Mermaid Theatre in London, but the connection was probably not lost on Marjorie.

Within nine months of her arrival at SIU Marjorie had enough competent students to mount the first of those full-scale productions of opera she had envisaged. For this she chose Bizet's *Carmen* using a double cast and chorus singing in English, the Southern Illinois Symphony conducted by its regular conductor, Carmine Ficocelli, scenery constructed in the university art department and wigs and costumes hired from the New York costumiers Eaves and Stivanellos. By international professional standards the production was a poor thing, by local standards it was a revelation, and as a learning experience for the participants it was invaluable.

It became the practice for Marjorie to mount one production per year, with her most talented students filling the principal roles and occasionally a singer brought in from outside if a role could not be taken by a student. Once Marjorie had chosen an opera and selected students for the principal parts, those students would be invited to participate in the next summer workshop at Harmony Hills, now conducted under the auspices of SIU, where they would begin work on their roles. The average cost of these productions in the mid-1960s was $25,000, comparable with the amounts spent by small regional opera companies across America at the time, suggesting that the standards rose after that initial *Carmen*.

In subsequent years Marjorie produced Mozart's *The Marriage of Figaro, The Magic Flute* and *Don Giovanni,* Verdi's *Aida* and *Falstaff,* Puccini's *Madame Butterfly* and *Gianni Schicchi,* Menotti's *The Medium,* Gounod's *Faust,* Offenbach's *The Tales of Hoffmann,* and *Carmen* again – six years after the first production – and with everything performed in English. Proving that she was not bound by tradition, Marjorie also mounted Scott Joplin's *Treemonisha* just a few months after its first stage production in Atlanta, also an opera called *Altgeld*, set during the time of the Haymarket riots in Chicago and written by a colleague at the school of music, and even a scene from the rock musical *Hair*, for which Marjorie insisted the students remained fully clothed.[15]

To this day participants in those productions feel a sense of privilege at having been chosen by 'Miss Lawrence' and cherish stories about mishaps and memorable moments like the time a camp set designer confounded Marjorie at rehearsal one day with the rejoinder, 'Just remember *darling*, you may be the madam around here, but it's we *girls* who do all the work!'

The Menotti opera and *Aida* were significant because Marjorie cast herself in both. *Aida* was the grandest of the productions staged and an enormous challenge for all concerned. Ninety extras were employed for the triumphal scene and if elephants could not be conjured up in Carbondale, Saluki dogs could, a pair of these sleek, graceful creatures whose breed originated in Ancient Egypt looking more comfortable on stage than many of the singers. The title role in the four performances of *Aida* was shared between three of Marjorie's soprano pupils. Radames was given to Thomas Page, who later had a modest career in Europe, and Gary Varnadore, who joined the Met chorus. Marjorie sang Amneris, carried on and off stage on a throne by members of the local football team.

Three of these performances were taped and the tapes are preserved at SIU. They give evidence of a brave attempt by all involved, the inexperienced singers giving their all and – along with some risible regional accents – showing the benefit of Marjorie's training. It would be gratifying to have had a record of Marjorie singing Amneris from the early 1950s, but her efforts in 1962 should remain where they are – preserved in an archive and to serve the purposes of the occasional knowledgeable researcher. The publication of these tapes would in no way benefit Marjorie's reputation. She can still command attention with her grand vocal gestures, but the voice is a mere shadow of its former majesty, sustained notes are truncated and top notes are hurled out with force but to little effect.

Menotti's opera (given in a double bill with *Gianni Schicchi*) was by all accounts highly successful. Marjorie was as riveting as Madame Flora in 1966 as she had been in 1953 and better able to cope with the musical demands of this role than she had with those of Amneris. No tapes seem to have survived of these performances, which is a great pity because they once existed. One who listened to them was mezzo-soprano Pam Sanabria, who studied with Marjorie for two years and who has sung with regional companies in the United States and in Germany. Like the 'Toby' of the 1953 production, Sanabria remembers a dramatically engrossing performance and a 'razor-sharp voice' that seemed perfect for the part.[16]

Marjorie also sent a copy of the tape to the composer and Menotti wrote back to congratulate her on her interpretation of Madame Flora. As is a composer's privilege, he also made suggestions about tempo changes, should Marjorie have the opportunity to do the role again and Marjorie nearly did, in what would have been a more worthy setting. The production, with the SIU cast, including Marjorie, was offered to the 1967 Ravinia Festival but the festival organisers in Chicago declined to take up the offer. The final performance in the Shryock Auditorium on 13 February 1966, therefore, took on an historical significance. It was Marjorie's last appearance on any stage in opera.[17]

Marjorie's work at Southern Illinois University also drew praise from other quarters. Her students regularly passed preliminary trials for scholarships provided by the Met, the New York City Opera, the Ford Fountain, the Julliard School of Music and the International Opera Centre in Zurich. Occasionally one would go on to pick up an award or a scholarship. Joe Thomas, the young baritone who sang Amonasro in *Aida*, for example, won a scholarship from the Met to study with Rudolph Szekely in Santa Barbara. A high-profile visitor to the college in 1963 also bestowed her approval on Marjorie. Friedelind Wagner came to give a lecture about her grandfather (to whom she bore a striking resemblance) and told the audience how fortunate they were to have Marjorie among them. 'Marjorie Lawrence is one of the greatest interpreters of the soprano roles in my grandfather's music-dramas the world has ever known', she told the assembled students and the local press.[18] The ultimate accolade came in 1971 when SIU announced that they were renaming the opera school. In future it would be known as 'The Marjorie Lawrence Theatre'.

It would be pleasing to be able to report that Marjorie was as successful a teacher as she had been a singer but, based on long-term results, this doesn't seem to have been the case. Her students produced excellent academic results, but the excellence often ended there. Unlike her old friend and colleague Martial Singher, for example, who turned out a string of successful opera stars, most of Marjorie's students never quite made 'the big time'. Most ended up as stalwarts of church choirs, leading lights in amateur music societies or singing teachers, but there were exceptions. Apart from those already noted, mention should be made of the bass Glenn Bater, who spent thirty years in the chorus at the Met and sang numerous *comprimario* roles there, and mezzo-soprano Raeschelle Potter, arguably Marjorie's most successful protégé. Potter acted as Marjorie's graduate assistant at SIU and at the summer workshops, before going on to sing at the Met and in major opera houses in Europe, where she enjoyed success in principal roles. Potter had an especially close friendship with Marjorie, who helped the then young, naïve African-American soprano from Mississippi through personal trials and smoothed the path for her early career. 'She was and will always be my inspiration', Potter recalls.[19]

Famous or not so famous, Marjorie's former students all agree that their encounters with Marjorie were rewarding and enriching. They remember her with deep affection, and the sound of her speaking voice with its Australian 'twang' lingers in their memories – 'You're wasting *your* time and *their* time if the audience can't *understand* what you're singing, dearies' … 'A singer *never* reveals her age to anyone' … 'Lips and teeth girls, please. Lips and teeth!' [meaning smile] … 'Get out there and sing wherever you can, no singer ever made a career by hiding themselves away' … 'You must have a *plan*!' … 'Never lose your musical concentration no matter how much you get carried away by your character' and perhaps most resonant of all: *'CAN'T*? No such word, dearie!'

Chapter Twenty
'Leb' wohl'

Outside the world of academe, Marjorie was not forgotten. She continued to give the occasional public lecture and people in cities and towns across the Midwest paid readily to hear her talks such as 'My Life as A Singer' or 'Interpretation of Wagner, My Personal Experiences'. These brought in useful fees ($500 each time) to supplement Marjorie's earnings from Southern Illinois University.

Marjorie also sang occasionally, generally just one or two items at Democratic conventions, women's forums and charity fund-raising concerts. She even maintained a loose connection with the Met, appearing three times as an interval guest during Saturday matinee broadcasts. Her first appearance coincided with the twenty-fifth anniversary of her Met debut. Between the acts of a splendid performance of Massenet's *Manon* with Victoria de los Angeles and Jussi Björling, Milton Cross, now in his twenty-eighth year as host of these broadcasts, chatted with Marjorie about her years at the Met. She returned on her fifty-fifth birthday and joined the Met's assistant general manager, Francis Robinson, to talk about *Salome*, the opera being broadcast that afternoon with Brenda Lewis in the title role. Her last guest spot was on 30 December 1967, when Robinson interviewed her at length about her life and career.

Each time she was heard in these broadcasts a new batch of fan mail would arrive. Mostly it was handwritten notes on decorated paper from older opera fans, reminding Marjorie of past glories and assuring her she was not forgotten. Sometimes a letter would come from an aging polio victim or a young person newly stricken with some debilitating disease, seeking comfort. Occasionally small gifts were enclosed; often there were desperate pleas for money, for help with a singing career or just an autograph. Replying to letters was not one of Marjorie's strengths, so she was selective about the letters she replied to and let Tom answer the rest on her behalf. None were ever thrown away; instead they were added to the many hundreds of pieces of fan mail Marjorie had collected over the years.

Marjorie was also invited to appear on the Met stage during the Farewell Gala Concert before the company moved out of the old Metropolitan Opera House.

This historic event took place on 16 April 1966, with 4000 people paying $200 each to hear excerpts from opera sung by the current stars of the Met and then watch a cavalcade of former stars entering one by one in alphabetical order. When Marjorie's turn came Tom wheeled her on, shepherded by Rudolf Bing, and the audience exploded. Lotte Lehmann, whose entry was next, had to wait several minutes, and did so gracefully out of respect for Marjorie – and because she knew that when her name was called the same reception awaited her.

Of the great Wagnerians of the 1930s and early 1940s only Marjorie, Lehmann and Alexander Kipnis were present. Melchior had been dismissed by Bing in 1950 and reluctantly declined his invitation to attend; Kirsten Flagstad and Friedrich Schorr were both dead. Many other old friends and colleagues were there; Tom Prideaux, writing in *Life* magazine, described the entry of these old timers with an apposite turn of phrase: 'The audience roared their approval as each star came on stage, looking like parched plants drinking in the rain'.[1] It might be said that this was actually the last time Marjorie sang at the Met, for she, all the other former stars and the current stars joined the audience in singing 'Auld Lang Syne' at the end of the evening.

Marjorie and Tom were back in New York the following September as guests of the company on the opening night of the new Metropolitan Opera House in the Lincoln Centre and to watch the premiere of a new opera commissioned for the occasion – Samuel Barber's *Anthony and Cleopatra* with Leontyne Price, a soprano Marjorie regarded highly. Marjorie's name was also perpetuated in the new house by the provision of facilities for patrons in wheelchairs, financed in her name by a fund set up by a group of her grateful students. Marjorie was also invited to be the guest of honour at the unveiling of a bust of Wagner at the Met in 1969 and again in 1976 when her portrait (in costume as Salome) was hung in the gallery of great singers on the opera house concourse.[2]

Between these visits Marjorie and Tom occasionally attended performances at the Met as members of the audience. Cyril (still living in New York) went more often and was Marjorie's eyes and ears on what was happening there. In 1961 he heard Joan Sutherland singing *Lucia di Lammermoor* in her first series of appearances with the company. 'I wish you could have been there, Marge,' Cyril wrote, 'she's spectacular and has the finest technique of this age or any other'.[3] He also heard Birgit Nilsson many times and reported on her performances in detail. He was less impressed with her and undoubtedly less objective. 'She's cold,' he wrote, 'even colder than Flagstad and she's got none of your warmth and pathos'.[4]

In January 1965 Marjorie also made her last visit to the White House to attend a reception for distinguished American women, hosted by Mrs Lyndon B. Johnson, where she added another President to her list of acquaintances and renewed her friendship with Greer Garson.

The following year she and Tom visited Australia, which was essentially a private visit to enable Marjorie to see her now aging brothers and sister, but the press got word of it. Marjorie was accorded a civic welcome in Sydney and taken on a guided tour of the construction site of the Sydney Opera House. She was also persuaded by EMI Australia to make a recording of 'Waltzing Matilda' with the Sydney Symphony Orchestra. That recording was issued on a seven-inch, 45 rpm disc, but its only distinction is that it is in stereophonic sound, the sole example we have of Marjorie recorded in that mode.

Marjorie postponed her return to America at the end of this visit by a few days to sing at one of the *Music for the People* concerts held in the Myer Music Bowl in Melbourne's Kings Domain Gardens. The invitation came from the organiser and conductor of the concerts, Hector Crawford, who as a very young man in 1939 had conducted one of Marjorie's concerts in Melbourne. A vast audience and many more listening on radio and watching on television witnessed Marjorie's final appearance in her homeland. She sang Sieglinde's aria 'Du bist du Lenz' from *Die Walküre* and 'My Ain Folk', substituting (as she had done in 1939) one line for 'at home in dear *Australia* with my ain folk'. She also sang 'Annie Laurie' and finished with 'Waltzing Matilda'. It was an occasion of greater sentimental than musical excellence, but after the concert Crawford told the press, 'I think today meant more to me and the orchestra than any of the dozens of other concerts we have given'. Marjorie and Tom returned home via Europe and stopped off in Milan to attend a performance of *Don Giovanni* at La Scala with Joan Sutherland singing Donna Anna. As Richard Bonynge recalls in his foreword, after the performance the Bonynges and the Kings enjoyed a memorable evening together.

Marjorie was never niggardly in praising singers she liked or begrudging about their success and she had enormous respect and admiration for Sutherland, but one aspect of the younger Australian singer's career might have prompted a twinge of envy. By 1966 Sutherland was on the way to becoming the most recorded soprano in history and Marjorie's own recordings (apart from the little seven-inch disc) had long disappeared from circulation. Amends were made when the Austrian Preiser company released an LP in their *Lebendige Vergangenheit* (*Living Past*) series. The disc offered excellent transfers of the best of Marjorie's Paris recordings from 1933 and 1934 and enabled a whole new generation of opera lovers to discover her voice and her remarkable Ortrud, Brünnhilde and Salome. Reviewers in hi-fi magazines around the world waxed lyrical about her startlingly youthful and vocally resplendent Immolation Scene and the *Salome* finale, where her voice and personality seemed to leap out of modern loudspeakers.

By 1973, the year Marjorie and Tom each turned sixty-six, the pressure of maintaining two houses and travelling back and forth between Hot Springs and Carbondale was taking its toll on them both. Tom did the 300-mile trip most often, returning to Harmony Hills to deal with farm issues, while Marjorie stayed on in Carbondale in the care of Clara Weekes and the assistant Southern Illinois University provided for her. Compounding the problem, Tom's health had also become an issue. As far back as 1955, he had been diagnosed with 'heart problems' and the situation had steadily deteriorated to the point where going on long and exhausting road journeys on his own was risky. The opportunity to change this lifestyle presented itself in the spring of that year. John Hughes, Dean of the Division of Fine Arts at the University of Arkansas, approached Marjorie with a plan to establish an opera school at his university in Little Rock.

The Arkansas state capital was a mere thirty miles north of Harmony Hills on Highway 7 South. Hughes also made a generous offer of $3000 per semester for a nine-hour week increasing to $6000 for an eighteen-hour week, the choice of hours being entirely Marjorie's. Hughes also offered a flat fee of $1800 for the summer workshops and suggested that, if Marjorie wished, she could also conduct her regular classes at Harmony Hills and the students would come to her. There was less responsibility in this post as well. Blanche Thebom was being appointed head of the new opera school and all the leadership and management functions Marjorie performed at SIU would be Thebom's responsibility. It was too good a deal to turn down and solved Marjorie and Tom's domestic dilemma.

In April Marjorie wrote to Phil Olsson explaining that she wished to retire from SIU on 1 September. The news naturally came as a disappointment to Marjorie's colleagues and students, but there was acceptance that she had given so much for so long to SIU and had earned the right to put her own and Tom's interests first. SIU organised a series of events to celebrate her achievements and mark her retirement. The University of Southern Illinois Press produced a new edition of *Interrupted Melody* and there was a gala showing of the film in Shryock Auditorium – the proceeds from both going to the School of Music Scholarship Fund. There were receptions for Marjorie and gatherings of students and colleagues to present her with parting gifts and to make their tearful farewells. Others have stepped into Marjorie's place at SIU in the years since, but none has been quite able to, as the old expression goes, 'fill her shoes'.

Marjorie joined the faculty of the University of Arkansas in November 1973 amid much local publicity. She was photographed with Dean Hughes and Blanche Thebom and the university proudly boasted that they now had the services of two former Metropolitan Opera divas. Thebom told the press that she was delighted to be working with Marjorie and that she looked forward to an active and growing alliance.[5]

Students came to Harmony Hills and received the same personal attention, the same practical instruction and the same encouragement that dozens of others had in New Orleans and Carbondale. The University of Arkansas supported the seventeenth and final summer workshop at Harmony Hills in 1973 and continued to send her students until 1977. Marjorie also began teaching at the Garland County Community College in Hot Springs in 1974 – a less prestigious establishment, but perhaps one that better suited her depleted energy and Tom's rapidly dwindling capacity to be her physical mainstay.

In 1974 Marjorie and Tom decided to sell off most of Harmony Hills, retaining a 40-acre block separated from the remainder by the highway. On that site they planned and built a smaller, modern-style and more wheelchair-friendly house. The rest of the property became 'The Harmony Hills Riding Stables'. The planned move into a smaller house meant that there would be no space to store the many boxes in which Marjorie had kept letters, contracts, programs, newspaper clippings, scrap books, photographs and all the other memorabilia and detritus from her career. Marjorie decided to contact Southern Illinois University and offer the whole collection to them.

The Dean of Library Affairs at SIU accepted readily, so all the dusty boxes were brought up from the cellar at Harmony Hills and Marjorie set about going through them. Anything that she believed should not be made public (including her correspondence with Charles Buttrose) was removed and probably burned. What remained was still a treasure trove, documenting all aspects of her life and career and giving invaluable insight into performing standards and conditions in Australia, Europe and the United States in the pre-war, wartime and post-war eras. Ken Duckett, Curator of Special Collections at the time, made several trips to Harmony Hills and brought back car loads of material. The whole collection was eventually catalogued, and as 'The Marjorie Lawrence Papers' it is now one of SIU's most important archival collections.

As Tom's health declined and periods of hospitalisation were needed, his sister Doris moved to the area to help out. Doris proved a stalwart support for her brother and sister-in-law for the rest of their lives. The new house proved a delight for both Marjorie and Tom. Vast expanses of glass gave them wonderful views of the Ouachita Mountains and level floors allowed Marjorie ease of movement. The potted banana palms were transported over from the old house and graced the patio of the new establishment, which meant that the fried bananas they both loved could remain on the menu. The living room doubled as a studio and old and new students continued to arrive, Marjorie helping to arrange performance experience for them in concerts and church services in Hot Springs.

After the trip to Australia in 1966, Marjorie had resigned herself to the fact that she would probably never see her homeland again. That saddened her, because, although she was accepted as 'a distinguished American woman', a part of her remained resolutely and proudly Australian. Half a lifetime of absence probably coloured her memories and nurtured her fondness for Australia, but what she felt was sincere, intense and indestructible. Marjorie was also one of those expatriate 'Aussies' who recognised how much of their success (and survival) could be credited to their native resourcefulness, their dry sense of humour, their lack of pretentiousness and to that fighting spirit that has always distinguished Australians on the battlefield, on the sporting field and in the world's opera houses.[6]

In 1976 the opportunity to see Australia one last time unexpectedly presented itself. Marjorie was contacted by the producers of the Australian version of *This Is Your Life* asking her to travel to Australia to appear as a guest on the program they were planning to honour Harold Blair. The request came at a time when Tom was not well, so Marjorie declined, offering instead to videotape a message to the tenor in her new living room for inclusion in the program. The producers accepted that and a crew duly arrived and the short video was made.

The producers of the program then contacted Tom and said they wanted to make a program honouring Marjorie. The 1955 American version pre-dated the arrival of television in Australia and the producers said they felt she would be an ideal candidate for their program. With Tom's connivance, a devious scheme was devised. Marjorie was told she was needed in Australia to appear in a documentary about Blair's life. Tom was feeling better by then and seemed very keen to go, so Marjorie agreed. A week later Blair died suddenly, so Marjorie stopped packing and called the trip off. The producers in Australia panicked and cabled Marjorie that she was still needed, now to take part in a memorial program for the tenor. Marjorie procrastinated. She admitted to Tom that she longed to see Australia again, but feared the trip would be too arduous for him. Tom finally got impatient with her and in Marjorie's words 'bludgeoned' her into going.

Marjorie and Tom landed at Sydney Airport on a frosty morning to find a barrage of reporters and photographers awaiting them. To Tom she whispered, 'Well, the buggers haven't forgotten me yet!' At the Wentworth Hotel the program's host, Mike Willesee, was waiting for her and pronounced those famous words: 'Marjorie Lawrence, this is *your* life', to which Marjorie responded: 'Gee whiz!'

In the days leading up to the filming of the program, Marjorie and Tom went to the races at Randwick and were special guests at the opening performance of Opera Australia's winter season in the Sydney Opera House. When Tom wheeled Marjorie into the Opera Theatre a spotlight was swung onto her and the audience rose to give her a standing ovation.

If the Australian version of Marjorie's *This Is Your Life* lacked the parade of celebrities that distinguished the American version, time was to blame – Melchior, Tibbett and Johnson were all dead. Guests in the studio included Sir Hubert Opperman, who reminded Marjorie about the bicycle he had given her in 1939, pianist Isador Goodman and a navy veteran, Geoff Waye, who had been one of the patients Marjorie sang to in the Australian General Hospital in Darwin in 1944. Lena and Allan were there and Cyril sent a video message from New York. Brothers Ted and Lindsay were too frail to take part. Raeschelle Potter sent a moving video message from the Vienna Staatsoper and the surprise guest at the end of the program was Francis Robinson, who made it abundantly clear to Marjorie's fellow countrymen and women, just how much she had been loved and appreciated at the Met.

While they were in Sydney, Marjorie and Tom recorded an hour-long radio program about Marjorie's life and career, loosely based on the lecture she had been delivering for years, 'My Life as a Singer', complete with a few long-practised inaccuracies. It is the only audio document we have of Tom speaking and the most extensive to survive of Marjorie. We can listen to that 'southern drawl' Marjorie found so attractive when she first met Tom and Marjorie's voice is still projected with such clarity that one suspects the technicians would have set the microphone well back from her chair. While in Sydney Marjorie was also invited to return in 1977 to conduct a series of master classes at the state conservatorium of music, a request she felt unable to fulfil when the time came.

No visit to Australia would have been complete without a trip to Melbourne and a visit to Deans Marsh and Winchelsea. At Marjorie's request, Lena's husband drove them to the Bambra Cemetery and Marjorie paid her respects for the last time at the graves of her parents, the visit cut short by teeming rain. Lena celebrated her seventy-fourth birthday while Marjorie was in Melbourne and forty family members gathered to celebrate the occasion with a barbeque at the seaside town of Anglesea. The weather stayed fine, everyone enjoyed mountains of sizzling lamb chops, succulent steaks and fat-spitting sausages washed down with cold beer and scalding tea. Marjorie led everyone in singing 'Happy Birthday' and any passer-by who might have witnessed the party would have concluded it was an Aussie-style gathering of a typical Australian family. For one memorable afternoon on the shores of Bass Strait where the waves roll in from the Tasman and the dense forests of the Otway Ranges spill down to the sea, Marjorie truly was 'back among her ain folk'.

Marjorie and Tom again returned to the United States via Europe and stopped over in Paris for two weeks. Old friends made them welcome, but their number was now few. They attended a performance at the Opéra, Marjorie wearing the jewelled miniature of her *Legion d'honneur* insignia. Marjorie might well have wondered as she listened to a whole new generation of singers, first in Sydney then in Paris, if she would ever again have the opportunity to sing in public, but a few weeks after they reached home, such an opportunity did present itself – and it was no ordinary opportunity.

In 1976 UNICEF, the United Nations Children's Fund, celebrated its thirtieth anniversary and the Australian Government's contribution to the festivities was a gala concert held in the General Assembly Hall of the United Nations building in New York. This was the first time such an event had been held in that resplendent chamber and Australian theatrical icon Sir Robert Helpmann was charged with organising it. Invitations to take part were issued to and accepted by many distinguished Australian performers, including Joan Sutherland and Richard Bonynge, June Bronhill, Rolf Harris and Marjorie.

Zoe Caldwell and Cyril Ritchard compered and Marjorie opened the concert with what Ritchard described as the song most Australians recognise as their true national anthem. Tom, looking frail but dapper in black tie and ruffled shirt, wheeled Marjorie out amid a welcoming roar from the audience. Then he retired, reluctantly but proudly handing over the woman he had loved for thirty-seven years to the public for one last time and leaving her centre stage where she belonged. In a shimmering gown, her 'diamonds' and her trademark smile flashing, Marjorie mustered all the vocal resources that remained to her in her seventieth year as the orchestra struck up the opening bars of 'Waltzing Matilda'. As Richard Bonynge recalls in his foreword, by the end of the song, the entire audience was moved to tears by Marjorie's courage, by memories of glories past and echoes of a once great voice, and the spirited performance she had just given.

After the concert a lavish reception was held, hosted by the Secretary General of the United Nations and the Australian Ambassador to the UN. Marjorie was photographed with Joan Sutherland, both divas glowing as only great divas can and obviously touched to be once more in each other's company. It was a great night for all Australians and for UNICEF, which benefited by $100,000, but more importantly it was an historic occasion. It was one of those precious occasions when two great musical ambassadors from the same nation – a generation apart in age and art – came together in public to create history.[7]

Shortly before the UN concert Marjorie had been informed that she had been nominated for an imperial honour. Some, including Tom, thought this was long overdue. As far back as 1949, Tom had petitioned the Australian Government to recommend Marjorie for an award. At the time a Labor government was in power in Australia and Arthur Calwell wrote back to say it was not his party's policy to recommend people for imperial honours. Tom next approached the Victorian Liberal government, but got no further with Melbourne than he had with Canberra.

Just who recommended Marjorie for the award she finally received is unclear, but it would seem likely that the process was begun when Marjorie and Tom were in Sydney for the Australian *This Is Your Life* program. The result was that Marjorie's name was published in the 1977 New Year Honours list among those to become Commanders in the Order of the British Empire, in recognition of her illustrious career in music. Marjorie was given several options for accepting the award, including attending an investiture at Buckingham Palace, but chose to travel to Washington and to receive it from the Australian Ambassador to the United States, Allan Renouf.

The academic world also honoured Marjorie with three awards. In 1969 the University of Ohio bestowed on her an Honorary Doctorate of Humane Letters and at the same time she accepted a fellowship from the British Royal Society for the Encouragement of the Arts. Soon after Marjorie got her CBE, Southern Illinois University conferred an Honorary Doctorate of Music on her. Marjorie was not a snob, but it might well have given her satisfaction that, by the end of her life, she too had 'more letters than a crossword' after her name.

During 1978 Marjorie continued to teach a small number of students, and the local community in Hot Springs, who had been happy to adopt her as their local celebrity, now revered her as their local legend. The mayor of Hot Springs designated a day in September as 'Marjorie Lawrence Day' and the plan was to celebrate her life and work on that day each year with a concert, but Marjorie wasn't around for the second. Her last appearance in public was at a Christmas concert in the Hot Springs Convention Centre. Marjorie had prepared the singers – students and former students – to appear with the Arkansas Symphony Orchestra. Those who saw Marjorie and spoke with her that evening recall that she seemed in fine form, giving last-minute instructions backstage, then applauding louder than anyone else after each performance.

A week into the new year, Marjorie complained of feeling, in own her words, 'not too hot'. Tom and their local doctor conferred and it was decided that as a precaution Marjorie should be admitted to St Vincent's Infirmary in Little Rock for a complete medical check-up. In recent years Marjorie had been prone to minor ailments like anyone else, but her general health had been good for her age and activity had kept her mentally alert. Nothing specific was found when she was examined in the infirmary, but as the days passed her condition deteriorated. Tom and the Little Rock doctors who attended her reached the conclusion that her life was coming to its natural end. Their prognosis was right. With Tom and his sister Doris at her bedside, Marjorie died at 3 am on Saturday 13 January 1979, a month short of her seventy-third birthday. The official cause of death was heart failure.

News of Marjorie's death was cabled around the world and obituaries appeared in newspapers across America and Australia. Most featured portraits of her in her glamorous concert gowns; a few found space to include photos of her in her major roles. Her singing was praised and memorable incidents – like riding Grane into the funeral pyre at the Met – were recalled, but Marjorie's illness, her comeback and the film of *Interrupted Melody* dominated these columns.

Marjorie's body was brought back to Hot Springs and lay in state in the Gross Mortuary to allow friends, acquaintances, former and current students to pay their last respects. The following day her funeral was held in St Luke's Episcopal Church in Hot Springs. The church was packed and hundreds more gathered in the street outside. A choir made up of Marjorie's students provided the music. After the service a cortege proceeded to Greenwood Cemetery at Hot Springs, where Marjorie was laid to rest. Later an impressive memorial in the shape of a classical temple was erected over her plot and the empty one beside it, reserved for Tom. Inscribed on the stone are the words: 'God, love and music. These have I lived for' – a variation on the first line of Tosca's aria 'Vissi d'arte'. Memorial services for Marjorie were conducted in various other places, including Dean's Marsh on the anniversary of her death.

Tom stayed on in the new house at Harmony Hills, his loneliness and frailty alleviated by help from his devoted sister and a few of Marjorie's former friends and students who remained faithful to him to the end. Congestive heart failure took his life six years after his beloved wife. Unlike Marjorie's, Tom's funeral was poorly attended. On 8 April 1985 he was laid to rest beside Marjorie.[8]

In the years since Marjorie's death her face and name have never slipped completely off the radar. The reissue of the Preiser LP as a CD brought it to the attention of many new listeners and the occasional reissue on CD of all those broadcasts from the Met and the Teatro Colón revealed the glory of Marjorie's voice to people who had never before heard of her. In 2001 the Marjorie Lawrence International Vocal Competition was established in Washington by James McCully, a former student of Marjorie's, with Sutherland and Bonynge as its honorary chairpersons. Marjorie's name was added to the 'Walk of Fame' in Hot Springs, a commemorative plaque was placed on the old Lawrence house in Deans Marsh and the road between Deans Marsh and Winchelsea was renamed 'The Marjorie Lawrence Way' in her honour.

To celebrate the centenary of Marjorie's birth in 2007 events were held in the United States and in Australia, culminating in the presentation of the 'Marjorie Lawrence Centennial Celebration Award' to Deborah Voigt in the Kennedy Centre in Washington. It was an appropriate choice of recipient, with Voigt now singing most of the roles Marjorie sang at the Met in her day.

With Marjorie's death now more than thirty years in the past, we can look back on her life with the benefit of hindsight and place her art in context and perspective. Of her character I hope the picture is clear. No biographer can trawl the recesses of their subject's mind and explore their personality from the inside. All we can do is present the outward manifestations of that personality through the subject's words, writings, actions and reactions, and report the effects these had on others. I hope that what has been recounted about Marjorie in this and the previous chapters is sufficient to support my own conviction that she was a person of exceptional courage, blessed with an indomitable spirit and the capacity to be a life-enhancing force. Richard Bonynge's comment that he and Dame Joan Sutherland felt privileged to share a tiny part in her life would be echoed by a legion of others in Australia and the United States. My only regret is that I was not one of them.

In discussing her art, subjectivity enters, but in my view the conclusions are just as clear. The 1930s at the Metropolitan Opera have been described as a golden age in the history of Wagner performance. In truth if we were transported back into the stalls of the Met during one of those performances caught on disc (of *Die Walküre* perhaps, with Marjorie, Flagstad, Melchior and Schorr, or *Lohengrin* with Lehmann, Marjorie and Melchior), what we would *see* would probably strike us as anything but golden: the stage cluttered, costumes mismatched and the singers resorting to stock poses and gestures, but in one regard the term 'golden' would seem entirely apt, perhaps even inadequate. The voices we would be listening to would be of a magnificence probably not heard before nor since in this repertoire. This was truly an age of Wagnerian vocal giants, one of those rare moments when a group of extraordinary artists appear on the scene at the same time and coalesce to produce performances without parallel.

Back in our seat at the Met, we would be watching and listening to mostly Germans, Norwegians, Danes and Swedes, progeny of races issuing from the fountainhead of Wagner's music dramas. That a young Paris-trained woman from a rural community in far-off Australia should have been accepted into that fraternity is remarkable. That she could muster the voice and the artistry to be acknowledged as an equal among these titans is even more so. Marjorie's life is littered with tantalising and frustrating 'might-have-beens', but they should not be allowed to overshadow her achievements. For a few short years she was a glittering adornment to the operatic stage – a true 'star', an ambassador for her nation and a dutiful servant of her art.

The title of this chapter is the opening of Wotan's moving farewell to his daughter, Brünnhilde, in the final scene of *Die Walküre*. 'Leb' wohl, du kühnes, herrliches Kind', the ruler of the gods sings – 'Farewell, thou valiant, glorious child'. A more fitting epitaph would be hard to find for Marjorie Lawrence.

Notes

CHAPTER ONE ⁓ 'PUSH THE PRAM FOR BABY'

1 William Lawrence, born Modewarre, Victoria, 1861, was one of five sons of Henry and Julia Lawrence. The Lawrence family can be traced back to the end of the eighteenth century and seems to have been entirely English, although in later years Marjorie claimed both Scottish and Irish forebears, usually when singing Scottish or Irish songs.

2 Elizabeth Smith, born Deans Marsh, 1869, was one of seven children of Robert and Mary Smith. Elizabeth's gravestone suggests she was born in 1866, but 1869 is the date on all extant documents pertaining to her life and death.

3 On a concert tour of Australia in 1939 Marjorie regaled a bemused journalist with two examples from her father's comic song repertoire: *Does anyone know of a nice old lady, of fifty-one or two or three* ('a dear old duck that would just suit me') and *Jackson Brown was a worn out clown* ('who stands upon his head').

4 The house was constructed for them by one of Bill's brothers: he purchased a smaller cottage on another site, cut it in two, transported the halves on a dray to the new location and built a new central section. Finished, it comprised four rooms and a lean-to with an earth floor at the rear, housing the utilities. The house still stands and is heritage-listed.

5 In later years Marjorie's birth year was frequently misreported as 1909. The first instance of this discrepancy appears in 1948 when Marjorie was forty-one and her career was at a low ebb. It may have been a deliberate ploy on her or her concert agent's part at that time to create the impression she was still a 'young' singer (yet to reach forty), or it may simply have been vanity.

6 Marjorie's memory failed her when in later years she tried to recall her grandfather's given name. In *Interrupted Melody* she mistakenly refers to him as Jasper, the name of one of her great uncles. Henry Lawrence was a shoemaker by trade and the son of a shoemaker from the market town of Calne in Wiltshire who had immigrated to Australia with his wife and eight children in 1853.

7 Marjorie Lawrence & Charles Buttrose, *Interrupted Melody*, Southern Illinois University Press, 1974, hereafter referred to as *Interrupted Melody*. All the subsequent

passages quoted in this chapter are from the same source, occasionally with minor editing.
8   Marjorie kept a large inscribed studio portrait of Reverend Pearce all her life. It is preserved in the Marjorie Lawrence Papers, Morris Library, Southern Illinois University, hereafter referred to as MLP.
9   In *Interrupted Melody* Marjorie gives a slightly different version of that morning's events, excluding her sixteen-year-old brother Allan from any part in it and suggesting she and Percy walked to the station. Allan himself, however, vividly remembered every detail and later took great pride and delight in recounting his part to his children.

CHAPTER TWO ∽ STITCHES AND SCALES

1   Ivor C. Boustead, born about 1885, died 1958, had a modest career as a baritone before turning to teaching. John Brownlee and Marjorie were his most famous pupils, but his teaching also produced a number of other singers who had successful careers in Australia.
2   Biographical notes prepared by Marjorie for the ghost writer of *Interrupted Melody* (MLP). There are often quite significant differences between reported facts and accounts of events in these notes and what was published in *Interrupted Melody*. Where such discrepancies arise I have chosen to use the information in Marjorie's notes as my source, on the assumption that they are more authentic than the ghost writer's treatment of the same material. Hence readers will find some quite glaring differences from here onwards between what appeared in *Interrupted Melody* and what they will read in this volume.
3   This and all the other quotes that follow in this chapter unless identified otherwise are taken from *Interrupted Melody*.
4   Marjorie reports in *Interrupted Melody* that this woman never failed to seek her out on her visits to Melbourne after she became famous and would boast about how she helped 'dear Marge' when she first came to Melbourne.
5   Letter to Marjorie from Eileen Lawrence, 21 March 1926 (MLP).
6   Barrie Gregory & Marjorie Gregory, *Coast to Country – Winchelsea, a History of the Shire*, Hargreen, Melbourne, 1985.
7   Boustead and Hart were professional rivals and there was no love lost between them. As well as teaching privately at his studio, Boustead was associated with the Melbourne University Conservatorium, a rival establishment to the Albert Street Conservatorium.
8   Sun Aria prizes were offered in Ballarat, Bendigo, Geelong and later Sydney. The Geelong Sun Aria was suspended in 1933 and the only other winner who went on to have an international career was the tenor John Dudley, who took the award in its final year. Dudley joined the Metropolitan Opera in New York for the 1940–41 season and remained until 1944 singing in the chorus and occasionally assigned minor roles. Although they were on the roster together for three seasons, Dudley only appeared on stage as a chorus member with Marjorie singing principal roles. Sydney winners included Joan Sutherland and June Bronhill.

9   Biographical notes prepared by Marjorie for the ghost writer of *Interrupted Melody* (MLP).
10 *Australian Musical News*, August 1928. John Brownlee (1900–1969) came to figure prominently in Marjorie's life as a mentor, colleague and devoted friend. After studying with Boustead and encouraged by Melba, he had completed his studies in Paris and commenced his career there. He famously appeared with Melba at her Covent Garden farewell in 1926 and in the mid-1930s with the fledgling Glyndebourne opera. He made his debut at the Metropolitan Opera in New York in 1937 and remained with that company for twenty-seven consecutive seasons. His voice can be heard on numerous recordings.
11 Not the TSS *Hobson's Bay*, as stated in both her biographical notes and *Interrupted Melody*.

CHAPTER THREE ~ INNOCENTS ABROAD

1   The name of the piano accompanist does not appear on these discs. It may have been Ray Dickson, but was more likely an in-house pianist at the Aeolian studios. The accompaniments are played unremarkably.
2   The house Cécile Gilly occupied is an elegant three-storey villa in a precinct that has housed music teachers and music shops for centuries. Today the area is rundown and electric guitars and amplifiers fill the dusty shop windows which once displayed violins, flutes and harps, but the house is beautifully preserved and still occupied.
3   Biographical notes prepared by Marjorie for the ghost writer of *Interrupted Melody* (MLP).
4   ibid.
5   The Académie française members were the lawyer, writer and politician Pierre Louis de Lacratelle (1751–1823), his younger brother, journalist and historian Jean Charles Dominique de Lacratelle (1766–1855), both of whom were important figures in the French Revolution, and the novelist Jacques de Lacratelle (1888–1985). Opera lovers might also note that Jean Charles Dominique (Marie's grandfather) was a close friend and colleague of André Chenier, subject of Giordano's opera, *Andrea Chenier*.
6   The complement of boarders at the Grodets was always an international mix and in 1933 included two secretive young Germans who claimed they were in Paris to study art. With hindsight, Marjorie concluded they were more likely to have been sent to study *the* art in preparation for looting by the Nazis.
7   When a few days later a solitary, skinny chicken was served for Christmas dinner and apportioned among ten people, Marjorie found herself longing for the feast she knew her family would be tucking into in Winchelsea that day. The next time a chicken was served Marjorie offered to stuff it with breadcrumbs, onion, sage etc. but when it was served no one else would eat it.
8   Since 1944 the school has been named Lycée Jacques Decour.
9   Biographical notes prepared by Marjorie for the ghost writer of *Interrupted Melody* (MLP).

10 Biographical notes prepared by Marjorie for the ghost writer of *Interrupted Melody* (MLP).

CHAPTER FOUR ~ MADEMOISELLE LAWRENCE

1 Comparison of the recordings of Thill with his Italian counterpart Beniamino Gigli will serve to illustrate these differences if readers wish to explore the topic.

2 Like the studio of Mathilde Marchesi, the Paris-based teacher of several antipodean singers including Nellie Melba, Ada Crossley and Evelyn Scotney, a generation earlier, Cécile Gilly's studio was mostly (but not exclusively) for females and seems to have been a magnet to singers from 'down under'. During her time there Marjorie encountered at least three other Australians and one New Zealander.

3 Had Cécile Gilly returned to New York she would have had the distinction of creating a small role in a Puccini opera. While the company was performing in Paris the prospective cast for the world premiere of Puccini's *La Fanciulla del West* was released to the press and Cécile Gilly was listed to sing Wowkle, the Indian squaw. When she did not return to New York, the role was given to another singer.

4 Biographical notes prepared by Marjorie for the ghost writer of *Interrupted Melody* (MLP).

5 Renée Gilly (1906–1977) made her debut in 1933 and then sang regularly at the Opéra, the Opéra-Comique and for one season at Covent Garden. She can be heard in 'live' opera recordings conducted by Ernst Ansermet, singing Marina in Mussorgsky's *Boris Godunov* and Judith in Bartok's *Bluebeard's Castle*. No recordings of Cécile Gilly are known to exist.

6 One of the tactics Marjorie used (and which many singers use) was to carefully underline in red pencil her part in her scores of each opera. For those roles which she went on to sing during her career she kept and used those early scores, most of which have the text in Italian and French or German and French. Also conspicuous by their absence in these scores are alterations or transpositions and only a few traditional cuts are marked in, suggesting that when Marjorie was permitted to, she remained as faithful as she could to composers' intentions. The majority of these scores, leather-bound and well worn, survive in the MLP.

7 Biographical notes prepared by Marjorie for the ghost writer of *Interrupted Melody* (MLP). Among Marjorie's recordings is a brief speech given in French at a concert in Paris in 1946 – see page 383. The only features of her speaking on that occasion which betray her origin are an occasional misplaced emphasis. Marjorie also learned to write fluent French and there is evidence in hastily written notes to herself, that she also 'thought' in French as often as she did in her native tongue.

8 Marjorie encountered Dinh Gilly several times at Madame Gilly's studio and, although she stood in awe of him as a singer, her respect for him as a man was affected by her loyalty to Cécile Gilly. When he divorced Cécile and married one of his London pupils (the contralto Edith Furmedge), the new 'Madame Gilly' was persona non grata with Marjorie.

9 *Australian Musical News*, January 1930.

10 Biographical notes prepared by Marjorie for the ghost writer of *Interrupted Melody* (MLP).
11 After that Marjorie accompanied Madame Grodet to mass many times both at Notre Dame de Lorette and at Sacré Cœur, the great basilica on the summit of Montmartre which Marjorie admired most among the hundreds of churches in the city, but she was never again tempted to convert to Catholicism.
12 *Interrupted Melody*.
13 *Geelong Advertiser*, 17 May 1949.
14 *Geelong Advertiser*, 21 May 1949.
15 Bank statements in MLP.
16 Public Record Office of Victoria VPRS 7591/P2 Box 823.
17 Reported in *The Argus*, Melbourne, 11 June 1930.
18 Correspondence from Blake & Riggall, Solicitors, 120 William St, Melbourne (MLP).
19 Biographical notes prepared by Marjorie for the ghost writer of *Interrupted Melody* (MLP).
20 Unidentified and undated newspaper clipping, probably from an Australian newspaper published in 1939 (MLP).
21 Gilly and Marjorie used the standard French translations of Wagner's operas by Alfred Ernst that were also used at the Opéra, in French provincial opera houses and by other French-language companies around the world.
22 *Interrupted Melody*.
23 A singer providing their own costumes was standard practice up until the arrival of 'The Age of the Producer' in the 1950s and the initiation of integrated productions with coordinated sets, props and costumes. A few years later there were reports in the Australian press that Marjorie had also received advice and encouragement from Emmy Destinn, but as Destinn died in January 1930 and given the circumstances this seems highly unlikely.

CHAPTER FIVE ~ TRIUMPH IN THE SUN

1 Jeer at them.
2 Marjorie had requested that Cécile Gilly accompany her to this audition, but Madame refused then and for all future auditions, reminding her that a singer must stand on his or her own feet. It is a very different thing to sing in your teacher's studio from singing among strangers in a strange place, she advised, and the only way to learn to do that well is without your teacher there as a crutch.
3 Marcel Journet, like Felia Litvinne and Dinh Gilly, belonged to an earlier generation of French singers who had found the ready acceptance on international stages largely denied those of the interwar years as a consequence of changing tastes among audiences outside France.
4 Many singers had stories about this Rumanian impresario and his eccentric and often anti-social behaviour, including Chaliapin who called him 'a cocksure little fool' but admitted to liking him and Maggie Teyte (one of those sopranos who made

their stage debuts at Monte Carlo), who had to fight Gunsbourg off when he tried to seduce her. Gunsbourg's anti-social behaviour also included sucking raw eggs from the shell and dribbling the contents onto his beard and filching morsels of food he fancied from other people's plates.

5   Gunsbourg had been the first to present Berlioz's 'dramatic legend', *La Damnation de Faust*, written for the concert hall, on stage in dramatised form in 1893.
6   *La Tetralogie* is the title the French give to Wagner's Ring Cycle. Marjorie claimed that at the time she did not recognise this term, but that seems highly unlikely, given that she had been studying the work in French for the past year.
7   *Interrupted Melody*.
8   It should be remembered that in earlier times opera seasons were arranged in a more haphazard way than they are today. Repertoire and casts were not locked in years in advance. Singers were sometimes engaged for a raft of roles, but might sing only a few. Operas that had been advertised sometimes didn't reach the stage and others which had not replaced them. If a production was successful, it would be repeated as often as the impresario calculated the public would keep paying to hear it; if a production was not well received, it might be withdrawn after one night. Impresarios like Gunsbourg had the final say, but the whims of individual singers or the demands of influential patrons often affected their decisions.
9   Marjorie's copies of both these contracts survive in the MLP. Each also carries a printed clause whereby Gunsbourg could terminate Marjorie's or any other singer's engagement if they failed at rehearsal or on debut, adding to the risks Marjorie would be taking.
10 Biographical notes prepared by Marjorie for the ghost writer of *Interrupted Melody* (MLP).
11 The name of the person who lent this brooch to Marjorie was never revealed. The owner believed the brooch had also once belonged to the actress Sarah Siddons, but its history and provenance are dubious.
12 Apart from Marjorie and Thill, the other principals were: Marguerite Sens as Venus, Louis Richard as Wolfram and Ernest Mestrallet as the Landgrave. The conductor was Gabriel Grovlez.
13 Dame Clara Butt was by then suffering from cancer of the spine and confined to a wheelchair, but illness and immobility did not stop her spending the season at Monte Carlo, pushed around by her devoted baritone husband Kennerly Rumford.
14 Undated clippings in the MLP.
15 *Australian Musical News*, July 1932.
16 The Australian press asserted that Marjorie also sang Aida and Isolde at Monte Carlo but she did not, then or ever.
17 The score of *L'Escarpolette* (bearing the names of both Gunsbourg and Delmet) was published by Enoch & Co in Paris in 1932, but I have found no records of the opera ever being performed outside Monte Carlo.
18 Biographical notes prepared by Marjorie for the ghost writer of *Interrupted Melody* (MLP).

19 There were reports in the Australian press that following Marjorie's debut in Monte Carlo she had received offers to sing in London and the United States, but there is no evidence to support these claims. No doubt there were plenty of Britons and Americans in Monte Carlo, but it seems likely suggestions were reshaped into commitments by eager supporters in Australia, with or without input from Marjorie.

CHAPTER SIX ∞ DEBUTS, DELAYS AND DISPUTES

1 Ortrud is generally designated as a mezzo-soprano role but the tessitura is high and many sopranos have essayed the role with outstanding success. In more recent times these have included Astrid Varnay, Leonie Rysanek, Eva Marton and Elizabeth Connell.
2 Biographical notes prepared by Marjorie for the ghost writer of *Interrupted Melody* (MLP).
3 Lafranco Rasponi, *The Last Prima Donnas*, Limelight, New York, 1990. Just how extensively Lubin collaborated with Nazi leaders is still a matter of conjecture but she did continue to sing at the Opéra during the German occupation and in Bayreuth and Berlin, where she was admired by Hitler. She claimed, as most artists in the same situation did, that she was apolitical and simply practising her art where she could, but not all the evidence is on her side.
4 The earliest photograph we have of Marjorie in costume also belongs to this period and shows Marjorie as Brünnhilde in the costume she wore at Nantes.
5 Biographical notes prepared by Marjorie for the ghost writer of *Interrupted Melody* (MLP).
6 The Opéra-Comique also had an exalted record for staging new works which slipped effortlessly into the standard repertoire of the time. In the company's former home the Salle Favart, Bizet's *Carmen* had first seen the light, and in their present home on Boulevard des Italiens, Charpentier's *Louise*, Debussy's *Pelleas et Melisande* (with Mary Garden) and Ravel's *L'Heure Espagnole* had been staged for the first time.
7 The Opéra-Comique also had a quota for foreign singers, so either that quota was not filled at this time or Marjorie failed to mention she was a foreign national. The former is the more likely, as the Opéra-Comique employed fewer foreign artists than the Opéra.
8 This letter is the first of several from Marjorie to Rouché preserved in the Bibliothèque-musée de l'Opéra, Paris.
9 Pneumatic letters were the fastest but most expensive form of communication in Paris. The document was placed in a metal cylinder and shot around a network of underground pipes by air pressure.
10 A copy of the contract is preserved in the Bibliothèque-musée de l'Opéra.
11 *Interrupted Melody*.
12 *Interrupted Melody*.
13 Since the publication of the first edition of this book, a number of people have expressed to me their belief that Marjorie did bear a son and that great pains were

taken to preserve the child's anonymity. I acknowledge that this may be the case, but still hold the view that belief should not be presented as fact without proof.
14 ibid.
15 Biographical notes prepared by Marjorie for the ghost writer of *Interrupted Melody* (MLP).
16 ibid.
17 Glowing press reviews and the excellent recordings Lubin made in the 1937, 1939 and 1944 also demonstrate that her voice was still in fine form during this period.
18 Archie Longden confirms that Marjorie had heard Frida Leider and Lotte Lehmann when they were guest performers at the Opéra but less frequently than Lubin and probably not in rehearsals.
19 *L'Intransigent*, Paris, 28 February 1933.
20 *Paris Soir*, 27 February 1933
21 *Paris Soir*, undated clipping (MLP).
22 *La Liberté*, Paris, undated clipping (MLP).

CHAPTER SEVEN ~ L'ÉTOILE DE L'OPÉRA

1 As far as I can determine none of this opera has ever been recorded, but one sample of the music exists on a Pathé newsreel film where Thill can be seen and heard rehearsing his part with the composer. The music is undistinguished, but the singing is spectacular.
2 *Le Temps*, Paris, 28 June 1933.
3 *La Liberté*, Paris, 24 June 1933.
4 Unidentified newspaper clipping dated June, 1933 (MLP).
5 In 1935 Canteloube also sent Marjorie a copy of his song cycle *L'Arada* inscribed affectionately to her. Both scores and the photograph are preserved in the MLP. Also, when Marjorie was going home to Australia for a concert tour in 1939, Canteloube wrote to the French Consul-General in Sydney, who was a friend of his, praising the contribution Marjorie had made to French music and suggesting the Consul-General entertain her, which he did.
6 The concert Marjorie gave at Ostend, singing the 'Liebestod' from *Tristan und Isolde* and the Immolation Scene from *Götterdämmerung,* prompted an interesting letter to the June 1935 edition of *Gramophone* magazine from an Edinburgh cinema organist who was in the audience. He reported being deeply disappointed at first with what he heard, then realised he had become so accustomed to listening to recordings, he had developed a false sense of balance between singer and orchestra. When his ears adjusted he found himself listening to what he reported as 'the finest singing of Brünnhilde's Immolation Scene I have ever heard'. It might also be of interest to readers to note that the opera theatre at Ostend was inaugurated in 1905 with a performance of *Rigoletto* with Caruso and another Australian soprano, Lalla Miranda, the only Australian to be a permanent member of the Paris Opéra before Brownlee and Marjorie.
7 Alan Blyth (ed.), *Opera on Record*, Hutchinson, London, 1979.

8   Among the many reviews of these recordings published in French newspapers and journals is one written by Lucienne Bréval, who had been the Opéra's principal dramatic soprano in the 1890s and Paris's first Kundry. Writing in *Le Candide*, Bréval stated that 'If prizes were offered for recordings, these by Marjorie Lawrence would surely win'.
9   Marjorie Lawrence & Thomas King, 'Marjorie Lawrence: Her life and art', a 1976 radio talk and biographical notes prepared by Marjorie for the ghost writer of *Interrupted Melody* (MLP).
10 Robert Tuggle, 'A Season of the Valkyries', *Opera News*, October 2005. Ziegler does not identify the friend who had written about Marjorie, but it is not inconceivable that it was another singer. Marjorie claimed that Lotte Lehmann, Lily Pons, Maria Müller and Lauritz Melchior all recommended her to opera houses outside France at different times. The last three of these were all established at the Met when Ziegler received his letter.
11 The heads of great opera houses like Rouché and Gatti-Casazza were always informed about going rates for singers and this offer fell well below that mark, especially when no guarantee of the number of performances was given. Leider was complaining about $750 per performance and other artists at the Met were receiving up to $1900 per performance.
12 During her years in Paris Marjorie sang a great deal of contemporary French music. As well as works discussed, others of a much more ephemeral nature included *Le Sommeil de Canope* by Gustave Samazeuilh and *Une Lamentation Hébraïque* by Daniel Lazarus.
13 *Comedia*, Paris, undated clipping (MLP).
14 *Le Temps*, Paris, 28 November 1933.
15 Around this time Marjorie acquired a letter written by Richard Strauss, probably as a gift and a keepsake of this production. It is dated the previous May, written on stationery from a sanatorium in Bad Kissingen and does not contain any musical references. It is preserved in the MLP.
16 *Gramophone*, London, May 1990; *Stereo Review*, New York, June 1990.
17 Details of all these Paris recordings are given in the appendix: A Discography of Marjorie Lawrence's Recordings, pages 279–297 (hereafter referred to as 'the discography').
18 The most likely explanation is that they were among the hundreds destroyed by the Germans when they raided the Paris premises of Voix de son Maitre, but Marjorie put the story about that her recordings were singled out on the instructions of Germaine Lubin, which is improbable.
19 Paul Jackson, *Saturday Afternoons at the Old Met*, Amadeus Press, Portland, 1992.
20 Biographical notes prepared by Marjorie for the ghost writer of *Interrupted Melody* (MLP).
21 ibid.
22 Jackson.
23 *Interrupted Melody*.

24 Years later when Marjorie was dining at the Monte Carlo restaurant in New York she ate food that disagreed with her. In the powder room she vomited and the cap came off this tooth.
25 Rouché had renewed Marjorie's contract for 1936, thus ensuring he was not losing his new star to America permanently.

CHAPTER EIGHT ~ APPLE PIE AND HORSEPLAY

1 *Interrupted Melody*.
2 ibid.
3 Biographical notes prepared by Marjorie for the ghost writer of *Interrupted Melody* (MLP).
4 As this accent was not commented on by the press during subsequent visits to America it seems it was shaken off fairly quickly.
5 Biographical notes prepared by Marjorie for the ghost writer of *Interrupted Melody* (MLP).
6 Shirlee Emmons, *Tristanissimo – The Authorized Biography of Heroic Tenor Lauritz Melchior*, Schirmer, New York, 1990.
7 *Interrupted Melody*.
8 At every subsequent performance Marjorie gave at the Met, Sachse gave her another 'penny' (a bronze one-cent coin). Marjorie joked later that she was saving them up to buy a new horse for Brünnhilde.
9 Rasponi.
10 *New York Sun*, 19 December 1935.
11 *New York Times*, 19 December 1935.
12 See discography for details of this and subsequent 'off-air' recordings.
13 In fact, Walker was mistaken. David Littlejohn (*The Ultimate Art: Essays around and about opera*, Univ. of California Press,1992) reports that a soprano did ride her horse in a performance of *Götterdämmerung* in Munich in the nineteenth century and that when told of this, Wagner's widow, Cosima, dismissed the accomplishment as 'a circus trick', so it was not repeated.
14 When the press got hold of this story a few weeks later they embroidered it making the police officer a bass-baritone and a Wagner buff who only agreed to let Marjorie go if she sang a duet from *Götterdämmerung* with him there and then in the middle of Central Park. This must have strained the newspaper's credibility with even their most devoted readers for several obvious reasons, not least being that the only duet Brünnhilde sings in *Götterdämmerung* is with the tenor.
15 *Gramophone*, September 1999.
16 Jackson; Jackson reports that on the tapes he listened to a short section of the duet was missing and a few notes sung by Flagstad taken from a later broadcast were inserted to fill the gap. I don't believe this to be the case with the tapes used for the CDs issued in 1999. While there are a few notes on these CDs which do not sound typically 'Marjorie' (due most likely to distortion and surface damage to the original discs), there are none that sound like Flagstad.

17   Cyril Lawrence, who became quite a good judge of voices attended many of Flagstad's performances and all of Marjorie's between 1935 and 1942, often referred to Flagstad as being a 'cold performer' compared with his sister. His opinion was no doubt biased, but it was shared by plenty of others who heard both singers in their prime.
18   This might also be an opportune moment to consider Marjorie's art in relation to that of Frida Leider, the other dominant Wagnerian soprano of the interwar years. Leider (nineteen years Marjorie's senior) is considered by many to have been the most 'complete' artist since Lilli Lehmann to essay the big Wagner soprano roles. She is one of those singers it is difficult to criticise and there was a patrician excellence about everything she did. There are also similarities in style (thrilling spontaneity, for example) and in their eclectic repertoire which drew Lieder and Marjorie closer than Marjorie to Flagstad. Had her career not been blighted by illness, it is reasonable to speculate that Marjorie could have become Leider's successor, just as Birgit Nilsson eventually became Flagstad's.
19   Lawrence & King, 'Marjorie Lawrence: Her life and art', a 1976 radio talk.
20   *Sydney Morning Herald*, 27 July 1936.
21   *New York Times*, 21 January 1936.
22   Letter from Marjorie to Rouché, New York, 27 December 1935 (Paris Opéra Archives).

CHAPTER NINE ~ STORM CLOUDS GATHERING

1   *Le Temps*, Paris, 7 March 1936.
2   *Interrupted Melody*.
3   Each of the singers was offered a stand-in to ride while they sang from behind the scenes, but six of the eight declined the offer and rode the horses themselves. Germaine Hoerner singing Sieglinde, also agreed to lie across the saddle of Marjorie's horse when Brünnhilde made her entry riding on from the most distant point in the vast, steep set.
4   Marjorie's interest in lieder sets her apart from most other Australian singers of her generation. Among her contemporaries only the mezzo-soprano Dorothy Helmrich made a career of lieder and Australian singers at large did not begin to distinguish themselves in this repertoire until well into the second half of the twentieth century.
5   For both of these new roles Marjorie had commissioned new costumes. She was photographed in her costume for the first and third acts of *Fanciulla del West* and it is preserved in the Southern Illinois University Museum collection. To modern eyes it looks more suited to 'Annie Get Your Gun' or 'Calamity Jane', but the photographs show it was certainly flattering to the wearer.
6   Thirty years later Hans Busch recalled how Marjorie had taken a kindly interest in him in Buenos Aires and, like Kipnis and Singher, had shown infinite patience with his lack of experience as a stage director.
7   It was Rameau's revised version of the opera dating from 1754 which excluded the allegorical prologue that was performed in an edition prepared by Panizza.

8   Fred Destal (1905–1978) slipped completely off the radar after his career ended around 1950. Today he is ignored by compilers of anthologies of historic Wagner singing, perhaps because he was a variable singer who was capable of giving good performances but who suffered long periods when his voice was not in a reliable state. He too was a refugee from Nazi Germany.

9   The first performance of *Lohengrin* with Lemnitz, Marjorie and Wittrisch was recorded but the discs are believed to be lost.

10 Henri Grodet remained a devoted friend to Marjorie for the rest of their lives and wrote to her regularly always addressing her as 'My little dear one'. He became Agent General for France of George Blackburn & Sons, a Nottingham manufacturer of hosiery knitting machines and many of his later letters are written on his company's letterhead (MLP).

11 Some excerpts from the Montevideo broadcast were crudely transferred to LP many years ago, but because the sound is so poor I have confined discussion of Marjorie's broadcast performances in this opera to those from the Met. The following year Marjorie was introduced to the Peruvian ambassador to France at a party organised by Pierre Delbée. Marjorie blurted out how much she had enjoyed singing in the ambassador's capital city – Montevideo. Cyril grabbed her and whisked her off saying 'Blimey, you're a goose Marge. Montevideo's in *Uruguay* not Peru!'

12 *New York Times*, 13 November 1936.

13 Fidelio was one of Flagstad's, Leider's and Lubin's great roles and it would seem to have been an ideal part for Marjorie, but there is no record that she ever sang it again, whole or in part. Less surprisingly, there is also no record of her singing Fiordiligi's aria again.

14 In January 1941 Marjorie was studying this role in preparation for singing it on stage for an unidentified American opera company – possibly the 'New Opera Company' of New York who gave the work in October that year at the 44th Street Theatre, conducted by Fritz Busch – when her illness intervened.

15 *New York Times*, 9 January 1937.

16 *New York Times*, 12 January 1937.

17 The third performance of *Die Walküre* in New York on 16 January, with Marjorie, Lehmann, Hoffmann and Thorborg was broadcast. Tapes exist but I have not been able to hear them.

18 The contract for these performances is in the MLP and the *Gazette de Lausanne* listed her in the prospectus for the Municipal Theatre's 1933 season.

19 Undated newspaper clipping (MLP).

20 In her diary the following year Marjorie scribbled the observation: 'Mimi and Henri are my only *real* friends – they are always there and it is good to be able to count on someone' (MLP).

21 Not acquiring a famous opera star as a wife may have slowed Delbée's career, but it didn't ruin it. He eventually became president of Maison Jansen in the 1960s, dying in 1974.

22 Grotrian Hall, Wigmore Street, known as Steinway Hall until 1924 and demolished in 1938.

23 Like most artists in those and earlier times, Marjorie saw nothing incongruous in singing chunks of Wagner's and Richard Strauss's operas with piano accompaniment. The piano transcriptions were usually well written, but it must have put an enormous strain on accompanists to try to sound like a 100-piece orchestra and not an irrelevance when the soloist was in full flight.
24 *The Daily Telegraph*, London, quoted in *The Argus*, Melbourne, 3 July 1937 and *The Times*, London, 18 June 1937.
25 Biographical notes prepared by Marjorie for the ghost writer of *Interrupted Melody* (MLP).

CHAPTER TEN LUCKY STRIKES AND JACKBOOTS

1 It may interest readers that before her departure for the United States this time, Marjorie made an inventory of the contents of her travelling trunks for insurance purposes. This gives an insight into the wardrobe a prima donna of the pre-aeroplane age travelled with. It included 'stage costumes for seven operas with wigs, props and accessories, six morning outfits, eight concert gowns, eight other evening outfits, eight capes or coats, one fox fur and one Persian lambswool coat (both by Van Fraecham of New York), other fur items, three dresses by Labille, six other dresses, thirteen sports-type outfits and sundry items of satin lingerie and sleepwear' – total value $US25,000 (MLP).
2 *New York Times*, 6 January 1938 and undated clipping from the *Herald-Tribune*, New York (MLP).
3 Biographical notes prepared by Marjorie for the ghost writer of *Interrupted Melody* (MLP). Among the hundreds of songs included in Marjorie's sheet music are copies of a few pieces by various composers that had belonged to Lillian Nordica, the American Wagnerian soprano whom many Americans claimed Marjorie reminded them of. Each of these carries Nordica's signature boldly written on the cover. They are preserved in the MLP.
4 *New York Times*, 4 December, 1937.
5 *New York Times*, 19 December 1937. See discography for details of the CD reissue.
6 ibid.
7 Johnson did make this offer in 1938 but Marjorie declined, believing she was not yet ready to tackle Elektra, a role that can be injurious to all but the most robust voices. She finally sang it in 1946.
8 Later Marjorie tried out her dance on George Balanchine, founder of the American Ballet, who gave it and her his approval.
9 Biographical notes prepared by Marjorie for the ghost writer of *Interrupted Melody* (MLP).
10 *New York Times*, 5 February 1938.
11 *Musical Courier*, New York, 15 February 1938. The only dissenter was Irving Kolodin. When he came to write his second history of the Met in 1953 and an updated edition in 1966 he was unaccountably critical of Marjorie's performance. Kolodin was, like Jokanaan, 'a voice in the wilderness' on this topic.

12 In years to come Marjorie would regularly include songs by John Carpenter, Richard Hageman, Harriet Ware, Ernest Charles, Randall Thompson, Bainbridge Crist, Elinor Warren and several other living American composers in her recital programs, sometimes in response to direct requests from the composers.
13 Biographical notes prepared by Marjorie for the ghost writer of *Interrupted Melody* (MLP).
14 The name of this small town near the Baltic port of Gdansk is today spelled 'Sopot'. Marjorie referred to it as being in Germany although it was actually in independent Poland. Gdansk (which Marjorie knew as 'Danzig') was predominantly German and at this time had a large local Nazi Party branch.
15 See discography for details.
16 MLP.
17 *Interrupted Melody*.
18 ibid.
19 MLP.
20 *Interrupted Melody*.
21 Deutsche Allgemeine Zeitung, Berlin, 30 July 1938.
22 Unidentified and undated newspaper clipping in the MLP.
23 Biographical notes prepared by Marjorie for the ghost writer of *Interrupted Melody* (MLP).
24 ibid.
25 See discography for details.

CHAPTER ELEVEN ～ HOMECOMING

1 Thérèse Radic, *Bernard Heinze – A Biography*, Macmillan, Melbourne, 1986.
2 Richard Davis, *Eileen Joyce – A portrait*, Fremantle Arts Centre Press, Fremantle, 2001.
3 Biographical notes prepared by Marjorie for the ghost writer of *Interrupted Melody* (MLP). Resolution of Bill's Lawrence's estate was still eight years away and the long-term effect of Marjorie's visit, rather than improving family relations, resulted in their deterioration. Soon after Marjorie departed, Lena wrote to say she had had fallings-out with both Lindsay and Alan and Ted wrote to say the delay over resolving their father's estate was causing him much hardship (letters to Marjorie dated 22 November and 17 December 1939, MLP).
4 *Sun-Pictorial*, Melbourne, 15 June 1939.
5 *Interrupted Melody*.
6 ibid.
7 The unmarried Emma Smith wrote regularly to Marjorie and Cyril from 1928 until her death in her hundredth year in 1959, sharing with them information she felt it was important they knew, about the weather, crops, livestock, births, marriages and deaths in the local community. Marjorie was a notoriously lazy letter writer but the lack of replies never deterred Aunt Emma and her perseverance earned her a special place in Marjorie's affection.

8 Before leaving Melbourne Marjorie was approached by a local recording company to make a recording of her singing this song. The recording was made on 18 July, but not issued. See discography.
9 When Felix Wolfes complained that he had never seen a live kangaroo, Thorold Waters drove him out to a bush reserve near Healesville to see some.
10 Originally aspirants for this award were required to sing an opera aria or an aria by Bach and a German lied, but as the war progressed the stipulation of a German lied was relaxed. It seems the award disappeared from the competition after a few years, possibly when Marjorie found herself in straightened circumstances in the mid-1940s.
11 Isabelle Moresby, *Australia Makes Music*, Longman, Melbourne, 1948. Marjorie was as passionate about hats as she was about perfume and told the Australian press she owned about seventy, many original creations by the famous French-born, New York-based milliner Lilly Daché. Later she patronised John Pico John, known as 'Mr John', whose clientele ranged over the years from Wallis Simpson to Marilyn Monroe.
12 Longden rose to the rank of Squadron Leader and was made Staff Officer for Welfare and Entertainment, organising troop entertainment tours.
13 MLP.
14 Act Two of this performance was broadcast and has been reissued on CD, but a complete off-air recording of *Die Walküre* with Marjorie singing Sieglinde and Flagstad as Brünnhilde, conducted by Leinsdorf, taken from a Met broadcast four months later is more representative of Marjorie's assumption of this role. It will be discussed in the next chapter.
15 *New York Times*, 29 October 1939.
16 *Interrupted Melody*.
17 *New York Times*, 14 December 1940. The concert was broadcast and the Grainger songs have been preserved on tape. I have been able to hear only one: 'Willow Willow'. Marjorie sings this with great feeling, scaling her voice down and producing seamless phrasing.
18 Letter from Grainger to Marjorie, 14 December 1940.

CHAPTER TWELVE ~ THE GLORY YEARS

1 Marjorie's standard fee in 1940 for an opera performance was $1000 and for a recital $1500, but these figures were often increased by fifty to 150 per cent. Such amounts were still less than a handful of elite international artists received, but well above the going rate in the US where depression and now war in Europe were affecting the economy. In comparison she was receiving only $500 per performance from the Met.
2 *Interrupted Melody*.
3 In 1944 Bachner wrote a small book entitled *Dynamic Singing* (L.B. Fischer, New York 1944), which Marjorie endorsed by writing the foreword.
4 *New York Times*, 9 February 1940 and *Herald Tribune*, New York 26 January, 1940.

5   This was Wolfes's only season at the Met. Most of his duties were behind the scenes and he was given only one public assignment. On 18 February 1940 he took the podium for one of the Met's Sunday concerts, conducting the Act One duet from *Die Walküre* with Irene Jessner and Paul Althouse (making his last appearance in the house) and excerpts from Act Three of *Tannhäuser* with Jessner, Dorothee Manski, Arthur Carron and Mack Harrell.
6   Biographical notes prepared by Marjorie for the ghost writer of *Interrupted Melody* (MLP).
7   This time it was Marjorie's friend Lawrence Tibbett cast as Jack Rance who fell ill and could not be replaced at short notice. This was to have been the first performance of *La Fanciulla del West* in English in the US. Marjorie never did get to sing Minnie, a role that might have suited her better than Carmen.
8   The matrix of Marjorie's recording of 'My Ain Folk', which had been approved for release was subsequently damaged in the factory and two months later she received a letter from RCA Victor requesting she return to their studios in New Jersey and re-record the item – for an additional fee.
9   Letter to Marjorie, Hollywood, 28 December 1940 (MLP).
10 *Buenos Aires Herald*, 7 October 1940.
11 *Buenos Aires Herald*, 14 September 1940.
12 *Buenos Aires Herald*, 22 September 1940.
13 In neither *Interrupted Melody* or the biographical notes she prepared for the ghost writer of that book, does Marjorie identify Serge Obolensky, referring to him only as 'Sergei', but correspondence between them and other documents leave no doubt as to his identity. To avoid confusion I have spelled his name 'Serge' even when quoting Marjorie.
14 Biographical notes prepared by Marjorie for the ghost writer of *Interrupted Melody* (MLP). By coincidence, Alexis Obolensky, a cousin of Serge's had sung in one of Melba's opera companies in Australia but not in either of the performances Marjorie had attended in 1928.
15 The Carnegie Hall war charity concert, on 21 February, was notable for the appearance of Walter Damrosch, who came out of retirement to accompany Marjorie in a selection of his songs.
16 It was the 'French' version of *Alceste* dating from 1776 the Met used for this production.
17 *New York Times*, 25 January 1941.
18 The fourth performance was broadcast and recorded, but unfortunately that was one of the performances Marjorie missed. Had she performed that day we would have had a complete recording of her Alceste instead of the solitary aria from the NBC studio broadcast of 1938. Fans of Bampton however should be grateful for the twist, for the recordings of this broadcast caught her in her finest form.
19 This and all subsequent quotes in this chapter are from *Interrupted Melody*.
20 Ortrud was to have been sung that afternoon by another singer but when she fell ill, Marjorie stepped into the breach, despite having sung *Alceste* the night before.

CHAPTER THIRTEEN ~ 'WAS ICH LIEBE, MUSS ICH VERLASSEN'

1. *Interrupted Melody*.
2. Western Union cable to Marjorie from Johnson, New York, 16 April 1941 (MLP).
3. McArthur denies that Flagstad travelled on a German passport, but it seems unlikely she would have been able to traverse most of German-occupied Europe on her Norwegian one.
4. To prolong the opportunity to be alone this trip offered the newlyweds, they planned to drive back to New York in July via the Pacific coast then across the Midwest.
5. *Interrupted Melody*.
6. Biographical notes prepared by Tom for the ghost writer of *Interrupted Melody* (MLP). The nature of the tests used in making this diagnosis is unrecorded. Whatever they were, they would be considered rudimentary by today's standards and the records of the American Hospital in Mexico City disappeared after its amalgamation with another hospital shortly after these events.
7. When the season finally got under way on 1 July, Pauly sang Salome and Carmen and Manski shared the role of Brünnhilde with an undistinguished young Swedish soprano named Thelma Jerguson.
8. Biographical notes prepared by Tom for the ghost writer of *Interrupted Melody* (MLP).
9. *Interrupted Melody*.
10. ibid.
11. *Interrupted Melody* and biographical notes prepared by Tom for the ghost writer of that book (MLP).
12. ibid.
13. Letter from Dr George B. Fletcher to Edward Ziegler, 9 July 1941 (MLP).
14. Biographical notes prepared by Marjorie for the ghost writer of *Interrupted Melody* (MLP).
15. Ibid.
16. Letter to Marjorie, New York, 14 October 1941 (MLP).
17. Another particularly interesting letter came from Martial Singher telling Marjorie that he had recently suffered an illness with similar symptoms including paralysis, but had recovered fully after a few weeks (MLP).
18. It should be remembered that these events were taking place in an era when the needs of people living with disability were not catered for in public buildings or in the street as they commonly are today.
19. Biographical notes prepared by Marjorie for the ghost writer of *Interrupted Melody* (MLP).
20. Confirming that at this stage the Met management were still expecting her to sing Isolde when she recovered comes in a letter from Edward Ziegler, dated 18 October 1941, checking that she has the same edition of the work that is used at the Met (MLP).
21. Biographical notes prepared by Marjorie for the ghost writer of *Interrupted Melody* (MLP).

CHAPTER FOURTEEN — 'MASTER OF MY FATE AND CAPTAIN OF MY SOUL'

1. Before leaving the north Marjorie also undertook a course of therapy offered by a Mr (not Dr) William MacMillan. The treatment was described as 'physical and spiritual' but no further details are available. MacMillan was possibly one of the many quacks who exploited polio victims, several of whom approached Marjorie over the years. Marjorie abandoned MacMillan's treatment when no improvement attributable to it was evinced.
2. As most of the good will was entailed in Tom himself, the sale of the practice realised little more than the value of the building lease – less than $2000 after commissions were paid.
3. Tom to Elizabeth Kenny, White Plains, 3 December 1941 (MLP).
4. Tom to Everett Smith, White Plains, 28 November 1941 (MLP).
5. Cyril to Marjorie, New York, various dates commencing 8 December 1941 (MLP).
6. Marjorie to Cyril, quoted in the above 17 January 1942 (MLP).
7. Amongst Marjorie's scores in the MLP are twenty-three unpublished and one published song by Cyril. Most have titles with Australian associations, such as 'In My Bendigo Bungalow', 'Where the Barwon River Flows' and 'Long Distance Call from Woo-loo-moo-loo'.
8. Blake & Riggall to Marjorie, Melbourne, 15 January 1942 (MLP).
9. Biographical notes prepared by Marjorie for the ghost writer of *Interrupted Melody* (MLP).
10. Marjorie sang again in Dr Smith's church during the Easter Service in April, this time offering the 'Inflammatus' from Rossini's *Stabat Mater* and Maybrick's 'The Holy City'.
11. Cyril attended two of the performances Traubel gave this season and in one of his letters to Marjorie (dated 13 February 1942) he reported on her performances: 'She missed the top C at the end of the duet in *Götterdämmerung* and she cracked completely on the second 'Yo-ho-to-ho' in 'Walküre', but the papers never mentioned that. If you had done it they would have made a big mouthful of it!' (MLP).
12. A repayment plan had been agreed between Marjorie and the Mexicans in January 1942 and the nature of the plan is a clear indicator of just how desperate Marjorie and Tom's financial situation was. The Mexicans had agreed to accept repayment of the debt at twenty-five dollars per month over two years, but Marjorie had been forced to default after the second payment and hence legal action was again being threatened. In early 1943 Marjorie was able to discharge the balance of the debt in one payment, swearing she would never set foot in Mexico again (MLP).
13. Various newspapers including *Sydney Morning Herald*, 15 June 1942.
14. It seems improbable that Tom, as a qualified doctor, would have been unaware of the risk to Marjorie's unborn child through her being anaesthetised. We can only conclude that he and Marjorie decided to take a calculated risk in the interests of her recovery.
15. Various newspapers including *Sydney Morning Herald*, 27 July 1942.

16 *Interrupted Melody*.
17 ibid.
18 To further support her when singing in this fashion, Marjorie later had plackets fitted into the bodices of some of her concert gowns into which strips of smooth, flat metal could be placed – much the same as whalebone had been used in women's garments in earlier times.
19 From which the title of this chapter comes.
20 *Interrupted Melody*.
21 Accompanist Paul Meyer with whom Marjorie had begun working before her illness was engaged for this recital. Marian Anderson described Meyer as an extremely sensitive musician who knew the scores of most of the standard operatic repertoire by heart and helped her learn the role of Ulrica for her Met debut in Verdi's *Ballo in Maschera*. Marjorie worked regularly with Meyer for the rest of her career and also with a young Canadian accompanist named Gordon Manley. Manley was a pupil of Egon Petri and Marjorie was the first important singer to engage him.
22 *New York Times*, 30 November 1942.
23 *Herald Tribune*, New York, 30 November 1942.
24 Biographical notes prepared by Marjorie for the ghost writer of *Interrupted Melody* (MLP). Venus had been assigned to some lesser singers over the years but recently to Karin Branzell and Kerstin Thorborg, neither of whom would have been pleased if they had heard this comment. Comparison with Fremstad was repeated by at least one distinguished music critic after Marjorie had sung the role (see page 178).
25 The character Venus only appears in this scene and very briefly at the end of the opera.
26 *New York Times*, 23 January 1943.
27 ibid.
28 ibid.
29 Biographical notes prepared by Marjorie for the ghost writer of *Interrupted Melody* (MLP).
30 *Herald Tribune*, New York, 28 December 1942.
31 That document (an autograph collector's dream) is preserved in the MLP.

CHAPTER FIFTEEN ~ CHIN-UP GIRL

1 Indirectly Marjorie already had a connection with this group and was beholden to them. Tom had applied for and been given a grant of $100 to help finance their trip to Pasadena the previous year.
2 As in Marjorie's case, current thinking casts doubt on the origin of Roosevelt's disability, but polio was assumed to be the cause at the time. Throughout Roosevelt's political career and especially during the war years, it was considered expedient for the public at large to be kept in ignorance of his disability.
3 The original letter is preserved in the MLP.
4 *New York Times*, 23 January 1943.
5 *Chicago Tribune*, 30 March 1943.

6   It is interesting to speculate how one of the radical opera directors of today might have overcome Marjorie's disability – perhaps by placing the rest of the cast of an opera in wheelchairs! After some of the unusual interpretations inflicted on the Ring Cycle by directors in recent times, a Brünnhilde on wheels might have seemed a tame enough innovation.
7   *Montreal Herald*, 28 May 1943.
8   ibid.
9   Biographical notes prepared by Marjorie for the ghost writer of *Interrupted Melody* (MLP).
10 Typed manuscript in the MLP.
11 Biographical notes prepared by Marjorie for the ghost writer of *Interrupted Melody* (MLP).
12 Marjorie also indulged her fondness for bananas by planting banana palms in pots so they could be brought indoors during the winter months.
13 *New York Tribune*, 15 March 1944.
14 *New York Sun*, 15 March 1944.
15 Tom began keeping a diary at this time and his comments about the *Tristan und Isolde* performance in Chicago provide a glimpse of the sort of antics that accompany operatic endeavours the world over, especially when a large company goes on tour: 'Performance was late starting. Melchior's costume and Isolde's couch didn't arrive until 8 o'clock. So Beecham made some more last minute cuts and conducted the whole thing at a terrific speed – all very confusing. Angel sang it even better than in New York. Critics divided. Most very good others not so, like Claudia Cassidy – the bitch.' In fact, it was Tom who was carping this time. Cassidy had (by her standards) been extremely generous in her praise of Marjorie. Tom also noted that his brother Carl and his sister-in-law drove up from Warsaw, Indiana, to attend. Tom's and Marjorie's extant diaries are preserved in the MLP.
16 Melchior soon got over his animosity towards Marjorie and after she sent him a handsome gift to mark his twentieth anniversary at the Met he wrote back: 'Dear Marjorie, I think of your comradeship and friendship to me through the past and of the wonderful way in which you showed it by your gift. I want to express to you my heartiest thanks both for your friendship and for the token of it. I hope that for the continuance of my years in opera the same harmony and devotion will be with us on the stage and that our friendship will continue as long as we will be together in this world. I thank you with all my heart. Your friend and colleague, Lauritz Melchior.' (Melchior to Marjorie, 22 February 1946, MLP)
17 *Interrupted Melody*.
18 MLP.
19 One of the ships in the large fleet carrying supplies to Britain.
20 These were also issued in Australia under the title *Marjorie Lawrence Sings for the Boys*. See discography.
21 *Interrupted Melody*.

CHAPTER SIXTEEN ~ OFF TO WAR

1. Biographical notes prepared by Marjorie for the ghost writer of *Interrupted Melody* (MLP).
2. Ibid.
3. *Interrupted Melody*.
4. Belgian-born Raymond Lambert (1908–1966) was a talented eclectic musician, well established in Australia by this time. He taught at the Melbourne University Conservatorium and was regarded as Australia's leading accompanist. He had played for some of Marjorie's colleagues including Brownlee, Rethberg, Pinza and Kipnis on their tours of Australia and once before for Marjorie, standing in for Felix Wolfes when the latter came down with the flu during the 1939 'homecoming' tour.
5. Tom's 1944 diary (MLP).
6. *Interrupted Melody*.
7. Tom's 1944 diary (MLP).
8. ibid.
9. Letter to Marjorie from Sgt L.W. King, 1 August 1944 (MLP).
10. Forde later had a letter prepared like an illuminated scroll and sent it to Marjorie thanking her for the concerts she had given. It was received with less than enthusiasm.
11. *Sydney Morning Herald*, 15 September 1944 (edited).
12. ibid.
13. Postcard to Marjorie from Marie Grodet de Lacratelle, 25 September 1944 (MLP).
14. Harold Blair to the author, Melbourne, 1970.
15. Marjorie later rerecorded 'Haere Ra' and 'Waltzing Matilda' for Columbia in the United States in soupy arrangements with a male voice quartet. The 'Maori Farewell' was issued, backed by a recording of 'My hero' from Oscar Straus's *The Chocolate Soldier*, neither doing Marjorie's reputation any favours.
16. Biographical notes prepared by Tom for the ghost writer of *Interrupted Melody* (MLP).
17. Various documents in the MLP.

CHAPTER SEVENTEEN ~ TWILIGHT OF THE GODS

1. Marjorie and Tom were also told that when they reached the continent they would be provided with a guard detail to protect them from any Germans resentful of their presence, but the guard detail never showed up.
2. Tom's 1945 diary (MLP).
3. *Interrupted Melody* and biographical notes prepared by Marjorie for the ghost writer of that book (MLP).
4. Back at Harmony Hills that gun proved useful to kill vermin and wild animals who threatened the stock. As well as this gun, Tom brought home a German helmet and various German military badges as souvenirs.
5. Marjorie's 1945 diary (MLP). Generally speaking Marjorie and Tom used their diaries only to record engagements, but from time to time they added brief notes and comments such as this about significant events.

6   Biographical notes prepared by Marjorie for the ghost writer of *Interrupted Melody* (MLP).
7   ibid.
8   ibid. It might also not have escaped Marjorie's notice that what she was giving that day was effectively a 'Command Performance' and the last Australian to be invited to give one of those for the British royal family had been Dame Nellie Melba.
9   Biographical notes prepared by Marjorie for the ghost writer of *Interrupted Melody* (MLP).
10 ibid.
11 Edward Young, Deputy Private Secretary to the Queen to the author, 15 March 2010.
12 Original manuscript (edited) for an article published in *The Musical Digest* and later reprinted in the April 1946 issue of *Australian Musical News*.
13 Biographical notes prepared by Tom for the ghost writer of *Interrupted Melody* (MLP). Marjorie tells in *Interrupted Melody* how she wore woollen socks and woollen GI underwear under her concert gown to ward off the cold in the cavernous unheated Royal Albert Hall.
14 *The Times*, London, 15 November 1945.
15 *The Star*, London, 15 November 1945.
16 *Daily Mail*, London, 15 November 1945.
17 Legge to Marjorie, 19 November 1945 (MLP).
18 Before leaving New York Marjorie studied these arias with the Russian singer and teacher Xenia Vassenko.
19 MLP.
20 Victor Carrell & Beth Dean, *Gentle Genius – A Life of John Antill*, Akron, Sydney, 1987; John Culshaw, *The Ring Resounding*, Secker & Warburg, London, 1967. Unlike opera broadcasts in North and South America, which as we have seen were routinely recorded, no recordings of either of these performances of *Tristan und Isolde* appear to exist. Extensive searching by a number of scholars, including Beecham's most recent biographer, John Lucas, have so far failed to turn up even the briefest extract. It is regrettable that we do not have anything of Marjorie's Isolde, other than a truncated version of the narrative and curse from a 1945 US radio program with a scratch orchestra and an inferior conductor. Another broadcast of *Tristan und Isolde* was planned by the BBC for the following year with Marjorie and Torsten Ralf as Tristan, but it was cancelled for some unknown reason.
21 *The Times*, London, 11 November 1946.
22 MLP.
23 Virginia Goodman, *Isador Goodman – A Life in Music*, Collins, Sydney, 1983.
24 MLP.
25 Biographical notes prepared by Marjorie for the ghost writer of *Interrupted Melody* (MLP).

CHAPTER EIGHTEEN ∼ INTERRUPTED MELODY

1. Marjorie's 1946 diary (MLP).
2. Among the many photographs of Marjorie standing is one that shows a different platform from this one – or the photograph has been retouched. The platform described here was used by her from 1947 until 1961 and is preserved in the collections of Southern Illinois University Museum. In the beginning Marjorie used the platform with the central railing in front of her. Later she used the platform the other way round, so the central railing became a back rest.
3. Before her first standing performance Marjorie received many cables. One came from Edward Johnson and read: 'The entire Met family shares with you the joy that must be yours tonight'. Another came from Buckingham Palace. It read: 'The Queen is delighted to hear of your great achievement and wishes you all success tomorrow. Her Majesty so well remembers your singing before her in 1945' (MLP).
4. On the way back to Harmony Hills after this engagement Marjorie and Tom had the frightening experience of having to drive through a tornado between Memphis and Little Rock. The heavy Cadillac was almost blown off the highway.
5. *Interrupted Melody*.
6. While she was in Paris to perform at the Opéra, Marjorie also received a telegram of welcome from Charles de Gaulle and did a broadcast of the first act of *Tristan und Isolde* for Radiodiffusion Français with Victor Forti as Tristan, Georgette Frozier as Brangäne and Arthur Endreze as Kurvenal, conducted by Gaston Poulet.
7. When Marjorie gifted her papers to Southern Illinois University she removed all the correspondence with Buttrose, but missed one letter, dated 14 January 1949. In this Buttrose addresses her as 'Miss Lawrence'. Appointments with him were noted in Marjorie's diary with just the word 'Buttrose' and no details.
8. Charles Buttrose, *Words and Music*, Angus & Robertson, Sydney. Marjorie and Buttrose remained on friendly terms and when Marjorie sang in Sydney in 1951 he took his young daughter backstage to meet Marjorie. Ita Buttrose (a respected and popular media personality in Australia) remembers the occasion; that she was in awe of the Marjorie who smiled a lot and was very nice to her (Ita Buttrose to the author, 15 January 2010).
9. Appleton-Century insisted on the deletion of a chapter dealing with music in Australia which appeared in the other editions, believing quite rightly that Americans were not particularly interested in the musical scene in Australia.
10. Note and medals are preserved in the MLP.
11. Greer Garson to Marjorie, 10 February 1950 (MLP).
12. Gertrude Johnson had also hoped to mount *Tristan und Isolde* this season with Marjorie, but the opera proved greater than the company's resources. For the six performances of Amneris Marjorie was paid 900 pounds, the equivalent of $US300 per performance.
13. Another emotional encounter took place when Marjorie reached Toowoomba on the Queensland leg of this tour and visited Sister Kenny now living there in retirement and handicapped by Parkinson's disease.

14 A copy of the Katcher script is preserved in the MLP.
15 Annie Laurie Williams to Marjorie and Tom, 12 May 1951 (MLP).
16 The final figure that appeared on the contract and was paid to Marjorie and Katcher was $20,500. Each party received $10,250.
17 Williams to Marjorie and Tom, 8 June 1951 (MLP). Williams also told Marjorie and Tom that Kathryn Grayson's agent had been circulating stories that Grayson would be given the role and would sing it as well as act it, but that these stories were unfounded and should be ignored. Grayson was a competent singing actress, but with a voice which would never have coped with Wagner or Strauss.
18 The titles of the pieces Marjorie sang at these tests are not recorded in MGM's files or Marjorie's diary.
19 If readers are surprised to find the Puccini aria included here, they will be doubly so to learn that arias from the same composer's *La Bohème* and Verdi's *Il Trovatore* were also included in the film – operas Marjorie never appeared in or even studied – plus the song 'Somewhere Over the Rainbow' from another MGM hit *The Wizard of Oz* which Marjorie never sang. For the test recording of the *Salome* finale, the studio also provided a tenor to sing Herod's order at the end of the scene. To date, his identity remains a mystery.
20 In perhaps the best line in the whole script, Marjorie's character turns to Cyril's and says: 'The trouble with you Cyril, is that *my* success has gone to *your* head!'

CHAPTER NINETEEN ~ PROFESSOR LAWRENCE

1 The program was in its third season and singers Jeanette McDonald and Lily Pons had been featured in the first and second series. Like Pons, McDonald was a friend of Marjorie's and when Marjorie sang in California, she and Tom sometimes stayed with McDonald.
2 In 1955 Marjorie wrote to Charles Moses of the ABC proposing a concert tour to coincide with the 1956 Melbourne Olympics, but Moses declined. She then wrote to Robert Quentin who was organising Australia's first national opera company (the forerunner of Opera Australia), offering her services as a guest artist for their inaugural season in 1956, but Quentin too declined, explaining that the company's repertoire for their first season was all Mozart and all roles had been filled.
3 Nelson to the author, 12 August 2010.
4 Recorded interview by Dr Lynch at Southern Illinois University, 31 August 1973 (MLP).
5 Marjorie had a firm policy of not accepting students who were too young. 'Let God do His work first', she said.
6 Later 'Artist in Residence' was added to Marjorie's title at Tulane University.
7 There are dozens of ribbons and certificates testifying to this in the MLP.
8 Later there was a 'Friends of the Summer Workshops' committee established which helped to raise funds.

9 Marjorie's own contribution to these picnics was always a huge bowl of potato salad, its unappetising consistency and colour showing that her culinary skills never matched her vocal.
10 Glenn to the author, 19 May 2010.
11 Various newspapers including *The Sentinel-Record*, Hot Springs, 11 February 1979.
12 Among those who wrote to congratulate Marjorie on her appointment to SIU was John Brownlee, now retired from the Met, director of the Manhattan School of Music and conducting his own Summer Opera Workshops. In July 1962 Marjorie officially resigned from Tulane University.
13 Shryock to Marjorie, 27 August 1970.
14 Despite their earlier encounter in London, it seems that it took until the late 1950s for Marjorie to 'discover' Britten and in the final years of her career, as previously mentioned, she occasionally included some of his folk song arrangements in her programs.
15 No doubt Marjorie would have loved to have mounted an opera by Wagner and at one stage did briefly consider *Die Fliegende Holländer*, but wisely decided she had neither the singers, the players or the stage resources to do justice to this or any other Wagner work.
16 Sanabria to the author, 17 February 2011.
17 Marjorie's 1964 production of *The Marriage of Figaro* (and possibly others of these productions) was filmed and shown on a local television station. That film seems to have gone the way of the tapes of *The Medium*. Audio tapes do survive of performances of *Madame Butterfly* (1963), *Faust* (1965), *Carmen* (1967), *The Tales of Hoffman* (1968) and *Don Giovanni* (1973) as well as *Aida* (MLP).
18 Printed transcription of Friedelind Wagner's lecture (MLP).
19 Potter to the author, 21 February 2011.

CHAPTER TWENTY ~ 'LEB' WOHL'

1 *Life*, New York, 29 April 1966. This article covers several pages and has many coloured photographs including one of Marjorie, Tom and Bing, showing Marjorie wearing a sky-blue taffeta gown with a short, white fur cape and beaming happily as Bing fusses over her.
2 Marjorie's portrait was commissioned by a former colleague at Tulane University, Dr John M. Yarborough Jnr and painted by Joseph Dickinson. It is currently in storage, along with many of the other portraits from the gallery.
3 Cyril to Marjorie, New York, 19 December 1961 (MLP).
4 Various letters from Cyril to Marjorie including New York, partially dated, November 1972 (MLP).
5 *Sentinel-Record*, Hot Springs, 14 November 1973.
6 Both the old and new houses at Harmony Hills were decorated with a collection of stuffed toy koalas, kangaroos, platypus and wombats, the odd boomerang or two and prints of landscapes by Hans Heysen and other Australian painters.

7   This was the last time Marjorie and Sutherland met. Sutherland gave a recital in Memphis the following year and received this cable form Marjorie: 'Dearest Joan, we had planned for a year to have the great joy of attending your Memphis recital but a nasty cold prevents this. Know you and your great art will be immensely successful. Warmest regards to you both and congratulations to Richard Bonynge for CBE. Marjorie Lawrence' (Joan Sutherland, *A Prima Donna's Progress*, Random House, Sydney, 1997).

8   The old homestead at Harmony Hills still stands at the time of writing, but is boarded up and badly in need of renovation. The garden is long gone and the whole property has a most forlorn aspect. The 'new' home is occupied.

Appendix
A Discography of Marjorie Lawrence's Recordings

Listed below are all the recordings of Marjorie Lawrence singing and speaking that came to my attention during research for this book. They are arranged by composer (in alphabetical order), with the spoken recordings listed at the end. Where a piece was recorded more than once, the versions are listed chronologically according to the recording dates.

Most of the recordings (issued and unissued) listed here are held in either the Marjorie Lawrence Papers at the University of Southern Illinois at Carbondale; the archives of the companies which recorded them; the Archives of the Metropolitan Opera, New York; the New York Public Library; or the Schlesinger Listening Library, San Diego Opera. The majority of these recordings, including most of the CD reissues, are not available commercially at the time of publication, but some can be heard on the internet and all warrant searching out in used copies.

I make no claims as to the completeness of this discography. There may be other private or pirate recordings of Marjorie in institutions around the world or in the hands of lucky individuals and no one will be happier than I if it is found that I have inadvertently missed some, and further recordings come to light to broaden our knowledge and enhance our enjoyment of Marjorie's art.

Readers may note some discrepancies between this and earlier published discographies. Where questions of dates, locations, repertoire and assisting artists have arisen, Marjorie's first-hand accounts and diary entries have been used as the preferred source.

ADAMS, Steven

'The Holy City'

Performed with the Bell Telephone Orchestra and Chorus conducted by Donald Voorhees and taken from a broadcast of the radio program *The Bell Telephone Hour*, New York, 27 August 1945.

ARNE, Thomas

'Rule Britannia!'

(1) Recorded with Raymond Lambert (piano) in Sydney, 22 September 1944 and issued on Columbia (Australia) 10-inch, 78 rpm disc, LO 68.

(2) see under Grainger.

BALFE, Michael

'Killarney'

Recorded with Ivor Newton (piano) in Kingsway Hall, London, 5 July 1946. Never issued.

BEETHOVEN, Ludwig van

'In questa tomba oscura'

Recorded with piano (pianist unidentified) in Melbourne, October (?) 1928. Issued privately on Vocalion 10-inch, pink label, 80 rpm disc, PR17 and reissued on LP Unique Opera Records Corp., UORC248.

BENJAMIN, Arthur

'From San Domingo'

Performed with the Bell Telephone Orchestra conducted by Donald Voorhees and taken from a broadcast of the radio program *The Bell Telephone Hour*, New York, 11 February 1946.

BIZET, Georges

Carmen: Act II Complete (as Carmen)

Broadcast of a public performance in the War Memorial Opera House, San Francisco, 31 October 1940 with Raoul Jobin (Don José); Ezio Pinza (Escamillo); Thelma Votipka (Frasquita); Alice Avakian (Mercedes); Lorenzo Alvary (Zuniga); George Cehanovsky (Dancairo); Alessio de Paolis (Remendado) and the chorus and orchestra of the San Francisco Opera, conducted by Gaetano Merola. Issued on CD *San Francisco Opera Gems, Vol. 1*, Guild, GHCD 2238-39-40.

Carmen: Act III Extract (as Carmen)

'Ecoute, écoute, compagnon, écoute! ... Fortune ! Amour ! (from the beginning of the Act to Carmen's entry in the card scene) with Jan Kiepura (Don José); Florence Kirk (Frasquita); Elizabeth Brown (Mercedes); unidentified tenor (Dancairo) and the chorus and orchestra of the St Louis Grand Opera Association, conducted by László Hálasz. NBC Broadcast from the Municipal Auditorium, St Louis, 25 April 1940.

BOHM, Carl

'Still wie die nacht' ('Calm as the night') (Sung in English)
Recorded with Felix Wolfes (piano) in the RCA Victor Studios, Camden, N.J., 29 May 1940. Never issued.

BRAHMS, Johannes

'Nicht mehr zu dir zu geben', Opus 32, No. 2
Recorded with Ivor Newton (piano) in Kingsway Hall, London, 5 July, 1946 and issued on Decca 10-inch, 78 rpm disc, M598.
'So willst du des Armen', Opus 33, No. 5
Recorded with Ivor Newton (piano) in Kingsway Hall, London, 5 July, 1946 and issued on Decca 10-inch, 78 rpm disc, M598.
'Der Schmeid', Opus 19, No. 4
(1) Performed with Raymond Lambert (piano) and taken from a radio broadcast, Melbourne, August 1944.
(2) Recorded with Ivor Newton (piano) in Kingsway Hall, London, 5 July, 1946 and issued on Decca 10-inch, 78 rpm disc, M598.

CHERUBINI, Luigi

Medée: E che? Io son Medea (sung in Italian)
Performed with Robert E. Mueller (piano) and taken from a radio recital broadcast by WSIU (University of Southern Illinois), Carbondale, Ill., during the early 1960s.

DAY, Maude Craske

'Ring, Bells, Ring'
Recorded with piano (pianist unidentified) in Melbourne, October (?) 1928. Issued privately on Vocalion 10-inch, pink label, 80 rpm disc, PR19.

FRANCK, César

'La Procession'
Recorded with Felix Wolfes (piano) in the RCA Victor Studios, Camden, N.J., 15 May 1939. Never issued.

GLUCK, Christoph Willibald von

Alceste: Divinités du Styx
Performed with the NBC Symphony Orchestra conducted by Frank Black and taken from a broadcast of the radio program *NBC Magic Key of RCA*, New York, 24 April, 1938. Issued on CD *The Stars Were Shining, Vol. 3*, Symposium, SYM 1369.

GOUNOD, Charles

Sappho: O ma lyre immortelle

(1) Recorded with Felix Wolfes (piano) in the RCA Victor Studios, Camden, N.J., 10 May 1939. Never issued.
(2) Performed with L'Orchestre National de Paris conducted by Albert Wolff and taken from a radio broadcast of the 'Concert pour la pénicilline' in the Théâtre National du Chaillot, Paris, 16 October, 1946. Issued on CD *Marjorie Lawrence*, Malibran, MR502.

GRAINGER, Percy

'Hubby and Wifey'

Performed with Percy Grainger (guitar), Henry Cowell (guitar) and the Durieux Ensemble and taken from a radio broadcast of the 'Bundles for Britain' concert, Carnegie Hall, New York, 13 December 1940.

'Rule Britannia' (arr. of Arne)

'Shallow Brown'

'The Old Woman at the Christening'

'Willow, Willow'

Performed with Percy Grainger (piano) and the Durieux Ensemble and taken from a radio broadcast of the 'Bundles for Britain' concert, Carnegie Hall, New York, 13 December 1940.

'Blithe Bells'

Performed with Percy Grainger (piano) and Ella Grainger (steel marimba) No details available.

GRIEG, Edvard

'Jeg elsker Dig', Opus 5, No. 3 ('I Love Thee') (sung in English)

(1) Recorded with unidentified orchestra conducted by Sylvan Shulman for Columbia in the USA, 16 April 1945. Never issued.
(2) Recorded with unidentified orchestra conducted by Sylvan Shulman for Columbia in the USA, 2 May 1945. Never issued.
(3) Recorded with Ivor Newton (piano) in Kingsway Hall, London, 2 July 1946 and issued on Decca 10-inch, 78 rpm disc, M602. Reissued on CD Marjorie Lawrence, Malibran, MR502.

GRUBER, Franz

'Silent Night'

(1) Performed with an unidentified accompaniment and taken from a Christmas Radio Program broadcast in the USA, 24 December 1939.
(2) Recorded with organ accompaniment (organist unidentified) in Kingsway Hall, London, 25 June 1946. Issued on Decca 12-inch, 78 rpm disc, K1558.

HALÉVY, Jacques

La Juive: Il va venir

Performed with the Bell Telephone Orchestra conducted by Donald Voorhees and taken from a broadcast of the radio program *The Bell Telephone Hour*, New York, 12 March 1945.

HANDEL, George Frederic

Giulio Cesare in Egitto: Piangerò la sorte mia (Sung in French)

Performed with the NBC Symphony Orchestra, conducted by Frank Black and taken from a broadcast of the radio program *NBC Magic Key of RCA*, New York, 5 February 1939

HILL, ALFRED

Arrangement of 'Haere Ra' ('Maori Song of Farewell') (First verse sung in English; second in Maori)

(1) Recorded with Raymond Lambert (piano) in Sydney, 22 September 1944 and issued on Columbia (Australia) 10-inch, 78 rpm disc, LO 68.

(2) Recorded with unidentified male voice quartet and orchestra, conducted by Shulman Sylvan in the USA, 16 April 1945 and issued on Columbia (USA) 12-inch, 78 rpm disc, LOX 809.

(3) Recorded with unidentified male voice quartet and orchestra, conducted by Shulman Sylvan in the USA, 2 May 1945 and issued on Columbia (USA) Masterworks, 12-inch, 78 rpm disc, 71684-D, in an album of three discs, entitled *Marjorie Lawrence Sings for Fighting Men*. In Australia the set was released with the title *Marjorie Lawrence Sings for the Boys*, SET M-579.

HOOK, James

'Doun the Burn'

(1) Performed with the NBC Symphony Orchestra, conducted by Frank Black and taken from a broadcast of the radio program *NBC Magic Key of RCA*, New York, 5 February 1939.

(2) Recorded with Felix Wolfes (piano) in the RCA Victor Studios, Camden, NJ, 13 April 1939. Never issued

(3) Recorded with Felix Wolfes (piano) in the RCA Victor Studios, Camden, NJ, 29 May 1940 and issued on RCA Victor 10-inch, 78 rpm disc, 2147; also on HMV (Australia) 10-inch, 78 rpm disc, EC 70, and reissued on RCA Victor Camden 12-inch LP, CAL-216.

(4) Performed with the Bell Telephone Hour Orchestra conducted by Donald Voorhees and taken from a broadcast of the radio program *The Bell Telephone Hour*, New York, 1 May 1944.

(5) Performed with Raymond Lambert (piano) and taken from a radio recital broadcast in Melbourne, August 1944.

(6) Recorded with Paul Meyer (piano) for Columbia in the USA, 17 October 1945. Never issued.

HUME, Alexander
'Flow Gently, Sweet Afton'
Recorded with Paul Meyer (piano) for Columbia in the USA, 19 October 1945. Never issued.

LAUDER, Harry
Medley: 'I Love a Lassie' – 'Wee deeoch and Doris' – 'Roamin' in the Gloamin''
(Preceded by an introduction spoken by Lawrence)
Performed with the Bell Telephone Orchestra and Male Chorus conducted by Donald Voorhees and taken from a broadcast of the radio program *The Bell Telephone Hour*, New York, 27 August 1945.

LEMON, Laura G.
'My Ain Folk'

(1) Recorded with piano (pianist unidentified) in Melbourne, October (?) 1928 and issued privately on Vocalion 10-inch, pink label, 80 rpm disc, PR20.

(2) Recorded for an unknown company in Melbourne, 18 July 1939. Never issued

(3) Recorded with Felix Wolfes (piano) in the RCA Victor Studios, Camden, NJ, 29 May 1940. Matrix accidentally destroyed.

(4) Recorded with Felix Wolfes (piano) in the RCA Victor Studios, Camden, NJ, 18 July 1940 (Replacement for the above). Issued on RCA Victor 10-inch 78 rpm disc, 2147; HMV (Australia) 10-inch, 78 rpm disc, EC 70 and reissued on RCA Victor Camden 12-inch LP, CAL-216

(5) Performed with the Bell Telephone Orchestra conducted by Donald Voorhees and taken from a broadcast of the radio program *The Bell Telephone Hour*, New York, 1 May 1944.

(6) Recorded with Paul Meyer (piano) for Columbia in the USA, 17 October 1945. Never issued.

(7) Performed with the Victorian Symphony Orchestra conducted by Hector Crawford and taken from a broadcast of a concert in the series *Music for the People*, Myer Music Bowl, Melbourne, April, 1966.

MALOTTE, Albert
'The Lord's Prayer'

(1) Performed with Raymond Lambert (piano) and taken from a radio recital broadcast in Melbourne, August 1944.

(2) Recorded with an unidentified orchestra, conducted by Sylvan Shulman for Columbia in the USA, 16 April 1945. Issued on Columbia Masterworks, 12-inch, 78 rpm disc, 71683-D in an album of three discs, entitled *Marjorie Lawrence Sings for Fighting Men*. In Australia it was issued with the title *Marjorie Lawrence Sings for the Boys*, SET M- 579. Also issued on Columbia (Australia) 12-inch 78 rpm disc LOX-810.

MASSENET, Jules

Hérodiade: Il est doux, il est bon

Performed with the Bell Telephone Hour Orchestra conducted by Donald Voorhees and taken from a broadcast of the radio program *The Bell Telephone Hour*, New York, 1 May 1944.

MENDELSSOHN, Felix

'Festgesang an die Künstler' (as 'Hark, the Herald Angels Sing')

Recorded with organ accompaniment (organist unidentified) in the Kingsway Hall, London, 25 June 1946 and issued on Decca 12-inch, 78 rpm disc, K1558.

O'HAGAN, Jack

'On the Road to Gundagai'

Recorded with an unidentified pianist and a chorus of Royal Australian Air Force servicemen in Liederkranz Hall, New York, 12 February 1943. Never issued.

PERI, Jacopo

Euridice: Invocation d' Orphee (Sung in French)

Performed with L'Ensemble Lili Laskine (nine harps) and taken from a radio broadcast of the 'Concert pour la pénicilline' in the Théâtre National du Chaillot, Paris, 16 October 1946. Issued on CD *Marjorie Lawrence*, Malibran, MR502.

PFITZNER, Hans

'Die Einsame', Opus 9, No. 2

(1) Recorded with Felix Wolfes (piano) in the RCA Victor Studios, Camden, NJ, 10 May 1939. Never issued.

(2) Recorded with Felix Wolfes (piano) in the RCA Victor Studios, Camden, NJ, 31 May 1940. Never issued on 78 rpm disc, but issued on RCA Victor Camden 12-inch LP, CAL-216.

'Stimme der sehnsucht', Opus 19, No. 1

(1) Recorded with Felix Wolfes (piano) in the RCA Victor Studios, Camden, NJ, 10 May 1939. Never issued.

(2) Recorded with Felix Wolfes (piano) in the RCA Victor Studios, Camden, NJ, 31 May 1940. Issued on RCA Victor 10-inch, 78 rpm disc, 2142 and reissued on RCA Victor Camden 12-inch LP, CAL-216.

'Michaelskirchplatz', Opus 19, No. 2

Recorded with Felix Wolfes (piano) in the RCA Victor Studios, Camden, NJ, 31 May 1940. Issued on RCA Victor 10-inch, 78 rpm disc, 2142, and reissued on RCA Victor Camden 12-inch LP, CAL-216.

PUCCINI, Giacomo

Madama Butterfly: Un bel dì

Recorded with an MGM studio orchestra (players from the Los Angeles Philharmonic) conducted by Adolph Deutsch in Hollywood, June 20 1954. Part of the second set of test recordings Lawrence made for the MGM film *Interrupted Melody*.

PURCELL, Henry

Dido and Aeneas: When I am laid in earth (Dido's Lament)

(1) Performed with harpsichord (player unidentified) and taken from a broadcast of the radio program *NBC Magic Key of RCA*, New York, 24 April 1938.

(2) (Sung in French) Performed with L'Orchestre National de Paris conducted by Albert Wolff and taken from a radio broadcast of the 'Concert pour la pénicilline', Théâtre National du Chaillot, Paris, 16 October 1946. Issued on CD *Marjorie Lawrence*, Malibran, MR502.

RACHMANINOV, Serge

'Floods of Spring', Opus 14, No. 11 (sung in English)

(1) Performed with unidentified accompaniment and taken from a broadcast of the radio program *The Bell Telephone Hour*, New York, 11 February 1946.

(2) Recorded with Ivor Newton (piano) in Kingsway Hall, London, 2 July, 1946. Issued on Decca 10-inch, 78 rpm disc, M602 and reissued on CD *Marjorie Lawrence*, Malibran, MR502.

REYER, Ernest

Sigurd: Salut, splendour du jour

(1) Recorded with Orchestre de l'Association des Concerts Pasdeloup, conducted by Piero Coppola in the Salle Pleyel, Paris, 1934. Issued on HMV 12-inch, 78 rpm disc, DB 4937 and reissued on CDs *Marjorie Lawrence*, Preiser/Lebendige Vergangenheit, 89011 and *Sigurd Excerpts*, Malibran, MR 546.

(2) Performed with Robert E. Mueller (piano) and taken from a radio recital broadcast by WSIU (University of Southern Illinois), Carbondale, Ill., during the early 1960s.

Sigurd: O palais radieux

Recorded with Orchestre de l'Association des Concerts Pasdeloup, conducted by Piero Coppola in the Salle Pleyel, Paris, 1934 and issued on HMV 12-inch, 78 rpm disc, DB 4937. Reissued on CDs *Marjorie Lawrence*, Preiser/Lebendige Vergangenheit, 89011; *The Record of Singing, Vol. 3*, EMI Testament, EX2901693 and *Sigurd Excerpts*, Malibran, MR 546.

SAINT-SAËNS, Camille

Samson et Dalila: Mon coeur s'ouvre à ta voix

(1) (Sung in French) Recorded with an MGM studio orchestra (players from the Los Angeles Philharmonic) conducted by Adolph Deutsch in Hollywood, 23 June 1954. Part of the second set of test recordings Lawrence made for the MGM film *Interrupted Melody*.

(2) (Sung in English) Recorded with an MGM studio orchestra (players from the Los Angeles Philharmonic) conducted by Adolph Deutsch in Hollywood, 23 June 1954. Part of the second set of test recordings Lawrence made for the MGM film *Interrupted Melody*.

SCHUBERT, Franz

'Der Erlkönig', D328

(1) (Orchestrated by Liszt) Performed with the Bell Telephone Hour Orchestra conducted by Donald Voorhees and taken from a broadcast of the radio program *The Bell Telephone Hour*, New York, 1 May 1944.

(2) (Orchestrated by Liszt and sung in French) Performed with L'Orchestre National de Paris conducted by Albert Wolff and taken from a radio broadcast of the 'Concert pour la pénicilline', Théâtre National du Chaillot, Paris, 16 October 1946. Issued on CD *Marjorie Lawrence*, Malibran, MR502.

(3) Recorded with Hubert Greenslade (piano) in the Decca Studios, Broadhurst Gardens, London, 30 November 1946. Never issued.

'Der Lindenbaum', D911, No. 5

Recorded with Hubert Greenslade (piano) in the Decca Studios, Broadhurst Gardens, London, 30 November 1946. Never issued.

SCOTT, Lady John Douglas

'Annie Laurie' (arranged by Liza Lehmann)

(1) Recorded with Felix Wolfes (piano) in the RCA Victor Studios, Camden, NJ, 1 June, 1940. Issued on RCA Victor 12-inch, 78 rpm disc, 17457, also on HMV 12-inch, 78 rpm disc, DB5870, and reissued on RCA Victor Camden 12-inch LP, CAL-216.

(2) Performed with an unidentified studio orchestra conducted by Andre Kostelanetz and taken from a broadcast of the radio program *The Pause That Refreshes on the Air* (Coca Cola Hour) from Liederkranz Hall, New York, 6 September 1942.

(3) Performed with Raymond Lambert (piano) and taken from a radio recital broadcast in Melbourne, August 1944.

(4) Recorded with an unidentified orchestra conducted by Sylvan Shulman for Columbia in the USA, 16 April 1945. Issued on Columbia Masterworks. 12-inch, 78 rpm disc, 71682-D, in an album of three discs, entitled *Marjorie Lawrence Sings*

for *Fighting* Men and in Australia under the title *Marjorie Lawrence Sings for the Boys*, SET M-579. Also issued in Australia as LOX-808.

(5) Recorded with an MGM studio orchestra (players from the Los Angeles Philharmonic) conducted by Adolph Deutsch in Hollywood, 23 June, 1954. Part of the second set of test recordings Lawrence made for the MGM film *Interrupted Melody*.

(6) Performed with the Victorian Symphony Orchestra conducted by Hector Crawford and taken from a broadcast of a concert in the series *Music for the People*, Myer Music Bowl, Melbourne, April 1966.

'Think on Me' (arranged by Perrazot)

Recorded with Ivor Newton (piano) in Kingsway Hall, London, 2 July 1946. Never issued.

STEWART, Dorothy

'God Bless Australia'

Recorded with Raymond Lambert (piano) in Sydney, 22 September, 1944 and issued on Columbia (Australia) 10-inch, 78 rpm disc, LO 67.

STRAUS, Oskar

The Chocolate Soldier: My hero

(1) Performed with an unidentified orchestra and taken from a broadcast of the radio program *The Pause That Refreshes on the Air* (Coca-Cola Hour), Liederkranz Hall, New York, 31 January 1943.

(2) Recorded with an unidentified orchestra conducted by Shulman Sylvan for Columbia in the USA,16 April 1945. Issued on Columbia 12- inch, 78 rpm disc, LOX 809; also issued on Columbia Masterworks 12-inch, 78 rpm disc, 71684-D, in an album of three discs, entitled *Marjorie Lawrence Sings for Fighting Men*. In Australia the set was released with the title *Marjorie Lawrence Sings for the Boys*, SET M-579.

STRAUSS, Richard

Salome: Ah, du wolltest mich nicht deinen Mund küssen (Final Scene)

(1) Recorded in French with Orchestre de l'Association des Concerts Pasdeloup conducted by Piero Coppola in the Salle Pleyel, Paris, 1934. Issued on 2 x HMV 12-inch, 78 rpm discs, DB 4933/4 and reissued on CD: *Marjorie Lawrence*, Preiser/Lebendige Vergangenheit, 89011.

(2) Performed with the BBC Symphony Orchestra, conducted by Sir Adrian Boult and taken from the broadcast of a concert in the Royal Albert Hall, London, 14 November 1945.

(3) Recorded with an MGM studio orchestra (players from the Los Angeles Philharmonic) conducted by Adolph Deutsch and an unidentified tenor singing

Herod's final line, Hollywood, 23 June 1954. Part of the second set of test recordings Lawrence made for the MGM film *Interrupted Melody*.

'Zueignung', Opus 10, No. 1

(1) Performed with the NBC Symphony Orchestra, conducted by Frank Black and taken from a broadcast of the program *NBC Magic Key of RCA*, New York, 5 February 1939.

(2) Performed with an unidentified studio orchestra conducted by Andre Kostelanetz and taken from a broadcast of the radio program *The Pause That Refreshes* (The Coca-Cola Hour) from Liederkranz Hall, New York, 6 September 1942.

(3) Performed with Raymond Lambert (piano) and taken from a radio recital broadcast in Melbourne, August 1944.

'Des Dichters Abendgang', Opus 47, No. 2

Recorded with Felix Wolfes (piano) in the RCA Victor Studios, Camden, NJ, 31 May 1940. Issued on RCA Victor 10-inch, 78 rpm disc, 17230; also issued on HMV (Australia) 10-inch, 78 rpm disc, ED-286, and reissued on RCA Victor Camden 12-inch LP, CAL-216

'Lied an meinen Sohn', Opus 39, No. 5.

Recorded with Felix Wolfes (piano) in the RCA Victor Studios, Camden, NJ, 1 June 1940. Issued on RCA Victor 10-inch, 78 rpm disc, 17230; also issued on HMV (Australia) 10-inch, 78 rpm disc, ED-286, and reissued on RCA Victor Camden 12-inch LP, CAL-216.

Elektra: Very brief extract from Elektra's monologue (bars 53 to 59).

Warner-Pathé newsreel film (sound and vision) of a concert with the Chicago Symphony Orchestra conducted by Artur Rodzinsky, Symphony Hall, Chicago, 11 December 1947.

TCHAIKOVSKY, Peter Ilyich

'None But the Lonely Heart'

Performed with the Bell Telephone Orchestra conducted by Donald Voorhees and taken from a broadcast of the radio program *The Bell Telephone Hour*, New York, 27 August 1945.

Eugen Onegin: Tatiana's Letter Scene (sung in Russian)

(1) Performed with an unnamed studio orchestra conducted by Josef Stopak and taken from a broadcast of the radio program *The Met Presents*, New York, 20 March 1945.

(2) Performed with L'Orchestre National de Paris conducted by Albert Wolff and taken from a radio broadcast of the 'Concert pour la pénicilline', Théâtre National du Chaillot, Paris, 16 October 1946. (On the original tapes, Lawrence introduces this scena, speaking in French.) Issued on CD *Marjorie Lawrence*, Malibran, MR502.

TRADITIONAL

'A Highland Lad my Love was Born'

Recorded with Paul Meyer (piano) for Columbia in the USA, 19 October, 1945. Never issued.

'Auld Lang Syne'

(1) Recorded with an unidentified male voice quartet and orchestra, conducted by Shulman Sylvan, in the USA, 16 April, 1945. Issued on Columbia 12-inch, 78 rpm disc, LOX 809.

(2) Recorded with an unidentified male voice quartet and orchestra, conducted by Shulman Sylvan, for Columbia in the USA, 2 May 1945. Issued on Columbia Masterworks, 12-inch, 78 rpm disc, 71684-D, in an album of three discs, entitled *Marjorie Lawrence Sings for Fighting Men*. In Australia the set was released with the title *Marjorie Lawrence Sings for the Boys*, SET M-579.

'Bluebells of Scotland'

(1) Recorded with Paul Meyer (piano) for Columbia in the USA, 19 October, 1945. Never issued.

(2) Performed with an unidentified accompaniment and taken from a broadcast of the radio program *The Bell Telephone Hour*, New York, 11 February 1946.

'Comin' thru the Rye'

(1) Recorded with Paul Meyer (piano) for Columbia in the USA, 17 October, 1945. Never issued.

(2) Performed with unidentified accompaniment and taken from a broadcast of the radio program *The Bell Telephone Hour*, New York, 11 February 1946.

'Danny Boy'

(1) Recorded with Felix Wolfes (piano) in the RCA Victor Studios, Camden, NJ, 10 May 1939. Never issued.

(2) Recorded with Felix Wolfes (piano) in the RCA Victor Studios, Camden, NJ, 29 May 1940. Issued on RCA Victor 12-inch, 78 rpm disc, 17457; also issued on HMV 12-inch, 78 rpm disc, DB5870, and reissued on RCA Victor Camden 12-inch LP, CAL-216.

(3) Performed with Raymond Lambert (piano) and taken from a radio recital broadcast in Melbourne, August 1944.

(4) Recorded with an unidentified male voice quartet and orchestra, conducted by Sylvan Shulman, for Columbia in the USA, 16 April 1945. Issued on Columbia Masterworks, 12-inch, 78 rpm disc, 71683-D, in an album of three discs, entitled *Marjorie Lawrence Sings for Fighting Men*. In Australia the set was released with the title *Marjorie Lawrence Sings for the Boys*, SET M-579. Also issued in Australia as LOX-810.

(5) Performed with the Bell Telephone Hour Orchestra, conducted by Donald Voorhees and taken from a broadcast of the radio program *The Bell Telephone Hour*, New York, 27 August 1945.

'Loch Lomond'

(1) Performed with the Bell Telephone Hour Orchestra, conducted by Donald Voorhees and taken from a broadcast of the radio program *The Bell Telephone Hour*, New York, 27 August 1945.

(2) Recorded with Paul Meyer (piano) for Columbia in the USA, 17 October 1945. Never issued.

'Men of Harlech'

No details available, believed to be a Columbia recording made in the USA (not on 10 June 1936 as stated in other discographies) Never issued.

'Robin Adair'

(1) Recorded with Paul Meyer (piano) for Columbia in the USA, 19 October 1945. Never issued.

(2) Performed with the Bell Telephone Hour Orchestra, conducted by Donald Voorhees and taken from a broadcast of the radio program *The Bell Telephone Hour*, New York, 11 February 1946.

'Waltzing Matilda' (attributed to Cowan, arr. by Kostelanetz)

(1) Performed with an unidentified studio orchestra conducted by Andre Kostelanetz and taken from a broadcast of the radio program *The Pause That Refreshes* (The Coca-Cola Hour) from Liederkranz Hall, New York, 6 September 1942.

(2) Recorded with an unidentified pianist and a chorus of Royal Australian Air Force servicemen in Liederkranz Hall, New York, 12 February 1943. Never issued.

(3) Performed with an unidentified studio orchestra (possibly conducted by Andre Kostelanetz) and taken from a broadcast of the radio program *The Pause That Refreshes on the Air* (Coca-Cola Hour), Liederkranz Hall, New York, 13 June 1943.

(4) Performed with Raymond Lambert (piano) and taken from a radio recital broadcast in Melbourne, August 1944.

(5) Recorded with Raymond Lambert (piano) in Sydney, 22 September 1944 and issued on Columbia (Australia) 10-inch, 78 rpm disc, LO 67.

(6) Recorded with an unidentified male voice quartet and orchestra conducted by Sylvan Shulman, for Columbia in the USA, 2 May 1945. Issued on Columbia Masterworks, 12-inch, 78 rpm disc, 71682-D, in an album of three discs, entitled *Marjorie Lawrence Sings for Fighting Men*. In Australia the set was released with the title *Marjorie Lawrence Sings for the Boys*, SET M-579. Also issued in Australia as LOX-808.

(7) Recorded with an MGM studio orchestra (players from the Los Angeles Philharmonic) conducted by Adolph Deutsch in Hollywood, 23 June 1954. Part

of the second set of test recordings Lawrence made for the MGM film *Interrupted Melody*.

(8) Performed with the Victorian Symphony Orchestra conducted by Hector Crawford and taken from a broadcast of a concert in the series Music for the People, Myer Music Bowl, Melbourne, April 1966.

(9) Recorded with the Sydney Symphony Orchestra conducted by Patrick Flynn for EMI (Australia) in Sydney, in 1966. Issued on EMI 7- inch, 45 rpm disc (in stereo) EMI 11463.

Unidentified

'The Greatest of These'

Performed with an unidentified accompanist (piano) Tape of recital, no details available.

VERDI, Giuseppe

Macbeth: Viena! t'affretta! (Letter Scene)

Performed with the National Orchestral Association conducted by Leon Barzin and taken from a broadcast of a public concert, New York, 11 December 1936.

Don Carlos: O don fatale

Recorded with piano (pianist unidentified) in Melbourne, October (?) 1928. Issued privately on Vocalion 10-inch, pink label, 80 rpm disc, PR18 and reissued on LP Unique Opera Records Corporation UORC 248.

Aida Complete (as Amneris)

Performed with Ruth Adele Batts (Aida); Frederic Rounsfull (Priestess); Thomas Page (Radames); Joe Thomas (Amonasro); Vern Shinall (Ramfis); William Davis (King); Phillip Falcone (Messenger) with Southern Illinois University School of Music Orchestra, conducted by Carmine Ficocelli. Recorded during a public performance in the Shryock Auditorium, Southern Illinois University, Carbondale, Ill., 24 February 1961. Private tape held by Southern Illinois University.

WAGNER, Richard

Der Fliegende Holländer Complete (as Senta)

Performed with Fred Destal (Dutchman); Alexander Kipnis (Daland): René Maison (Erik); Hans Fleischer (Steersman); Irra Petina (Mary); Orchestra and Chorus of the Teatro Colón, conducted by Fritz Busch. Taken from a broadcast of the public performance in the Teatro Colón, Buenos Aires, 19 September 1936. Issued on CD: Pearl GEMM CDS 9910

Tannhäuser Complete (as Venus)

Performed with Astrid Varnay (Elisabeth); Lauritz Melchior (Tannhäuser); Julius Huehn (Wolfram); Alexander Kipnis (Hermann); John Garris (Walther); Mack Harrell (Biterolf); Emery Darcy (Heinrich); John Gurney (Reinmar); Maxine Stellman

(Shepherd); Chorus and Orchestra of the Metropolitan Opera conducted by Paul Breisach. Broadcast of a public performance at the Metropolitan Opera House, New York, 5 February 1944. Issued on CD: Gebhardt, JGCD 0034.

Lohengrin: Erhebe dich, Genossin meiner Schmach

Recorded in French, with Martial Singher (Telramund) and Orchestre de l'Association des Concerts Pasdeloup, conducted by Piero Coppola, in the Salle Pleyel, Paris, 20 September 1933. Issued on HMV (Voix de son maître) 12-inch, 78 rpm disc, DB 4900. Reissued on CD: *Wagner Singing on Record, Part 1* EMI, CMS 7 64008 2; *Marjorie Lawrence*, Preiser/Lebendige Vergangenheit, 89011; *Lohengrin – Excerpts*, Malibran, MR649 and *Martial Singher* Presier/Lebendige Vergangenheit, 89635

Lohengrin: Elsa! Wer ruft? ... Entweihte Götter! ... Ortrud! Wo bist du? ... Du armste kanns wohl.

Recorded in French, with Yvonne Brothier (Elsa) and Orchestre de l'Association des Concerts Pasdeloup, conducted by Piero Coppola, in the Salle Pleyel, Paris, 20 September 1933. Issued on two HMV (Voix de son maître) 12-inch, 78 rpm discs, DB4890/91 (Side B of DB4891 contains the Prelude to Act 1 of *Siegfried*). Reissued on CD: *Marjorie Lawrence*, Preiser/Lebendige Vergangenheit, 89011 and *Lohengrin – Excerpts*, Malibran, MR649

Lohengrin Complete (as Ortrud)

Performed with Lotte Lehmann (Elsa); Lauritz Melchior (Lohengrin); Ludwig Schorr (Telramund); Emanuel List (King Henry); Julius Huehn (Herald), Orchestra and Chorus of the Metropolitan Opera, conducted by Artur Bodanzky. Taken from a broadcast of the public performance in the Metropolitan Opera House, New York, 21 December 1935. Issued on CD: Gerhardt, JGCD 0023-3 and Melodram, MEL 37049 3

Lohengrin Complete (as Ortrud)

Performed with Tiana Lemnitz (Elsa); Marcel Wittrisch (Lohengrin); Fred Destal (Telramund); Alexander Kipnis (King Henry); Fritz Krenn (Herald); Orchestra and Chorus of the Teatro Colón, conducted by Fritz Busch. Taken from a broadcast of the public performance in the Teatro Colón, Buenos Airies, 14 August 1936.

Lohengrin Complete (as Ortrud)

Performed with Germaine Hoerner (Elsa); René Maison (Lohengrin); Fred Destal (Telramund); Alexander Kipnis (King Henry); Fritz Krenn (Herald); Hans Fleischer (First Noble); Luis Santoro (Second Noble): Jorge Andronoff (Third Noble) and Vittorio Baciato (Fourth Noble); Orchestra and Chorus of the Teatro Colón, conducted by Fritz Busch. Taken from a broadcast of the public performance in the Teatro Colón, Buenos Aires, 17 September, 1936. Issued on CD: Archipel, ARPCD 0182 and Premiere Opera CDNO 1621-3.

Die Walküre: Ride of the Valkyries (as Gerhilde on side A; Brünnhilde on side B) Act III, Scene 1 from the beginning up to the vocal entry of Sieglinde.

Recorded in French with unidentified members of the chorus of the Paris Opéra singing the other Valkyries and the Orchestre de l'Association des Concerts Pasdeloup, conducted by Piero Coppola in the Salle Pleyel, Paris, 11 October 1933. Issued on HMV 12-inch, 78 rpm disc, DB 4905. Reissued on CD: *Wagner in French*, Romophone, 88001-2 and *Marjorie Lawrence*, Malibran, MR502.

Die Walküre: Nur zäume dein Ross, reisige Maid ... Ho-jo-to-ho!

Recorded in French with Jean Claverie (Wotan) and Orchestre de l'Association des Concerts Pasdeloup, conducted by Piero Coppola, in the Salle Pleyel, Paris, 11 October 1933 Issued on HMV 12-inch, 78 rpm disc, DB 4925. Reissued on CD: *Marjorie Lawrence*, Preiser/Lebendige Vergangenheit, 89011 and *Marjorie Lawrence*, Malibran, MR502.

Die Walküre: War es so schmählich, was ich verbrach

Recorded in French with Orchestre de l'Association des Concerts Pasdeloup, conducted by Piero Coppola, in the Salle Pleyel, Paris, 11 October 1933. Issued on HMV 12-inch, 78 rpm disc, DB 4925. Reissued on CD: *Marjorie Lawrence*, Preiser/Lebendige Vergangenheit, 89011 and *Marjorie Lawrence*, Malibran, MR502.

Die Walküre Complete (as Brünnhilde)

Performed with René Maison (Siegmund); Germaine Hoerner (Sieglinde); Fred Destal (Wotan); Weber (Fricka) Alexander Kipnis (Hunding); unidentified singers in the other roles; Orchestra and Chorus Sinfonica Oficial de Difusion Radio y Espectáculos, conducted by Fritz Busch. Taken from a broadcast of the public performance in the Opera House, Montevideo, Uruguay, 29 September 1936.

Excerpts from these tapes were issued on LP by Unique Opera Records, UORC-139.

Die Walküre Complete (as Brünnhilde)

Performed with Lauritz Melchior (Siegmund); Lotte Lehmann (Sieglinde); Friedrich Schorr (Wotan); Emanuel List (Hunding); Kerstin Thorborg (Fricka); Thelma Votipka (Gerhilde); Irene Jessner (Ortlinde); Doris Doe (Waltraute), Anna Kaskas (Schwertleite); Dorothee Manski (Helmwige); Helen Olheim (Siegrune), Irra Petina (Grimgerde); Ina Bourskaya (Rossweisse); Orchestra and Chorus of the Metropolitan Opera, conducted by Erich Leinsdorf. (Note: Seltsam claims the conductor on this date was Bodanzky and does not list Leinsdorf for the Met until the next season, 1937–38) Taken from a broadcast of the public performance in the Metropolitan Opera House, New York, 16 January 1937.

Die Walküre: Complete (as Brünnhilde)

Performed with Lauritz Melchior (Siegmund); Kirsten Flagstad (Sieglinde); Friedrich Schorr (Wotan); Ludwig Hofmann (Hunding); Kirstin Thorborg (Fricka); Thelma Votipka (Gerhilde); Irene Jessner (Ortlinde); Doris Doe (Waltraute), Anna Kaskas (Schwertleite); Dorothee Manski (Helmwige); Helen Olheim (Siegrune); Irra Petina (Grimgerde); Lucielle Browning (Rossweisse); Orchestra and Chorus of the Metropolitan Opera, conducted by Artur Bodanzky. Taken from a broadcast of the public performance in the Metropolitan Opera House, New York, 18 December 1937. Issued on CD: Acts II & III only Walhall, WHL 21 and Archipel, ARPCD 0039.

Die Walkure: Act II Complete (as Sieglinde)

Performed with Kirsten Flagstad (Brünnhilde); Lauritz Melchior (Siegmund); Fred Destal (Wotan); Hertha Glaz (Fricka); Norman Cordon (Hunding); Orchestra of the San Francisco Opera, conducted by Edwin McArthur. Taken from a broadcast of the public performance in the War Memorial Opera House, San Francisco, 24 October 1939.
Issued on CD: Excerpt on *Marjorie Lawrence*, Malibran, MR502.

Die Walküre: Complete (as Sieglinde)
Performed with Lauritz Melchior (Siegmund); Kirsten Flagstad (Brünnhilde); Julius Huehn (Wotan); Emanuel List (Hunding); Karin Branzell (Fricka); Thelma Votipka (Gerhilde); Maxine Stellman (Ortlinde); Doris Doe (Waltraute), Anna Kaskis (Schwertleite); Dorothee Manski (Helmwige); Helen Olheim (Siegrune), Irra Petina (Grimgerde); Lucielle Browning (Rossweisse); Orchestra and Chorus of the Metropolitan Opera, conducted by Erich Leinsdorf. Taken from a broadcast of the public performance in the Metropolitan Opera House, 17 February 1940. Issued on CD: Walhall, WHL 14; extract: 'Der Männer Sippe sass hier im Saal' to 'Keiner ging, doch Einer kam siehe' with Melchior Issued on Malibran MR502.

Die Walküre: Complete (as Brünnhilde)
Performed with Lauritz Melchior (Siegmund); Lotte Lehmann (Sieglinde); Friedrich Schorr (Wotan); Emanuel List (Hunding); Kerstin Thorborg (Fricka); Thelma Votipka (Gerhilde); Irene Jessner (Ortlinde); Maxine Stellman (Waltraute), Doris Doe (Schwertleite); Dorothee Manski (Helmwige); Helen Olheim (Siegrune), Winifred Heidt (Grimgerde); Lucielle Browning (Rossweisse); Orchestra and Chorus of the Metropolitan Opera, conducted by Erich Leinsdorf. Taken from a broadcast of a performance in the Boston Opera House, 30 March 1940. Issued on CD: Walhall, WHL 1; Guild immortal Performances GHCD 2215/7 and excerpts on Myto 3 MCD 953.133.

Die Walküre: Complete (as Brünnhilde)
Performed with René Maison (Siegmund); Irene Jessner (Sieglinde); Herbert Janssen (Wotan); Emanuel List (Hunding); Lydia Kindermann (Fricka); Judith Hellwig (Gerhilde); Yolanda di Sabato (Ortlinde); Maria Rubini (Waltraute), Rïse Stevens (Schwertleite); Maria Malberti (Helmwige); Clara Oyuela (Siegrune), Emma Brizzio (Grimgerde); Lydia Kindermann (Rossweisse); Orchestra and Chorus of the Teatro Colón, conducted by Erich Kleiber. Taken from a broadcast of the public performance in the Teatro Colón, Buenos Aires, 23 August 1940. Issued on CD: Gebhardt, JGCD 0028
Note: The producers of the Gebhardt set identify the Fricka of this performance as Rïse Stevens, but Teatro Colón records and press reports indicate that it was Lydia Kindermann.

Die Walküre: War es so schmählich, was ich verbrach

Performed with Friedrich Schorr and the Philadelphia Orchestra conducted by Eugene Ormandy. Taken from the broadcast of a concert in Carnegie Hall, New York, 16 February 1943

Die Walküre: War es so schmählich, was ich verbrach (Abridged version omitting Wotan's part)

Taken from a broadcast of the radio program *Invitation to Music*, 3 June 1943.

Die Walküre: Du bist der Lenz

Performed with the Victorian Symphony Orchestra conducted by Hector Crawford and taken from a broadcast of a concert in the series *Music for the People*, Myer Music Bowl, Melbourne, April 1966.

Götterdämmerung: Starke Scheite (Immolation Scene)

Recorded in French with Orchestre de l'Association des Concerts Pasdeloup, conducted by Piero Coppola in the Salle Pleyel, Paris, 19 January 1934. Issued on 2 x HMV (Voix de son maître) 12-inch, 78 rpm discs, DB4914/5 and reissued on CD: *Marjorie Lawrence*, Preiser/Lebendige Vergangenheit, 89011.

Götterdämmerung: Complete (as Brünnhilde)

Performed with Lauritz Melchior (Siegfried); Ludwig Hofmann (Hagen); Eduard Habich (Alberich); Friedrich Schorr (Gunther); Dorothee Manski (Gutrune and First Norn); Kathryn Meisle (Waltraute); Editha Fleischer (Woglinde); Irra Petina (Wellgunde and Second Norn); Doris Doe (Flosshilde and Third Norn); Max Altglass (First Vassal); Arnold Gabor (Second Vassal); Orchestra and Chorus of the Metropolitan Opera, conducted by Artur Bodanzky. Taken from a broadcast of the public performance in the Metropolitan Opera House, New York, 11 January 1936. Issued on CD: Naxos Historical, 8110041/3 and Walhall, WHL24.

Götterdämmerung: Starke Scheite (Immolation Scene)

Performed with the Bell Telephone Hour Orchestra, conducted by Donald Voorhees and taken from a broadcast of the radio program *The Bell Telephone Hour*, New York, 11 February 1946.

Götterdämmerung: Starke Scheite (Immolation Scene) (Sung in French)

Performed with L'Orchestre National de Paris conducted by Albert Wolff and taken from a radio broadcast of the 'Concert pour la pénicilline', Théâtre National du Chaillot, Paris, 16 October 1946.

Tristan und Isolde: Isolde's Narration and Curse

Performed with the Bell Telephone Hour Orchestra, conducted by Donald Voorhees and taken from a broadcast of the radio program *The Bell Telephone Hour*, New York, 8 January 1945.

Parsifal: Complete (as Kundry)

Performed with René Maison (Parsifal); Martial Singher (Amfortas); Fred Destal (Titurel); Alexander Kipnis (Gurnemanz); Fritz Krenn (Klingsor); Hans Fleischer (First Knight and Third Squire); Jorge Andronoff (Second Knight); Lucy Ritter (First

Squire and Second Flower Maiden); Irra Petina (Second Squire and Fourth Flower Maiden); Luis Santoro (Fourth Squire); Editha Fleischer (First Flower Maiden); Maria Malberti (Third Flower Maiden); Emma Brizzio (Fifth Flower Maiden); Yolanda di Sabato (Sixth Flower Maiden); Chorus and Orchestra of the Teatro Colón, conducted by Fritz Busch. Taken from the broadcast of a public performance in the Teatro Colón, Buenos Aires, 22 September 1936. Issued on CD: Marston, CD 53003-2.

WOLF, Hugo

'Gebet' (orchestrated version)

'Der Rattenfänger' (orchestrated version)

Performed with the NBC Symphony Orchestra conducted by Eugene Goossens and taken from a broadcast of the radio program *NBC Magic Key of RCA*, New York, 1938.

'Gesang Weylas'

(1) (Orchestrated version) Performed with the NBC Symphony Orchestra conducted by Eugene Goossens and taken from a broadcast of the radio program *NBC Magic Key of RCA*, New York, 1938; with orchestra conducted by Eugene Goossens.

(2) (piano version) Recorded with Felix Wolfes (piano) in the RCA Victor Studios, Camden, NJ, 29 May 1940. Never issued on 78 rpm disc, but issued on RCA Victor Camden 12-inch LP, CAL-216.

WOLFE, Jacques

'British Children's Prayer'

Performed with unidentified accompaniment and taken from a broadcast of the radio program *The Pause That Refreshes on the Air* (Coca-Cola Hour), New York, 13 June 1943.

Spoken recordings

1. Brief speech about Lawrence's radio comeback following her illness Broadcast of the radio program *The Pause That Refreshes* (Coca- Cola Hour) from Liederkranz Hall, New York, 6 September 1942.
2. Introduction to a medley of songs by Harry Lauder. Broadcast of the radio program *The Bell Telephone Hour*, New York, 27 August 1945.
3. Apology to the audience that she has a bad cold affecting her voice. Broadcast of public concert: 'Concert pour la pénicilline' in the Théâtre National du Chaillot, Paris, 16 October 1946. Issued on CD: *Marjorie Lawrence*, Malibran, MR502.
4. Introduction of Tatiana's Letter Scene (*Eugen Onegin*) in French. Broadcast of public concert: 'Concert pour la pénicilline' in the Théâtre National du Chaillot , Paris, 16 October 1946.
5. Brief interview by Dr Lynch in August, 1973, about her teaching career at Southern Illinois University. The Marjorie Lawrence Papers, SIU.
6. Radio Talk 'My Life and Career', ABC Radio, Australia, June 1976 also includes the voice of Lawrence's husband, Dr Thomas King.

Bibliography

Ashbrook, William 1968, *The Operas of Puccini*, Cassell, London.
Bachner, Louis 1944, *Dynamic Singing*, L.B. Fischer, New York.
Batelt, Chuck & Bergeron, Barbara 1988, *Variety Obituaries 1906–1986*, Garland, New York.
Bibliothèque de l'Opéra, Paris, Dossier 'Marjorie Lawrence', Collection of letters on microfilm.
Bird, John 1976, *Percy Grainger*, Macmillan, Melbourne.
Briggs, John 1969, *Requiem for a Yellow Brick Brewery*, Little, Brown & Co., Boston.
Blyth, Alan (ed.) 1979, *Opera on Record*, Hutchinson, London, 1979.
Buttrose, Charles 1984, *Words and Music*, Angus & Robertson, Sydney.
Capell, Richard 1973, *Schubert's Songs*, Duckworth, London.
Carell, Victor & Dean, Beth 1987, *Gentle Genius – A Life of John Antill*, Akron, Sydney.
Cargher, John 1988, *Bravo! Two Hundred Years of Opera in Australia*, Macmillan, Melbourne.
Chaliapin, Feodor & Gorky, Maxim 1968, *Chaliapin – An Autobiography as told to Maxim Gorky*, trans. N. Froud & J. Hanley, Macdonald, London.
Christiansen, Rupert 1995, *Prima Donna – A History*, Pimlico, London.
Cook, Ida 2009, *Safe Passage*, Mira, Sydney (originally published as *We Followed Our Stars*, Mills & Boon, London, 1950).
Culshaw, John 1967, *The Ring Resounding*, Secker & Warburg, London.
Daniels, Josephus 1947, *Shirt-sleeve Diplomat*, University of Carolina Press, Chapel Hill, NC.
Davidson, Jim 1994, *Lyrebird Rising*, Melbourne University Press.
Davis, Richard 2001, *Eileen Joyce – A Portrait*, Fremantle Arts Centre Press, Fremantle.
Davis, Richard 2006, *Geoffrey Parsons – Among Friends*, ABC Books, Sydney.

Easton, Quaintance 1959, *Opera Caravan – Adventures of the Metropolitan on Tour 1883–1956*, John Calder, London.

Elms, Lauris 2001, *The Singing Elms*, Bowerbird, Sydney.

Emmons, Shirlee 1990, *Tristanissimo – The Authorized Biography of Heroic Tenor Lauritz Melchior*, Schirmer, New York.

Evans, Lindley 1983, *Hello, Mr Melody Man*, Angus & Robertson, Sydney.

Farrell, Eileen & Kellow, Brian 1999, *Can't Help Singing*, Northeastern University Press, Boston.

Game, Peter 1976, *The Music Sellers*, Hawthorn Press, Melbourne.

Garden, Mary & Biancolli, Louis 1951, *Mary Garden's Story*, Simon & Schuster, New York.

Glennon, James 1968, *Australian Music & Musicians*, Rigby, Adelaide.

Goodman, Virginia 1983, *Isador Goodman – A Life in Music*, Collins, Sydney.

Gregory, Barrie & Gregory, Marjorie 1985, *Coast to Country – Winchelsea, a History of the Shire*, Hargreen, Melbourne.

Gruen, John 1978, *Menotti – A Biography*, Macmillan, New York.

Gyger, Alison 1990, *Opera for the Antipodes*, Sydney, Currency Press.

Harrison, Kenneth 1975, *Dark Man, White World – A Portrait of Tenor Harold Blair*, Novalit, Melbourne.

Hubble, Ava 1988, *The Strange Case of Eugene Goossens and Other Tales from the Opera House*, Collins, Sydney.

Jackson, Paul 1992, *Saturday Afternoons at the Old Met*, Amadeus Press, Portland, Oregon.

Kolodin, Irving 1940, *The Metropolitan Opera 1883–1939*, Oxford University Press, New York.

Kolodin, Irving 1966, *The Metropolitan Opera 1883–1966*, Alfred A. Knopf, New York.

Lawrence, Marjorie & Buttrose, Charles 1955, *Interrupted Melody*, Invincible Press, Sydney (reprinted by Southern Illinois Press, Carbondale, 1972).

Littlejohn, David 1992, *The Ultimate Art: Essays around and about opera*, University of California Press.

Lucas, John 2008, *Thomas Beecham – An Obsession With Music*, Boydell, Woodbridge, Suffolk.

McArthur, Edwin 1965, *Flagstad – A Personal Memoir*, Alfred A. Knopf, New York.

McKenzie, Barbara & Findlay 1967, *Singers of Australia*, Lansdowne Press, Melbourne.

Marsi, Lina 1990, *Index to the Australian Musical News 1911–1962*, Lima Press, Melbourne.

Matheopoulos, Helena 1991, *Diva*, Gollancz, London.

Moffat, James 1995, *Florence Austral*, Currency Press, Sydney.
Moore, Roger & Owen, Gareth 2008, *My Word is My Bond*, Collins, New York.
Moresby, Isabelle 1948, *Australia Makes Music*, Longman, Melbourne.
O'Connor, Garry 1979, *The Pursuit of Perfection*, Gollancz, London.
Radic, Thérèse 1986, *Bernard Heinze – A Biography*, Macmillan, Melbourne.
Rasponi, Lanfranco 1990, *The Last Prima Donnas*, Limelight, New York.
Robinson, Francis 1979, *Celebration – The Metropolitan Opera*, Doubleday, New York.
Ross, John (gen. ed.) 1993, *Chronicle of Australia*, Chronicle Australasia, Melbourne.
Sadie, Stanley (ed.) 2001, *New Groves Dictionary of Music and Musicians*, 2nd edn, Grove, London.
Sametz, Phillip 1992, *Play On! – Sixty Years of Music-Making with the Sydney Symphony Orchestra*, ABC Books, Sydney.
Seltsam, William H. 1947, *Metropolitan Opera Annals*, W.W. Wilson, New York.
Steane, John 1998, *Singers of the Century (Vol. 2)*, Amadeus Press, Portland, Oregon.
Stratten, Frank van 1994, *National Treasure*, Victoria Press, Melbourne.
Sutherland, Joan 1997, *A Prima Donna's Progress*, Random House, Sydney.
Teyte, Maggie 1958, *Star on the Door*, Putnam, London.
Thompson, Oscar 1949, *Cyclopaedia of Music and Musicians*, Dodd, Mead & Co., New York.
Traubel, Helen 1959, *St Louis Woman*, Duell, Sloan & Pearce, New York.
Trotter, William R. 1995, *Priest of Music – The Life of Dimitri Mitropoulos*, Amadeus Press, Portland, Oregon.
Tuggle, Robert 2005, 'A Season of Valkyries', *Opera News*, October.
Waters, Thorold 1951, *Much Besides Music*, Georgian House, Melbourne.
Zietz, Karyl Lynn 1995, *Opera Companies and Houses of the United States*, McFarland, Jefferson, NC.

Index

A

Abravanel, Maurice 80
Ackland, Essie 126
Adams, Jack 216, 224, 225
Albanese, Licia 176
Alda, Frances 177
Althouse, Paul 92, 267
Alwin, Karl 153, 154, 186
Antill, John 213
Arndt-Ober, Margarete 119
Austral, Florence 127
Australian Broadcasting Commission (ABC) 126, 127, 130–133, 190, 197, 199, 223
Aveling, Valda 203

B

Baccaloni, Salvatore 218
Bach, Johann Sebastian 38, 49, 168, 194, 196, 206
  St Matthew Passion 50
Bachner, Louis 138, 139, 176, 221, 232
Balanchine, George 265
Balogh, Erno 124
Bampton, Rose 147
Barber, Samuel
  Anthony and Cleopatra 242
Barbirolli, John 107, 116
Barkan, Maria 169
Bater, Glenn 239
Bäumer, Margarete 119–120
Bavarian State Opera, Munich 121, 152
Bayreuth Festival 117, 121, 152
BBC Symphony Orchestra 209, 210, 212, 288
Bee, Betty 98, 151, 176, 177
Beecham, Thomas 176, 182, 183, 186, 187, 199, 201, 210, 211, 212, 213
Beethoven, Ludwig van 22, 26, 38, 194
  Fidelio 107
Behrens, Hildegard 96

Bellini, Vincenzo
  Norma 80, 101
Belmont, Eleanor 174
Belsen Concentration Camp 206
Benjamin, Arthur 280
Bentine, Michael 206
Berlin Philharmonic Orchestra 214
Berlioz, Hector
  La Damnation de Faust 21, 41, 51
Bernstein, Leonard 210
Billig, Dr H.E. Jnr. 170, 185
Bing, Rudolf 222, 242
Bizet, Georges
  Carmen 141–142, 144–146, 153, 155, 198, 208, 221, 237, 259, 280
Björling, Jussi 241
Blair, Harold 198–199, 223, 246
Blamey, General Sir Thomas 193, 196, 197
Bodanzky, Artur 77, 83, 84, 88, 89, 91, 93, 94, 95, 98, 105, 113, 134, 139, 144, 293, 294, 296
Boddington, Ada 10, 24, 25, 27–30, 32–35, 70, 130
Boggs, Oscar and Mabel 149, 167, 168, 169, 180
Bohnen, Michael 138
Bonelli, Richard 123
Bonynge, Richard ix, xiii, 243, 247, 248, 250
Bordeaux Opera 69
Bori, Lucrezia 89, 92
Boston Opera House 140, 141, 295
Boulanger, Nadia 36
Boult, Adrian 209, 288
Boustead, Ivor 11–14, 16–24, 26, 27, 31, 42, 101, 126–128, 221, 232
Brahms, Johannes 77, 102, 110, 136, 189, 194, 205, 210, 281
Branzell, Karin 115, 138, 295
Breisach, Paul 188, 293
Bret, Gustave 49, 55, 58, 59, 69
Bréval, Lucienne 260–261

Britten, Benjamin 204, 237
  Peter Grimes 204
Bronhill, June 247, 254
Brothier, Yvonne 74, 92, 293
Brownlee, John 11, 12, 21, 23–25, 30, 31, 34, 37, 41, 55, 57, 76, 81, 127, 135, 175, 176, 178, 183, 273, 277
Busch, Fritz 103–106, 170, 292–294, 297
Busch, Hans 103
Busch Greenough, Edmee 98, 148, 215, 222
Butt, Clara 8, 26, 55
Buttrose, Charles 129, 218–219, 245

C

Cabanel, Paul 62, 65, 212
Caldwell, Zoe 247
Calwell, Arthur 221, 248
Campbell, Mary 16, 17
Caniglia, Maria 123
Canteloube, Joseph 72, 73, 79, 136
  Vercingetorix 72–73, 79
Carnegie Hall 106, 136, 146, 148, 152, 183, 198, 282, 296
Caro, Georgette 62, 81
Carron, Arthur 182, 212, 268
Caruso, Enrico 50, 260
Castagna, Bruna 116
Cehanovsky, George 116, 280
Celibidache, Sergiu 214
Chaliapin, Feodor 50, 55
Chaplin, Saul 224, 226
Chausson, Ernest
  Le Roi Arthus 79–80
Chereau, Pierre 60, 63, 64, 67, 72, 81, 122, 212, 217
Cherubini, Luigi
  Medée 281
Chicago Symphony Orchestra 216, 289
Chifley, Ben 221
Chopin, Frédéric 194
Cigna, Gina 116
Cincinnati Zoo Opera 216, 217, 218
Civic Opera House, Chicago 41, 107
Claverie, Jean 75, 294
Clay, General Lucius 213, 214, 222
Code, Percy 22
Colón Theatre, Buenos Aires 99, 101–106, 143–144, 161, 292, 293, 295, 297
Colonne Orchestra 79

Columbia (Record Company) 190, 199 (also, see discography)
Columbia Artists Management 175
Copeland, Aaron 210
Coppola, Piero 74–76, 81, 82, 286, 288, 293, 294, 296
Covent Garden 69, 73, 110, 111, 201–203, 212, 213
Cowell, Henry 136, 282
Crain, Maurice 219, 223
Crawford, Hector 243, 284, 292, 296
Crespin, Régine 68, 76
Crooks, Richard 89
Cross, Milton 113, 141, 241
Crusinberry, Jane 41
Culshaw, John 213
Cummings, Jack 224, 226

D

Damrosch, Walter 268
D'Ans, Armand 110, 145
Dal Monte, Toti 23, 217
Danieli, Elena 24
Dawson, Peter 223
Debussy, Claude 194
  Pelleas et Mélisande 47, 259
Decca (Recording Company) 210, 213 (also, see discography)
Defrère, Désiré 113, 176, 188, 189
De Gaulle, Charles 275
Delbée, Pierre 105–106, 108–110, 215
Delibes, Léo
  Lakmé 49
De los Angeles, Victoria 241
Destal, Fred 104–106, 125, 292–296
De Stefano, Giuseppe 218
Destinn, Emmy 37, 81, 257
Detroit Symphony Orchestra 107, 215
Deutsch, Adolph 226, 286, 287, 288, 291
De Valmalète, Marcel 224, 225
Dickson, Ray 19, 20, 21, 255
Di Sabato, Yolanda 295
Djamel, Lily 138
Donizetti, Gaetano
  Lucia di Lammermoor 8, 23, 49, 217, 242
Dowd, Ronald 223
Dudley, John 254
Duparc, Henri 112, 136
Durieux, Willem 136, 282

Index

E

Elgar, Edward 30
Elizabeth, Her Majesty Queen (The Queen Mother) 206, 207, 208, 209, 213
Elizabeth II, Her Majesty Queen 207, 208
Elmendorff, Carl 85
Endrèze, Arthur 56, 274
Entertainments National Service Association (ENSA) 202, 203–206, 208
Evans, Lawrence 175
Ewing, Doris 167, 245, 249

F

Falcon, Cornélie 39
Farrar, Geraldine 123
Farrell, Eileen 227, 228
Fauré, Gabriel 112, 136
Faust, Herthe 119
Fauré, Maurice 60, 64, 66, 67
Featherstone, Amy 200, 203, 206, 222
Ferrar, Marisa 212
Fichefet, Marcel 61, 65
Ficocelli, Carmine 237, 292
Field, Douglas 226
Flagstad, Kirsten ix, 78, 83, 84, 87–90, 96–98, 102, 103, 108, 109, 111–113, 116, 122, 124, 126, 127, 134, 139, 140, 144, 147, 152, 153, 159, 161, 169, 175, 182, 183, 188, 202, 235, 237, 242, 250, 294, 295
Fletcher, Dr George 158, 159, 171
Ford, Glenn xi, 225, 228
Forde, Frank 197
Forti, Victor 109, 275
Franck, César 124, 281
Franz, Paul 60, 66, 70, 76
Fremstad, Olive 90, 176, 178
Friedlander, Heinz 98, 102, 105, 110, 116, 117, 128
Frozier, Georgette 274

G

Gadsden, Norma 41, 109
Gadski, Johanna 90
Garden, Mary 47, 48, 50, 79, 81, 115, 116, 174, 259
Garson, Greer 222–224, 226, 227, 242
Gatti-Casazza, Giulio 77, 78, 83, 84
Gaubert, Philippe 42, 43, 49, 58, 59, 72, 74, 79, 81
Gheusi, Pierre-Bathélemy 62–64

Giannini, Dusolina 116
Gigli, Beniamino 256
Gilly, Cécile 14, 24, 31–32, 35, 37–47, 49, 50, 52, 58, 61, 62, 69, 79, 109, 122, 132, 138, 143, 146, 217–218, 221, 225, 232
Gilly, Dinh 24, 37–40
Gilly, Renée 38, 41, 46, 47, 52, 143, 218
Ginster, Ria 138
Gluck, Christoph Willibald von 133, 174
  Alceste ix, 38, 40, 49, 51, 59, 110, 118, 146–147, 150, 209, 211, 281
  Orfeo et Euridice 146
Godard, Benjamin 50
Goodman, Isador 213, 246
Goossens, Eugene 223, 297
Gounod, Charles 168, 196
  Faust 237
  Sappho 124, 211, 281–282
Graarud, Gunnar 62
Graf, Herbert 114, 115, 147, 182
Grainger, Percy 132, 135–137, 282
Grayson, Kathryn 276
Greenslade, Hubert 203, 205, 213, 287
Grieg, Edvard 210, 211, 282
Grodet, Emile 32, 33, 35, 37, 41, 43, 45, 58, 64, 70, 77, 79, 109, 122, 132, 143, 168, 198, 224
Grodet, Henri 32, 34, 35, 41, 45, 46, 58, 61, 64, 83, 106, 108, 122, 132, 143, 207
Grodet, Mimi 34, 35, 48, 50–54, 56, 57, 59, 61–65, 85–87, 92, 94, 99, 102, 105, 106, 108, 109, 122, 132, 143, 198, 207, 214, 230
Grodet de Lacratelle, Marie 32, 33, 35, 37, 41, 43, 45, 52, 58, 64, 70, 77, 79, 109, 122, 132, 143, 168, 198, 207, 214, 224
Grovlez, Gabriel 258
Gunsbourg, Raoul 51, 52, 54–57, 64, 72
  L'Escarpolette 52, 56, 72

H

Hadley, Henry 116
Hageman, Richard 136
Hálasz, László 280
Halévy, Jacques
  La Juive 39, 41, 42, 60, 73, 97, 98–99, 107, 283
Handel, George Frideric 7, 38, 49
  Guilio Cesare 124, 283
  Messiah 20
Hanson-Dyer, Louise 34, 80

Harmony Hills Ranch (Villa Rustica) 158–159, 166, 171, 184–186, 200, 216, 224, 225, 232–234, 237, 243, 244–245, 249
Harreveld, Dr A. van 170, 185
Harris, Rolf 247
Hart, Fritz 16–17, 18, 23
Hartmann, Carl 112, 119
Hawkes, Ralph 201, 204
Hedrick, Mary 158, 159, 171, 184–185, 216
Heger, Robert 118–120
Heinze, Bernard 127, 133, 199
Helpmann, Robert 247
Hild, Oscar 216, 217
Hill, Alfred 199, 283
Hirsch, Georges 212, 217
His Master's Voice 64–65, 74, 81–83, 204 (also, see discography)
Hoerner, Germaine 69, 70, 103, 104, 106, 212, 217, 263, 293, 294
Hofmann, Ludwig 94, 294, 296
Holt, Harold 110, 111, 204, 209, 224
Honegger, Arthur 79
   Judith 79
Huberman, Bronislaw 126
Huehn, Julius 115, 182, 187, 188, 292, 293, 295

I

Ingpen, Joan 203
Interrupted Melody (book) xi, xiii, 5, 23, 28, 44, 53, 58, 61, 62, 64, 68, 76, 79, 84, 85, 95,101, 148, 150, 151, 154, 166, 173, 180, 183, 194, 197, 218–219, 220, 222, 223, 225, 228, 244, 249
Interrupted Melody (film) xi, 222–228, 229, 230, 244, 286–288, 292
Iturbi, José 107
Ives, Joshua 16

J

Jagel, Frederick 176
James, William G. 24
Janssen, Herbert 144, 161, 215, 295
Jepson, Helen 123, 124
Jeritza, Maria 123, 215
Jessner, Irene 125, 161, 267, 268, 294, 295
Jobin, Raoul 280
Johansen, Einar 33, 34, 224, 225
Johnson, Edward 83, 84, 87–90, 94, 96, 98, 99, 114, 116, 123, 134, 139, 146, 147, 152, 153, 159, 161, 169, 170, 174–178, 183, 184, 186, 188, 200, 215, 218, 222, 230, 246

Johnson, Gertrude 223
Johnson, Lyndon B. and Mrs Johnson 242
Jones, Gwyneth 96
Joplin, Scott
   Treemonisha 237–238
Journet, Marcel 51, 52, 70
Joyce, Eileen 126
Joyce, James 36, 80, 101

K

Katcher, Leo 223, 224, 225
Kellaway, Cecil 225
Kenny, Sister Elizabeth 160–162, 166, 169, 181, 275
Kerr, Deborah 224
Kiepura, Jan 123, 141–142, 280
King, Thomas 148–151, 152–165, 166–168, 179–181, 184–186, 189–191, 192–198, 200–201, 203–209, 212–214, 216–228, 229–230, 232–234, 236, 241–249, 297
Kipnis, Alexander 103–106, 126, 188, 242, 273, 292–294, 296
Kleiber, Erich 144, 161, 295
Klemperer, Otto 85
Kostelanetz, Andre 172–173, 227, 287, 289, 291
Kotikov, General Aleksandr 214
Koverman, Ida 222, 229
Krauss, Clemens 121
Kreisler, Fritz 215
Krenn, Fritz 104, 293, 296
Kreuger, Karl 215
Kullman, Charles 116, 176

L

La Guardia, Fiorello 176, 191
Lalo, Édouard 72
   Le Roi d'Ys 62, 63
Lambert, Raymond 193–195, 197, 199, 219, 280, 281, 283, 284, 287–291
Lamoureux Orchestra 64
Lapeyrette, Ketty 72
La Scala, Milan ix, 69, 73, 103, 243
Laskine, Lily 211, 285
Lauder, Harry 213, 284, 297
Lauri-Volpi, Giacomo 53, 56
Lausanne Opera 109
Lawrence, Allan (Thomas) (brother) 3, 6, 11, 17, 44, 45, 128, 130, 223, 246
Lawrence, Cyril (Percy) (brother) 2–4, 6, 7, 11–13, 15, 17, 24, 44, 45, 70–71, 83–87, 89,

Index 307

92–95, 99, 102, 105, 106, 108–111, 115, 118, 120–122, 125, 128–130, 132–135, 144–146, 148, 151, 153–157, 167, 225, 228–230, 242, 246
Lawrence, Ted (Edwin) (brother) 2, 3, 6, 7, 10, 11, 17, 45, 128, 130, 229, 230, 246
Lawrence, Eileen (sister) 2, 3, 5, 10, 11, 15–17, 19, 20, 24, 43, 44, 45, 128, 129, 197, 223, 246, 247
Lawrence, Elizabeth (mother) 1–4, 43, 70, 170, 247
Lawrence, Henry (grandfather) 4, 43
Lawrence, Julia (grandmother) 3, 4, 27, 43, 103
Lawrence, Lindsay (brother) 2, 3, 6, 7, 20, 44, 45, 64, 128–130, 167, 220, 225, 246
Lawrence, Marjorie
　American commercial recordings 124, 142–143, 190
　ancestry 1
　appearance 2, 21, 24–25, 32, 34–35, 48, 62, 88, 133, 231
　attitude to sex 65–66
　auditions for the Met 76–78, 83–84
　auditions for the Paris Opéra 58–59
　birth and childhood 1–7
　British commercial recordings 210–211, 213 (also, see discography)
　character 106, 179, 231–232, 250
　commences teaching 232
　death 249
　debut at the Met 88–91
　discovery of her voice 5–8
　education 5
　employment 13–15, 18
　father's opposition to her singing career 10
　first recordings (in Australia) 26–27 (also, see discography)
　first romance 10, 11
　illness and treatment 153–162, 170–171, 185
　learns French 33, 39, 46
　learns German 46, 84, 85, 98
　learns Italian 18, 22
　lieder singing 21, 102, 110, 142
　London debut 110–111
　meets and marries Tom King 148–151
　Met opera broadcasts 91–92, 94–96, 104, 113–114, 139, 140–141, 188, 250 (also, see discography)
　Paris commercial recordings 42, 64–65, 74–76, 81–83, 91, 92 (also, see discography)
　Paris Opéra debut 66–67
　piano lessons 6
　pregnancy 170–172
　recommences singing 163–164
　resumes her career 168, 172–178
　runs away from home 11
　singing competitions 16, 18–21
　South American opera broadcasts 104–106, 144, 250 (also, see discography)
　stage debut 54–56
　studies singing in Paris 37–69
　studies singing in Melbourne 12–24
　transition from contralto to soprano 14, 38
　1939 Tour of Australia 125, 126–133, 218, 253, 260
　1944 Tour of Australia 190–191, 192–193, 208
　1945 Tour of occupied Germany 204–207
　1946 Tour of occupied Germany 213–214
　1949 Tour of Australia and New Zealand ix, 44, 219–222
Lawrence, William (father) 1–5, 8, 9, 10, 11, 15–19, 21, 24, 25, 27–28, 43–45, 70, 71, 129, 130, 170, 172, 225, 247
Lazarus, Daniel 261
Lecocq, Charles
　La Fille de Madame Angot 37
Legge, Walter 204, 207, 210
Lehmann, Lilli 90, 263
Lehmann, Lotte 45, 73, 87, 91, 96, 102, 126, 127, 131, 140, 242, 250, 261, 293, 294, 295
Leider, Frida 45, 73, 77, 78, 80, 90, 111, 263, 264
Leigh, J. Colstan 201
Leinsdorf, Erich 134, 139–141, 144, 210, 294, 295
Lemnitz, Tiana 103, 104, 293
Levien, Sonya 225
Levine, Marks 86
Lewis, Brenda 241
Lille Opera 65, 101
List, Emanuel 88, 91, 108, 187, 293–295
Liszt, Franz 124, 211, 287
Litvinne, Félia 47–48, 50, 60, 64, 68, 76, 81
London, George 217
London Symphony Orchestra 210
Longden, Archie 45–46, 69, 127–129, 131–133
Longone, Paul 101, 102
Los Angeles Philharmonic Orchestra 224, 227, 286–288, 291

Lubin, Germaine 37, 60, 61, 66–69, 73, 76, 80, 81, 96, 100, 102, 109, 111, 146–147, 212
Luccioni, José 73, 103, 217
Ludwig, William 225
Luizzi, Alfredo 128, 132, 231
Lyon Opera 101, 109, 182

M

MacArthur, General Douglas 192, 197, 295
McArthur, Edwin 134, 139
McDonald, Jeanette 276
MacMillan, William 167, 270
Mahler, Gustav 77, 121
Maison, René 103, 104, 106, 115, 147, 292–296
Majito, Surgito 81
Manhattan Opera House (Manhattan Ballroom) 174, 179
Manley, Gordon 271
Manski, Dorothee 88, 95, 155, 268, 294–296
Margaret, Her Royal Highness Princess 208
Marseilles Opera 101, 108
Martinelli, Giovanni 87, 92, 98, 107, 116
Mascagni, Pietro
  Cavalleria Rusticana 42, 63, 235
Masini, Galliano 123
Massenet, Jules
  Hérodiade 38, 56, 64, 70, 85, 285
  Manon 176, 241
  Thaïs 97, 122–124, 221
  Werther 37, 46, 62
Meisle, Kathryn 88, 94, 296
Melba, Nellie 8, 9, 16, 17, 23, 27, 50, 61, 133, 143, 174, 223, 274
Melbourne Symphony Orchestra (Victorian Symphony Orchestra) 133, 199, 223, 284, 288, 292, 296
Melchior, Lauritz 76, 87–89, 91–94, 96, 98, 107, 108, 111, 113, 122, 125, 134–135, 139, 140, 141, 170, 175–177, 182–184, 187, 188, 212, 230, 242, 246, 250, 261, 292–296
Mendelssohn, Felix 7, 285
  Elijah 16, 38, 222
Menotti, Gian Carlo 238–239
  Amelia Goes to the Ball 116
  The Medium 226, 237, 238
Menzies, Robert 132
Merli, Francesco 23
Merola, Gaetano 134, 280
Mestrallet, Ernest 258

Metro-Goldwyn-Mayer (MGM) 222–227
Metropolitan Opera, New York 37, 38, 76–78, 83, 86–99, 101, 108, 110, 112–116, 118, 122–124, 127, 131, 135, 138–141, 146–147, 149, 152, 153, 158, 159, 161, 169, 170, 171, 174–176, 182–184, 186–189, 200, 218, 222, 228, 235, 239, 241, 242, 244, 246, 249, 250–251, 289, 293–296
Metz, Hermann 118
Mexican National Opera 153–155, 171
Meyer, Paul 271, 284, 290, 291
Meyerbeer, Giacomo
  L'Africaine 41–42, 64, 73
  Les Huguenots ix, 21, 38, 39, 51, 60, 65, 69, 100
Milanov, Zinka 116
Milhaud, Darius 112
Miller, Henry 34, 36
Miller, Rita 37, 40–41, 49
Mitropoulos, Dimitri 108, 163
Miura, Tamaki 53, 57
Modesti, Dominique 109
Monnaie Theatre, Brussels 207
Monroe, Marilyn 145, 267
Monte Carlo Opéra 50–57, 64, 108, 176
Montemezzi, Italo
  L'Amour Dei Tre Rei 149
Monteux, Pierre 74
Montevideo Opera House 106, 294
Moore, Gerald 213
Moore, Grace 87, 92, 123, 149
Moore, Roger 225, 228
Moresby, Isabelle 133
Morrisey, Gibson 214
Mozart, Wolfgang Amadeus 38
  Così fan tutte 107
  Die Zauberflöte 176, 237
  Don Giovanni ix, 25, 38, 39, 41, 42, 80, 107, 237, 243
  Le Nozze di Figaro 118–119, 237
Müller, Maria 76, 261
Mussorgsky, Modest 130, 134

N

Nantes Opera 61, 62, 65, 69
Narici, Louis 51, 52, 56
National Orchestra of Paris 211, 282, 286, 287, 289, 296
NBC Artists Services 86, 107, 112, 117, 126, 127, 143
NBC Symphony Orchestra 281, 283, 289, 297

Neal, Harry 231
Neate, Kenneth 200
Nelson, Allison 132, 231–232
Nemeth, Maria 53, 56, 62
Nespoulos, Marthe 72
New York Philharmonic Orchestra 106–107, 116, 151, 186, 218
New York Town Hall 112, 222
Newby, Nora 203, 205, 207, 208
Newton Ivor 210, 280–282, 286, 288
Nice Opera 101, 108
Nilsson, Birgit 242, 263
Nilsson, Sven 119
Nimes Opera 73
Nimura, Yeichi 114
Nin, Joaquin 220
Nissen, Hans Hermann 119, 121–123
Nordica, Lillian 90, 174, 265
Norena, Eidé 53
Novotna, Jarmila 176

O

Obolensky, Prince Serge 145–146, 148, 149, 151
O'Connor, Basil 179–181
Offenbach, Jacques 207
  The Tales of Hoffmann 237
Onegin, Sigrid 138
Opéra-Comique, Paris 62–64
Opperman, Hubert 130, 162, 246
Orange Amphitheatre 80, 101
Ormandy, Eugene 199, 200, 296
O'Sullivan, John 73, 80

P

Paderewski, Jan 146
Page, Thomas 236, 238, 292
Palma, Athos 99, 101–103, 106
Palustre, Marguerite 32, 39–41, 45, 46
Panizza, Ettore 103, 115, 147
Papi, Gennaro 123
Paray, Paul 79
Paris Conservatoire Orchestra 42, 74
Paris Opéra ix, 25, 30, 39, 42, 45, 50, 53, 56, 58–81, 83, 85, 86, 92, 99, 100–101, 103, 110, 117–118, 121, 131, 211, 212, 217, 218, 247, 293
Paris Symphony Orchestra 74
Parker, Eleanor xi, 227–230
Pasdeloup Orchestra 74, 75, 79, 81, 286, 288, 293, 294, 296

Pauly, Rose 114, 155
Pearce, Reverend Alex 6, 7, 130, 164
Pelletier, Wilfred 123
Peri, Jacopo
  Euridice 211, 285
Pernet, André 59, 72, 212
Petina, Irra 88, 292, 294–297
Petrie, Gladys 40–41
Pfitzner, Hans 85, 102, 110, 124, 142, 285
Philadelphia Orchestra 199, 200, 296
Philharmonia Orchestra 204, 296
Phillips, Linda 132
Pilotti, Angelo 217
Pinza, Ezio 87, 92, 98, 126, 135, 141, 176, 273, 280
Pistor, Gotthelf 120
Pittsburgh Opera 222
Ponchielli, Amilcare
  La Gioconda 38, 39
Pons, Lily 87, 92, 173, 176, 189, 261, 276
Ponselle, Rosa 87, 92
Potter, Raeschelle 239, 246
Poulenc, Francis 220
Poulet, Gaston 275
Price, Leontyne 242
Puccini, Giacomo
  Gianni Schicchi 237, 238
  La Bohème 123, 228
  La Fanciulla del West 102, 103, 142, 145, 256
  La Rondine 50
  Madama Butterfly 42, 51, 53, 57, 227, 237, 286
  Tosca 43–44, 48, 50–52, 56, 57, 62, 64, 122–124, 232, 249
  Turandot 103, 109
Purcell, Henry 189, 204
  Dido and Aeneas ix, 118, 211, 212, 237, 286

R

Rachmaninov, Serge 130, 198, 210, 211, 286
Rameau, Jean-Philippe
  Castor et Pollux 103, 106
Ravel, Maurice 36, 259
RCA Victor 124, 142 (also, see discography)
Reger, Max 85
Reiner, Fritz 186
Rethberg, Elisabeth 87, 88, 126, 169, 273
Reyer, Ernest
  Salammbô 46

Sigurd 46, 65, 81, 82, 85, 101, 286
Richard, Louis 258
Ritchard, Cyril 247
Robinson, Francis 241, 246
Rocamura, Wynn 230
Rocco, Rosanna 236
Rodzinsky, Artur 289
Roosevelt, Eleanor 107, 124, 176, 179, 180, 200, 201, 222
Roosevelt, Franklin Delano 107, 124, 179, 180, 181, 200, 201
Rosing, Vladimir 228
Rossini, Gioacchino 38
  Semiramide 40, 42, 50
  Stabat Mater 270
Rouché, Jacques 58, 59, 61–64, 66, 67, 69–71, 76, 78, 81, 84, 98–101, 117, 212
Royal Albert Hall 111, 209, 210, 288
Ruhlmann, François 67, 212, 217

S

Sachse, Leopold 89, 93–96, 139, 225
Saint-Saëns, Camille
  L'Ancêstre 64
  Samson et Dalila 21, 64, 227, 229, 287
Salle Gaveau 42, 84
Salle Pleyel 74, 79, 82, 286, 288, 293, 294, 296
Samazeuilh, Gustave 261
Sanabria, Pam 238
Sandor, Arped 124
San Francisco Opera 134, 142, 145, 280, 295
Sargent, Malcolm 126
Schary, Dore 224, 226, 227
Schlusnus, Heinrich 138
Schnabel, Artur 131
Schorr, Friedrich 87–91, 94, 107, 108, 113, 141, 183, 242, 250, 293–296
Schubert, Franz 102, 130, 134, 189, 205, 211, 213, 287
Schumann, Robert 21, 102
Seider, August 119, 120
Sens, Marguerite 258
Shaw, John 223
Sibelius, Jean 168
Simon, Erich 77, 78, 83, 84, 86, 87
Singher, Martial 66, 67, 69, 70, 72, 74, 103, 104, 222, 239, 269, 293, 296
Skyring, Emily 45, 132
Smith, Everett 166, 168

South Illinois University, Carbondale 235–239, 241, 243–245, 248, 281, 286, 292
Spalding, Albert 173
Spani, Hina 23, 103
Stainer, John 7
Stein, Aaron ('George Bagby') 184
Stevens, Rïse 295
Stivanello, Tony 216, 217
Stokking, Jean 56
Stokowski, Leopold 144
Strauss, Richard 84, 85, 102, 114, 124, 142, 173, 174, 211, 288–289
  Ariadne auf Naxos 233
  Elektra 84, 109, 114, 215–216, 221, 223
  Salome 46–47, 79–82, 84, 85, 114–117, 122, 124, 127, 133, 143, 144, 146, 153, 155, 188, 209–211, 223, 227, 241–243, 288
Stravinsky, Igor 36, 220
Supervia, Conchita 53
Sutherland, Joan ix, xiii, 242, 243, 247, 248, 250, 254
Swarthout, Gladys 89, 123
Sydney Opera House 243, 246
Sydney Symphony Orchestra 132, 199, 243, 292

T

Tait, Sir Frank 190
Taschner, Gerhard 214
Tauber, Richard 126
Tchaikovsky, Peter Ilyich 289
  Eugen Onegin 210, 211, 214, 289, 297
  The Maid of Orleans 210
Teichmüller, Robert 85
Teyte, Maggie 237, 257
Théâtre du Champs Elysées 79, 81
Thebom, Blanche 200, 244
Thill, Georges 37, 53–56, 69, 72, 73, 100
Thomas, Arthur Goring
  Nadeshda 20, 31
Thomas, John Charles 123
Thorborg, Kerstin 108, 111, 113, 141, 183, 187, 294, 295
Tibbett, Lawrence 87, 89, 92, 123, 127, 176, 181, 183, 230, 246
Traubel, Helen 139, 147, 169, 175, 182–184, 186–188, 200
Trevi, José de 59, 76, 81
Tulane University, New Orleans 232–233, 235–236
Turner, Lana 225–226

U

Ugarte, Fiore 143–145, 170
United Services Organisations 189, 190, 197, 207
University of Arkansas, Little Rock 244

V

Vallin, Ninon 37, 85
Varnadore, Gary 238
Varnay, Astrid 169, 188, 292
Vassenko, Xenia 274
Verdi, Giuseppe 234, 235
  Aida 23, 38, 39, 64, 65, 73, 101, 102, 107, 116, 215–218, 221, 223, 237, 238, 292
  Don Carlos ix, 18, 20, 26, 31, 110, 292
  Falstaff 237
  Il Trovatore 235
  La Traviata 89, 176
  Macbeth 107, 292
  Otello 101, 102
  Rigoletto 49
Vezzani, Cezar 101
Vichy Opera 85, 93
Vienna Staatsoper 62, 69
Vinay, Ramon 217
Vincent, J.J. (Vincent Attractions) 143, 146, 161, 167, 171, 172, 175
Voigt, Deborah 250
Votipka, Thelma 88, 280, 294, 295

W

Wagner, Friedelind 239
Wagner, Richard 46, 47, 80, 114, 119, 131, 134, 147, 152, 173, 188, 189, 194, 212, 222, 241, 242, 250, 251
  Der Fliegende Holländer 102–106, 121, 145, 277, 292
  Die Walküre 46, 47, 51, 52, 60–62, 64, 65, 67, 68, 70, 74, 75, 77, 78, 83–85, 87, 88, 92, 96, 98, 101, 102, 106–108, 113, 114, 116–122, 125, 134, 135, 139, 140, 144, 145, 147, 148, 153, 165, 243, 250, 251, 293–296
  Götterdämmerung ix, 47, 48, 51, 52, 58, 75–78, 83–85, 93–96, 101, 107, 110, 114, 119–121, 130, 133, 135, 139, 140, 145, 147, 175, 184, 205, 210, 211, 214, 218, 231, 237, 243, 296
  Lohengrin 34, 51, 52, 58–60, 66–69, 74–78, 84, 85, 89, 91, 92, 94, 96–98, 101, 102, 104, 105, 108, 116, 117, 118, 147, 149, 151, 243, 250, 293

Parsifal 46, 47, 78, 83, 98, 102–106, 120, 144, 152, 158, 168, 296–297
Siegfried 46, 47, 51, 52, 64, 78, 83–85, 93, 112, 114, 117, 119–121, 134, 147, 169, 293
Tannhäuser 46, 47, 51, 53–55, 60, 64, 69, 77, 84, 101, 102, 175–178, 181–184, 186, 189, 200, 217, 292–293
Tristan und Isolde 46–48, 51, 52, 57, 60, 68, 78, 83, 96, 98, 100, 109, 111, 145, 152, 158, 163, 164, 182–184, 186–188, 191, 198, 200–202, 205, 210, 212–214, 218, 222, 226, 296
Walker, Edyth 84–88, 91, 93, 94, 99, 176
Walter, Bruno 80, 174
Warren. Leonard 147
Waters, Thorold 18, 20–21, 42, 125, 126, 128, 132, 133
Webb, Purcell 20, 21
Weber, Carl Maria von
  Oberon 12, 14
Weekes, Clara 184, 216, 243
Wilder, Austin 175, 182, 184, 190, 201
Williams, Annie Laurie 223, 224, 226, 227
Witherspoon, Herbert 83, 84
Wittrisch, Marcel 103, 104, 293
Wolf, Hugo 102, 124
Wolfes, Felix 85, 92, 100, 102, 110, 111, 114, 124, 128–134, 139, 142, 143, 281–285, 287, 289, 290, 297
Wolff, Albert 64, 211, 282, 286, 287, 289, 296
Wysor, Elizabeth 182

Z

Ziegler, Edward 77, 78, 83, 84, 134, 159
Zoppot Festival 117 -121, 122, 128

Wakefield Press is an independent publishing and
distribution company based in Adelaide, South Australia.
We love good stories and publish beautiful books.
To see our full range of books, please visit our website at
www.wakefieldpress.com.au
where all titles are available for purchase.
To keep up with our latest releases, news and events,
subscribe to our monthly newsletter.

Find us!

Facebook: www.facebook.com/wakefield.press
Twitter: www.twitter.com/wakefieldpress
Instagram: www.instagram.com/wakefieldpress

www.ingramcontent.com/pod-product-compliance
Lightning Source LLC
Chambersburg PA
CBHW051627230426
43669CB00013B/2206